ORGANISE
OR DIE?

RAPHAËL BOTIVEAU

ORGANISE OR DIE?

Democracy and Leadership in South Africa's National Union of Mineworkers

WITS UNIVERSITY PRESS

Published in South Africa by:
Wits University Press
1 Jan Smuts Avenue
Johannesburg, 2001

www.witspress.co.za

First published 2017

978–1-77614–204-0 (print)
978–1-77614–206-4 (EPUB)
978–1-77614–205-7 (PDF)

This book was published with the support of the Institut des mondes africains (CNRS/IRD/EHESS/EPHE/Université Paris 1 Panthéon-Sorbonne/Université Aix-Marseille) and the French Institute of South Africa-Research (IFAS-Recherche). IFAS-Recherche was founded in 1995 in Johannesburg. Under the authority of the French ministry of foreign affairs and the CNRS (French National Centre for Scientific Research), it promotes research in the humanities and social sciences about southern Africa and within this framework supports scientific cooperation.

Project manager: Inga Norenius
Copy editor: Inga Norenius
Proofreader: Lisa Compton
Indexer: Tessa Botha
Cover design: Fire and Lion

To Hélène and awaiting Alix, July 2017

CONTENTS

FIGURES AND TABLES

ACKNOWLEDGEMENTS

I f I were to pick only one word to describe the National Union of Mineworkers (NUM), one that I have heard many times in its ranks, it would be the word 'humbling', since my experience of the organisation has been a humbling one. Although many members brought an individual contribution to this research, I wish to thank them as part of the formidable collective of men and women that they have been building over the years. Organisation and political involvement certainly have their ups and downs but their contribution to the struggle for South Africa's liberation is immense. I hope they will appreciate this book and, although I have tried my best to portray their union in their own words, I also hope they will forgive mistakes and inaccuracies that are likely to have slipped into this manuscript.

I also thank all those outside NUM, working in the labour movement, in civil society, in labour mediation or in mining, who agreed to talk to me and whose contribution to this work was crucial.

The research presented in this book was first released as part of a doctoral dissertation in political sociology (Université Paris 1 Panthéon-Sorbonne – La Sapienza Università di Roma). For their support and complementarity, I wish to thank my two supervisors, Richard Banégas – with whom I have had the pleasure to work since 2005 – and Claudio Pellegrini.

I am grateful to the French Institute of South Africa (IFAS, Johannesburg) for its superlative support, as well as the Institut des mondes africains (IMAF, Paris) which sponsored my research.

There are many other people that I must thank individually for their direct input into this work. I thank, in South Africa and the USA: Franco Barchiesi, Claire Bénit-Gbaffou, Andries Bezuidenhout, Luli Callinicos, Rudi Dicks, Kally Forrest, Dunbar Moodie, Noor Nieftagodien, Paul Stewart and Lucien van der Walt. In France,

Italy and England, I wish to thank Alexander Beresford, Françoise Blum, Fadime Deli, Judith Hayem, Miles Larmer, Daniel Leblanc, Roger Meunier, Clarence Paul, Adriana Piga, Michel Pigenet, Fabrizio Pirro, Enrico Pugliese, Marie-Emmanuelle Pommerolle, Anna-Maria Romani, Johanna Siméant, Ian Simms and Isabelle Sommier.

Last but not least, I wish to thank the two reviewers who read my manuscript for Wits University Press, as well as Inga Norenius, who patiently and competently edited this book.

ACRONYMS AND ABBREVIATIONS

Abet	Adult Basic Education and Training
Amcu	Association of Mineworkers and Construction Union
ANC	African National Congress
BOB	branch office bearer
Bonume	Bophuthatswana National Union of Mining Employees
CCMA	Commission for Conciliation, Mediation and Arbitration
Cosatu	Congress of South Africa Trade Unions
Cusa	Council of Unions of South Africa
EBMTC	Elijah Barayi Memorial Training Centre
EFF	Economic Freedom Fighters
Esop	Employee Share Ownership Programme
FET	Further Education and Training
Fosatu	Federation of South African Trade Unions
GS	General Secretary
IFP	Inkatha Freedom Party
ITU	International Typographical Union
MDA	Mineworkers Development Agency
MIC	Mineworkers Investment Company
MIT	Mineworkers Investment Trust
MRC	Murray & Roberts Cementation
MWPF	Mineworkers Provident Fund
NEC	national executive committee
NUM	National Union of Mineworkers
Numsa	National Union of Metalworkers of South Africa

PWV	Pretoria-Witwatersrand-Vereeninging
RDO	rock drill operator
SACP	South African Communist Party
Sactu	South African Congress of Trade Unions
SALB	South African Labour Bulletin
SG	Secretary General
SWOP	Society, Work and Development Institute
Uasa	United Association of South Africa
Wits	University of the Witwatersrand
YCL	Young Communist League

1

Introduction: South African Trade Unions in Apartheid and Democracy

THE NATIONAL CONGRESS

From 3 to 6 June 2015, the National Union of Mineworkers (NUM) held its 15th National Congress in Boksburg, Gauteng. It was an important meeting for both South Africa's trade union movement and the ruling party. Until 2012, NUM had been the country's largest workers' organisation and the Congress of South African Trade Union (Cosatu)'s main affiliate. The mineworkers' union lost its leading status in the aftermath of the August 2012 Marikana strike and massacre, when its rival Association of Mineworkers and Construction Union (Amcu) took over most of its members in the platinum belt. In the meantime, the ruling Tripartite Alliance entered its deepest crisis since its inception in the early 1990s. NUM's 2015 congress followed shortly after the expulsion of the National Union of Metalworkers of South Africa (Numsa) – now the country's largest trade union – from Cosatu, in November 2014. NUM's congress was also the elective meeting of a pivotal African National Congress (ANC) political ally, which had contributed to the Party's top national leadership like no other organisation since 1991.[1] Despite mounting criticism of Jacob Zuma's presidency, NUM national leaders remained among its most vocal supporters.

Stakes were thus high and outgoing NUM leadership had planned things well. Both its president, Pete Matosa, and its general secretary, Frans Baleni – the political protégé of ANC secretary general Gwede Mantashe – were ready to continue for, respectively, a third and a fourth term. Political alliances were sealed ahead of the congress and regional delegations thought to belong to the opposition motion, such as Rustenburg, were strategically placed at the back of the room.

As is customary, the congress started with long discussions between the various delegations about 'credentials' to agree on the exact number of voting delegates. Proceedings thereafter went smoothly on the first day. As usual in such union gatherings, leaders from allied workers and political organisations, as well as Cabinet ministers, queued to address the more than 800 NUM delegates. Speeches bore no surprises and very little space was dedicated to programmatic debate. Calls to 'discipline' and 'class consciousness' were now and then directed at invisible or visible external enemies such as the 'vigilante' and 'yellow union', Amcu. Internal dissidents who had tried to enforce a 'cult of personality' in the federation were also warned (an attack directed at recently expelled Cosatu general secretary Zwelinzima Vavi and at Irvin Jim, the general secretary of Numsa). Speakers such as Gwede Mantashe or Cosatu president Sidumo Dlamini called on all to 'contest on the basis of ideas' rather than person, while systematically equating divergent views with mere dissent and factionalism. In short, and as I shall later analyse in more depth, opponents were dismissed as either too politically uneducated to participate efficiently in the life of their organisation (that is, as lacking 'class consciousness') or too greedy for power to lead it effectively. The congress was seemingly moving towards its status quo as nominations for leadership positions were announced and accepted by the incumbents and their challengers. Four positions out of the nine put to vote were contested: deputy president, general secretary, deputy general secretary, and health and safety national chairperson. President Matosa's position went uncontested, and nine NUM regions out of eleven nominated Frans Baleni and his deputy. Their opponents received only the minimum required support of two regions.

Day two mirrored day one in content. The stage monopolised microphones with reports from the leadership and speeches by guests. Delegates got to speak only in short interludes. At the end of this second day my impression, as an external observer versed in NUM politics and as an analyst of organisation, was that I was being the witness of an organisational suicide. This impression was supported by informal exchanges I had with insiders. How – given the critical situation NUM faced on the ground – could this congress spare itself from genuine self-critical debate? How could it even consider returning a leadership under whose tenure the union had lost up to one-third of its membership?[2] This was a leadership that had proven incapable of dealing with unprecedented strikes and the Marikana massacre other than by claiming they were a conspiracy orchestrated by Amcu and mining bosses.[3]

The third and last day of NUM's 2015 national congress started with the treasurer general's financial report, which put figures to the union's setbacks since 2012 but also insisted on NUM's 'resilient nature'. Halfway through this last day, national leaders finally gave their regional counterparts – including their opponents – a chance to address the state of the union. A turning point in the congress occurred when newly elected Rustenburg regional secretary Desmond Mfuloane took the floor. After acknowledging that things had gone wrong at most Rustenburg mining operations, he pledged his commitment to 'go back to the basics' and denounced the fact that when leaders contest for positions, they are labelled 'troublemakers': 'This is wrong and upsets the members who cannot express their views,' he complained. Mfuloane was anything but a revolutionary or a troublemaker. He had been a NUM member for 26 years, an elected union cadre for many terms and voted into the leadership of his region twice. As opposed to many others, whose dress code spelled 'comrade' in a display of grassroots activism, he attended the congress dressed in a blue suit and shirt. His criticisms of the incumbent leadership were calmly argued and not militant in tone or content. To illustrate his point, Mfuloane said that members on the ground did not understand why Numsa had been expelled from Cosatu, a decision which they did not support and which he reduced to a harmful battle between political elites: 'We should have excluded the culprits if there were [culprits], not the 360 000 members.' He then recalled that the challenge Amcu posed to NUM was not a new phenomenon and compared it to the rise of the competing Mouthpeace Workers' Union in the mid-1990s. However, 'during that time' he argued, 'the leadership of the organisation was all over and we recruited back'. This was a reference to the work of former NUM deputy general secretary Archie Palane, who had once enjoyed popularity in the platinum belt before Gwede Mantashe – then the union's general secretary – had the NUM constitution changed to oust him and ensure the political victory of his protégé Frans Baleni. In an attack against top national leadership – who now only go to the field accompanied by bodyguards – and former NUM president Senzeni Zokwana, who had addressed the 2012 Marikana strikers from within a police Hippo, Mfuloane added: 'We were not there to assist our members who were threatened. The trend in the organisation is that as leaders we are surrounded by security. Members are not secured. We are not accessible to members because of that.'

These words were not mere rhetoric; they relayed strong criticism of the incumbent leadership, a call for change and a call to go back to the grassroots to serve defenceless members. Dozens of NUM members and local leaders had indeed been killed since 2012 because of police violence and union rivalry (which also claimed many lives among NUM opponents). Mfuloane's speech was crucial: it broke the silence that had prevented many delegates from speaking, for fear of being disciplined or victimised by the legitimist camp. As he later put it to me: 'There's a lot of suppression. People don't talk their minds out and the congress was the only platform for people to express their views, which they did at the end of the day.'[4]

Later in this book I show how Mfuloane's words speak for many of his fellow NUM leaders opposed to the type of organisational governance that had been gradually imposed on NUM by its second generation of national office bearers. This type of governance, in which democratic centralism increases and internal debate is gradually reduced, resorts to communist ideology as a powerful source of symbolic violence to muzzle political opponents. It constantly discriminates between political friends and foes to silence diverging views and uses the Party as a tool to seize power positions and further personal and collective political ambitions. This trend, which has affected NUM in the wake of Gwede Mantashe and several of his fellow NUM and South African Communist Party (SACP) central committee members, including Baleni, Zokwana and Crosby Moni, has reached the ANC and Cabinet too.[5] This political ascent of Party cadres, however, has not been followed by any significant progressive adjustment of national policies under Jacob Zuma's two presidencies over South Africa.

After Mfuloane's intervention during the congress, the mood remained rebellious as discussion over proposed resolutions started – an exercise which, as time usually runs short, is generally postponed to a post-congress central committee meeting. Resolution 10 came up, sponsored by the Matlosana, Highveld and North East regions, on the constitutionalisation of the recently formed NUM Youth Forum (see chapter 8). Faced with a situation in which none of those for or against managed to convince one another, a very rare situation presented itself: delegates were to vote individually on the matter rather than adopt the resolution by consensus, as is the norm. Delegates further decided that the vote was to be held by secret ballot and not by a show of hands as the union's constitution stipulates. A NUM veteran who had attended all union congresses since 1982 told me he had witnessed such a situation only two or three times, the last of which dated back to the 1980s, 'when I was still a mineworker', he remembered. As soon as the prospect of voting appeared, one SACP guest requested the mike and accused the delegates of dividing the organisation. This immediately occasioned a strong response by Matlosana regional secretary Joseph Montisetsi, who was also an SACP member: 'We are following the constitution of NUM,' he pointed out. While logistical preparations for the vote were in progress, the discussion on resolutions proceeded. Two of the resolutions, which delegates eventually adopted against the will of the national leadership, concerned the allocation of extra financial resources for cars and organisers' positions in the regions, with a view to rebuilding the union at the grassroots. No matter how hard national leaders argued against these resolutions, most regions held firm and managed to have them passed. Such a down–top dynamic and show of defiance towards national leadership was rare: I have seen this seldom enough in NUM meetings I have followed since 2010 to consider it noteworthy. It was a sign that the wind was changing.

As is usual in union conferences and congresses, the last day went on until late at night. Democracy takes time and collective decisions are sometimes reached through the exhaustion of individual and collective strengths. The vote on the Youth Forum was eventually cancelled after the two regions that opposed its constitutionalisation (along with Zokwana and Baleni) had been successfully lobbied and convinced by the others. Delegates queued in front of the voting station for long hours before the Independent Electoral Commission, hired to monitor the poll, locked itself in with observers from each camp to count the votes. At about eleven o'clock that evening, the commission announced that it was ready to proclaim the results.

President Matosa symbolically dissolved the leadership he had headed for the past three years and the national office bearers descended from the stage to return to their respective regional delegations. One electoral observer solemnly declared the election 'free and fair' and the announcement of the results began. This moment, which most delegates and observers had expected to confirm the outgoing leadership, turned into an incredible one, thrilling as only unexpected political or sports victories can be. It was a reminder that one was in the presence of an extraordinary organisation of human beings, the workings of which can be reduced neither to its collective mechanisms nor to the sum of its individual parts. Only two out of the top five incumbents were returned to their positions and, against all odds, outgoing general secretary Frans Baleni lost his position to his challenger, David Sipunzi, by twelve votes. There is no adequate word in the English language to render the depth of this moment – a defining one for democracy as a political regime – when a U-turn such as this change in political power occurs.[6]

This was an unexpected congress outcome for the incumbent national office bearers, just as it was for their opponents. It is seldom that the weakest team scores and wins at the last minute of the final. One could guess by the look on his face how lonely returned President Matosa felt at this precise moment of his political career in which he realised that his closest allies – who were also his political mentors – were gone. A crowd of delegates invaded the stage singing and dancing joyfully, as if symbolically taking over power. One of them next to me exclaimed with visible emotion, 'That's democracy!' Baleni himself proved a good loser and, looking slightly knocked out, with his eyes a bit wet, he mounted the stage to briefly congratulate the winners, a sign that he acknowledged his defeat and submitted himself to the verdict of the organisation. This behaviour on the part of an individual also displayed the collective ethos deeply entrenched in the culture of the ANC and of the Charterist movement: leaders come and go but the organisation remains. In other words, if the movement boasts that it produces extraordinary leaders – who are no doubt ambitious individuals – the latter also remain interchangeable and the organisation never durably succumbs to the 'cult of personality'. This tradition was exemplified at the very top of the ANC and the State when, in 2008, the organisation decided that Thabo Mbeki should resign from the presidency and be replaced by Kgalema Motlanthe.[7] The ability to humble oneself before the collective is arguably a rare capacity, demonstrated to me by another unlucky candidate at the 15th NUM congress, who insisted on the democratic nature of discipline: 'I've been a shop steward for some time now and outcomes of the congress do not mean anything to me. NUM is a democratic organisation and as a disciplined member I have a duty to abide by the outcomes as members have spoken.' After nine years in office, those Baleni had politically marginalised throughout the years, Archie Palane and Oupa Komane (Baleni's former deputy whom he defeated in 2012), had their revenge. The outgoing general secretary of NUM – a full-time employee of the union – was now officially unemployed. It was half past eleven at night when Pete Matosa metaphorically wrapped things up in his closing address: 'The members of NUM in the three sectors we are organising have spoken.'

These concluding words were metaphorical only because ordinary NUM members were not present in the congress room to speak their views or cast their votes. It was the delegates mandated by NUM branches and regions – local leaders – who did so in their names. Even though members are supposed to be consulted ahead of the congress, NUM regions are the level at which congress delegations are assembled, nominations for leadership positions agreed upon and proposed resolutions written. In this case regions were internally divided and although nominations were in favour of the incumbents, they were so only on paper. One Rustenburg regional committee member told me: 'As the region we did not really do justice to the process of nominations.' He explained that the regional chairperson and his secretary were divided on who to nominate and that even though Rustenburg nominated the incumbent team, individual delegates felt they were not bound by this decision. At least three other regions were in the same situation. Although some argued after the congress that the challengers knew beforehand that they had winning numbers but were clever enough not to advertise them, their slate was in fact never unified; there was no real certainty and they could only hope for victory.

More importantly, this congress was a reminder that voting ultimately remains an individual choice. As one delegate and veteran branch representative expressed it: 'You can unite on a slate but as I always say when I campaign for the ANC: when you go in the voting booth it's you, your mind, your pen and the voting paper. You can't remove an individual's right.' The act of voting has particular significance in South Africa, where the 'one man, one vote' motto guided anti-colonial and anti-apartheid struggles throughout most of the twentieth century. Twenty-two years after the end of apartheid, voting rates in national elections are still higher in South Africa than anywhere else in the world where voting is a free and non-compulsory act. Citizens or delegates at NUM congress feel they have the right to choose, and when offered the opportunity, they do. NUM leadership had long praised stability as a core union value, but delegates at its 15th National Congress thought otherwise and they overruled Frans Baleni, who was held responsible for undermining democratic debate in the union. Although his victor, David Sipunzi, and his new deputy general secretary, William Mabapa, arguably based their opposition on personal ambition rather than on a clear programmatic alternative, they were seen as embodying a needed change, just like Jacob Zuma when he gathered the ANC's left behind his bid against Thabo Mbeki in 2007.

RAISING QUESTIONS ABOUT UNIONS AFTER MARIKANA

The above account of NUM's 15th National Congress raises key questions about the functioning of this union, Cosatu, the ANC, the Tripartite Alliance and, more generally, about trade unions, organisations and the relationship between the individual and the collective. I address these questions in this book by examining the dynamics of the articulation between organisation building and the production of leadership in the case of NUM. The study is based on a PhD dissertation in political sociology[8] for which I conducted fieldwork in South Africa between 2010 and 2012.[9] When I started my research, the union was approaching its thirtieth anniversary; it was the country's largest and most powerful trade union and was generally portrayed as a wonderful workers' organisation, one that compelled admiration.

In January 2012, however, a massive strike started at Impala Platinum, the world's second-largest platinum operation near Rustenburg. It was followed by another comparable industrial action at Lonmin, the world's third-largest producer of the metal, which on 16 August 2012 was marked by fierce police repression that left 34 mineworkers dead. The strikers demanded major wage increases and, crucially, they rejected the intermediation of their historic representative: NUM. As far as the latter was concerned, two consequences were soon evident: the union had lost considerable legitimacy during these conflicts, as well as a significant share of its membership. Many observers of the mining strikes were quick to point to the obsolescence of a union its own members had disavowed. They saw it as the logical endpoint of a twenty-year process of post-apartheid union bureaucratisation (as classically described by Robert Michels' 'iron law of oligarchy') and the institutionalisation of a neo-corporatist type of relationship between the ANC-controlled State, NUM and the mining industry. Such an unnatural relationship between party, labour and capital was also pictured as class betrayal.[10]

These observations certainly have a degree of relevance – time erodes power – but they also proceed from an oversimplification. They were often expressed by analysts of trade unions and labour relations who had been in close association with Cosatu and its affiliates for years – including with NUM – during and after the anti-apartheid struggle. As I shall argue, this close association probably played a part in shaping two intellectual biases that are often found in analyses of the South African trade union movement: on the one hand, analysts tend to subscribe to an artificial binary division of South African time between an apartheid and a post-apartheid era. In their studies on the impact of the transformation of South Africa on trade unions, they tend to overestimate discontinuities rather than to historicise processes in the formation of organisations, which also necessarily include key continuities. This often leads them to romanticise the anti-apartheid struggle as a democratic golden age, and to subscribe to pessimistic approaches to organisation building, which is then interpreted as a teleological process of post-apartheid degeneration. However, as I will argue based on a close rereading of Robert Michels' classic study, these takes on the process of organisation are reductionist, be it in South Africa or elsewhere, as they fall short, for instance, of considering conscious orientations towards 'strategic bureaucratisation'. In other words, organisations are not only victims of their own success, they also consciously and actively shape it in a process – both collective and individual – that can be described as 'organisational agency'.

The Marikana massacre did not fundamentally alter my research questions and hypotheses. Rather, through making some features more visible, it helped me to reformulate them in more simple terms. This was true, for instance, when considering the gap between the distinctively militant nature of the strikers' repertoires of action and demands, and NUM's organisational response to their movement. The latter was characterised by legalist and legitimist postures, calls to discipline, and equating the workers' more informal and sometimes leaderless actions with chaos, as opposed to union claims that organisation was the only way. This reinforced my earlier intuitions about the historical tension between militant and even revolutionary NUM portrayals in traditional struggle iconography, and what I had personally observed: a union that, in practice, puts organisational discipline, leadership development and negotiation at the heart of its own strategy and its success.

In other words, the main questions I raise are: how are we to understand, by looking at the development of NUM over time, this tension between militancy on the one hand and organisation on the other? What, in NUM's organisational agency – as typically embodied by the leaders it nurtured – can help us understand what happened in 2012 and has happened since, not only as an expression of the fundamental and untenable contradictions that played out at Marikana, but also as the result of a deliberate process of organisation building and development? (The latter, what I call 'organisational agency', does not exclude the fact that conscious and rational decisions also yield unintended consequences.)

It was fieldwork that informed these research questions and I am of the view that contemporary debates on the democratic culture of NUM – one the union would allegedly have lost – miss crucial points, starting with the fact that tensions between leadership development and worker control date back to the union's very inception. Analysing history requires that we both account for past events and refrain from interpreting them in light of present developments. It is thus difficult to know whether the choices actors made thirty years ago were clear-sighted or whether they were just timely answers to conditions and constraints that then prevailed. Did they have a choice? Whatever the answer, it is my argument that NUM founders deliberately built a centralised and efficient organisation to survive in a hostile environment. This in turn created tensions, which were to remain, between the grassroots and the top structure of the organisation. Nonetheless, I argue that to fulfil its organisational goals, the union was compelled to invest in the production of leadership, at the expense of membership development. Historical contingencies, then, are crucially linked to the rise of a communist fringe of leaders whose own conception of discipline deepened the gap between members and leaders from a political point of view. There is no doubt that South Africa's transition from apartheid to democracy impacted on actors such as NUM – it provided, for instance, new avenues for individual careers. Yet in twenty years South Africa has probably changed far more than NUM or other worker and political organisations have done.

SOUTH AFRICAN TRADE UNIONS BEYOND TRANSFORMATION

No trade union movements in Africa have received as much scholarly attention as those in South Africa.[11] The South African 'school' of trade union and labour studies – of a mainly socio-historical orientation – has been characterised by a strong interpenetration between anti-apartheid trade unions and the academic world. It revolves around an intellectual generation whose founding figures are Edward Webster and Ari Sitas.[12] This group of activist-scholars was born during the 1973 Durban Dockers strike, known as the 'Durban moment,' and laid the foundations for South Africa's independent black trade union movement. Influenced by Marxism and by Rick Turner's more libertarian and workers' education orientated thought,[13] Webster participated in the launch of the *South African Labour Bulletin* (SALB) in 1974, as well as in that of the Society, Work and Development Institute (SWOP) in 1983, which he headed for many years at the University of the Witwatersrand (Wits).[14]

If the contribution of the mostly white anti-apartheid intelligentsia to the development of black trade unions can be conceived as decisive, start-up intellectual capital, critics have also recalled that these young, progressive whites who took many risks seldom learned the African languages spoken by their black 'comrades' and continued to live in their privileged white suburbs.[15] This relationship between university and trade unions, however, was never one-way. Former NUM general secretary Gwede Mantashe earned his MA from the University of the Witwatersrand[16] and former union activist Sakhela Buhlungu[17] has established himself as one of the most critical contemporary specialists of post-apartheid trade unions.

The contributions of South Africa's academia to global studies on labour and trade unions are several.[18] Just like their counterparts elsewhere in the world, South African scholars were influenced by Western European and North American approaches, often pessimistic, to trade unions in terms of bureaucratisation,[19] and marked by the paradigms of economic development and dependency. To escape such 'big narratives', a new generation started to interview workers on the shop floor and get involved in workers' education. Beyond mechanistic conceptions of class, they insisted on the characteristics peculiar to African working classes, discussed in a special issue of *Labour, Capital and Society* on 'South African Labour', edited by Roger Southall in 1985 (vol. 18, no. 2). What emerged at the time was also a willingness to take into account workers' subjectivities, representations and cultural productions.[20] In more recent times and as apartheid reached its final years, South African approaches to trade unions resorted to analytical concepts such as that of 'social movement unionism' to take into account the peculiarities of workers' mobilisations combined with social movements that emerged in authoritarian countries like the Philippines, Brazil or South Africa.[21] The manifold consequences of neoliberalism, rising unemployment and new employment patterns have also driven interest in the transformation of South Africa's trade union movement.[22]

Early connections between labour and politics are crucial to an understanding of contemporary dynamics and were especially important in the development of black independent trade unions (from the 1970s onwards). 'Independent trade unions' are those unions which, despite diverse geographical, sectoral or ideological realities, converge in terms of their chronology, the new repertoires and strategies they adopted, and their commitment to nonracialism and organisational democracy ('worker control').[23] Another dimension of these unions is their claim to roots in earlier experiences of African political trade unionism and, particularly, that of the South African Congress of Trade Unions (Sactu, 1955–1964), whose 'populist' dimension had clashed with its capacity to build a strong base on the shop floor.[24] When the ANC adopted guerrilla warfare in 1961, it chose to 'jettison a powerful weapon in the trade union organisation',[25] one that would later become central, during the 1980s, to its comeback in South Africa. The first 'genuinely national non-racial federation of trade unions' – the Federation of South African Trade Unions (Fosatu) – was formed in 1979, organising 120 000 workers represented in 11 affiliates, and it paved the way for the launch of Cosatu in 1985. A champion of workers' control and democracy, Fosatu also proposed that unions should be non-racial and independent of political parties.[26] Fosatu's opposition to political affiliation was criticised by proponents of political and social movement trade unionism.[27] When Cosatu was formed at the University of Natal, it gathered 33 unions representing over 460 000 workers, and NUM's general secretary, Cyril Ramaphosa, who had been central to this move, declared: 'A giant has risen and will confront all that stand in its way.'

The end of apartheid fed hopes that civil society could become a key actor in the political transition:

> Through a strategy we label *radical reform*, disciplined and sophisticated social movements may be able to inject more progressive content into the democratization process and wrest important concessions from reformers and moderates alike. In other words, a conservative outcome is in no way given in advance.[28]

This question on the role of trade unions in a democratic South Africa fuelled the debate around 'strategic unionism', a new 'strategic vision of a labour-driven process of social change' after apartheid.[29] A few years later, however, hopes for radical transformation had been dashed by the ANC's rallying to neoliberal economics. Eddie Webster and Glenn Adler proposed that South Africa was going through a double transition: on the one hand, the country was moving, politically, from authoritarianism to democracy while, on the other hand, its once isolated economy was opening up to the globalised world.[30] Central to their argument, and to the contribution of several authors I include in what I call the 'SWOP hypothesis', was the idea that trade unions in a free and democratic society now enjoyed considerable room to manoeuvre and press for change, while paradoxically being constrained, threatened, and eventually weakened by new external challenges – neoliberal globalisation in particular – which undermined their internal organisation and their political capacity. In the first part of this book I deconstruct the 'SWOP hypothesis' and several of its assumptions about organisational change. Many dimensions of Cosatu's loss of organisational power, which they themselves did nothing to sweeten,[31] were explored.[32] SWOP teams tested the political attitudes of Cosatu members towards parliamentary democracy in three Cosatu-commissioned longitudinal surveys (the *Taking Democracy Seriously* surveys) in 1994, 1998 and 2004. They found that the social composition of Cosatu's membership was changing in terms of age, occupational category, security of tenure, education standards, gender and length of membership. They showed that Cosatu's alliance with the ANC still enjoyed massive support and that internal democracy remained robust despite the challenges of globalisation.[33] More critical of Cosatu's post-apartheid destiny and legacy, and in many ways alarming as far as the federation was concerned, was the latest survey conducted by SWOP in 2008.[34]

These studies on Cosatu and its affiliates are without doubt of great analytical value. However, as I was learning more about NUM through observing the life of the organisation, interviewing its cadres and reading through union archives, two important reservations led me to question some of their underlying assumptions. The first relates to the historical links between South African academia and Cosatu. It indeed appeared to me that this might at least partly explain the development of a romanticised view of unions under apartheid. This in turn led many analysts to express disillusionment in the face of what they were becoming under democracy and to overestimate changes in their organisational patterns. Moreover, SWOP teams tested their hypothesis on the impact of the transition to democracy not only on South Africa as a country, but also on workers, unionists and their organisations. The latter were in turn influenced by these findings. This generated a circular flow of knowledge, in which academics and unionists mutually reinforced one another's conceptions of reality and routinised their questions.[35] In the case of NUM, it is striking to note that for the national leadership of the union, SWOP expertise became a primary source of technocratic knowledge, which often spared leaders the trouble of collecting first-hand data on the field. This contributed to deepening the gap between ordinary members and the union's power arcane.

My second reservation relates to the binary division of South African time that SWOP reports and subsequent scholarly analyses then began to establish. Consequently, many works on trade unions since 1994 over-insist on historical discontinuities between mobilised actors under apartheid and post-apartheid organisations. In other words, they apply a 'transformation' paradigm onto trade unions and fall short of assessing organisational continuities, which, in the case of NUM, helped me to understand organisation building, leadership development and the union's political life in the long term. Whatever the explanatory framework one chooses to account for South Africa's transformation from apartheid to democracy, past analyses of regime change elsewhere have shown that there are always important continuities between, for instance, colonial and postcolonial powers[36] or the revolutionary States and the autocratic rulers they overthrow. Failure to account for historical continuities in most works on post-apartheid trade unions is even more striking in view of the fact that this is commonly problematised in analyses of political actors such as the ANC. Scholars have pointed out, for instance, that the organisational culture of underground activism developed during the years of exile was hard to reconcile with the functioning of a political party in a democratic regime.[37] This suggests that if actors such as the ANC and NUM are likely to have been impacted, as organisations, by the 1990s political transition, their organisational ethos, as developed under and against apartheid, also persisted in democracy along with or despite other, more recent transformation processes.

What I crucially question here, therefore, are the 'paradox' and 'transformation' put forward by the SWOP school as a framework for the analysis of post-apartheid trade unions. Such paradigms rely on the assumption that the transformation of South African unions post-1994 was mostly the result of the new democratic dispensation in South Africa. This transformation is viewed as paradoxical insofar as one would have expected democracy to give birth to a stronger labour movement. In my view, and as I will show, although NUM's organisational trajectory may be paradoxical from an ideological point of view, from the vantage point of socio-history its trajectory reveals the results of a series of traceable steps and decisions.

HISTORICISING TRANSFORMATION AND PARADOX

Approaching the internal transition of trade unions as paradoxical stems from workerist ideology, which was strong among leftist activists and academics in the 1980s.[38] There is a tendency, therefore, to depict South African trade unions in the 1980s as united, collectivist, altruistic, decentralised, bottom-up – in a word, democratic. As soon as one adopts a more distanced point of view, however, more ambivalent collective mechanisms and individual strategies are quick to emerge: they intertwine in what I have called 'organisational agency'. This postulate does not imply that South African trade unions were or would be mere instruments of social control and domination. It is simply based on the socio-organisational assumption that the social construction of NUM is historically coherent and includes, for instance, willingly resorting to bureaucratisation in order to advance mineworkers' rights. Bureaucratisation was conceived of as a weapon: it was, in other words, strategic bureaucratisation.

This view allows me to reintroduce the debate on NUM's organisational development and transformations with a more fundamental questioning of the dynamics of organisation, rather than subscribing to teleological views in which NUM would finally have deviated from its presumed original destination. I propose that the founders of the mineworkers' union willingly chose to rely on its head office resources to build a centralised structure inscribed in a particular vision of bureaucratic modernity. Their goal was to give birth to a competent organisation, one that would be able to serve its members and improve their conditions. To do so they built up a strong machinery that gradually matched and withstood the organisation of the great multinational mining companies the union was fighting. Part I of this book shows how, and under what historical conditions, this necessity to build NUM from the top arose: the union was created from above and its national level was developed into a well-staffed bureaucracy that was to be the ultimate rampart against apartheid repression (a role that local structures were too weak to play). It then describes the construction and functioning of this bureaucracy before showing how it turned into an incredible financial power in the 1990s and 2000s – a power that, despite considerable challenges faced by NUM at the grassroots level since 2012 especially, has so far guaranteed its survival, just as it had done when mining houses and government destroyed local union branches under apartheid.

Applied to Cosatu and NUM, the transformation approach reveals a 'paradox' between these two organisations' visible successes on the national political stage and their state of chronic organisational weakening under the joint dynamics of the centralisation of decision-making, the disarray of local structures and the opening of South Africa to international markets which contributed to casualising the country's labour force and fuelled unemployment.[39] In the case of NUM, this approach insists on using both external and internal factors to explain the difficulties the union faced during the 2000s, in particular the growing gap between its base and its leadership. The new educational and social mobility opportunities opened to workers' representatives since apartheid ended have encouraged careerist behaviours

that have in turn weakened NUM structures, now characterised by a constant struggle for full-time union positions and for promotion to management positions. The
mining houses' increasing resort to subcontractors also divided their workforces
between permanent and temporary employees, hence threatening workers' solidarity.[40] The 'paradox' allows one, Buhlungu argues, to consider the great successes
achieved by South African trade unions while avoiding a typical bias in pessimistic
approaches that picture them as trapped in a binary dilemma between empowerment *or* institutionalisation. The paradox, according to Buhlungu, lies precisely
in this joint process of empowerment *and* institutionalisation. He points to elitist
dynamics at work in trade unions after apartheid, as well as to their strategic choices
in terms of the modernising projects they embraced. For him, however, these developments are virtually all post-1994: 'During the struggle against apartheid, activism
was driven by notions of solidarity, altruism and sacrifice. In the post-apartheid
period, activism is shaped by individualism and a quest for upward social mobility,'
he writes.[41] He also describes organisations that, in the 1970s and 1980s, 'were generally non-hierarchical, to the extent that many unions had flat salary structures for
their full-time officials'.[42] Buhlungu shows that professionalisation and modernisation were timely answers by trade unions to a changing context marked by

- their membership growth;
- reforms in labour law and collective bargaining from 1979 onward;
- the induced democratisation of State–union relations; and
- the rapid liberalisation and internationalisation of the South African
  economy.

He nonetheless fails to draw logical conclusions from the fact that the development of at least the first two of the above factors – and to some extent the last
two – preceded the end of apartheid. The apartheid regime's attempted reform also
opened a space – albeit a constrained one – for trade unions to organise workers.
This means that the generation of trade unions launched in the 1980s, including
NUM, had to adapt to this changing environment from the very start, not only after
democratisation. The environment was also characterised by nascent institutionalisation in the relationship between labour and capital, with some mining houses
favouring the establishment of trade unions to mediate their relationship with their
employees.

Analyses in terms of 'transformation' or 'paradox', which combined make the
'SWOP hypothesis', are therefore problematically anchored in a binary division of
South African time. In the case of trade union analysis, this caesura leads one to
embellish the years of the anti-apartheid struggle (insisting on democratic union

power, worker control and grassroots militancy), while pointing at increasing disillusion in the post-apartheid sequence (in a nutshell, bureaucratisation). But can one reasonably depart from the assumption that the political involvement of individuals was mostly selfless prior to 1994, before becoming essentially guided by selfish careerism after 1994? Accepting such a conclusion would relegate the analysis of the individual trajectories of most former anti-apartheid activists in the new democratic South Africa to assessing levels of schizophrenia. Moreover, union strategies such as the creation of union-funded investment companies, which are often associated with the democratic period, were in fact designed at the turn of the 1990s and cannot be understood outside of this historical context. This is not to say that NUM's organisational structure was not reformatted in the 1990s and 2000s. Rather, I argue that such developments followed a path that had largely been set before.

Most approaches to post-apartheid NUM consequently tend to view organisa-tional processes as dysfunctional, rather than resulting from organisational agency – the combination of individual and collective choices. In doing so they probably insist too much on factors that are external to the union to explain its internal evo-lution. There is, in fact, a certain contradiction in the available and limited literature on NUM after apartheid which, on the one hand, points to it as an instance of mil-itant trade unionism controlled by its members and focused on workplace issues, while stressing, on the other hand, that it had and still has a tendency to concentrate on national politics. Buhlungu and Bezuidenhout explain the years 1985–1990 thus:

> During this period, NUM consolidated its structures, giving meaning to the idea of worker control, one of the key principles of Cosatu. It set up vibrant health and safety structures and spent significant resources and effort on building branch and regional structures, as well as education committees. It made a number of senior appointments, with researchers, legal officers, education officers, and health and safety officers in its head office, as well as in regions, which became the envy of many of the smaller unions.[43]

Their description is accurate insofar as it reflects the voluntaristic character of NUM in its early years, but one can also question the sanctified image of an unblemished militant mineworkers' union. I will show, for instance, that not all NUM structures in the mid-1980s or early 1990s were as 'vibrant' as suggested and that organisa-tional weaknesses already existed back then. The literature on trade unionism often relies on a basic typology that broadly divides trade unions into those with a more workerist tendency (focused on workplace issues)[44] and those with a more political orientation (affiliation to political parties and relying on national strategies).[45] In South Africa, NUM is generally considered to be more aligned to the ANC than its sister unions[46] – it was instrumental both in launching Cosatu and in the federation's alliance with the ANC. Such a distinct political dimension is also an indication that its historical inclination towards national politics may have translated into more centralised intra-organisational dynamics.

ORGANISATION BUILDING: THE IRON LAW AS STRATEGY

Analysts of South African trade unions after apartheid usually agree that these organisations became bureaucratised and that the gap between their leaders and members deepened. As I have shown, they mostly explain these internal developments by pointing to external factors. I intend to look, first, at internal factors to explain the historical and contemporary development of NUM. In doing so I wish to insist on organisational agency in order to show that bureaucratisation is not necessarily to be viewed as the inevitable result of a degenerating organisational democracy. Rather, I venture that it can fit into a strategic collective project, which ought to be socio-historically rendered as a conscious and positive process of organisation building.

Such a process was classically analysed in Robert Michels's *Political Parties*. Michels's landmark book, which has been very widely discussed,[47] is generally reduced to its most notorious thesis: the 'iron law of oligarchy'. In my view, however, Michels's most important assertion is not that oligarchy in organisations is inevitable; I think, rather, that what the German sociologist chiefly demonstrated, in a Weberian lineage and with a distinctively optimistic view, is the fact that it is the very process of organisation that is first and foremost inevitable: without it, the weak are doomed to live and suffer, isolated and hopeless. Michels's study was first published in German at the end of 1910. Addressing major issues for left-wing parties in Europe at a time of political effervescence and creativity, it was almost immediately translated into Italian (1912), French (1914) and English (1915).[48] These translations, which are now dated, were only partial ones. The first integral translation of Michels's book was published in French only a century later.[49]

Michels's *Political Parties* is usually labelled as belonging to 'the *pessimistic tradition* in the study of trade unionism'[50] and reduced to the notorious sociological law it expounds.[51] This, however, is only a superficial reading. Firstly, because in his introduction Michels positively assesses the ineluctable extension of the realm of democracy through the spread of the parliamentary system, a practice – if not an idea – which all, including its aristocratic opponents, were compelled to endorse. The other side of the coin was, of course, that aristocratic – or oligarchic – features survived and kept developing in democratic organisations. This in turn raised questions on the claim that progressive organisations could democratise society while being themselves subjected internally to oligarchic tendencies. Secondly, however, Michels, who was working-class biased, was adamant that there was no alternative to organisation in modern societies. The need for organisation is a modern one, a practical or technical necessity when it comes to governing mass societies. Michels also valued it from a political point of view: 'Democracy is inconceivable without organization,' he wrote, before adding: 'Be the claims economic or be they political, organization appears the only means for the creation of a collective will.' He further explained that organisation 'is the weapon of the weak in their struggle with the strong'. 'It is easy to understand, then, that organization has become a vital principle of the working class, for in default of it their success is *a priori* impossible.'[52] Michels concluded his book on a poetic and encouraging note – rather than a naïve one – regarding the sense of history. Although successive democratic 'waves' were doomed to 'break ever on the same shoal,' he wrote, each one of them played the part of delegitimising, always in greater depth, the aristocratic past as a viable alternative to the imperfect democratic present. Moreover, he added, as soon as democracy is betrayed anew by its former promoters-become-oligarchs, 'new accusers arise to denounce the traitors' and stand in defence of it.[53] Michels's view therefore included two possibilities for organisations: they could either die and be replaced by others, or they could regenerate. The title of this book is a reference to NUM's famous 1980s motto 'Organise or die!' The motto suggested that organisation was the only way for workers to fight for their rights, just as in Michels's argument. In the process of organisation building, however, the perpetuation of the union gradually came into question, as also analysed by the German sociologist. It is this dilemma that NUM has been facing since 2012: will NUM survive as a democratic organisation, will it just survive as an organisational body emptied of its original goals, or will it keep disaggregating and eventually disappear? Apply the concepts of 'strategic bureaucratisation' and 'organisational agency' to these questions and it becomes patently clear that in building organisations, conscious individual and collective choices are made. This implies that choices can also be made to regenerate organisations. In other words, groups such as South Africa's mineworkers indeed had to organise or die (symbolically but also literally if one thinks of the levels of fatality in the mining industry in the 1980s). However, they do not necessarily have to organise *and* die (as a collective of workers). Organisational agency can also be deployed to regenerate organisations and renew collective struggles. Only time will tell if this will be the case with NUM.

Marxist thinkers had, of course, positively valued organisation as the revolutionary tool of the working class and they had no qualms about the tool being appropriated by leaders as long as the latter remained progressive.[54] In the reading I propose of it, Michels's book allows us to go further: firstly, it shows that organisation is the only channel through which the dominated – such as the mineworkers organised by NUM in the early 1980s – can speak.[55] Secondly, it allows us to sociologically deconstruct such a project and its complexities and ambiguities, with a focus on leadership development. Michels's book is indeed interesting here in view of the light it sheds on the project of the NUM founders, who decided to build a complex organisational apparatus capable of dealing with and sometimes even rivalling the organisation of the State and mining houses. In one famous quote Michels describes the ambiguous achievement of the process of organisation building, which could well be applied to NUM or, for that matter, to Cosatu:

> For half a century the men of the party have been working in the sweat of their brow to create a model organization. Now, when three million workers have been organized – a greater number than was supposed necessary to secure complete victory over the enemy – the party is endowed with a bureaucracy which, in respect of its consciousness of its duties, its zeal, and its submission to the hierarchy, rivals that of the state itself; the treasuries are full, a complex ramification of financial and moral interests extends all over the country. A bold and enterprising tactic would endanger all this: the work of many decades, the social existence of thousands of leaders and sub-leaders, the entire party, would be compromised.[56]

For some the paradox lies precisely in this description. As Gwede Mantashe, quoted in a SWOP report, explained in 2004, one needs to consider not only the impact of trade unions on the South African transition to democracy, but also how this very transition impacted on the trade unions themselves.[57] In my analysis of the iron law as a strategy, I propose an alternative analysis of the development of NUM.

I borrow from Michel Crozier's proposed methodology to approach the 'bureaucratic phenomenon'.[58] Based on a thorough sociological description of an organisation, he questioned the 'natural' destination of modern forms of organisation. Organisations often naturalise their existence and functioning in a belief that they work like automatons. In NUM one is often faced with a description of its internal workings as a harmonious machinery based on constitutional rules. The concept of 'bureaucracy' is here used in a Weberian sense, with a view to underlining the specificity of a type of organisational power, the legitimacy of which is grounded in rules, impersonal hierarchies and merit. In such a view, leaders hold power by election and skills. Around the leaders, administrators are organised in line with strict disciplinary rules and well-defined tasks; they are paid (with pension and other benefits), employed full-time and guided by a career path.[59] This is, of course, a description of the ideal; the other side of this organisational model is found in union politics, which is what lies behind the description of modern bureaucracy and allegedly neutral forms of organisation. Members and leaders sometimes decide that they are no longer bound by the rules of the game, use them to fulfil personal ambitions or even choose to change them to accommodate their own political agendas.

After focusing on the formation of NUM administration, Part I examines the internal politics of the union. Here again, I challenge commonplaces such as the idea that NUM would be naturally structured from the bottom up, based on the sacrosanct principle of worker control. I consider the union's rank-and-file participation and branch politics before looking at regional power and its exercise. National union politics is considered in relation to substructures at branch and regional levels. NUM's political dimension has usually been considered from the outside, through its role in tripartite politics. In Crozier and Friedberg's 'strategic analysis', it is the organisation that is conceived as intrinsically political because it depends on the articulation of individual interests and strategies within a common 'system of action'. As they put it, 'Any consistent analysis of collective action must therefore place power at its centre. Collective action is nothing else in the end than daily politics. Power is its raw material.'[60] 'The term organization refers both to a state and dynamics,' is how Friedberg puts it.[61]

The 2012 strikes saw seemingly resourceless ordinary members get the better of their local, regional and national leaders who proved unable to predict or read the strikers' behaviour in all its complexity and merely saw it as chaotic (lacking discipline) and manipulated 'by dark forces' (Amcu in this case). However, as soon as one considers previous instances of ordinary members rebelling against their leadership, other readings of the 2012 strikes, as part of a type of intra-union governance, become possible. NUM unionists, who experienced previous disavowals from their members in the 1980s and 1990s, hope that members will 'come back' in the medium term. The existence of conflicts between leaders and members can hence be read as a failure to fully institutionalise and internalise tensions in the organisation. As observed by Gramsci, 'discipline' is necessary in a trade union but it requires leaders to conceive and develop a clear programme of action to which members can relate. His observations on the *Confederazione Generale del Lavoro* are interesting to reflect on in relation to the 2012 strikes: he conceived it as an organisation in which bureaucracy was so developed (and compared with State administration) that it could no longer be conquered by constitutional means. Rather, he suggested, as the 2012 strikers did in a way, workers ought to take control at the point of production and set up workplace committees before eventually seizing majority in the confederation.[62] The question of leadership in the union is a 'problem' in its own right. The production of 'leaders' has been, I will show, not only an internal task to design a cadreship for NUM, but also an aim in itself for the union. The Marikana strikers got it right and they founded their movement on a vow to reject the intermediation of those NUM leaders who, they argued, had betrayed their representative role.

LEADERSHIP OF A SPECIAL TYPE

Observers of NUM have often noted that it has produced extremely talented leaders and, in particular, all three secretary generals and two deputy presidents of the ANC since 1991. Yet it has very seldom been asked why this is and, more importantly, how one becomes a leader in the mineworkers' union. In other words, what types of leader does this union nurture?

Part II of this book addresses NUM's long-lasting endeavour to grow individuals and produce leaders in several fields.[63] These leaders in turn subscribe to an original conception of leadership – a multifaceted one to be sure – that has become a trademark of the union. NUM leaders are prized for their ability to campaign, organise, manage human resources, administer an office, provide sound guidance and even negotiate their way out of contentious situations. Moreover, NUM leaders are expected by those they lead to perform the role of not merely 'representative' or 'messenger', but rather the dual role of carrying both the message of 'the masses' and guiding them, ultimately thus playing the role of mentor and adviser. Launched in 1982, NUM expanded thanks to the hard work of a handful of skilled and ambitious leaders who soon realised that the union had no choice but to invest in education and cadreship development if it was to be perennial and resist the implacable machinery of mining houses.

Leadership development in a trade union context can be viewed through a Marxist lens. From such a vantage point, unions are often regarded with suspicion, as potential reformist agents. Their function is therefore generally restricted to that of revolutionary schools for the masses.[64] As such, trade unions ultimately become an educative tool in the hands of the Party, with a view to producing class-conscious workers. This view partly applies to NUM for, as I will show, it has increasingly turned into a communist union since the early 2000s. However, the Marxist approach also misses an important point in the local South African picture. In South

Africa indeed, developing black skills and leadership was and still is conceived as a way to redress the deeds of apartheid, a regime that institutionally maintained black people in subaltern social, professional and political positions.[65] Present-day leaders of NUM often lacked formal school education when they joined the union, even though many if not most actually surpassed the educational standards of their fellow mineworkers through, minimally, the possession of literacy skills. It is thus firstly in such a literal sense that the organisation *grew* them, by providing space for them to develop skills that are typically attained otherwise through schooling. This first basic NUM mission is clearly reflected in the gratitude many who grew up in the union express towards it. At the end of my interview with Mez Ramatena, treasurer of NUM Impala Services branch, and after I had stopped my digital recorder, he proudly made the following statement in a way that suggested he wanted to put it on record: 'NUM produces a lot of leaders like Mez Ramatena.' 'NUM teaches me a lot,' he added before quoting the names of NUM-made top South African leaders such as former NUM general secretaries Cyril Ramaphosa, Kgalema Motlanthe and Gwede Mantashe, as well as that of former Cosatu general secretary and NUM organiser Zwelinzima Vavi.[66] My interviewees regularly expressed deep gratitude towards their organisation.[67] When I asked a branch chairperson I met in 2010 if I could quote his words in my work, he answered, as if stating the obvious: 'I'm proud of NUM you see, I'm what I am thanks to the union.'[68] Another local leader, who was nominated by ordinary members to stand for a position despite having decided to take a break from leadership, told me in 2011: 'I am a product of NUM. NUM made me what I am today.'[69] A freshly elected branch secretary from the Carletonville region, whom I once drove back to a township near Westonaria after we had attended a union meeting together in September 2011, told me about his new position: 'It changed my life, I'm learning so many things.'

Leadership development in NUM also bears a second meaning, beyond personal development: that of a core curriculum leaders are expected to have completed when they graduate and reach the level of experience required to rise through the ranks. The curriculum goes beyond just practical requirements; it also embraces a more general ethics of leadership, which, as I will show, implies that there is also an art to leading members that one must learn in order to win one's spurs. This curriculum and the approach to leadership I have described above are also found in many of South Africa's Charterist organisations. Hence former NUM, Cosatu, or ANC leaders do not refer to themselves as just former members of these organisations but, rather, often boast that they are 'graduates' of them. This means that one may leave the organisation but that the latter will always live in one, be it only through the imprint it has left on one's personality in terms of know-how and of a specific set of values. This imprint is also an emotional one, of course, which connects to one often-heard motto among present and former leaders of ANC-aligned formations in South Africa: 'Once an ANC, always an ANC.'

Beyond mass participation, the production of leadership was one of the most important achievements of the anti-apartheid struggle to an extent seldom matched in other post-conflict or postcolonial contexts. As Buhlungu expresses it:

> One of the most phenomenal successes of the black unions in the 1980s was their ability to build several layers of leadership. It was this that not only made it possible for the movement to withstand repression and employer victimisation, bust also catapulted the movement to the front line of the struggle for democracy. In part this was achieved through intensive pro-cesses of union education and training, particularly in those cases where unions had achieved paid leave for union training.[70]

The rise of NUM-trained leaders within this organisation also opened alterna-tive careers to many beyond the union. As the scope of professional opportunities expanded for black leaders in the 1990s, union-acquired skills increasingly became transferrable to other fields beyond the usual political career prospects available to former unionists, particularly in business and government (Figure 1.1 shows the impact of such 'deployments' of former union cadres on their material culture – here, their dress code). This partially explains the growing gap between ordinary NUM members and their leaders, which was pointed out as a decisive factor in explaining the current crisis faced by the union: in addition to the material benefits attached to the position of elected shaft steward (time off work for people who are already working on-surface, company offices, cars and phones, extra pay and so on), education and the prospect of social mobility also prove critical. In other words, the more NUM developed its cadreship, the more it cut itself off from its ordinary membership. Despite its determination to educate the workers, access to education and professional mobility de facto proved a reality for only a minority of NUM leaders (probably in the range of a few thousand since its inception). Because of this trend, most members remained largely excluded from opportunities for personal and occupational development. What was originally conceived as a commitment for the majority turned into a mechanism for the production of an elite and even-tually, through co-option mechanisms, into a dynamics of leadership reproduction. However, and as I have suggested, NUM also adapted its conception of education specifically to the post-apartheid context, in which making people grow is viewed as fulfilling a right rather than as reproducing a class.

Special focus on trends and fashions in high places in the New South Africa.

COMRADES-ABOUT-TOWN

NUM's *Godfrey Oliphant*   COSATU's *Jay Naidoo*

BEFORE...   BEFORE...

RED EYE is reliably informed that the noticeable change of dress among COSATU (or ex-COSATU) seniors in recent months flows from a call by the South African Clothing and Textile Worker's Union to stimulate the recession-plagued clothing industry via changes to comrades wardrobes. RED EYE's roving camera snapped a few "before and after" shots demonstrating our comrades' solidarity with the clothing workers' struggle to defend their jobs.

...AFTER   ...AFTER

Figure 1.1:   The workers' voice in Parliament?

Source: *South African Labour Bulletin* 18 (1994). Reprinted by permission of the *South African Labour Bulletin*.

Robert Michels's study of social democracy was largely dedicated to analysing the development of leadership. He showed how leaders were technically and intellectually essential to organisation. However, their rise and multiplication at all levels eventually led them to take over the organisation and reduce grassroots democracy to a mere ideal. This analysis was contested chiefly by Seymour Martin Lipset, Martin A. Trow and James S. Coleman. Based on a thorough study of the International Typographical Union (ITU), they found that 'a democratic political system also requires leaders'. But they insisted that such leaders should be relatively equal in status or pay to those they lead and that the latter should have ways to exercise direct control over their leaders, through direct elections and referenda. Moreover, the main reason why power in an organisation like the ITU did not become absolute was the creation of an original internal two-party system that gradually institutionalised internal opposition.[71] The current organisational identity of NUM was and still is, as I have argued and will further show, the result of centralising power and decision-making at the top level of the organisation. In contrast to the ITU, NUM can be approached as a 'one-party union'. This does not necessarily mean, however, that it is an oligarchic organisation in which power cannot be contested internally. The fact that incumbents were defeated in NUM's 15th congress, a gathering of leaders of various importance in the organisation, shows that it also developed internal democratic safeguards.

As mentioned earlier, Part II explores how NUM, and beyond South Africa's Charterist movement, gave birth to a special type of leadership. The task of producing not only 'good' but also skilled leaders was in fact always an intrinsic and key feature of anti-apartheid organisations in the 1970s and 1980s.[72] The fall of apartheid hit South African trade unions hard and deprived them of many skilled leaders in what was labelled a 'big brain drain',[73] but it certainly did not lead to a skills vacuum as far as leading the 'new' South Africa was concerned. To succeed him when he retired, Nelson Mandela – who himself was just one of many talented leaders among his generation – was spoilt for choice. Internal ANC politics eventually decided for him, but options were several among leaders whose competence made them suitable for the job: the smart and popular commander-in-chief of the ANC's armed wing whose assassination almost derailed the transition's peace talks;[74] the founding general secretary of NUM, a prime organiser and the ANC's finest negotiator at the time,[75] who was eventually defeated in the run-up to the movement's deputy-presidency by a reserved party-man who was also much more experienced in the arts of diplomacy and politics.[76] In Part II I show why the type of leadership NUM produced includes transferrable skills.

Leadership and command need to be addressed transversally, as a set of skills and aptitudes that are produced and can be separately or jointly mobilised and exercised in fields as diverse as trade unionism, political parties, government or business. The intertwined questions of leadership, authority and domination have a long history that I cannot fully address here. Leadership, however, took a new and specific meaning in the twentieth century, when it became an essential and transversal feature of all human forms of organisation. From 1890 onward, a widespread preoccupation with leadership (*commandement* in French, *Führung* in German, or *rukovodstvo* in Russian), and the need to have it embodied in dedicated individuals, emerged in countries as diverse as France, Germany, the Soviet Union and the United States. Historians of the twentieth century gave considerable attention to the phenomenon of charisma and to the role of leaders in totalitarian regimes, yet in doing so they also underestimated the impact and extent of leadership beyond totalitarian contexts. It is significant to note in this regard that the last decade of the twentieth century and the first part of the twenty-first century saw, all over the world, collective mobilisations claiming, in opposition to the overwhelming presence of leaders in society, that they were '*leaderless*'.[77] Examples abound: the recent Arab uprisings, as well as at mobilisations against authoritarianism and financial greed as various as those of Madrid's Puerta del Sol 'indignados', New York's 'Occupy Wall Street' or Istanbul's Taksim Square and Gezi Park, and even the 2012 strikes in the South African mining industry.[78] As Yves Cohen explains about the twentieth century, 'It is not as if leaders and command had not existed until then, but it is only at this time that they became problems.'[79] The historical development of a type of leadership that did not rely on only a few individuals but on many emerged not as a result of the concentration of leadership but, on the contrary, through its dissolution across spheres of society. Command, be it in a political organisation or in a factory, was now increasingly linking people unknown to one another.

My interest in leadership was firstly dictated by my own ethnographic experience of NUM and its crucial focus on issues of education and personal development, which I have identified as a key feature of the union. But it also fits, as I have said, within a global history of leadership linked to factory work or, in the case of NUM, to the environment of the mine. When the union took control of the mining compounds, it replaced the izinduna (the traditional leaders appointed by mining bosses) with elected committees and shaft stewards.[80] But leadership in trade unions and in NUM was also decisively affected by the joint development of industry and communism. As Cohen writes, 'The 20th century indeed presents a cruel paradox. After October 1917, an immense and new hierarchy was created, covering the world in differentiated ways, precisely based on the promise of removing the State and all hierarchies.' Yet, he adds, 'independently of a history of "totalitarianisms", which mainly brings together Nazism and Stalinism, the history of authority and of communist hierarchies ought to be written jointly with that of liberalism'.[81] And indeed it is no coincidence that NUM leaders such as its former general secretaries Gwede Mantashe and Frans Baleni were able to lead their organisation politically through a conception of power derived from Marxism–Leninism, while being perfectly at ease in their daily interactions with staff members or mining industry captains in a neoliberal managerial register.

The growing distance between NUM leaders and their membership results to some extent from the symbolic power the former have acquired through accumulating cultural capital. The role of an ideology – in this case communism – is also noticeable in the case of NUM, for, as I will explain, it has been produced and reproduced by a group of national office bearers and imposed on the organisation both as a form of knowledge that legitimises the domination of those at the top over those at the base, and as a specific practice of power that ensures its control of structures. The cultural capital of national leaders is also reflected in the academic titles they have amassed through their years in office. Gwede Mantashe, as already mentioned, is an MA graduate; Frans Baleni is a BA graduate; and former NUM president Senzeni Zokwana earned several certificates in executive management and risk assessment from the University of South Africa. The three are no exception among their peers.

The trajectory of NUM cadres and leaders is not, as far as internal representations of it are concerned, the expression of a contradiction but rather the logical continuation of a career path started in the union. The concept of 'career', which is drawn from the work environment, is greatly useful in accounting for the professional and personal development and mobility of workers' representatives. It is a conceptual tool that helps to make sense of the dynamics of anticipation, contingency and relationship with and between social groups, as well as helping to approach the trajectory of an individual in sequential rather than linear terms. In post-apartheid South Africa, the non-linear professional destination of an individual is much more socially accepted than, say, in France, where going from trade unionism to business quickly earns one the 'social traitor' label (*social-traître*). This is so because 'personal development' is not conceived as merely individualistic but also as part of wider catch-up dynamics. Notions of age and generation are also considerations, and how they work may differ in other contexts, where one would rise through the ranks in a steadier fashion. In South Africa, the pace of one's social upward mobility often translates into the contrast between the careers of those who were part of the struggle (and experienced a late ascent, although often a rapid one) and the younger post-apartheid generation, who may rise fast thanks to the benefits of higher education and Black Economic Empowerment. The concept of 'career' is also useful to render the link between the 'objective' social position of individuals at a given time and its evolution, on the one hand, and, on the other, the 'subjective' conception they have of themselves and of their progression in life.[82]

METHODOLOGY AND OUTLINE OF THE BOOK

Fieldwork for this book was conducted over a three-year period, from May 2010, when South Africa was boiling on the eve of hosting the World Cup, and at the time of NUM's apogee and uncontested monopoly in mineworkers' representation, to May 2012, when the union had started losing ground in the aftermath of the January 2012 Impala strike, and as the August 2012 Lonmin strike and Marikana massacre were looming. I hence covered most of a NUM three-year organisational and internal political cycle. Complementary fieldwork was conducted in May and June 2015. This time frame also allowed me to follow one biyearly round of wage negotiation. All in all, I interviewed more than one hundred individuals (some of whom were interviewed twice)[83] in the different categories of actor that this book covers: these included about 70 former or current NUM leaders, members and employees (including 15 ordinary NUM members, 25 local NUM leaders – shaft stewards and branch office bearers – 12 regional office bearers or union employees, 13 national office bearers or NUM employees). The remaining 30 interviews included 11 mining company officials, 8 representatives from other mining unions, and another 10 relevant actors including labour lawyers, representatives of NGOs and union-related organisations, as well as labour facilitators and mediators. Many informal conversations complemented this body of formal interviews.

I also observed and shadowed most of the actors interviewed in the live performance of their work. I conducted close to 50 non-participant observation sessions[84] relevant to the organisational life of NUM: mass meetings; local, regional and national meetings; conferences and congresses. These allowed me to approach the democratic workings of the organisation from local grassroots to national executive level. In addition, I observed either fully or partially four separate wage negotiations involving NUM, four mining houses and other trade unions. Other types of social performance I observed included union schools and training, a labour court hearing, recruitment campaigns, marches and demonstrations, and union–company meetings at local and company level. I also went on two underground visits at a gold and at a platinum mine, accompanied by managers in one case and by managers and unionists in the other. My work focused mostly on NUM in the gold and platinum mining sectors. There is, of course, a practical concern behind this choice: it was not possible, alone, to cover all the mining sectors (the largest of which are platinum, gold, coal and diamonds) and other sectors (construction and energy) that are organised by NUM. However, from a methodological point of view, my chosen focus allowed me to view the union in a declining sector (gold) and in a booming industry (platinum). In terms of chronology it allowed me to get a sense of how NUM organised its historical stronghold on the one hand, and of how it had managed to penetrate the more recently unionised platinum sector on the other.

This mostly oral body of primary sources was complemented by the written documents I collected randomly during interviews and observations, including union literature and reports, minutes of negotiations or wage agreements. I have tried to build coherent and, in some cases, almost exhaustive bodies of primary NUM literature. Thenji Mlabatheki and Ntombi Masango kindly gave me access to NUM's resource centre at the head office, where NUM documents and other publications on labour and trade unions are stored. I compiled an archive containing an almost exhaustive set of national congress documents (secretariat reports, financial statements, resolutions and others) from 1986 to 2015. It is worth insisting on the fact that as they obviously constitute a discourse that NUM developed on itself, these documents cannot be regarded as 'politically correct'. They address the union's situation quite frankly, from the point of view of the structure that produced them (and, in it, of NUM secretaries at regional and national levels), at a given point in time: sensitive questions, such as corruption, are dealt with straightforwardly, which already gives one an idea of how internal democracy is understood in NUM and, beyond, in the ANC-aligned trade union movement. Other similar documents produced at regional and, more rarely, at local levels also added up to more than two hundred NUM primary written sources I use in this book (these include training manuals, central committee documents, or NUM position papers on a wide range of issues). I also managed to reconstitute a set of minutes taken at about 15 national executive committee meetings held between 1990 and 1994. This is a precious internal archive that allowed me to capture organisational dynamics at the time of South Africa's transition to democracy, in fields as diverse as the management of the union's human resources, the state of union structures, internal debates or NUM interactions with other actors. In addition to this NUM archive, I collected more than one hundred primary sources produced by mining companies, government, the judiciary (the South African labour courts in Braamfontein, Johannesburg), as well as by unions other than NUM. Through the Digital Innovation South Africa web portal hosted by the University of KwaZulu-Natal, I also accessed about one hundred primary NUM documents, most of which are articles from past issues of the union's periodical publication, *NUM News*, from 1985 to 1993.

This book is divided in two parts, starting with a description and analysis of NUM's structuring as an organisation and its internal political life in Part I. I analyse the organisation at a crossroads of the approaches proposed by Michels and Lipset, Trow and Coleman, to show how, out of both necessity and strategy, NUM's founders decided to build a competent and centralised mineworkers' union (chapters 2 and 3). This created early tensions between the top and base levels of the organisation, which were managed through the union's commitment to the worker-control principle and its unequivocal involvement in the anti-apartheid struggle and the struggle for the improvement of the mineworkers' working and living conditions. I deconstruct common views on NUM branches as a 'seat of union power' and show that internal politics were never univocal, but always marked by power struggles for position and resources (chapters 4 and 5).

In Part II, which is dedicated to the union as a leadership school and to its production of leaders, I argue that, right from its start and as a matter of survival, NUM assigned itself the task of giving birth to a numerous stratum of competent and dedicated leaders; an army of organic intellectuals; and an elite of trade unionists able to withstand the firepower of mining companies. I first show, in chapters 6 and 7, that NUM saw itself as a 'learning organisation' – a paradoxical one, however, for while it aimed to develop leaders and members equally, education first benefited the former, hence producing increased 'distinction' between leaders and the grassroots. Thus began the digging of a gap between 'distinguished leaders' and 'ordinary members'. Grasping the extent of this process is, I argue, pivotal to an understanding of how differentiation between leaders and members became critical over a few decades, to the point that some top NUM leaders expressed contempt for their members during the 2012 strikes and their aftermath. In chapters 8 and 9, I analyse the trajectories of a few NUM leaders and draw 'ideal types' of union leadership in order to qualitatively temper my analysis of the previously described internal dynamics, which otherwise would remain caricatural. I show how, over the past decade, NUM gradually passed into the control of its 'communist faction', which disciplined the organisation and muzzled internal debate, in what constituted a major deviation from earlier approaches to and practices of intra-organisational negotiation.

PART I

ORGANISATIONAL AGENCY IN UNION BUREAUCRACY AND POLITICS

Comrades,

I have stood on this rostrum as President for every Congress since I was elected 6,353 days ago on 4 December in 1982 – the day the Union was officially inaugurated in the Catholic Church in Jouberton Township near Klerksdorp. In a very strong sense, the Union's history and my life have been inextricably intertwined. For the first five years of the Union's life I was a worker president, combining my work as a personnel assistant at Western Deep Levels with the task of building our union organisation in a team led by Comrade Cyril Ramaphosa. After Western Deep Levels dismissed me during the 1987 strike, the union constitution was amended to enable me to continue as President on a full-time basis. That has been my job ever since.

*Address by NUM president James Motlatsi at the
10th NUM National Congress, Sinodale Centre,
Pretoria, 26 April 2000*

2

Local Weaknesses Solved through Centralisation

THE SWOP HYPOTHESIS APPLIED TO NUM

Three articles on NUM, published by Sakhela Buhlungu and Andries Bezuidenhout, constitute most of the available scholarship on the union and its transformation after apartheid.[1] Their analysis is based on material collected in three longitudinal surveys of NUM members, commissioned by the union and released respectively in 1998, 2005 and 2010. The surveys, which addressed the broad issue of 'servicing' to members, were conducted by the University of the Witwatersrand-based SWOP Institute, to which Buhlungu and Bezuidenhout belonged. They contained mostly quantitative data, complemented with some qualitative interviews. Such data provide a useful picture of NUM's membership with regard to, for instance, age, gender, languages, domicile. From a more qualitative point of view, the surveys explore members' perceptions of NUM presence and action at the grassroots, and the degree of members' involvement in union activities.

The 1998 report's executive summary starts by recalling what the effective functioning of union structures means according to NUM (see Figure 2.1). Local structures have to be 'strong, independent branches which solve their problems on their own, and which use the regional and national structures as a form of support. Regions are serviced by the national office, and branches are serviced by regional offices.'[2] An empowered branch is further described as one that is 'able to take initiatives and engage management effectively. The branches have the capacity to run their administration, education, and health and safety programmes. There is a dynamic interaction between the region, the branch leadership and membership.'[3] The report's summary then contrasts this ideal with reality on the ground:

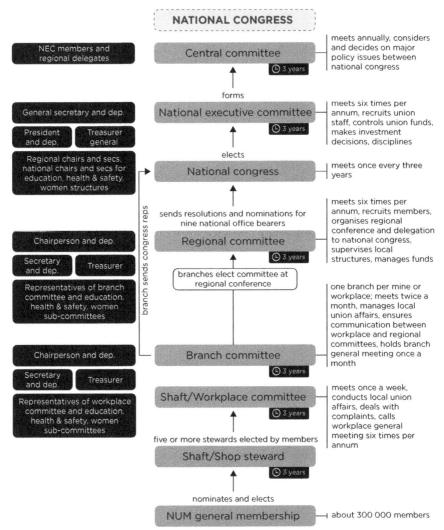

Figure 2.1: Constitution of the National Union of Mineworkers, as amended by the 2009 national congress and approved by the Registrar of Labour Relations on 28 March 2011

Source: Diagram created by the author

'if the picture presented from the data gathered in this project is compared to the characteristics of a strong branch, it is clear that the vision of strong, self-sufficient branches remains to be met'.[4] The report also notes that where branch structures existed at the time, other factors negatively impacted on their operations, such as 'destructive branch politics, office bearer turnover, unclear portfolios, the lack of consultation with members, low levels of responsibility and commitment, and office bearer disempowerment' due to a lack of training. In 1998, between 15 and 33 per cent of NUM members surveyed said union structures at their branch were not in place. Particularly alarming for the surveyors was the fact that 'political infighting among leadership at some branches' – 'leadership factionalism' – 'seemed to lead to perceptions and claims by membership and branch office bearers that leadership courts management and that it favours certain members'. This perceived conniv-ance of NUM local leaders with management clearly echoes perceptions underlying the widespread rejection the union has experienced since 2012. Another related issue was that some workers saw their branch office bearers as 'using their positions to gain access to promotion into management hierarchies'. Among the three regions surveyed in 1998, Rustenburg – where the 2012 strikes started – already appeared to be the most problematic in terms of the services provided to members and its capacity to fight dismissals.[5]

The 2005 SWOP report started with the general statement that members seemed satisfied with the services provided to them. Overall, it was more optimistic than the previous one with regard to the functioning of NUM's organisational appara-tus. Once again Rustenburg was depicted as particularly problematic: an expanding region in the context of the booming platinum industry, it had been unionised later than other, older mining regions and by 2005 was largely dysfunctional and disor-ganised after several regional office bearers had been suspended or had resigned from the union. In general, the report concluded that while members were 'loyal' to NUM because of 'its history and its legacy', there were serious gaps in servic-ing them and regional offices were under-capacitated to address labour-law-related issues. The problem of internal rivalries between leaders and aspiring leaders was a matter of particular concern.[6]

SWOP's latest report on the state of servicing in NUM dates back to 2010 and it is the most comprehensive of the three in terms of number of members, branches and regions surveyed. Most members said they were satisfied with the services received from the union but only 37 per cent said their branch was 'strong', with one-third saying it was 'average' and another third that it was 'weak'. Some com-plaints were again heard about cases in branches where members perceived their leaders as aligned with management. Others pointed to a lack of communication between members and leaders who failed to consult them on a regular basis. With regard to the relationship between branch and region, some 80 per cent of members in Rustenburg said they did not know who their regional representatives were, as against the average of 62 per cent in the whole union. This negative figure was even higher when it came to regional organisers – a union official whose presence on the ground is supposed to be particularly visible: 82 per cent of members did not know who this person in Rustenburg was (as against 60 per cent in the Free State and Carletonville). Paradoxically, workers seemed relatively content with the assistance they received from their respective regions, be it for fighting dismissals or providing legal advice. The 2010 report concluded by pointing out members' increasing concern about corruption and allegedly rigged local elections. 'Mega-branches' often seemed in serious disarray, an indication that is significant in view of the fact that the 2012 strikes started in large platinum branches.[7]

The three SWOP surveys conducted between 1998 and 2010 therefore depict a situation in which NUM certainly faced serious challenges, especially at local branch level, but was still able to cope with its duties at workplaces. In their three articles on NUM based on the SWOP reports (cited at the beginning of this chapter), Buhlungu and Bezuidenhout further analyse these challenges, viewing them as resulting largely from the impact of the post-apartheid transformation on NUM. It is arguable, however, that many of the features identified as illustrations of what a weak NUM is, especially at the local level, are neither entirely new nor particularly 'post-apartheid'. As a matter of fact, most do not result from the transformation of South Africa since 1994. Moreover, it is arguable that they do not result from a transformation of NUM itself. By this I do not mean that important post-1994 trends such as the growing social mobility of NUM members and leaders or the rise of subcontracting did not affect the union's structures through, for instance, increased battles for leadership positions. I suggest, however, that intra-union rivalries ought to be considered as a historical feature, which has always been part of NUM, rather than as a paradoxical consequence of the democratisation of South Africa.

LOCAL WEAKNESSES AND TENSIONS IN TIME

In a 1991 report, NUM's national executive committee (NEC) urged regions 'to examine why the quality of service to members is declining; why branches are not growing etc.'. In terms of legal servicing, 'it was noted that our service to members has deteriorated to an extent that complaints from members have become commonplace. It was found that the question of cases is the most crucial and needs immediate attention.'[8] At the time, of course, NUM was going throught its 'survival phase' (1987–1992), as it is known in the union. It was still in the process of recovering from the 1987 strike in which it had lost more than 50 000 members. The union was also suffering from severe retrenchments in the gold sector. Continuous victimisation by mining houses also played a part in the weakening of local union structures. To quote but one case, in June 1992, the Westonaria and Secunda regions had lost a majority of their leadership due to retrenchments.[9] The NEC, however, seemed to take for granted that the relative stagnation of the membership in those years was the consequence of poor delivery on the part of the union and not primarily due to external factors. The March 1991 NEC report, in preparation for the June 1991 national congress, complained that if most regions had held their respective conferences upstream of the congress, most of them had 'not yet commenced to hold branch conferences'. This is an illustration of serious organisational malfunctioning since, in terms of the union's constitution and in order to apply the worker-control principle, branch conferences should have come first in the build-up to a national congress (see Figure 2.1). Moreover, the report stressed that 'not all the regional conferences were well attended and it seems also in some regions documentation was not adequately prepared'.[10]

Tense relationships between local branches and their supervising regional and national offices sometimes perturbed the good functioning of NUM. A letter dated 11 June 1992 from the general manager of Grootvlei Proprietary Mines Ltd (a Springs-based subsidiary of Gengold) to the general secretary of NUM exposed the situation at one local union branch. The manager complained about the behaviour of the local NUM chairperson, Mr. Hlaele, in a case of alleged miscommunication between the national and local offices of NUM, which resulted in some employees not clocking in as they believed they had been awarded a holiday.[11] The union's regional chairperson intervened promptly and took steps to disband the branch committee after making sure that most members would go back to work. The dismissed branch chairperson then allegedly disturbed a union meeting and prevented new elections from being held. Whatever the actual causes of this conflict between mine management and NUM at its various levels and which, according to management, 'jeopardised' its relationship with the union due to the 'unconstitutional interference of Mr. Hlaele', it provides an example of how a local conflict developed and was managed in NUM twenty years ago.[12] Such conflicts between local and upper NUM structures are often considered as characteristic of post-apartheid union dynamics, as is the intervention of management in the life of local union structures. The ingredients described in this 1992 episode – tensions around NUM rules, resultant clashes between local leadership and upper union structures, and tensions between union and employer around the rules governing their 'industrial relations' – show that such dynamics were already in place before the end of apartheid. Comparable episodes in the post-apartheid period should therefore be read in tandem with such historical precendents. One example is the events that took place at platinum producer Lonmin in 2011, which played a part in the build-up to the 2012 strike and Marikana massacre. A local election was due to take place at the mine's Karee branch but the outgoing branch chairperson – Steve Khululekile – allegedly refused to hold it. In support of their chairperson, who had been dismissed by NUM's Rustenburg region, most likely in agreement with their national leadership, workers did not report for work. This tension between members and their leadership, which is generally approached as a post-apartheid dimension of the life of NUM, had many historical precedents.

In the early 1990s, the Rustenburg region developed in the difficult context of repression by apartheid's auxiliaries from the Bophuthatswana 'homeland'. In addition to police and mine security repression, NUM leaders were sometimes also the target of their own members. In July 1992, it was reported that a group of between 21 and 40 workers – including 'five girls' – from the Jabula branch of Rustenburg Platinum Mines and described by the NEC as a 'group of ill-disciplined workers' violently attempted to close NUM's Rustenburg office, which they successfully achieved twice before coming back a third time with a view to preventing regional office bearers from accessing the facility. One of them allegedly carried a gun, and some had sticks, iron bars, sjamboks and other 'instruments like knives, knobkerries', which they used to threaten office occupants. Someone known as Jerry Ntshatha led this group of angry workers, which was allegedly composed of NUM marshals and members from the Rustenburg Platinum Mines branch. After storming into the NUM office they decided to occupy it and kept at least one NUM office bearer with them, comrade Tambo A. Silekwa, who was beaten up and received death threats. On entry, they told the people in the Rustenburg office that they 'had been charged' and demanded that office keys be handed over to them. (At this point, it is interesting to note that ad hoc workers' committees and Amcu representatives formulated this very same demand against local NUM leaders in 2012.) Jerry Ntshatha then wrote a note that was placed at the entrance of the office and bore the names of three Rustenburg-based NUM officials and administrators, followed by these words: 'we dismiss them no return'. The angry members occupied the office in the following days until the police eventually dislodged and arrested some of them. The Rustenburg office subsequently had to be guarded by marshals from other branches and later by two paid security guards. The reasons behind this occupation are not clear – it was possibly meant to have national leadership attend to and solve an issue at mine level – but it shows that targeting union facilities and representatives through direct action and, more specifically, trying to close NUM offices was already in 1992 a repertoire of action in use among angry members willing to contest their union.[13] This hijacking of union facilities and personnel was no exception. A 1993 Carletonville regional report recounts:

> [Union] staff was held hostage on two consecutive weeks by dismissed workers in Doornfontein. The first incident was resolved when their demand was met. They were demanding that the deputy president must attend to their problem as promised. His absence created an impression that the Union was less concerned about them.[14]

A year later it was reported that at NUM's Grootvlei branch, 'on 28 and 30 March 1994, our Gold Fields Security members attempted a sit-in in the branch union office demanding to be serviced by the branch committee'.[15] Such episodes provide clear historical indications that, as far as internal union democracy is concerned, members dissatisfied with the workings of NUM viewed and still view it as their prerogative to embark on direct action. Moreover, such precedents were not limited to only the newer and more volatile NUM Rustenburg region; core gold regions, which were unionised in the 1980s, were also affected by the internal tensions and malfunctions that are generally considered to be post-apartheid trends.

Hard hit by the post-1987-strike massive dismissals as well as by the decline of the gold industry, regions like Carletonville nonetheless remained well established, leading NUM structures in the early 1990s. This did not prevent them, however, from facing structural and organisational challenges. In September 1993, Carletonville had ten branches falling under three mining houses (Gold Fields, Anglo American and Rand Gold) and energy supplier Eskom. A report on regional activities submitted to the NEC stated: 'the Region has structures which are not geared to a particular objective thus fail to function. The current structures were not given support by officials.' It added: 'Although most branches are still at the embryo stage, they do meet on weekly basis. It is however not clear as to what programmes do branches have which guide them. It is also not clear as to how s/s [shaft stewards] engage management in their programme. The Regional meetings could not take place as planned due to failure by branches to attend.'[16]

This description reminds us that instability in local union structures and, in many instances, their inability to operate are nothing new. At the time, of course, the failure by branches to attend regional meetings could also have been a consequence of State repression or victimisation by employers. This said, however, one should note, based on this series of examples, that NUM was historically always weak at the local level (with major variations from branch to branch). This was not necessarily true in terms of its capacity to mobilise – the union successfully united mineworkers against racist employers and the apartheid regime. It rather implies that the union's organisational strength, which was best exemplified by its national office, did not necessarily translate into strong and perennial union structures at the grassroots and even at the intermediary regional level. If one looks at a 2002 report, at the start of NUM's second decade, one reads that 'Carletonville has a history of volatility, where structures get entangled in infighting from time to time, to a point of collapse in certain instances'.[17] Such a comment surely did not apply, in the mind of the region's secretary, to the post-apartheid era only.

Because of weakness at local branch and, very often, regional level, NUM head office had no choice but to take the lead. This further accentuated tensions between local aspirations to autonomy and the organisation-building ambition of the national layer. A 1993 report on the state of the Pretoria–Witwatersrand–Vereeniging (PWV) region makes this clear: 'There is a concern in the region over the way the Head Office intervenes in the region. This concern is a result of three serious interventions by the Head Office where the Head Office virtually takes over from the region, either in the middle of a process or on the invitation by management.' These 'interventions' referred to the interference of head office in wage negotiations, including during one negotiation at Durban Deep 'where the Collective Bargaining Dept imposed a R30.00 across the board settlement to the branch. That settlement has destroyed faith in the Union. The region has to absorb the knocks.'[18]

Running NUM at regional and local level was never an easy task, be it during or after apartheid. Regional reports submitted to the NEC punctuate the life of the union and they typically point to organisational weaknesses. If one randomly picks one such report in the early 1990s and looks, for instance, at July 1993, one will find that it deals with external factors: the constant threats to the union and its weakening following management-imposed retrenchments and derecognition of its structures (in Nelspruit, Phalaborwa, Northern Cape and the list continues …); violence and repression in the political confrontation between the ANC and the Inkatha Freedom Party ([IFP], Southern Natal) or resulting from police action (Bophutatswana police in Rustenburg and Northern Cape). But such reports also point to internal factors, including delays in or bad reporting, the lack of human resources to effectively service members and keep structures alive, or the lack of commitment on the part of leadership (Northern Natal, Orange Free State, Rustenburg, Witbank).[19] In other words, the usual assumption that NUM structures would paradoxically have been weakened after apartheid is far from obvious: one could, on the contrary, assume that they have grown in capacity (in human resources, for instance). The lack of local democracy or the centralising tendencies of head office were already well-entrenched NUM organisational features under apartheid, just like personal conflicts around power. This largely results from the context in which NUM was built. Faced with intense local and national repression on the one hand, it had to rely on strong national structures. Yet, on the other hand, it was often forced to deviate from its own organisational rules in order to adapt to volatile and informal local arrangements and situations, with a view to penetrating the closed environment of mining compounds. Once this was done, union leaders tried to build local union structures around NUM rules and this brought new conflicts due to the clash between union bureaucracy and these very same local arrangements and situations. The existence, and possibly the prevalence, of historical continuities in the organisation's weaknesses will soon become more obvious but one can already venture that the union's organisational strength (measured by its bureaucratic density and its capacity to effectively engage employers on workplace issues or to service its membership) is far superior nowadays to what it was in the 1980s or 1990s.

RUSTENBURG: LATE AND LIGHT UNIONISATION IN THE BANTUSTAN

When viewed historically, the case of Rustenburg – NUM's Achilles heel – demonstrates that the weakness of NUM at local level is an ingrained organisational feature rather than just a post-apartheid product. The case of Impala Platinum, the world's second-largest platinum producer, whose main operation is in Phokeng, near Rustenburg, is a clear illustration of this. There are indeed interesting parallels to be drawn between the 2012 Impala Platinum mine strike, the first of many work stoppages that followed in platinum (but also gold, chrome or coal) and the strike that, some twenty years earlier, had forced Impala management to recognise NUM. Parallels between the two situations include Impala's resort to lockouts and mass dismissals, but also the 'insurrectional' and violent dimensions of the 1991 mobilisation in which workers fought management in the broader context of mobilisation against Lucas Mangope's bantustan regime. In 2012, Impala's security still included former Renamo and Unita fighters from Mozambique and Angola in its ranks and employers were ready to use violence. Another feature of the earlier strike is that, just as in 2012, it relied on a local workers' committee – the Bafokeng action committee, characterised by the strong homogeneity that made this mine unique (in 1991, more than 70 per cent of Impala's employees were local Tswana who shared life experiences under Mangope's rule).[20] The degree of local autonomy the Impala workers displayed in 1991 was notable, and if it allowed NUM to quickly reap the rewards of their grassroots organisation, it is also a reminder of how fragile union structures were and remained. It is in fact following a similar path by which Amcu penetrated Impala in 2012:

> The [1991] strike action was remarkable, in that it was initiated by worker activists organising on their own. NUM had virtually no members and extremely tenuous links with the workforce. However, the union was able to take advantage of the space opened by the strike, gain access, and sign up 30 000 workers within a few weeks.[21]

NUM embarked on a 'blitz' recruiting campaign and sustained industrial action at Impala in 1991–1992 (it followed several other strikes, including that of 1986[22]). 'The battle to achieve recognition in the mine has begun despite the … Bophuthatswana legislation. It is vital for the union to mobilise around this issue to ensure that we win a decisive victory in Bophuthatswana,' a September 1991 NUM NEC meeting reported.[23] On 4 July 1991 workers, angry after the locally registered Bophuthatswana National Union of Mining Employees (Bonume) signed an eight per cent wage increase agreement with management, struck for higher wages and better working conditions. In August 'one worker was found shot dead'; no one was arrested and 'white workers were going to work armed'. The rejection of Bonume, which was seen as a 'sweetheart union', is an interesting element if one juxtaposes it with the 2012 rejection of NUM, just as it had struck a wage deal with Impala. Workers, who were not, as we shall later see, properly consulted, rejected this deal and they accused NUM of collusion with management. In the first instance, Impala workers who organised the 1991 action had mobilised and organised themselves on a virtually spontaneous basis. But NUM was also present on Impala's shaft through undercover organisers such as Sipho Shabangu or Isaac Mayoyo[24] and one cannot exclude that Amcu resorted to a similar type of organisation to undermine NUM monopoly representation in 2012. Despite much violence NUM continued recruiting members at the mine and soon reached 20 000 members (as against Bonume's 3 000 members). For NUM 'the strategic objective [was] to ensure that this growth of the union is consolidated in as short a time as possible'.[25] On 15 August, 40 000 Impala workers embarked on a go-slow, which continued the next day, and 'alleged management-sponsored vigilantes launched brutal attacks at the striking workers', killing eight (or eleven, depending on estimates).[26] Another similarity with the 2012 situation is that the Impala ad hoc committee quickly felt overwhelmed in negotiations with management (in 2012 this was one factor that drove workers to call Amcu in to negotiate on their behalf): 'The first [1991] meeting with management had its shocks. Workers were not well organised and their demands were haphazard. They had no prepared agenda and the language was a barrier as some members of the committee don't have elementary education,' Mayoyo explained. After workers from all Impala operations had formed a unified committee to represent them, negotiation still proved an arduous task: 'Management was using the law and the skills of negotiating. They drove negotiations into more technical and complex levels. Lack of experience and little knowledge put us at a disadvantage … What frustrated me was that I have very little knowledge of English and at times failed to follow or understand arguments, especially when management used percentages,' Shabangu argued. Workers subsequently referred management to NUM for negotiation (Jessie Maluleka and Martin Nicol, from NUM head office, were involved). Workers nevertheless continued to closely monitor the negotiation process: 'The workers "wore management down" by asking to caucus with the union officials every time a fresh point was raised. Eventually management agreed that the officials could join the workers' negotiating team, and "the union was recognised de facto".'[27]

The strike continued sporadically despite the workers having achieved wage increases ranging from 15 to 16 per cent and having won recognition for their ad-hoc local committee. Repression from company security and Bophuthatswana police remained harsh in the following months (Mayoyo was detained and tortured at the Phokeng police station). Violence included clashes between pro- and anti-NUM elements that left 14 workers dead on 28 September. NUM, which had reached a membership of 43 000, had to wait for official recognition first and could not represent its members directly in the meantime. At this stage the company had recognised only the Impala workers' committee.[28] This created a situation of autonomy among the workers – one that doubled NUM's unrecognised chain of command at Impala. As Allen explains,

> Isaac Mayoyo, who had left BONUME to join NUM, began to recruit militant young black mineworkers to act in a new role of marshals to assist with crowd control at mass meetings and suchlike events but with no specific union functions … However, because NUM officials had no legitimate access to the mines, the marshals developed a degree of autonomy that enabled them to operate broadly in parallel with the official organisation of the formally unrecognised NUM, though not always in harmony with it … They were uncompromising in their recruitment tactics and allegedly used force to back up their powers of persuasion.[29]

The 1992 commission of enquiry into events at the Bafokeng North Mine described the September brawl in the following terms:

> On 28 September 1991 large-scale violence broke out within the hostel complex and fourteen persons were killed. The events have variously been described as a faction fight between the Tswanan and Lesothan workers, and as an ideological fight between those who supported NUM and the marshall system, and those who resented these new forces. The majority of those killed were Lesothans.[30]

There were tensions among members of the workers' committee, and between the latter, workers and NUM leadership, that are reminiscent of later instances of violence and suspicion of management–union collusion. When NUM leaders went underground to convince workers to halt a sit-in they had embarked on in support of a dismissed committee member, in October 1991, NUM's Rustenburg region secretary recounted: 'We had to be very tactful and apply diplomacy. Workers were very hostile, having been told we were collaborating with management.'[31]

In October a group of workers had also assaulted Impala's general manager, Mr. Drummond, who was saved from the mob only by Isaac Mayoyo's intervention. (Ironically, in 2009, NUM deputy president Pete Matosa was assaulted by angry workers at Impala and his life was saved only thanks to the intervention of the Protea mine security.) After months of unrest, NUM and Impala management signed a recognition agreement in 1992. The sour relationship between the union, the employer and Bophuthatswana continued[32] until the homeland was formally reintegrated into South Africa in March 1994, which finally gave Impala workers and others in the bantustan the same legal rights of association as black mineworkers in the rest of South Africa.

It was against this sour background that NUM truly imposed itself in Rustenburg, a region it had launched in 1986. The platinum province proved to be both NUM's main membership growth prospect (at the end of 2011, Rustenburg claimed 107 866 paid-up members[33] – more than one-third of total NUM membership at the time)[34] and the union's Achilles heel, with a membership that may have been easy to recruit but always remained hard to organise and discipline. Rustenburg, beyond some early precedents of unionisation such as that of Impala, remains a more recently established mining area where unionisation is also a relatively recent process. The installation of local NUM branches in the platinum sector followed the industry's growth (most currently active platinum mines did not exist prior to 1994) and, indeed, half of the NUM members in Rustenburg were actually recruited between 2006 and 2012.[35] At

Murray & Roberts Cementation, for instance – a contractor that services many mines and whose main operation is at the Kroondal-Marikana mine – NUM was established only in the mid-2000s. In other words, the NUM–Amcu confrontation, which started at Impala, NUM's oldest position in the sector, is not only a fight between two unions; it is also, at a more fundamental level, an endeavour to unionise the platinum sector durably (a mission to evangelise, one would say in religion). The weakness of this relatively new NUM region was underlined in a 2006 report:

> As we vigorously drive our recruitment campaign, we also have to ensure that we do not grow this organization with ill-informed members because it will be disastrous in the long run. There is a growing tendency to confuse the organization with figures. Numbers are important but we need to take a comprehensive view of the organization, which includes: 'Sustainability', 'growth', 'capacity', and 'influence'.[36]

Such number games were clearly at play in NUM's recruiting strategy, which I will describe shortly through the example of Sithethi Mxhasi, Rustenburg's regional coordinator, responsible for overseeing recruitment and meeting targets set at head office.

Another element that has probably durably weakened NUM's position in Rustenburg was the 2006 ousting of its former deputy general secretary, Archie Palane, whose leadership was key in organising where he enjoyed significant popularity (for a detailed analysis of Palane's defeat in the national leadership, see chapter 9). Most head office leaders rose through the ranks in the older gold industry, but Palane was the most knowledgeable and field-experienced leader in the platinum industry. Here is how he described his role in organising the unionisation of the workforce and in responding to the challenge of rival unions:

> I was then given the Platinum, which is the Rustenburg mines ... And I must say of great interest was the challenge that we faced in the Rustenburg area because in 1995, as I was leaving for southern Africa, there was a splinter group called Five Madoda [5 M], which was initiated I learned later from some of the management with the intention of breaking NUM because in Rustenburg you had the homeland. When NUM started growing in the area, particularly after the [1994] election, managers began to fear NUM, and especially in Anglo Plats they sponsored this 5 M [note that such a co-option hypothesis is contended. The 5 M are usually described as an ad hoc workers' committee]. It started as 5 M and translated into Mouthpeace [Workers' Union] afterwards

because 5 M was not a registered union. It was a terrible scene; NUM membership dropped. When I came in, in 1998, NUM membership was about 13 per cent, which meant we had lost even organisational rights. The major challenges there were the killings. If you were wearing a [NUM] tee shirt you were dead. So I realised we were not going to win membership by violence, we had to devise some strategy. I found the best tool was to organise members around collective bargaining issues, wages and conditions of employment, because that's what they could relate to the most. When I left in 2006, our membership in Anglo Plats was around 80 to 85 per cent. When I arrived there were about 13 unions recognised; when I left, three or four.[37]

As shown by this insight into the fragile unionisation of Rustenburg, violence and union rivalry are nothing new to NUM. Putting the present in historical perspective can help shed light on why old national leaders of the union seemed surprisingly relaxed given the challenge their organisation started facing in 2012. Part of this attitude, beyond a degree of (over)confidence, is probably explained by their sense that union rivalry is nothing new and that 'NUM shall come back'. Only the future will tell. However, one key element from the past, which crucially connected the top of the organisation to its base, now seems to be lacking: organising.

ORGANISING THE ORGANISATION

The SWOP reports referred to at the beginning of this chapter found that between 2005 and 2010, the proportion of members who had never seen a regional organiser rose from 28 to 41 per cent. The fact that the quantity or at least the quality of NUM's organising capacity diminished – with more professional but less committed individuals – is a hypothesis one can make to explain the union's current loss of ground. Historically, the weak state of subnational structures was addressed by paying thorough attention to organising. NUM invested a lot of resources in one non-elected position that became key in the union: the organiser. The figure of the organiser is central to any organisation-building process. 'The core functions of an organizer are membership recruitment, organizing and service ... Recruitment entails bringing new members into the union and organizing is about building structures, empowering stewards and making them ready to engage management and mobilizing members.'[38]

NUM was not initially developed as a grassroots movement. It was conceived from above, by the Council of Unions of South Africa (Cusa), which mandated

Cyril Ramaphosa, then a young law graduate, to form a mineworkers' union. The decision to form NUM also arose from an increasing demand for organisation formulated by mineworkers and a strike wave that had shaken the mines just a few months before NUM was launched. When the union was formed in December 1982 it had four regions, no regional offices and 25 organisers. The organisation was very chaotic at the time as 'none of [the recruits] knew anything about the pyramidal structures of unions stretching from shaft stewards' committees to branches through regional offices to a national executive committee as the union constitution prescribed'.[39] The role of organisers in the early years was therefore crucial for the successful development of the union; they travelled throughout all the regions.

Organising had initially been conceived as a normal activity for all union officials. It was professionalised at the Fifth National Congress (1987), when a dedicated union department was formed under the leadership of the Witbank regional secretary, Gwede Mantashe. Based in the regions or at the head office, organisers, who reported directly to the general secretary, acted as a conveyor belt between the organisation's several levels with which they were directly in touch. The main task of the organising department was to recruit members in the hostels, using processes and techniques that had been in place since 1982 (see Figure 2.2). Organisers were often experienced unionists who had been dismissed after the 1987 strike. Where the union was not welcome to recruit, they put clandestine structures in place in the form of small cells, just as they had done during the strike.[40] Sithethi Mxhasi – who himself was not dismissed in 1987 – recalled these years prior to the 'big strike':

> I was elected as a shop steward and then I was so active [that] I converted my house into a recruiting office of the union. So the guys I was staying with were able to assist members, fill in stop orders. If members were having cases we started to delegate each other to go and represent workers. Within the hostels we identified certain rooms to do union work, because it was safer within the hostels than outside. Remember that the apartheid regime was so brutal out there looking for everybody that is an activist. In the compound it was safer, you have the gate, it's always locked, there are tribal police at the gate so when you get in you have to be searched … One of the hostels I was staying [in] was accommodating something like 4 000 employees, it was a whole world … Over the weekends when we were entertaining ourselves inside the hostels and outside in soccer and rugby stadiums it was a very busy environment. Comrades from neighbouring mines, some more advanced than us in terms of recruitment … used to visit us, like the current

Figure 2.2:   NUM recruitment poster, 1980s

Source: Digital Innovation South Africa. Reproduced with permission.

secretary general of the ANC, Gwede Mantashe. He was working in a coal mine not far away from us, he used to come, he was a strong rugby player, so they used to come, organise matches and all those things. I think he utilized his own position because he was a welfare officer.[41]

Sithethi later held the position of regional coordinator in NUM's Rustenburg region. Before he was appointed as a regional coordinator in 2007, he spent ten years working as an organiser. Being in charge of recruiting members in Rustenburg made him an important person in the union, given the strategic position the region then occupied as NUM's main prospect for growth. During a 2011 interview, he recalled: 'Our efforts towards [increasing] the membership … saved this union in many ways. At some point there was a financial crisis, the industry was retrenching in other sectors, like gold, but because we recruited more members we kept the organisation alive.'[42] At our first meeting, Mxhasi proudly told me that his region was by far the biggest in the union. He claimed nearly 94 000 paid-up members[43] a week ahead of the 2011 regional conference in which Rustenburg would publicise a paid-up membership of 108 000.

The regional coordinator is, among other tasks, in charge of overseeing organisers. The regional staff he supervises is crucial for the good functioning of regions given that there are typically only two full-time elected officials, who are supposed to 'lead' the region: the regional chairperson and the regional secretary (other regional office bearers are sometimes also deployed to the union on a full-time basis, but they are more frequently part-time). This limited number of full-time leaders at the regional level empowers administrative staff all the more, particularly since they have specific skills (especially financial skills) that elected leaders do not typically have. The regional coordinator therefore becomes a central facilitator in the union whose mission is to articulate different organisational levels:

> As an organiser you will play a key role in making sure that decisions by the national congresses or the central committee are clearly interpreted at the level of the region where they must be implemented. From there it is also your role as an organiser of making sure that a similar understanding flows down to the branches and that the branches put it on the ground.[44]

Organisers often pride themselves on their abilities, which have, in fact, become a NUM trademark that is also prized outside this union – as I have argued before, it is no coincidence that all three secretary generals of the ANC after 1991 were all former NUM general secretaries. Organising is a source of power since it exposes one to all levels and workings of the organisation. Archie Palane, a former NUM organiser and deputy general secretary, remembered:

> When I came to NUM I still recall Cyril [Ramaphosa] was saying I would rather go into the Education Department because I had already done the ground work in terms of organising, coming from the Young Christian Workers Movement. But I said no, I said I needed to acclimatise to the mining environment and understand the language … I did not want to give a theoretical guidance. So I then chose to go in organising to mobilise workers. I came in as an organiser [in February 1986]. It was hardly two months, then there was an education conference in Soweto where I met some of my old schoolmates coming from Phalaborwa and when they heard I had joined NUM, they said to Cyril and James Motlatsi they wanted me to go there. Because in Phalaborwa workers did not have an office, there was no administration, there was nothing. I went to Phalaborwa and I think that's when my career started because then there I was able to learn. Then Cyril asked me to establish the regional office in the Lydenburg area, then I was sent to Rustenburg to establish NUM structure there. I came back, then I was sent to Witbank, which is the coal fields, because the union membership there was declining … Then I came back to head office and was given what is called now Pretoria Witwatersrand Vaal (PWV), which dealt with the gold mines, coal mines and power stations. Then a crisis emerged in Carletonville, structures were collapsing again, membership declining and I was sent there to go and build the organisation again.[45]

Palane followed the path of other former NUM employees such as Marcel Golding, who, initially recruited as a press officer, was eventually elected as assistant general secretary in 1987. Golding even acted as general secretary when Ramaphosa was deployed to the ANC in 1991. Palane was elected as deputy general secretary from 1997 to 2006.

In NUM the figure of the organiser is revered and the union was successively led by reputed administrators, from Ramaphosa to Mantashe. Collin Mohala, regional coordinator in Carletonville, insisted on the career prospects that derive from organising:

> I think I must thank the union for employing me as an organiser before. Because if you are an organiser you work as a generalist. Our former general secretary, comrade Gwede Mantashe, used to refer to organising as the dirty

work because there you do everything. So any other position that arises in the union except for areas of specialty like your finances, research, it is easy for a person who has been an organiser just to plug in very smoothly.[46]

Mohala's comment gives one a sense of the potential tension between organisational commitment and individual careerism, which is found in NUM as in any other organisation. Buhlungu has argued that the early generation of organisers who, post-1973, embarked on building independent black trade unions was composed of 'activist organizers' who, because they were politically committed to the anti-apartheid struggle, speeded up the emergence of worker leaders and promoted internal union democracy. The situation changed, this argument goes, particularly after 1994, and followed a new pattern of class formation, which

> manifested itself in the form of individualism and a quest for personal material advancement, values and ideologies that were antithetical to the collectivism and solidarity that had been the hallmark of the democratic organizational culture in the unions. The effect of these competing values and approaches was the fracturing of the activist-organizer fusion such that it could no longer be assumed that all full-time officials supported or promoted internal union democracy.[47]

This resulted in the emergence of three kinds of post-apartheid union official: ideological unionists, career unionists and union 'entrepreneurs'. The first two types, Buhlungu argues, are 'implicit in debates on the sociology of trade unionism, particularly in relation to notions of union democracy on the one hand [here embodied by ideological unionists] and oligarchy on the other [career unionists]'. In this classification, the third type would feature as a new ideal that includes union leaders and officials who, having achieved these positions sometimes incidentally, then used them as a platform to switch to business especially.[48] However, the classification poses several problems.

Firstly, it is problematic in its general assumption that political or trade union involvement could be fully selfless or, for that matter, fully selfish. It is obvious that former NUM leaders such as Marcel Golding, who used the union's investment arm launched in the 1990s to build a business career for himself, are successful entrepreneurs, or that Gwede Mantashe, who used his position as NUM general secretary to embark on a political career, is a career unionist. Cyril Ramaphosa, the union's first general secretary, also became both a successful businessman and politician. If some leaders are more 'dedicated' to their organisations than others, the notion of interest can never be excluded from the picture.

Secondly, there is also a romantic approach to careerism or self-interest in the context of the struggle against apartheid, which relies on the questionable idea that because people had fewer opportunities, because the colour bar deprived most talented men and women of upward social mobility, they were also less opportunistic than their post-apartheid counterparts. There is no doubt that conviction and political ideals, along with the daily and historical experience of racial oppression, were key to anyone's involvement against apartheid in the 1980s. Certainly the risks that came with involvement and very limited prospects for financial reward were hardly an incentive. This said, however, the decision for one to get involved in the anti-apartheid struggle remained a choice. Some degree of upward social mobility existed back in apartheid days outside unions or political organisations. Public administration offered limited career prospects for black people, as did the corporate sector. Some mining house executives, such as Impala Platinum's employee relations executive Humphrey Oliphant, whom I met in May 2012, started to rise in the corporate sector in the 1980s. His upward mobility may have speeded up after apartheid but it was the result of a career choice he had made long before 1994. In fact, the idea of selflessness has been invalidated *a posteriori*: as soon as career opportunities opened up post-1994, former unionists and anti-apartheid activists proved just as attracted by money and power as anyone else.

Thirdly, there are several distinct types of recompense for activism in organisations, not only for top leaders but also for intermediary layers of leadership, as well as for the rank and file. Recompense can be monetary or non-monetary material remunerations, as well as symbolic remunerations. The latter usually occur in organisations driven by powerful and allegedly selfless ideologies such as the anti-apartheid struggle or communism. Participation in the organisation is classically remunerated through the award of positions and/or time off work in the case of trade unions, which helps to explain why individuals such as Ramaphosa chose to pursue a career in trade unionism rather than in places where available opportunities were definitely more limited, though not non-nexistent, for a young and talented lawyer like him. Symbolic rewards – the sense of belonging to a cause, a group, and the acquisition of cultural capital are also powerful drives for the involvement of individuals, especially in mass-based organisations.[49] In other words, getting involved in trade unions such as NUM was a career strategy that made sense and it also had the advantage of coinciding with the political ideals of many. What the multiplication of business and political opportunities in post-apartheid South Africa did, however, is revalue individual career strategies driven by material and financial reward. Conversely the demise of apartheid devalued ambitions based on prospects of non-monetary remuneration. This is possibly one reason why mass mobilisation became increasingly difficult: the mostly symbolic rewards one could aspire to under apartheid are now outnumbered by the material rewards one can hope to gain through one's contemporary NUM involvement.

LEGALISTIC AND BUREAUCRATIC BEGINNINGS

The birth of NUM in December 1982, and in the context of a renewal of the anti-apartheid struggle largely instilled by the new 'independent trade unions', can be seen as an organisational success story. Appointed by Cusa, a federation close to the black consciousness movement, the young lawyer named Cyril Ramaphosa worked hard with a group of black employees and clerks from the gold mines – including James Motlatsi, founding president of NUM, and Elijah Barayi, its deputy president and a member of the ANC, who eventually became Cosatu's first president. They launched an organisation that soon became the country's leading trade union. Just one year after its creation it had 55 000 members; by 1994, it was 281 000 strong. The new union was grounded in mounting contestation on the mines and it took advantage of recent openings in South African labour law, as well as of the change in some mining bosses' attitude to workers' representation.[50] NUM's founders managed to unify black mineworkers sustainably for the first time in the history of South Africa's mining industry. Thanks to NUM, mineworkers could speak as one with the powerful Chamber of Mines, the representative of mining bosses. The union soon started negotiating pay rises that the Chamber had so far announced unilaterally every year. It also put new, organised pressure on mining companies about issues such as safety at work, a fundamental issue at a time when the mines killed more than 700 mineworkers a year, and an issue on which NUM has been consistent ever since (see Figure 2.3). Collective action gave mineworkers a new sense of dignity that they expressed through boycotting mine stores and their excessive prices, or through fighting daily apartheid racism and divide-and-rule policies.

Two elements are particularly striking in NUM right from the start: its will to unify mineworkers, who had often been deemed impossible to organise, on the one hand, and, on the other, its will to channel their energy into a legalistic strategy, with a view to protecting the nascent organisation[51] in an environment that had been marked by spontaneous strikes and high levels of violence between mineworkers.[52] The migrant labour system, one of apartheid's pillars, relied on a foreign workforce drawn from southern Africa's rural areas. This workforce was

Figure 2.3: Joint NUM–management safety march, October 2011
Photographer: Raphaël Botiveau

highly vulnerable, since employment was on the basis of yearly contracts and min-ing houses also used to divide workers along tribal lines, which increased their propensity to get involved in faction fights. The will to organise mineworkers and make them available for mobilisation found its first expression in a minority sec-tion of the mines' workforce composed of skilled or semi-skilled black minework-ers, employed in junior managerial positions, often on the surface, making them more mobile in the mining compounds. Many of this first generation of local lead-ers came from Lesotho and NUM sometimes used the established structures of the Basutoland Congress Party to build its own structures.[53] The trade union opted for a remarkably legalistic approach on the initiative of its general secretary, Cyril Ramaphosa, being himself a jurist. In NUM's first years, the union avoided direct confrontation with the mines even though regular strikes, often spontaneous, took place locally, usually about recognition of the union. The July 1982 strike, just a few months before NUM was launched, resulted in the death of one hundred mine-workers and the deportation of thousands – a scenario the new union wanted to avoid repeating. However, by September 1984 it had exhausted all legal methods after wage negotiations with the Chamber of Mines had reached a deadlock,[54] and NUM-organised gold mines as well as others, where it was not yet recognised, went on strike. The conflict ended in the death of a dozen workers and the dismissal of thousands.[55] A year later, a second legal strike took place (August 1985), although the wisdom of pursuing a legal strategy came under discussion among NUM leaders and members, because it gave employers time to adjust and because they responded violently.[56]

Emphasising the legalistic character of NUM does not mean to underplay other aspects of its organisational character. It is meant, however, to draw attention to the fact that there is some continuity between NUM nowadays and its historical determination to act within the framework of its own rules as well as in line with State laws. This helps us to understand the stance of NUM leaders in the face of the 2012 strikes. They remained stubbornly rooted in their legalistic stance: despite having been targeted in a violent attack orchestrated by Amcu, they called on their members to comply with the law. Faced with illegal strikes, they repeatedly enjoined their members to go back to work. This reading of recent events is not the only one possible; the legalistic rejection of Amcu was also an admission of powerlessness on the part of NUM. Its members overtook the union and it had no choice but to resort to the law to try to contain a more militant contender using the more militant repertoires of action that NUM had also once embraced in the 1980s.

NUM's legalistic orientation indeed coexisted in those earlier years with a more militant stance that gained ground from the 1985 national congress onwards. After a second wave of local leaders, less educated and closer to the base, was elected, and following their recommendations, NUM decided to confront the system of racial oppression that prevailed in the mines directly. The union started responding to physical or verbal violence through attacking the structures of oppression at work, both on-surface and underground.[57] Back then, the union was not reluctant either to resort to violence when necessary or to manipulate ethnicities in order to fight rivals.[58] This tension between legalistic and militant approaches to trade unionism is visible, for instance, in a 1992 document published after a joint NEC-staff workshop in which various problems were raised, including:

> Legalistic approach to struggle
> – Weakness in the legalistic approach which is defensive …
> – Union is becoming more defensive now and everything is going down.
> Reference to the books every time but everything is not encouraging. The union should revert to aggressive struggle.[59]

However, the making of a modern central administration, in the Weberian sense, was also one of Ramaphosa's original preoccupations. Legalism was thus not only a response to the external environment, but rules were also designed to ensure the development of union bureaucracy, which was, of course, much needed in order to cope with the rapid growth in membership. The national office had four employees in 1983, its 13 organisers lacked training and, in the absence of an administration worthy of the name, the management of union resources already proved problematic. NUM's small car fleet, for instance, accounted for one-quarter of its total expenditure – a recurring source of concern for head office. Members' subscriptions were collected from hand to hand and did not always make it to the union's treasury. At the end of 1983 NUM started receiving regular funding from several Scandinavian trade unions – 74 per cent of its resources came from donors based overseas.[60] While Ramaphosa insisted on the need for each region to have its own offices to better service members and relieve head office, the constant repression experienced at the local level in these early years made decentralisation a vain wish. In 1986, 228 000 members were serviced by 32 employees unevenly dispersed across six departments. NUM's two leaders applied a relatively strict division of labour. Ramaphosa was in charge of administration and negotiations, and Motlatsi, who was an Anglo American employee, took care of recruitment and mobilisation. Allen gives an interesting description of how NUM's central administration worked:

> The head office in Johannesburg, consisting of the secretariat and full-time staff, was the only section of the union organization that the mine owners could not effectively destroy and which, therefore, had a continuing existence during which the acquisition of organization skills was possible. This concentration of knowledge and expertise by the full-time, appointed staff, mostly with little or no experience of mining, gave them exceptional influence in managing the affairs of the union. The head office, in consequence, became the source of all vital decisions in the union and the main provider of its administrative services.[61]

Allen's view is, of course, nuanced by the fact that he adopted a top-down approach in his history of NUM, but it is useful to put the situation NUM now faces in perspective.[62] The union's centralised character is hence to be viewed not only as a drift from its assumed initial destination, but also as a constant in its history that regularly conflicted with other elements such as the worker-control principle, which is central to NUM's ideology. The tension between militancy and legal-rational bureaucratic repertoires of action was thus also a tension between local aspirations to autonomy and head office's centralisation and control tactics.

The fact that NUM was, from its inception, built from the top rather than bottom-up had consequences that are still at work in today's organisation. Bearing these upward-tending dynamics in mind is important when one considers the bottom-up strategy, so clearly different, that gave birth to NUM's sister, the National Union of Metalworkers of South Africa (Numsa) in 1987. Numsa was born out of the merger of several unions strongly rooted in the tradition of 'worker control', which still reflects nowadays in its opposition to the centralising trends of Cosatu and the ANC.[63] NUM and Numsa are classically opposed as the 'populist' versus the 'workerist'. Whereas the former traditionally conceives the workers' struggle as part of a wider struggle and promotes the political involvement of trade unions, the latter pledges to remain focused on the shop floor and is generally suspicious of politics.[64] This reflected as early as 1985, when NUM became a leader in the formation of Cosatu and an architect in its subsequent alliance with the ANC. In 1987 NUM also popularised a slogan, '1987 – the year mineworkers take control', which suggested an involvement far beyond the workplace.

THE 1987 STRIKE AND THE REINFORCEMENT OF CENTRAL POWER

In the first years of its existence, NUM focused on recruiting, having the union recognised in as many mines as possible, confronting local managers and negotiating wage increases and better basic conditions of employment. NUM also tested its capacity to mobilise in two short industry-wide strikes. It soon became clear, however, that a major confrontation with mining houses was looming. In 1986, Ramaphosa declared, in response to the apartheid government's threat to expel foreign mineworkers, that 'there will definitely be a national strike if migrant workers are repatriated'. Answering a question about NUM's organisational priorities, he added: 'Organizationally, our priorities will be to consolidate our position, to make the union strong enough to withstand the attacks that the mining bosses may launch against us this year, and to be better prepared for the struggles that lie ahead of us – in July for instance, when the wage negotiations are due.'[65]

At the end of June 1987, the annual wage negotiations between NUM and the Chamber of Mines reached a deadlock and the Chamber, as it was wont to do, unilaterally implemented a pay rise corresponding to its final offer on the 1 July. The Chamber seemed ready to cross swords with NUM, and Bobby Godsell, a former Anglo American official often presented as a moderate, later explained:

We thought that this was not only a strike about this year's wage but a strike about future bargaining patterns. We had lived for a couple of years with what I could call bargaining by brinkmanship. We thought we had to go through a strike experience at least once in order to indicate that the threat of a strike was not always going to move us where NUM wanted us to be.[66]

NUM refers to this strike as the '21 days that rocked the Chamber' (see Figure 2.4). The conflict, which was severely repressed, mobilised 300 000 mineworkers and caused the death of 11, as well as mass dismissals involving 50 000 to 60 000 mineworkers. Its aftermath was disastrous for the organisation: the Chamber had demonstrated all the extent of its repressive power and NUM was weakened for years to come. 'The strike ended during the third week when Anglo used the legal strategy of lock-outs, systematically dismissing workers, hostel by hostel and shaft by shaft. In the end, NUM was forced to settle for the Chamber of Mines' original wage offer with one or two improvements in benefits.'[67]

Figure 2.4:   NUM strike poster, 1987

Source: Digital Innovation South Africa. Reproduced with permission.

Until the 2012 strikes at Impala and Lonmin and before the 2014 Amcu strike, 1987 remained a landmark in the mineworkers' struggle, comparing only with the 1946 miners' strike. Local and regional NUM structures were, for many, literally wiped out. In structural terms, the 1987 strike also proved catastrophic for mineworkers as it made companies realise they could operate the mines with fewer workers. In the strike's immediate aftermath several companies embarked on undercover restructuring. Thanks to the autonomy of its national structure, and largely helped by foreign funding, NUM nevertheless managed to take the blow the destruction of its local structures had caused.

Organising NUM's central administration, which Ramaphosa had conceived as a centrepiece in the union's architecture, became even more crucial after 1987 and the general secretary made sure it was further expanded. The head office had nine departments, of which five were staffed by one person only. The most important were administration (seven employees) and finances (four employees).[68] The legal department in charge of representing members consumed most of NUM's budget, but it hardly managed to retain its legal experts who were attracted to better remuneration in the private sector. The education and culture department, headed by future NUM general secretary Kgalema Motlanthe, had only five instructors to train union cadres and 'conscientise' members. After the 1987 congress, a department dedicated to organising was created and placed under the stewardship of Gwede Mantashe. Present in 15 of the union's 16 regions, it employed about 15 mineworkers who had been retrenched in 1987.[69] It is also at that time that young white university graduates involved in the anti-apartheid movement were recruited, such as Martin Nicol, an economist who was hired to head the collective bargaining department, and Kate Philip, who oversaw cooperative projects in rural areas that NUM designed for dismissed mineworkers. Recruiting new cadres without a mining background further reinforced head office power and some were even elected to top leadership positions, including Marcel Golding, in charge of publications and press relations, who became assistant general secretary after defeating Gwede Mantashe, a former mineworker, in 1987.[70] The union's operating costs dramatically increased during this period of bureaucratic expansion: between 1986 and 1988, the share of wages in NUM's budget was multiplied by two and a half. NUM slowly managed to recover from the 1987 shock, but it was still far away from its self-assigned target of 400 000 members by the end of 1989. Between 1991 and 1994 it managed to sign up only 12 000 new members, and a plan was drafted to reach an organising rate of 75 percent across the mining industry, with precise goals assigned to each branch and monitored by an organisation department employing 42 staff members.[71]

3

The Power of Head Office: Building National Bureaucracy

FROM AMATEURISM TO PROFESSIONALISM

NUM is a strong union not only because it has at least one full-time elected official in each structure from branch to national (in addition to many other part-time elected officials and some full-time officials at shaft level), but also because it rests on numerous and competent staff. The importance of staff in NUM is illustrated in early NEC and congress reports, which deal extensively with staff matters and update delegates on the union's growth. The latter is generally quantified both in numbers – membership figures – and organisational capacity – staff and departments. Making bureaucracy work was always a core preoccupation at head office and, in 1989, Ramaphosa was 'pleased to report that all regions but one now have administrative staff' and emphasised that 'the administration department [30 staff] remains a mainstay of all the union's activities. With time it has become more efficient and professional and has proved to be the engine room of the union.' Apart from the administration department, the organising department (27 employees) was in fact the only other one with staff deployed in all 16 regions but one.[1]

From the early 1990s on, NEC meetings always started by dealing with the management of NUM human resources, including the appointment of new employees, probation periods, resignations or dismissals for motives as diverse as being under the influence of alcohol, absenteeism, or the mismanagement of union resources. Such problems were far from uncommon and they challenge the iconic figure of the 'activist organiser' described by Buhlungu. His analysis of the decline of the democratic tradition within South African unions – in which, he wrote, employment was 'non-hierarchical, collectivist and driven by altruism' – is based on his observation that 'activist organisers' became an endangered species after apartheid ended, when union employment became just a 'conventional job in the labour market'.[2]

Unions in the 1980s and early 1990s, however, were also ordinary workplaces. One permanent source of preoccupation with respect to building union structures was the high turnover in NUM staff, which was a reality back in the 1980s as is still the case today. This turnover was caused by union staff opting for the corporate sector, in mining or elsewhere, or for other, more lucrative jobs. This trend is another challenge to the icon of the selfless organiser: people always had and still have individual ambitions and career plans. A May 1992 report, for instance, records three resignations (Mary Cobbet, Funeka Siyongwana and Manoko Nchwe) all of whom mentioned unsatisfactory salary to motivate their decisions, in addition to a lack of recognition for their work performance. Instances of corruption or misappropriation of union funds were not uncommon at the time and the same document reports the dismissal case against Benjamin Maqolo, who worked as a messenger for the finance department. He was accused of having deposited subscriptions to the worth of R2 452.61 into his personal account.[3] In 1994, 'the General Secretary reported that Akila Leshaba had been dismissed for embezzling Union subscription funds. The sum total involved is R24000.'[4]

Turnover in union staff was also explained by the fact that working for NUM was very demanding: earnings were limited, unconditional and full involvement was expected from employees, and rewards were mostly symbolic. That is one of the reasons why the national office established a staff development programme in 1991, which included career development ('Every staff member should be able to have a career path in the union and will include training and enhancement of skills'); sabbaticals ('in order to ensure that staff members do not burn out'); and rest periods ('when the need arises'). It was also decided to establish a 'Staff–Office Bearers Joint Committee', as the NEC noted that 'there was no structure through which the staff could have their problems and grievances heard in a structured way', which is quite ironic for a trade union.[5] The same year the NEC also recommended a 'total revaluation of the staff conditions of employment and various job categories … It should give effect to adequate wage increases to ensure that our skill retention takes place and more people [are] at rates which permit them to leave alternative sources of employment.'[6]

In an annual national staff seminar held in February 1991, the general secretary conducted a harsh assessment of NUM's internal working conditions and missions. He quoted letters from two 'comrades' who had recently resigned, in which they complained: 'Union managed in a very authoritarian way, different standards applied for different people, leadership indifferent to work that is done, no team spirit, no openness, bad relationship between staff and elected leadership, resistance to training, staff treated with lack of respect, leadership fails to pick up signals of distress.' The two comrades further complained that as a result of 'dishonesty in the way comrades serve mineworkers in the union', 'mineworkers have taken the back seat'.[7]

Such complaints were common (violence was also an issue, with instances of rape, worker assaults on union officials or harassment by elected union officials, especially at the regional level) but working for the union also had many positive aspects, including the development of a supportive relationship with the workers, the informality of the way in which NUM operated, the comradeship involved, the idea of working for social and economic justice and contributing to the struggle, as well as the travelling.[8]

As time passed NUM started to take its staff more seriously and a change in its salary grid was envisioned when national office bearers 'came to the conclusion that there is a need for the Union to introduce a structure that will be simple, equitable and just if the high staff turn-over is to be stemmed'. The NEC set the minimum wage at R2 000 and the maximum at R3 700.[9] A decision was also taken to grant a housing subsidy to NUM officials.[10] At the same time stricter disciplinary rules for staff members were also drawn up; for instance, it was decided that staff absentee-ism on Saturday would bring about a disciplinary hearing, with the possible penalty of losing two days' salary. For years there had also been a problem with the misuse of union cars: they were regularly damaged due to improper attention, or used for private ends, and 'the NEC decided to develop policy guidelines for car smash-ers'.[11] Frans Baleni drafted an employment contract for NUM staff in September 1992, which clearly delimited the rights of staff (holidays, paternity and maternity leave, housing allowance, reimbursement of expenses such as hotel, food or travel). Although Baleni called for a union-specific approach to staff issues,[12] NUM started to function more and more as a standard office employing white collars.

These changes to internal rules coincided with wider bureaucratisation dynam-ics, of which Frans Baleni was one key craftsman. At the start of the 1990s – that is, at the height of the era of the 'activist organiser,' according to Buhlungu's typol-ogy – NUM started enforcing more rigid procedures on internal management. Staff members were now expected to give accurate, monthly reports on their timetables and activities. Rules to rationalise internal processes were created, as were disci-plinary procedures to solve problems such as alleged cases of employee abuse of union resources. NUM staff, however, did not remain passive in the face of such attempts from union leaders to tighten their control over employees. The issue of wages proved a particularly sensitive one in this regard. A letter to NUM, signed by several prominent staff members, including Archie Palane, Frans Baleni, Manne Dipico and Kate Philip, argued in favour of experience being clearly reflected in their payslips. They complained that 'the category dealing with experience has not been implemented as yet. All staff members are paid a flat R150 per month, for experience, irrespective of their experience in the union, the general efficiency in their present and past responsibilities with the union.'[13]

What all this chiefly emphasises is the fact that, as opposed to what is usually suggested in analyses of trade unions in the transition from apartheid to democracy, the transformation of these actors was not mainly a consequence of regime change, but had started years before as part of a broad institutionalisation process. In the case of NUM, the domination of the centre over the rest of the organisation can be traced back to the very beginnings of the union and it was reinforced after the 1987 strike when it had to restructure – a restructuring that came to an end roughly, as far as the operational staff structure was concerned, in 1994 – that is, exactly at the end of apartheid. This time frame emerges clearly when one reads through 1994 documents that celebrate the achievement of 'restructuring in the NUM'. In June 1994, the 'new' NUM was equipped with four pillars, each one divided into subunits: Production (headed by Martin Nicol), Services (headed by Irene Charnley), Finance (headed by Ephraim Mafatshe), and Administration (headed by Daisy Manzana).[14]

The revised proposed salary structure reflected the professionalisation of NUM and the increasing internal division of labour. The salary structure now ranged from a minimum R2 500 to a maximum R4 000, divided into three levels (Level 1 was applicable to all staff members, Level 2 to unit coordinators, and Level 3 to pillar heads and regional coordinators) and 12 grades or 'notches'. Particularly indicative of the type of hierarchy and organisation now sought was that 'experience … is not going to be based on years of service, but [will] be based on the following criteria: 1. Quality of service delivered. 2. Initiative and innovation. 3. Will and ability to do more than basic requirements of one's job. 4. Ability to motivate others. 5. Contribution in building team-work'.[15] The shift between the egalitarian salary scale of the early 1980s and the performance-and-motivation-based one of the early 1990s is stark.

All other union rules and procedures were also reinforced as a result of this restructuring, including those designed for staff members. Initiatives were taken to save costs and improve productivity, which included tighter control over hotel and transport expenditure, the management of union cars, telephone usage (billing of private calls), and work hours (monitoring lateness and long lunches). This was accompanied by the installation of better equipment in the national and regional offices (including stationery, computers, printing and photocopying facilities). Staff members were also encouraged to subscribe to a medical aid scheme.[16] The formalisation of staff working conditions went hand in hand with stricter management and enforcement of rules. A very detailed grievance procedure was set up for employees, which necessarily implied more formal relations or at least a clear intention to formalise work relations. These internal processes were also legislated as, for example, in the different steps to be taken in the event of disciplinary action against an employee (verbal, written and final written warnings; suspension; termination of employment). Union rules and regulations further suggest that the work atmosphere in NUM was never tranquil, for rules are often designed to provide automated answers to pre-existing situations. Motivation for disciplinary procedures included 'poor performance, incompetence and incompatibility', as well as breaches of union rules such as absenteeism, bribery, leaking confidential information, failing to account for cash spending, a criminal record, damage to union property, insubordination or insolence, using offensive language, misrepresentation or fraud, negligence, lack of punctuality, sexual harassment, substance abuse, theft and violent actions.[17] In other words, whether designed to address existing problems or to prevent them from arising, such precise rules rigidified NUM's organisation. This is a reminder that NUM was far from being a harmonious organisation; it was traversed by conflict, including between employees and their union employer. For example, in September 1993 Kgalema Motlanthe received a letter from Deneys Reitz Attorneys, representing their client Kenny Mosime, former head of the NUM legal department. The latter had been dismissed and initially sought reinstatement before reaching an agreement on the end of his work contract: NUM would give him a letter of recommendation plus 'some form of compensation'. After the two parties had failed to agree on adequate compensation, however, Kenny Mosime's lawyers threatened to take NUM to the Industrial Court, based on the union's alleged failure to enforce the Labour Relations Act (1956).[18]

HEAD OFFICE: THE HOME OF NUM'S FIVE PILLARS

NUM's head office is situated in a heritage and newly refurbished building located at 7 Rissik Street, Johannesburg (see Figure 3.1). Its elegance matches that of the Chamber of Mines, AngloGold Ashanti or BHP Billiton headquarters, located just a few blocks away.[19] One can enter the building from a large wooden door opening directly onto Rissik Street or from the perpendicular Frederick Street, where there is a parking lot reserved for union employees and national office bearers. Cars, just like shoes, are a good indication of one's material condition and cultural capital. As one gazes out over the NUM head office parking lot, the days when Ramaphosa was travelling the length and breadth of the Free State and Witwatersrand in a kombi van to recruit union members and stewards seem long gone. National office bearers now park their gleaming NUM-owned Japanese SUVs in reserved spaces, next to other, personally owned Dodges or BMWs and, it is noteworthy, a majority of more ordinary cars. The parking, shared with an annexe of the Department of Correctional Services, overlooks a small garden – named after Carletonville Chair Selby Mayise, who was murdered in 1999, and 'dedicated to the memory of all workers that have died working in the mining, energy, construction sectors' – at the centre of which stands a rusted metal sculpture of a mineworker in underground attire, pushing a wheelbarrow.

In the parking lot ageing graffiti, reminiscent of the popular mine art often found on the walls of mining compounds, portrays the bust and face of a mineworker dressed in blue work overalls, helmet and torch. The graffiti contrasts with a wall

Figure 3.1: NUM head office, 2011

Photographer: Raphaël Botiveau

displaying finer, artistic representations of mineworkers and a NUM logo made of mosaics. The latter echo other pieces of art that are found on every floor of the building, including the refined black and white photographs and paintings of Sam Nhlengethwa, an artist represented by the Johannesburg-based Goodman Gallery.

Strict security protocol controls the entry of external visitors to the building. A first guard opens the gate and, before letting a vehicle in, takes note of the driver's name, car registration number, institution, person to be visited and arrival time. (This process became smoother as NUM security personnel got to know me.) After walking through the outdoor corridor the visitor goes through a small gate embellished with industrial scrap metal (pipes, bolts and picks), down a few steps and enters the hall where another guard seated behind a table fills in another form – identity and phone numbers. The visitor then passes through an airport-like security portal before a female security agent asks to record his computer's serial number, without ever requesting to search his belongings. After this introduction to the building, the visitor – in this case I – finally face Phuleng's smile at the reception desk as she calls the person I am visiting and cracks a few jokes on, say, the last French class she took as part of the union's joint staff and officials language-training programme. Phuleng then guides me through the different floors using a fingerprint recognition system to unlock the doors, and leaves me in the hands of the person I have come to see. It took several visits before I was allowed to use one of the building's two main elevators on my own to go and look for the people I was visiting.

If this first contact with the top tier of the organisation sounds cold and somewhat severe, everything in NUM's head office is in fact either semi-formal or semi-casual depending on the circumstances of the day. The trade unionist dress code in South Africa is unpredictable: officials met in an elegant suit on one day often wear NUM tee shirts and jeans on the next. Dress codes depend on contexts but probably even more on the effect that one wants to have on the audience. In wage negotiations, for instance, a negotiator from head office may choose to dress in a certain way with a view to showing either affinity with the company and distinction from his 'co-workers' or the exact contrary.

Visitors, be they external to the union or not, are sometimes asked to wait in the downstairs lobby, next to the attractive resource centre where Thenji Mlabatheki attends to requests for documents on NUM, trade unionism and mining, and where head office employees come time and again to read the papers and journals subscribed to by the union. The lobby is spacious and furnished with four couches and armchairs organised around two coffee tables. Two bar tables surrounded by eight bar-stools complete this tastefully designed environment, the modern aesthetic of which is broken only by a rudimentary kitchen where staff can prepare tea and coffee. A flat-screen TV hanging from the ceiling is sometimes tuned into news channels. When I first visited the NUM head office, I was struck by how distant its orderly, comfortable and trendy style was from the messy, old-fashioned 1980s style of Cosatu House, on the other side of the railway that cuts Johannesburg's CBD in two (Cosatu House has since been refurbished too). In Rissik Street, a solemn scroll in the lobby recalled the vision, mission and values of NUM ('reliability, competence, courtesy, credibility, understanding, honesty, integrity, responsiveness, access, communication, security, tangibles, respect'), which are closer to the values publicised by the upholders of the new public administration approach than to 1980s militant slogans from the anti-apartheid struggle. The latter appeared in the lobby on discretely placed posters, one reading 'Long Live ANC' and another from Cosatu's 2002 campaign against privatisation.

Head office staff are accommodated on five floors, most employees sharing open spaces, with pillar heads or national officials having their own private offices. Several boardrooms are also available.[20] On the last floor one finds the offices of the 'top five': the president, his deputy, the 'GS' (general secretary), his deputy, and the national treasurer. Outside their offices, one meets with Zukiswa Maduna, who is in charge of organising the busy lives of NUM's top two leaders: Senzeni Zokwana and Frans Baleni during most of my research. A highly professional personal assistant, always on the alert in a mixture of controlled cold and courtesy, she evokes the personal assistants of powerful political or financial men seen in American TV series on Wall Street or Washington DC, acting as a real barrier and filter for the two leaders.

The bureaucratic capacity of NUM leaders, and their political skills as negotiators, are renowned and it is not coincidental that all three former NUM general secretaries subsequently held the position of ANC secretary general. There is, of course, a tight historical relationship between NUM and the ANC, which the former joined early in the 1980s by making Nelson Mandela its honorary life president (1986) and by adopting the Freedom Charter (1987). But what first and foremost makes the strength of NUM 'organisers' is their skills in the management and administration of an organisation. In other words, they are not politicians but form the essential backup of any successful politician. In 1997, at the end of Motlanthe's mandate as NUM general secretary, the union had around 200 employees in its head office and regions.[21] Gwede Mantashe then imposed his mark on this administration by determinedly reinforcing its discipline. After proclaiming his success in suppressing personal dissension in the regions and instituting more depersonalised, modern working relations, he told delegates at the 11th National Congress in 2003: 'We are now dealing with operational politics. We cleared the operational relationship. The regional chairperson is the political leader of the region. The regional secretary is the operational and administrative leader of the region. The regional coordinator is the operational manager of the region.' Turning to the state of head office, he explained that 'developing managerial capacity has been quicker and easier at the Head Office than in the regions' and that 'an exciting team of young Heads of Pillars' had been established with Gino Govender heading the secretariat pillar. The latter included a parliamentary office (in charge of lobbying and advocacy), a strategy unit (the purpose of which, in Mantashe's conception, was to launch counteroffensives after media allegations against NUM, but proved a failure) and an international relations and administration unit (a transversal unit servicing all pillars and regions). The production pillar was headed by Welcome Mboniso and in charge of issues such as collective bargaining, membership, skills development and HIV and Aids). The services pillar was seen as 'critical' for 'the retention of membership'. It consisted of a social benefits unit (which included the satellite Mineworkers Provident Fund), the housing unit (in charge of speeding up the dismantlement of single-sex hostels), the JB Marks Education Trust (in charge of awarding scholarships to mineworkers and their dependants) and the legal unit (in charge of representing workers). The publicity and information pillar oversaw media liaison, the information and resource centre, media production and information technology. Human resources and finance represented two distinct pillars.[22]

The number of pillars and units has constantly changed since they were first created. In 2015, the union was divided into five pillars: (secretariat, human resources, finance, services and production). Reports about their good functioning alternated with concerns about their mismanagement due to the constant brain drain the union faced, but also due to more damaging tendencies, such as corruption.[23] In other instances, however, the work of employees was praiseworthy, as in 2006 when Mantashe congratulated Frans Baleni, the heir he had mentored for years. After having moved him from the Elijah Barayi Memorial Training Centre (EBMTC) back to head office, he strategically positioned him in the production pillar and proudly announced:

> This has, for the first time, brought passion to the pillar in two important areas, namely, organising and recruitment and trade union education … Rightfully so, the pillar has irritated a number of our regions by asking them for one report or the other. Staff management in the pillar has also been tightened, with some comrades being shaken out of comfort zones.[24]

The NUM in which I conducted my doctoral fieldwork at the turn of the 2010s can, to a great extent, be regarded as a product of Mantashe's and Baleni's successive administrations. They were also, as I have shown, the heirs and developers of the Ramaphosa and the Motlanthe administrations. Continuities between these four historical secretariats are clear: NUM was carefully built into a centralised and efficient bureaucracy. What changed under Mantashe and Baleni, however, was that efficiency was increasingly conceived as tight discipline and control of discordant views on the one hand – what I will later identify as part of their specific conception and practice of communism. On the other hand, the two imposed a form of staff and organisational management that can be interpreted as closely allied to the corporate neoliberalism that is typical of contemporary companies and multinationals. When Ramaphosa vowed to make NUM as powerful as the mining companies it was negotiating with in the 1980s, Mantashe and Baleni mimicked their postmodern avatars.

'REPORTING TO THE GS': MANAGING THE UNION

The picture drawn in this chapter and the previous one is that of a union that decided, right from its origins, to rely on its Johannesburg-based central administration. It is that of an increasingly sophisticated bureaucracy that was in fact never as selfless and amateurish as it was portrayed in accounts of that period. This in no way suggests that selfless dedication and many other organisational characteristics, not mentioned here, are not crucial to an understanding of the anti-apartheid trade union movement. The portrayal I present, however, is that of an ever-growing, bureaucratic NUM organised around the central figure of its general secretary who can arguably be seen – not only by analogy but also based on the type of management he imposed – as a genuine CEO. This identity between union and corporate functions was at the heart of a polemic when former general secretary Baleni, the only one among NUM's top five leaders who was not paid by a mining house but by the union itself (with a view to ensuring that the union's machinery was always functional), decided to align his monthly wage with that of his national peers paid by their respective mining companies. His salary was raised from R40 000 to R77 000.[25]

Public administrations, political organisations, trade unions and private companies can all be viewed through the lens of the Weberian 'ideal type' of bureaucratic organisation, but what the structuring of NUM shows is that it decided to rely on models of human resources management inspired by the corporate sector. I have demonstrated how, during the organisational structuring of NUM, staff relations were formalised partly to meet demands from union employees and partly based on the will of union leaders to build a more efficient organisation. It is also my argument here and in other sections of this book that South African contemporary communists, including NUM and ANC administrators of the likes of Mantashe and Baleni, can in fact be viewed as proponents of a type of organisation that mixes neoliberal corporate sector procedures with democratic centralism.

The ongoing process of skills improvement and professionalisation among NUM staff was always a conscious project. Under the eight years of Gwede Mantashe's secretariat and under the nine years of his protégé Frans Baleni's term in office, however, management techniques evolved. There had always been a clear division of labour between NUM's top employee, the general secretary, and its president. Ramaphosa – with his university background and no intimate knowledge of mining – controlled union administration and conducted negotiations, and Motlatsi – with his experience as a mineworker and later as a personnel assistant – represented NUM and addressed and mobilised members whenever necessary. This division of labour has persisted but staff management became more scientific under Mantashe and Baleni. In 2004, the former explained this in words that give a very clear view of his conception of union management:

> Running a professional Human Resource Management in a democratic organisation is complex. Many comrades equate democratic organisation to looseness, disorganisation and no rules. As one tightens policies, the more we hear of accusations of being like 'Bosses' and being managerialist. Our consistency over the years is beginning to give concrete results. We are insisting on running the National Union of Mineworkers professionally and efficiently. We are prepared to take the pains that go with success.[26]

The professionalisation of human resources management under Mantashe was marked by the introduction of a new human resource information system designed to centralise data on staff pay, leave and so on. This also came with improvements in conditions of employment, such as medical aid and pension fund benefits. Recruitment of NUM staff has also become more 'professional'. Mercy Sekano, who heads the union's training centre in Johannesburg, recalled how he was recruited:

> We are 'officials' as we say here, employees, appointed, non-elected. They normally put the advert, if you don't come from NUM you apply, then you go for an interview. A very rigorous interview, very tough … For instance myself I was interviewed twice in 2008 and 2009 until I was appointed in 2010 … Before I was in Sadtu [South African Democratic Teachers Union],

a regional secretary and full-time shop steward. But my profession is education; I am a qualified educator. I studied and then went through the ranks. When I left in 2006 I was supposed to head a school in Rustenburg.[27]

Over the past decade, the management of human resources was also crucially impacted by the introduction of what is known as the 'performance management system'. This system of staff evaluation based on performance was first introduced in 2002 when NUM adopted a scorecard as a system for evaluating its structures. The system was tested twice but it was met with reluctance among those who were supposed to enforce it and only the human resources pillar conducted the two trials with success. Only two regions (Natal and the Free State) as well as one other pillar completed at least one trial. After this dismal failure to mobilise union structures, the NEC decided to reward those who had complied with it and penalise others. This triggered a late submission of results by two additional regions, North East and Rustenburg.[28] Three additional trials for assessment were scheduled in 2003 but Mantashe lamented in 2004 that only half of NUM operation centres had attempted to implement the system. Financial penalties were applied, with managers receiving zero bonuses and staff being paid only half of what their colleagues in compliant structures received.[29] It took years for the system to be successfully enforced and Baleni noted in 2009 that the 'performance management system has been a challenge in the union'. In June 2008, a first performance assessment was conducted and it showed poor results. Eighty assessments of staff, from administrator to senior managers, were submitted with the following results: 16 came out at a rating of 3 (satisfactory performance), 12 at a rating of 4 (commendable), and only one at a top rating of 5. Depending on their performances, successful employees respectively qualified for a 1, 2 or 3 per cent bonus, calculated on their basic annual salary. However, 41 employees did not earn any bonus since they came out at a rating of 2 (performance below expected standard).[30]

The system has now become routine and in 2010 a total of 118 staff were assessed. When 85 were found to have performed at a rating of 3, Baleni summed up: 'It is clear that there is no outstanding performance in the organization.'[31] This followed a previous assessment of 101 employees out of 173 in 2009, which had led Baleni to conclude that NUM had '50 good performers' against 49 'poor performers'. He continued rather harshly: 'In essence out of the R2 375 452.43 that the organization is spending on salaries per month including benefits only R589 822.24 is paid to performers (competent staff), excluding non-submitted assessments.'[32]

'Performance management' is associated with the work of Aubrey C. Daniels, an American clinical psychologist who developed new ways to manage behaviour as a function of result.[33] Ideas about and practices of performance management come from the corporate world and have filtered into public administration and other forms of organisation through what has been labelled 'new public management'.[34] NUM sometimes uses course material from business schools in its own training designed for union cadres and staff, which is permeated with new management-inspired processes, including so-called participatory processes.[35] Performance management is also used in the mining houses NUM negotiates with. Anglo Platinum explains in a note for prospective employees: 'The human resource function within each organisation is unique although there are similarities from company to company in the major activities that are undertaken. These major activities are: job analysis and work design; human resource planning; recruitment and selection; human resource development; performance management; information management; employee relations; employee wellness; employee benefits management.'[36] This description of career prospects for staff at one of the world's leading mining companies offers a very good description of the type of human resource management NUM has been trying to enforce. The similarity is not just coincidental and one must also wonder whether looking and behaving like a mining company means being more closely aligned to mining companies, as former NUM members in rebellion against the union since 2012 have claimed.[37] A Lonmin document on human resources notes the articulation between individually rated performance and the overall efficiency of the organisation, which is so typical of both a corporate stance and NUM's contemporary managerial approach, but so distant from ideals of trade union solidarity in which the collective is expected to take precedence over the individual: 'Performance management includes the ongoing management, measurement, monitoring and development of employees to drive performance at the individual level, to ensure that the organisation meets its goals and objectives.'[38] In NUM, performance management involves assigning targets to each individual NUM employee through the signing of 'individual performance agreements' (a term that suggests a discussion between an employee and his manager to agree upon a reachable target – as if the two parts were equals) rather than setting collective targets to meet. As a result, collective targets set in congress resolutions and the policies through which they are implemented are now supposed to be reached by the sum of every single action taken by the union's individual employees and leaders.

The logic of performance management is based on bonuses awarded to individuals. Individual bonuses attached to recruitment targets are not new, however. The pay of 'recruiters' that NUM employed in the late 1980s was largely dependent on their fulfilment of recruitment goals.[39] Yet rewards can also be collective. Sithethi

Figure 3.2: Sithethi Mxhasi with the award for Rustenburg region, 2012
Photographer: Raphaël Botiveau

Mxhasi, who oversees membership recruitment in Rustenburg, brought his region NUM's 'best recruiting region' award several times in recent years. In Figure 3.2 Mxhasi looks proudly at the shield awarded to the Rustenburg region in 2012.

Under Baleni, Mantashe's management 'spirit' further penetrated NUM. He introduced the systematic use of statistics in his reports, some of which seem more cosmetic than operational – such as attendance sheets to NEC meetings that show NUM president Senzeni Zokwana as having attended 88 per cent of all NEC meetings in a given year (in fact seven meetings out of eight).[40] The relevance of using a percentage rather than numbers is questionable from a statistical point of view but it is certainly a way to make a report look more 'professional'. This example is not arbitrary: one of the workers' main grievances against their mining bosses and union representatives in wage negotiations is that they express wage increases in percentages rather than in absolute terms. In its campaign for a 'living wage' in mining since 2012, Amcu has always insisted that workers should be presented with cash increases and not with percentage figures they don't understand and therefore neither like nor trust. The managerial techniques used by Baleni encouraged regional and branch leaders to adopt representations of reality through numbers, which are derived from the corporate imaginary and clash with the world views of many NUM members. This had not always been the trend in NUM: in 1989, for instance, the union reported: 'Several small victories advanced the union's new wage policy but the union has not yet broken the back of the Chamber's racist wage policy or achieved a national minimum wage. However, for the first time the Chamber was forced to negotiate in money terms and not percentage.'[41]

Baleni's reports were also filled with an unusual mixture of quotations, some of them taken from revolutionary classics like Thomas Sankara, but others from the Bible, military history (Napoleon, Eisenhower), literature (Ben Okri), scholarship (Francis Meli, Luli Callinicos), or the self-help American author Wayne Dyer whom he quoted as prescribing: 'change the way you look at things and things you look at will change'. As opposed to the austere and mostly text-filled reports of his predecessor, Baleni's reports were full of graphs, tables, and sometimes even quasi-esoteric diagrams such as that, presented to the 2012 national congress, on the 'spontaneous abortion of democracy' (see Figure 3.3).[42]

Under Baleni's secretariat NUM, its organisation and its staff have basically been turned into quantifiable figures and statistics that are presented to congress delegates on colourful PowerPoint slides in stage performances that recall the presentations of CEOs in the corporate world – one more example of the spread of neoliberalism, consulting and expertise in politics and trade unionism.[43]

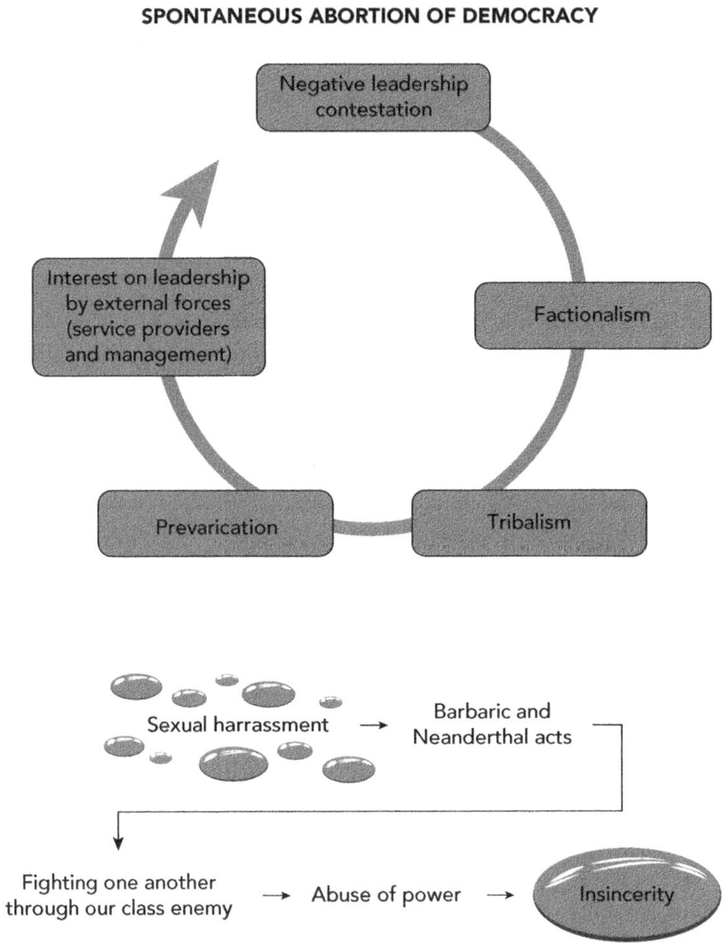

SPONTANEOUS ABORTION OF DEMOCRACY

Figure 3.3: 'Spontaneous abortion of democracy' diagram, NUM 14th National Congress, 2012

Source: NUM, Secretariat Report to the 14th National Congress, 2012, '30 years of unbroken revolutionary trade unionism struggle'. Reproduced with permission.

MONEY TO EMPOWER THE 'POOR' MINEWORKER

Another dimension of NUM's organisational modernisation project is the significant increase in its financial resources. The union successfully invested money in a guaranteed capital investment fund, which had almost R80 million in cash in 2008.[44] Such capital accumulation was made possible by the huge increase of membership contributions, which reached R92 million in 2009 and R209 million in 2011. This increase is in part linked to the new membership management system that now matches membership numbers with data on cash collections.[45] Until 1991, NUM's balance sheets had constantly showed a loss. Since then, the union has generated important cash reserves: by the end of 1994, NUM had R34 million in net assets. Its reserves were worth R94 million at the end of 2006 and R267 million at the end of 2011.[46] Prior to this impressive accumulation lies a history of financial difficulty.

Faced with reduced international donations at the end of apartheid but also, more immediately, with a decreasing income due to numerous retrenchments in the gold sector, the union had no choice but to raise its subscription fees. The latter initially consisted of a mostly symbolic 25 cents, later raised to 50 cents. It had already been raised from R1 to R2 in 1988 and was then increased to one per cent of a member's basic monthly pay at NUM's 7th Biennial Congress in 1991. The impact of such an increase on union financial resources was not immediately felt. NUM's income increased by 13 per cent in 1991, but there were delays and even refusals 'by various managements in deducting membership subscriptions after the submission of stop order forms' (see Figure 3.4).[47]

The union's dependency on the good will of companies for the transfer of membership fees was highly problematic, especially under apartheid. In 1991, NUM estimated that untransferred fees had deprived an approximate 46 000 members from being paid-up members of the union and resulted in a monthly loss of R92 000 in subscriptions between 1989 and 1990.[48] Another problem linked to 'subs' increases was that, because of bad communication, many members were not aware of the change in their contribution to NUM, which created temporary confusion and resignations from the union. The money generated by the new subscription system was nonetheless very significant. In September 1991, in companies that had already enforced the new system (employing roughly 85 000 NUM members), the subscriptions generated an income of R469 000 instead of the previous R143 000. This increase of union funding required a new cash management system and 'tighter financial control'.[49]

The accumulation of reserves by the union was firstly justified by the fact that this money was designed to benefit members. Reserves were indeed part of NUM's grand plan to improve the condition of mineworkers and, as Motlatsi put it in 2000:

> Our gains, however, were not all talk. We gave financial security to black mineworkers by improving their wages and conditions of work and, in the longer-run, by establishing a Provident Fund. Before then, the deaths of black mineworkers brought financial ruin as well as tragedy to their families. Now the casualties of mining can be buried with some dignity, and

NATIONAL UNION OF MINEWORKERS

P.O. Box 2424 Johannesburg, 2000
Tel.: (011) 377-2000/1 • Fax: (011) 836-6051

MEMBERSHIP № 586752

APPLICATION FOR MEMBERSHIP

Surname: _____
First Name(s): _____

Gender: _____ Nationality: _____
(Male or Female)
Education level passed: _____

Company (COY) No.: _____
TEBA Number: _____
(If you do not have a TEBA Number, please put your ID Number.
(If you do not have a South African ID, write your passport number)
Passport/ID No.: _____
Date of Birth: _____
Home Language: _____

Branch Name: _____

Region: _____

Where are you located in the branch? Please fill in ONE of the following four lines.

Shaft: _____
(write name of shaft)

Plant: _____
(write name of plant)

Other part of branch: _____
(eg. security)

Eskom distributor depot: _____
(eg. Johannesburg Benoni)

Are you an underground or surface worker? _____

Hostel Address: _____
(Address near work)

Post Code: _____

Home Address: _____
(Address where family
can be contacted)

Post Code: _____

Contractor: [YES] [NO]

Wage per month (basic) R _____

Job category: _____

Wage group: _____
(Patterson grade or job category)

_____   _____   _____
Member signature   Witness Signature   Date

STOP ORDER AUTHORISATION FORM

Surname: _____

Company Number: _____

First Name(s): _____

Passport/ID Number: _____

TEBA Number: _____

Name of employer: _____

MEMBERSHIP № 586752

NATIONAL UNION OF MINEWORKERS

SURNAME: ....
NAME: ....
ID NO: ....
BRANCH: ....
SIGNATURE: ....

I am a member of the National Union of Mineworkers (NUM). I hereby authorise you to deduct an amount equivalent to 1% of my basic earnings, or such further amounts as the National Congress may determine, from my remuneration every month in respect of union subscriptions, and to pay that amount to an account designated by the National Executive of NUM. I hereby revoke any previous authorisation for deductions in respect of any other union.

_____   _____   _____
Member Signature   Witness Signature   Date

Employer Acknowledgement of receipt   To be completed when stop order is delivered to management
On behalf of this company, I acknowledge receipt of this stop order and confirm that it is complete. If the union is not contacted by management within seven (7) days, the union will assume that the stop order has been verified.

_____   _____   _____   _____
Signature   Printed name   Position   Date

Figure 3.4: Membership application form with stop order authorisation
Source: National Union of Mineworkers. Reproduced with permission.

their dependants can have some financial security. What they receive is not enough but we have made a beginning.[50]

Major NUM-driven gains such as the Mineworkers Provident Fund (MWPF) are regularly praised by older mineworkers. A 1989 congress report read: 'The 1988 agreement [with the Chamber of Mines] on the Provident Fund which will cover 500 000 workers is a milestone for our union and members as it is the first time in 100 years that black mineworkers will be entitled to retirement benefits. This is a victory worth celebrating!' This pension fund started with a modest 1.5 per cent contribution by both workers and employers, before the latter was gradually increased first to 3 per cent and in 1990 to 5 per cent of members' monthly salary. The MWPF, launched in 1989, is not a NUM structure per se and it relies on workers' and employers' subscriptions, not on union reserves. It is jointly run by an equal number of trustees from the Chamber of Mines and NUM, and is designed to guarantee several types of benefits: pension, death, disability, funeral, retrenchment and housing loans, among others.[51] In 1991, the fund had 330 000 gold- and coal-mine members, who were contributing R10 million a month (the same amount as their employers) to a total capital worth R250 million. The NUM general secretary at the time raised the following question, which hints at an issue that I will later consider: 'Most of the money is invested in firms like Barlow Rand and Anglo American. The union has no say on where the workers' money is invested. We need to discuss if this is correct.'[52] The 7th NUM National Congress hence adopted the following resolution regarding the MWPF's investment strategy: 'The funds of the Mineworkers Provident Fund should not be invested in organisations that support apartheid or exploit workers; the funds of the MWPF should be largely invested in organisations or ventures that will benefit mineworkers in projects such as housing.'[53] Nowadays MWPF's monies are mostly channelled into a dozen investment vehicles such as Old Mutual Absolute Stable Growth, Sanlam Stable Bonus, Momentum Asset Management or Investec Asset Managers.

The administration of the MWPF has remained an issue, with questions being raised around the bias of employers' trustees on its board, or the fact that trustees are being lobbied – if not corrupted – by service providers, with a view to triggering investments or influencing decisions in companies where the fund is a shareholder. It is worth recalling here that trustees govern not only the MWPF but many other, smaller retirement funds at company level. It was also argued that the more experienced employers' trustees – who also often held high positions in management – were able to influence their union counterparts. This encouraged NUM to provide training for its own trustees and, between 2006 and 2008, 36 trustees graduated with an official qualification. This initiative was taken after NUM 'felt that the training offered by service providers was more of an indoctrination of how they wanted trustees to behave in the boardroom rather than empowering them on their fiduciary responsibilities'. Yet NUM trustees often fail to communicate with and report to union members adequately.[54] This problem is made all the more serious by the fact that union members usually have little or no understanding of how high finance works and are suspicious of non-cash or deferred remunerations. Mineworkers often battle to make ends meet, cannot afford decent accommodation and therefore don't understand why there should be deductions on their low and hard-earned wages for a purpose that is not immediately obvious to them. A 2008 MWPF members' booklet takes the following example, which gives a good idea of the amount of each worker contribution in proportion to his wage: 'Paul is employed in the Gold Mines and … earns R3 000 per month. The Retirement contribution will be: R3 000 x 14.5% = R496 … The Risk benefits and Fund expenses contribution will be: R3 000 x 7% = R210 per month.'[55] In this example, Paul's total contribution to the MWPF is 21.5 per cent of his monthly wage, which, needless to say, is a large share of money unavailable for monthly expenses, in particular if one also has to fund one's relatives. In other words, while retirement funds definitely represent progress in terms of workers' rights – a struggle that has been waged by unionists all over the world – they can also be seen as an unaffordable luxury for mineworkers who lack cash to meet basic needs. Participation in the fund is, of course, not compulsory but as members of NUM, workers stand to 'benefit' from these agreements reached between the union and companies. It is arguable, however, that due to the difficulty for an ordinary worker to access the type of information needed to choose a pension plan wisely, NUM members are in some respects held 'captive' of the MWPF. 'Previously mineworkers were given tokens like wristwatches, gum boots and overalls at retirement,' one reads on the MWPF website as an indication of the progress the creation of the MWPF embodies. This progress should nevertheless be read in the wider socioeconomic context of mining. MWPF money is, for instance, not directly available upon retirement and workers must wait six months to access it. The MWPF now has a membership of around 134 000, mostly in the lower grades of employment. In addition to gold and coal companies, which make up the bulk of the mining houses participating in the fund, other mining houses such as Northam Platinum have joined it. In many large companies such as Impala Platinum, however, agreements were reached on company-based pension funds (for example, Lonmin Masakhane, Impala Workers Provident Fund, Anglo Group Provident Fund or other funds such as the Sentinel Mining Industry Retirement Fund).[56] The MWPF portfolio was worth more than R23 billion on 31 March 2013.[57] However, despite the planned consultation of members through regional advisory committees, workers' participation in decisions taken by the fund's trustees remains mostly theoretical. Rumours about this unavailable cash reserve seen as a union war treasury often circulate. For instance, there have been rumours that money will be paid only every ten years[58] or, as happened in 2008, that members would receive 50 per cent of their retirement fund monies in a once-off payment by the 15 December – that is, just before the Christmas break.[59]

In 1999, Carletonville's regional chairperson, Selby Mayise, was stabbed to death during a meeting in which he reported on changes in the legislation governing the Mineworkers Provident Fund.[60] Current Carletonville regional secretary, Mbuyiseli Hibana, was there:

> It is unfortunate that in 1999 we lost one of the very good leaders of NUM who was the chairperson of the region here, comrade Selby Mayise. Many in NUM thought he should have been the president after James Motlatsi … He was killed in a mass meeting in Driefontein on 12 May 1999. We had a challenge on the provident fund, there were new rules that came up in terms of how it was to be handled. He was a trustee then and [one of] the trustees who had decided to change the rules … Comrade Zokwana was also part of that mass meeting, myself too. I was hospitalised for a week as a result of the assault by a group of people that we cannot say are members of the union. People were arrested but we lost the case since they could not be identified as the assaulters.[61]

At the same mine NUM faced the challenge of 'disillusioned' members joining legal aid schemes, such as LegalWise, Scorpion Legal Protection and a new 'quasi-union' formed in 2002 by 'a pastor, and an attorney of the high court', which was known as the Legal Voice Workers' Trade Union (LVWTU).[62]

Provident funds such as the MWPF, which count many migrant workers among their members (including a sizeable number of non-South African citizens), have been at the centre of a number of scandals as they have sometimes failed to trace their members to pay them their dues after they had retired and gone back home. In 2010, it was estimated that such 'unclaimed' benefits amounted to R5.7 billion stored in various retirement-type funds. Another fund, established in 1970, administered by the Chamber of Mines and accessible only to semi-skilled black employees (that is, a small minority of mineworkers), closed after the MWPF had been created and still contains the 'unclaimed benefits' of mineworkers who went back to Lesotho, Swaziland or Mozambique, where they often live in deprived rural environments and are often in bad health because of work-contracted illnesses.[63] The 1970 MWPF fund still contained R200 million in 2008, owed to 59 702 former workers. After a 2005 communication media campaign, no more than 119 beneficiaries were identified.[64] The MWPF also lost R1.4 billion in 2007 after Fidentia, a firm in which the MWPF was invested, went bankrupt.[65]

NUM resources were never used to constitute a strike fund, as in other unions worldwide. However, its attention to its retrenched members – most of whom were migrant workers – went far beyond the union's struggle for the creation of provident funds. After the devastating post-1987-strike retrenchments, NUM created the Mineworkers Development Agency (MDA), an original developmental project for the creations of jobs and small, medium and micro enterprises (SMMEs). It started as a producers' co-op project in the aftermath of the strike. This initial phase was quite narrowly focused on workers' cooperatives, with about 30 projects involving over 400 people and producing mainly vegetable crops, poultry, and cement blocks. The MDA then moved towards an enterprise-development strategy, targeting communities affected by job losses. NUM Co-op Unit was based at head office and managed by Kate Philip, who then became CEO of the MDA, a position she held between 1995 and 2002.[66] The MDA was externalised in 1995 and became part of the 'family' of projects funded by the Mineworkers Investment Trust (MIT). It receives R7 million per annum 'to create at least 1 700 sustainable livelihoods annually in South Africa, Lesotho and Swaziland' with a view to helping both retrenched mineworkers and their families.[67] MDA's initiatives included buying land for farming as well as the creation of Marula Natural Products – the MDA's success story and a company that produces juices and oil for cosmetics from the local marula berry.[68]

A TRADE UNION'S FINANCIAL EMPIRE

At the union's 2015 congress, the treasurer general described NUM as a resilient organisation. Its financial strength indeed makes it an organisational body that could now virtually function without members. With the advent of a democratic South Africa, NUM started to be directly involved in finance. The MIT was established in 1995 as the union's financial arm. The Trust relies on two subsidiaries that manage and develop its assets: its investment fund, the Mineworkers Investment Company (MIC) and Numprop, established in 1993, which takes care of the union's real estate properties, such as the head office building or the EBMTC in Yeoville and Midrand. The financial resources thus generated are reinvested in the union's training centre, the MDA, and its programme of bursaries designed for members, the JB Marks Education Trust Fund (see chapter 7). The MIC is the MIT's main asset and it has shares in media, industrial and leisure groups.[69] Started in 1997 with a union seed capital of R3 million, it had net assets worth R3 billion at the end of 2012.[70] 'Since 1995 it is estimated that the Mineworkers Investment Trust (MIT) improved the lives of more than 1,2 million people through grants made to three key beneficiaries,' the fund proclaimed in its 2010 annual report. By 2010, the MIC had donated a total of R368 million to the MIT, including a R245 million dividend for 2008. In 15 years of existence the MIT had also supported 4 000 young people in their studies through the JB Marks Bursary Fund.[71]

The MIC's first CEO was none other than NUM's former treasurer general Paul Nkuna. Its net asset value declined by 40 per cent between 2008 and 2009 due to the global economic crisis but it proved resilient with a nearly 20 per cent growth in the following year. Its goal is to distribute an annual dividend of ten per cent to its unique shareholder, the MIT, but it also claims to have become 'a strong engine of transformation' by striking deals compliant with the South African government affirmative action policy (Broad-Based Black Economic Empowerment). Regarding potential contradictions of NUM's involvement in finance, Nkuna stressed:

> There has always been formal separation between the National Union of Mineworkers and the MIC. But we remain proud of our union roots. It therefore goes without saying that we hate to see working people lose their jobs. At the same time, we are an investment company and seek sustainable returns. In tough times when business volumes are under pressure, returns are often a function of expense management and cost-cutting by employers. Our attitude is that jobs are the last item to be cut.[72]

This issue was publicly raised at NUM's 14th National Congress in May 2012. After NUM president Senzeni Zokwana had introduced Sidumo Dlamini, his counter-part in Cosatu, the congress became a scene in an episode of 'reality trade unionism' when Dlamini stated: 'Comrade President, I reported to you that I would have dif-ficulty to address the congress before this matter is solved: yesterday when I left the congress, I was arrested by one delegate who told me to come to an office of Fawu [the Food and Allied Workers Union] where two employees, employed by a labour broker, had been fired.' At the time, Cosatu was involved in a campaign to have labour brokers banned and Zokwana came to the stage to reassure his counterpart. One of the founding principles of trade unionism is 'an injury to one is an injury to all,' he recalled, before declaring: 'Our general secretary has been in touch with Peermont Hotels' CEO [through MIC, NUM is a majority shareholder in Peermont

Global, a group that owns the Emperor's Palace, where the congress was held in Johannesburg] and the matter will be solved. Our union will not be associated with labour brokers.' Dlamini then continued: 'Thanks, President, I can happily speak to the congress because when we say we are at war with labour brokers we mean it.' After Dlamini had finished his speech, Baleni further reassured him: 'As per your directive, President Dlamini, we have engaged the CEO of Peermont and I can confirm that these workers have been reinstated.' It is important to remember at this stage that decisions to create both the MIC and the MIT were taken by the NEC in 1995 and not by congress. The decision to invest in the business sphere was therefore not discussed with union members and their direct representatives and a resolution was adopted only afterwards, at the union's 1997 national congress, to ratify the creation of the MIC. It resolved 'that the union must refuse to engage in any capitalist activities which would compromise its commitment to the class struggle' and that guidelines and control of its investments should be well defined.[73]

According to a booklet the MIC published in celebration of its 15th anniversary, the story of the company started 'in 1987 with a policy decision by the national executive committee (NEC) of the National Union of Mineworkers (NUM) that miners, armed with skills, must take full control'. In this document, the decision to create the company is linked to the need to boost 'skills development [that] was seen as the prerequisite for workers to take control of their future'. The union thus had to find sustainable funding for an ambitious bursary scheme named after the renowned 1940s and 1950s communist and unionist JB Marks. While the decision to create an education-dedicated fund may have been an easy one to take, investing on stock markets was more ambiguous:

> It was decided that the goal could be best achieved by creating an investment holding company focused on earning solid returns from a diversified portfolio of investments. This was a controversial departure for any trade union as it could be interpreted as embracing capitalism. Frans Baleni acknowledges that at the time, it was almost political suicide for a left-leaning organisation like ours to take this decision, but it was inspired by our experience as mineworkers. The mineworkers were poorly paid and were breeding another generation of unskilled miners. If nothing was done then the status quo would remain.

The MIC was supposed to be a 'separate legal entity' but separation was doubtful if one looks at the administrators of the Trust: 'On the MIT Board of Trustees back then were James Motlatsi (NUM president at that time), Kgalema Motlanthe (then NUM general secretary) and Gwede Mantashe (NUM assistant general secretary until 2006). Other trustees included Paul Nkuna, Marcel Golding, and Senzeni Zokwana (former NUM president).[74]

Once again, what is generally presented as a post-apartheid evolution of unions in fact has older roots. The question of how to invest financial surplus had already been raised by NUM at the end of the 1980s. In 1987, for instance, the NEC decided to invest R2 million from the NUM Relief Account in a Eurobank account at a high return rate. This investment proved unwise when the bank was liquidated the following year, and NUM was still battling to recover these funds in 1991, three years later.[75] The debate on the opportunity to create a trade union investment vehicle dates to the early 1990s. In 1991, for instance, the NEC discussed a proposal by the Labour Research Service to launch such a fund and invest a share of retirement funds in a socially responsible way; it then pleaded for a clear investment code as agreed upon in a 1991 congress resolution.[76] With the opening of many new opportunities after 1994, however, things went fast and unions undertook some highly contentious investment deals. Even though 'a great deal of confusion' surrounded 'union investment', 'very little serious discussion or enquiry' occurred and 'secrecy' prevailed in many cases. In 1996, the 'Johnnic deal' was a particularly problematic one in which the black-consciousness-orientated National Council of Trade Unions federation was involved, in pursuit of 'strategies at variance with the unions themselves'. It involved a consortium, headed by New Africa Investments Limited (which had four individual shareholders including former NUM leader Cyril Ramaphosa), that took control of industrial holding group Johannesburg Consolidated Investment Corporation (Johnnic) and, through it, acquired shares in South Africa Breweries, Toyota and Omni Media. At the time, there were also indications that the group would make a bid for control of Anglo American's JCI Ltd gold-mining group.[77]

Two unionists were to become central to the dynamics of trade union investment companies in South Africa: Marcel Golding (former NUM deputy general secretary) and Johnny Copelyn (general secretary of the Southern African Clothing and Textile Workers' Union – Sactwu – from 1980 to 1994). Their trajectories are those of pioneers in the business of union investment companies who, after cutting their teeth for a few years in the unions, moved into the corporate world. In the early 1990s they represented their respective affiliates in Cosatu discussions about provident funds and the drafting of a union investment strategy. International examples were closely monitored, as revealed in a 1993 letter from Robert Oakeshott to Johnny Copelyn. Oakeshott was promoting employee ownership in England and he gave Copelyn a detailed brief on possible models for an income fund.[78] The same year, Sactwu established the Sactwu Investment Group (SIG), two years before NUM launched the MIC. Johnny Copelyn soon became CEO of the SIG and Golding was appointed director of the MIC. After having been barred from 'political' ascent in the union following his failure to get elected as NUM's general secretary in 1992, Golding opted for what in retrospect appears to be an exit strategy. In 1994 he was elected to Parliament on the ANC ticket, before he resigned in 1997 to dedicate himself to business. The same happened to Johnny Copelyn, who left Parliament the same year, and the two became executive directors of Hosken Consolidated Investments, a Johannesburg Stock Exchange listed investment fund, in which the main shareholder happens to be the SIG. Such a radical shift in their respective careers raised many questions at the time among their former 'comrades', regarding their decision to leave Parliament when they had been 'seconded' there by Cosatu in order to represent the workers' interests and, more significantly, on how their personal move into capitalism contrasted with the cause they had served for many years.[79] In answer to his critics, Copelyn said that he and Golding were, once again, doing 'frontier work', which was too innovative for workers to understand its true value. Copelyn argued, based on overseas examples, that their work was part of a strategy to develop workers' power as 'consumer power' and, at the risk of sounding 'romantic', he put forward the need to fund institutions with social functions 'such as crèches, clinics, retirement homes and the like for workers'. In a comment that eventually applied to only a few happy black people, he stated: 'Black empowerment can mean the opportunity for the working class to get ownership of billions of rand in independently owned investment companies.'[80] Marcel Golding answered in a similar vein, concluding on a cryptic note: 'You are unlikely to discover new oceans and distant lands if you are unwilling to lose sight of the shore.'[81]

This alignment between trade unions and market- and business-designed strategies, through investment companies at first, but then also through individual former unionists' choosing to go into business, had long-term impacts on how unions managed their resources. Critics pointed to the fact that these dynamics were part of an *embourgeoisement* of unionists and that 'unionism is not about making money. It is about social issues, about using worker solidarity at plant, industry and national level to improve living and working conditions.' The secrecy of the deals passed between union investment companies and their 'empowerment partners' was also criticised.[82]

Paul Nkuna may describe 'the separation between the MIC, the MIT and NUM as a "Chinese wall"',[83] but NUM leaders are on the boards of both the MIT and the MIC, which de facto confirms the increasing penetration of business, its social practices and etiquette into the field of trade unionism. In 2012, all top five NUM leaders served on the board of trustees of the MIT, on which website their biographies significantly differed from those presented on NUM's official website.

Comrades Baleni and Macatha (NUM treasurer general) respectively became Mr. Baleni and Mr. Macatha on the MIT website page about the trustees. Whereas on the NUM website their biographies concentrated mainly on their background in the organisation, the MIT website branded their corporate profile through listing the degrees they had earned, their positions and their hobbies. Baleni, for instance, was described as holding a BA in developmental studies, and '[he] enjoys swimming, reading and soccer'. Oupa Komane, former deputy general secretary of NUM, is presented as having an MSc in Engineering Business Management and an MBA, and '[he] speaks six languages and is able to relax whilst enjoying soccer and all genres of music'. The same union leaders who were pictured in red tee shirts on the NUM website appeared in suits and, for Macatha, in a tie on the MIT website.

The potential for conflicts of interest is particularly high when a union engages in business – a question that Philip Dexter, an ANC member of Parliament, raised very clearly in relation to career shifts such as those of Golding and Copelyn 'The real question is whether unions should be involved in capitalism in the same way that capitalists are, or whether they can be involved in business and investment for strategic reasons.' He further remarked:

> The business people who are currently running many of the investment companies are paid a commission, or receive shares in the company. While they are making a lot of money, they are not always acting in the interests of the union. Worse still, there have been cases where they get union officials to agree to certain investments by cutting them in on the deal or providing other incentives. Comrade X, who was recently a union official, is now a millionaire because he/she saw a gap and took it![84]

Yet, celebrating 15 years of existence, the MIT states, 'it was always understood that any investments would exclude possible conflicts of interests with the National Union of Mineworkers (NUM)'.[85] The MIC follows this broad orientation but it was invested, for instance, in Set Point, a company that provides technology-based solutions to the mining industry. The MIC had also acquired a 25 per cent stake in SA Teemane, a diamond-cutting and polishing business. Such decisions, however, were far from unanimously taken by NUM's leadership, even though some openly favoured investments in mining. In 2000, exiting NUM president James Motlatsi concluded his last speech as union leader by declaring:

> With the MIC we, however, did not clearly define its area of investment, that is where to invest and where not to invest … To date sharp differences exist

within our ranks on this issue … I want to take position based on realities. I do not think that MIC's investing in the mining and energy industry is a conflict of interest. We are not in the position of determining the price of these commodities … We continue travelling all over the world in a bid to restore investors confidence and to lobby for foreign investment. If we truly believe that this is a sunshine industry and not a sunset industry, why are we not investing on it? … I urge you as the National Union of Mineworkers to invest in this industry in order to heighten investor confidence.[86]

Such a stand by the founding president of NUM raises questions on whether his opinion gradually shifted with his 'class interest', to frame the debate in Marxist terms. After leaving NUM, Motlatsi indeed held several positions on the boards of investment vehicles and companies, including Ramaphosa's Shanduka Group, Masana Petroleum Solutions, and Verimark Holdings Limited.

FROM MEMBERS TO CUSTOMERS

As NUM was turning into a professional organisation, operated by skilled staff, managed by a general secretary – the 'top employee' of the union – and backed by strong financials, it conceived its members ever less as activists and more as customers. The latter were now contributing one per cent of their monthly salary and they were paying for union services, as the union itself put it. Such an assumption bears important consequences since these two categories of actor have different aspirations: militant workers belong to a collective – an occupational community – that makes them stronger in their struggle with employers, whereas customers are just aggregated individuals who mutualise resources to be stronger in the face of large companies from whom they buy goods and services. This tension in trade unionism is not unique to South Africa and it juxtaposes what is known as the 'organising model' with the 'servicing model'.[87] In social movement unionism, trade unions were historically conceived as institutions representing workers, but also more broadly as a social community and an instrument aimed at transforming society. Trade unions constituted to some extent a counter social order and belonging to one was constitutive of one's belonging to society. This comprehensive conception of membership has, however, declined since the 1980s and, in countries like France, the member has increasingly become a mere 'subscriber' and the union a service provider. In South Africa's mining sector, recent years have seen the development of two kinds of dynamics that reflect this tension between servicing and activism.

On the one hand, 'new quasi-union formations' sometimes emerged in the form of legal services providers, with a view to answering the needs of an allegedly dissatisfied NUM membership in search of better servicing. On the other hand, and more significantly, Amcu ruptured NUM's monopoly on workers' representation by adopting a more militant stance that allegedly met a demand among mineworkers for direct action.

The NUM head office and its regional subsidiaries view their membership base increasingly through data and statistics, including those produced in SWOP reports since 1998. If collaboration between the union and the university dates back to the 1980s and has been seen as mutually beneficial (expertise in labour sociology is traded for privileged access to research fields in the mines and the union), the very fact of producing expert knowledge is also based on a particular conception of the social world. The work of expertise[88] is very well captured in Frans Baleni's reports, which are then reproduced by his regional alter egos in a move that also participates, I argue, in deepening the gap between the top and the bottom of the organisation. Leaders increasingly know their members through figures in reports. The members' degree of satisfaction is expressed in percentages, just as surveys of consumer or customer satisfaction are conducted by firms or organisations that defend consumers' rights. Moreover, the central thesis of the last two SWOP reports (2005 and 2010) remains problematic when one looks at the current crisis in mineworkers' representation.

SWOP experts centrally identify 'NUM's changing membership base' as the result of 'massive changes' at work. The typical member is no longer a migrant living in a single-sex hostel. Since the end of apartheid, the workforce has become increasingly feminised and it is now also ageing (with induced tensions between the older and more traditional mineworkers and the more educated and careerist young workers). The membership has been impacted by the demise of mining hostels and the growing impact of subcontracting in mining.[89] SWOP's conclusions about changes in the NUM membership base are, however, too hasty: a dynamic is probably in motion but it is far from accomplished.[90] If the NUM membership profile has changed as a result of new social and class mobilities or through managerial reorganisation, this is true mostly for surface jobs: administrative and mineral-processing operations. The 2012 strikes, which were led by core sections of the mines' underground workforce, suggest on the contrary a great degree of stability in its composition and expectations (one must nevertheless bear in mind that rock drill operators are a minority of the mines' total workforce). The two central claims that were at the heart of the strike movement – demands for major wage increases on the one hand, and the rejection of NUM as legitimate intermediary on the other – remain basic and can in fact be analysed as historical continuities. What the strikes show, of course, is that working conditions on the mines have not been decisively altered since the end of apartheid. But what is of greater significance to my argument is that they also illustrate the fact that workers' mobilisations are relatively similar to what prevailed in the past. The strikes reflect an inclination of significant segments in the workforce towards militancy rather than service. This is clear, for instance, in the reinvestment of old repertoires of action based on the reactivation of old workers' solidarities.[91] These factors plead against the idea that NUM's membership base has experienced a radical transformation in its composition. Recent strikes did not witness the rise of the more 'sophisticated' young NUM members, more acquainted with the subtlety of labour law than with direct action, as described in SWOP reports. The conclusions reached in SWOP reports satisfy the views of leaders like Frans Baleni on the transformation of NUM. In such views, expertise calls for new methods of management, the production of sophisticated policies informed by a scientific knowledge of the needs of members and so on. In other words, SWOP reports have participated in a circular flow of information in which NUM leaders – including intermediary layers of leadership at region and branch levels – started to think that the majority of their members were in the process of becoming like them: looking like them, living like them, thinking like them, which, in my view, is a highly questionable assumption.

NUM leaders often quote from SWOP reports in their own organisational reports, which are distributed to delegates in congresses and conferences, from branch to national level. SWOP reports are considered as authoritative when it comes to assessing the state of the organisation and its membership base. 'We have commissioned the sociology of work (Swop) section of the Wits Sociology department to assess the levels of membership satisfaction about the service they receive from the union,' Gwede Mantashe wrote in 2005.[92] Mantashe himself was instrumental in linking NUM and SWOP after he had graduated from Wits in 2008. In 2006 he wrote: 'The second way of celebrating these brave struggles would be by improving our service quality. The Swop research, overall, is critical of the quality of service we render.'[93] Resolutions adopted during the 2010 central committee meeting were 'converted' into 'Key Performance Areas (KPAs)', one of which considered the 'implementation of recommendations contained in the Swop report' that were incorporated into regional programmes of action.[94] SWOP's latest report is particularly telling in respect of the new business- and customer-orientated 'ethics' at work in NUM. In his foreword to the study, and speaking directly to his more than 300 000 members, many of whom are still illiterate and live in shacks, Baleni wrote:

We have pleasure in presenting the outcome of this study titled 'Meeting Expectations? A report on the state of servicing in the National Union of Mineworkers' … The union is more than happy to do this so that we know how we can improve to help our members. In business circles, the customer is said to be king. We agree, and we take it further to say 'Members first in everything we do'.[95]

The idea of members as customers deserving a certain level of servicing by NUM cadres and structures may be a call for new fights in the workplace, but it also fits into the new 'culture of enterprise' that now permeates NUM. A Carletonville region report observed in 2005: 'Members pay subscriptions to the union and in return they expect us as leaders and shaft stewards to service them. They want quality for their hard-earned money.' The report then raised an interesting comparison between the 1980s and the 2005 union, which, if one reads between the lines, suggests a decrease in the organisation's militant character:

Comparison is sometimes made that in the 80s our members were getting quality service even though branch leaders were not full-time in the offices. This quality service is attributed to the fact that we were all in the coalface and therefore we could feel the heat. We had experiences of how the conditions were in our workplaces, and we were also subjected to all kinds of abuse and brutality by our supervisors. Unlike those years today we are all full-time in the offices; and we have plenty of time to do the union work including improving our service to members, but instead we are getting complaints about poor service.[96]

The provision of services by an ever more skilled and wealthy organisation has been improved since the 1980s and there is little doubt that a now more mobile mining workforce includes workers whose expectations of the union are also dependent on the levels and sophistication of the services they receive. However, the 2012 strikes, led by rock drill operators – that is, the modern-day wretched of the earth – suggested that a significant chunk of NUM membership is still concerned first and foremost with bread-and-butter issues. Calls by NUM leaders to abolish the migrant labour system or to get rid of Fanakalo, the mines' pidgin imposed by the industry, may be part of a legitimate will to decolonise mining, but they also threaten the way of life and, in one word, the 'culture' of a still significant chunk of NUM's membership, which has now joined Amcu.[97] Moreover, as I observed during wage negotiations, members are above all sensitive to cash increases on their payslips and often angered by 'deferred payments' such as pension contributions. Despite the major gains NUM has earned for them, the living conditions of many remain too harsh for them to be able to see beyond their monthly payslip to appreciate social benefits, whereas many NUM leaders have already crossed that step and are now fighting the battle for improved benefits and services.

In the meantime, NUM has slipped from a militant type of trade unionism to a model closer to service unionism, which involves a new organisational ethos and a relationship to members approached no longer as activists but as clients – a model that neither suits nor adequately reflects the needs of many union members whose actual living conditions and lifestyle is in fact much the same as it used to be. The much-quoted 2001 report prepared by former production pillar head Eddie Majadibodu, 'Implementing the Ten Dimensions for Quality Service to Members', is in itself illustrative of this shift towards a corporate-sector-inspired type of relationship.[98] And later, as reported in 2003: 'We have introduced and deepened the understanding about service quality. We have adopted the King's ten dimensions of service quality as the standard we must strive for.'[99] These ten dimensions – reliability, responsiveness, competence, access, courtesy, communication, credibility, security, understanding and tangibles – are directly taken from customer-centred approaches. However, as far as NUM's membership base is concerned, the ambitious promises in policies the union has set up to better service its members (such as a member-designed bursary programme) remain a faraway reality for the majority. Nonetheless, this is not to say that no members view themselves as customers; the word was sometimes used during interviews I had with members who described themselves as a 'client of the NUM'.

In an annual national staff seminar held in February 1991, Cyril Ramaphosa presented a harsh assessment of the state of NUM ten years after its creation.[100] The general secretary then cited Eskom, South Africa's parastatal electricity supplier (and Africa's largest electricity producer), as an example of good organisational management. This is ironic when one considers that Eskom later became NUM's black sheep, with the union denouncing it as an embodiment of the bad management of South Africa's parastatals, as unprofessional and unfit for negotiations. Yet this example also indicates, as early as 1991, the union's determination to move towards more corporate techniques of internal management. At the 1991 annual staff seminar, Ramaphosa stated: 'If all unions and the ANC and Civics were to try and be as professional as these companies – we would achieve wonders. Companies are efficient and ruthless – they know where they are going, they have a plan and they achieve it.' Such representations of private sector efficiency are also significant in Ramaphosa's mouth if one retrospectively thinks that the founding general secretary of NUM would later enjoy one of South Africa's most successful post-apartheid business careers.

4

Doing Union Politics: The Branches as Idealised Seat of Union Power

THE COMPLEXITIES OF WORKER CONTROL

The 'worker control' principle is at the heart of NUM's and Cosatu's ideologies. It is based on the double assumption that workers ought to (i) democratically control their own organisations (hence preventing officials from dominating union and federation structures); and (ii) effectively expand such control, as members of the working class, to overall society (as expressed in NUM's famous motto: '1987 – the year mineworkers take control').

This idea and its practice has also been historically at the heart of trade unionism worldwide. It found a radical meaning in anarcho-syndicalism, which promoted decentralised, autonomous and factory-based forms of workers' organisation, and a classist meaning in Marxism-Leninism according to which unions represented the workers but were to be subject to the Party's authority. Far from the anarchist or workerist ideals of a locally grounded power, independent of top structures in the organisation, worker control in NUM is firmly rooted in the socialist tradition of centralised, hierarchical and disciplined organisation. As a 1999 report acknowledged: 'Over the years the union has tended to become centralist with a very powerful head office and national structures.' The report vowed to fight against this tendency and to 'devolve this power and responsibility to branches'.[1] The tension between the reality of a centralised organisation and its will to decentralise is well summarised in the following quote by former NUM general secretary Frans Baleni, who once wrote that branches

> are the base of the union's pyramidal organisation. They are in contact with rank and file members and potential members, responsible for recruitment,

mobilisation, assessing grievances … They also play a vital role in demands formulation, resolutions and transmitting such information to the regional office and then on to decision-making organs of the union. Democracy cannot function in the union without vibrant, active branches.[2]

Such a description makes branches the seat of union power in a bottom-up type of relationship with upper structures. Figure 4.1 illustrates this insistence on the base as the root of union power. Baleni's words, however, also describe a top-down 'pyramidal' structure in which decision-making effectively lies with the top structure. In other words, while NUM always claimed to root its power locally by electing mines-based union structures first, before electing higher representative organs, it was always a representative organisation resting on the basic principle of delegation. As such, its leaders' views on pyramidal organisation and discipline-based decision-making processes sometimes conflicted with their members' aspirations. However, to workers, what sometimes mattered and probably still matters more than concretely impacting on daily union decisions was having direct, physical access to upper layers of leadership. 'Mass meetings', in which the assembled membership at a given workplace could talk to its leaders, make them listen and hear them speak – in one word, make leadership 'accountable' – were a key site where direct representation could take place. This 'direct' representation means that each individual member, and the mass of members, can be physically in the presence of their leaders to expose their work-related grievances. The image of the mass meeting in an open field is thus an image of how the union should function, and is diametrically opposed to the image of the closed office, in which tricks and sleights of hand are played, and in which one must know how to read and write in order to have one's voice heard. Members did not necessarily expect to impact on every decision relevant to the life of the union and its management. They neither necessarily conceived democracy as a totally participatory process nor were they ready to always go through the intermediation of local and regional structures to reach the ears of their national leaders. Occurrences in which union members boycotted constitutional processes and structures – that is, the process of institutional representation – in attempts to directly reach the attention of top leaders in the organisation are not new. As Allen, writing about the 1980s, recounts:

> Ordinary members believed that the union was theirs and existed exclusively to serve them. It was stimulated by Ramaphosa's dictum that the union offices belonged to the ordinary members … Whenever they wanted any kind of assistance they went straight to the head office and waited patiently

NATIONAL UNION OF
MINEWORKERS CONSTITUTION

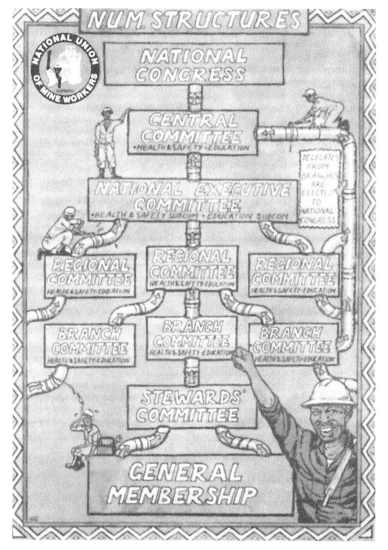

As Amended in January 2002

Figure 4.1:   The union relies on its members, NUM constitution, 2002

Source: NUM constitution booklet, 2002. Reproduced with permission.

to see Ramaphosa or Motlatsi. Sometimes they hung around for days … It was a common sight to see them in small groups, wrapped in their blankets in the corners of the offices.[3]

This situation, however, soon became unmanageable when, early in 1986, a large delegation of members employed by Gencor, in Rustenburg, travelled to Johannesburg after the company had dismissed 23 000 mineworkers. They wanted to talk to Ramaphosa whom they believed could have them reinstated. Once in town they literally occupied NUM's head office in Wanderers Street. Ramaphosa tried to oust them by offering each one of them a R300 stipend. Motlatsi was opposed to this, seeing it as an incentive to future disruptions, but he was over-ruled. The president's concerns proved right when almost 400 dismissed workers came to Johannesburg in the following two months in search of similar compensation. They occupied the NUM office for three weeks before the national leadership eventually decided to resort to force and called on the nearby Grootvlei branch, which 'had a reputation for providing a heavy-handed security service for the union', to evacuate them.[4]

As clearly shown during the 2012 wave of miners' strikes, union members have long strived for some form of direct contact with their leadership, who have on the other hand generally conceived a successful organisation as mainly representational. According to some observers of present-day NUM, workers are no longer (properly) consulted and heard on union matters and decisions, because 'NUM leadership [is] out of touch with its members'. Members now increasingly experience mass meetings, in which they are supposed to raise demands and mandate their leaders, as assemblies in which shaft stewards simply convey messages from management and 'come with decisions already made'. 'The formation of the Workers' Committee outside union structures and directly controlled by the workers at Marikana and elsewhere in the platinum belt highlights the extent to which post-apartheid unionised mineworkers are critical of their union leaders.'[5] These recent developments no doubt partially explain the ongoing labour unrest in mining. However, the 1980s also tend to be approached in a hagiographical way, as a golden age of militant and grassroots trade unionism, in contrast with current prevailingly centralised and bureaucratic tendencies.

Worker control has nevertheless always been, in South Africa as elsewhere, a contended domain and the line between democracy and oligarchy in organisations is always a thin one. Buhlungu describes workers' control in practice as:

- an emphasis on shop-floor structures led by elected shop stewards;

- the creation of representative structures in which worker delegates were the majority;
- leadership accountability through mandated decision-making and regular report-backs to members;
- factory-level bargaining which allowed workers and shop stewards to maintain control of the bargaining agenda and the conclusion of agreements;
- the subordination of full-time officials to control by worker-dominated structures; and
- involvement of workers, at all levels, in the employment of full-time officials.

For him, 'the principle of worker control was built into the founding constitution of Cosatu to prevent leaders and full-time officials from dominating structures of the federation and its affiliates'. He concedes, however, that some highly integrated and largely mechanised sectors such as the Numsa-organised factories (as opposed, for instance, to the more fragmented municipal services) also implied that worker control took different forms in different sectors.[6] In the case of NUM, and in the light of what has been evidenced in chapters 2 and 3, one could moderate Buhlungu's last three bullet points. The 1980s NUM, as opposed to some of its fellow black unions that boycotted national industry forums, was a forerunner in that it bargained with the gold- and coal-mining sectors in the Chamber of Mines. Its national structure, populated mainly by bureaucrats, already had a decisive say in many union decisions and policies.

Buhlungu does not argue that trade union democracy has simply vanished in the post-apartheid era. Relying on the case of Numsa, he explains that its nature has qualitatively evolved. For him, the 'collectivist and democratic organizational culture' that emerged in the 1973 Durban strike to later burgeon within South Africa's black unions was no monolith. It was indeed 'dynamic, highly contested, and contradictory', and the 'decline of the democratic culture in the unions began in the early 1990s and was accentuated by South Africa's transition to democracy as well as the increasing reintegration of the country into the global economy'.[7]

Moreover, the origin of the unions' grassroots organisational culture was also largely pragmatic since many leaders were arrested during strikes, with unions having to rely on their membership to survive. Recall, as previously argued, that in the case of NUM the only section of the organisation that survived the onslaught of blows such as the massive post-1987-strike dismissals was precisely its central apparatus, which in turn increased centralisation. Most union leaders in the 1980s – workers, students or youth activists with high school education, whom Buhlungu calls 'activist organizers' – were also ideologically committed to building democratic structures. In the 1980s, the call for democratic organisation in fact went far beyond trade unions, with the emergence of the United Democratic Front (1983) and township-based civic organisations. Buhlungu also notes that during the unity talks that preceded the disbanding of Fosatu and the birth of Cosatu in 1985, 'the principle of worker control of union structures was one of the least contentious'.[8] The hegemony of worker control remained, however, 'an uneasy and tenuous one'. It was also contested by management, which pressured union leaders to make decisions in the name of their constituencies.[9] But despite company and State repression, unions were among the few organisations that continued to operate legally, which, as opposed to their underground political counterparts such as the ANC and the SACP, made the practice of internal democracy easier. When political organisations were unbanned in the early 1990s, Cosatu and its affiliates soon discovered that the SACP and ANC organisational and leadership cultures were far more centralised than theirs.[10]

With regard to NUM, it is worth recalling that exercising worker control did not only and strictly mean organising the union through internal democratic mechanisms. It was also a principle that was aimed, in the mines, at undermining the despotic and disciplinary power of mine managers. To this end, and as NUM took control of mining compounds through unionising the mines' workforce, it also meant turning the compound system, and the mines' disciplinary apparatus, 'on its head'. Decisive in NUM's rise was its successful subversion of the mine's closed space in which workers lived in large numbers and where they were already well 'organised' through systems of managerial control. Once mining compounds were under NUM organisers' control, it was easier there than elsewhere to collectively organise and mobilise workers. In turn, Buhlungu and Bezuidenhout point out, the

> mass meetings meant that leadership faced immediate pressure to be accountable to membership, as they interacted with them on a daily basis in the compounds as well as at the rock face ... All these efforts combined with a militant membership, which became increasingly confident. They saw the union as belonging to them and as being controlled by them.[11]

The two authors nonetheless acknowledge that 'the union also tailored the principle of worker control to suit its own circumstances', as when NUM president James Motlatsi, who was dismissed in 1987 and no longer an employed mineworker, saw his part-time position converted to full-time (paid by NUM) and was thus able to retain his union position. According to these authors, worker control then declined with the advent of democracy and under the pressure of the new dynamics emerging from that.

Worker control thus always featured as a complex principle and practice in NUM as well as beyond the mineworkers' union. As principle and practice, it has different possible meanings and geometries. It is not obvious that workers had more effective control over their organisation and leaders in the 1980s than they have today in terms of decision-making or, viewed from the other side of the coin, that leaders were more inclined to listen to their members in the past. As early as May 1984, for instance, while NUM was due to take part in its second round of wage negotiations at the Chamber of Mines, the majority of delegates at its Second National Congress said they 'had been dissatisfied with the 1983 wages award and complained that they had not been given the opportunity to express their views about it before it was implemented'. As a result, the union leadership delayed the upcoming negotiation and committed to arrange report-back meetings throughout the wage talks.[12] This, among many other examples in the past, shows that the principle of worker control in a NUM that had historically been built from top to bottom was constructed, negotiated and always fragile. External factors also played a part. If the anti-apartheid struggle mass democratic movement meant that members were spontaneously more enthusiastic, that they could immediately feel they were part of a wider struggle, institutionalised union life in a democratic South Africa had the potential effect of digging holes in worker control or, at least, of making them more visible and critically felt on the ground.

MASS MEETINGS AND THE AMBIGUITIES OF LIVED LOCAL DEMOCRACY

Periodically, NUM membership exerted control over union leadership. In 1990, for instance, the Western Cape region faced troubles and a dispute arose when members decided to remove their regional committee through a no-confidence vote. The committee was accused of not performing its tasks, of maladministration (including in finance) and of being uncooperative with workers. A new committee was elected and requested confirmation from head office that its election, which had been contested by the outgoing team, was constitutional. A head office representative was sent and concluded, in quite a remarkable move if one considers the legalism of current NUM national office bearers faced with the emergence of workers' committees, that '1. The removal was unconstitutional; 2. But that we had to address the concerns of the workers'. The head office envoy further concluded, after meeting with the two opposing sides, that 'it is our policy that worker control and openness is fundamental to the way our organisation operates'.[13] In a mixture of constitutionalism and flexibility, the national executive committee ruled, following the recommendations of its envoy, to disband the two competing regional committees and to organise a regional congress as soon as possible.[14] In other words, the unconstitutional removal of a team of regional leaders by NUM members was sanctioned by the organisation as a legitimate move.

If worker control was well exercised in some instances, one should not hastily conclude that the 1980s or early 1990s were a time when members were always aware of union activities and informing NUM decisions. In a rather fascinating 1986 document, NUM's central committee drafted 'proposed resolutions' in preparation for the 1987 national congress, on the basis that:

> Our union's members, Shaft Stewards, Branch Committee members and Regional Committee members do not know what is taking place in their union. A serious breakdown of communication is taking place in our union. Our union has started slowing down and is losing its original fighting spirit because members do not know what is happening in their union and members have become docile and inactive because they do not have any information.[15]

A series of resolutions recalling basic NUM rules on the regularity of meetings, the election of representatives or report-back procedures from the shaft to the national office were then listed. One can, of course, argue that this document issued by head office was somewhat catastrophist and designed to remobilise troops – in a style that was quite typical of Ramaphosa – but it certainly gives a relevant indication that the situation in the mid-1980s was not exactly a bed of roses when it came to worker control and internal democracy, understood as the enforcement of bottom-up decision-making. Such warnings are not so different from what one might read in post-apartheid NUM reports. Striking in the latter, however, is that members now complain that their leaders have increasingly become conveyor belts for management: 'Members see the attendance of the NUM mass meetings as waste of time as they don't get report backs on issues they mandate their leaders to take … to the employer, but they are always bombarded by new issues from the employer. Leaders are seen to be representing the employer [more] than members'.[16] In the context of institutionalised post-apartheid industrial relations, it is indeed not unusual to have mass meetings convened where trade unionists inform their members about decisions taken by management.[17] This in turn leaves members with the impression that their leaders are mere messengers serving management, which is a significant departure from what a 'mass meeting' is supposed to be.

Branch committees lead branches on a daily basis and are constitutionally required to hold branch general meetings, more commonly known as 'mass meetings', in which all union members at a certain branch gather and take decisions either by consensus or by a majority vote.[18] If some of my own observations suggest that members' participation in union activities at the local level is now problematic in some branches, available figures on attendance in local meetings union-wide do not suggest massive disaffection in the post-apartheid period, despite arguably decreasing participation figures. In 2005 only six per cent of the NUM members SWOP surveyed said they did not know when mass meetings were held. Sixty-eight per cent of ordinary members said they always attended workplace or hostel meetings; only four per cent said that they never did so. Thirty-four per cent said they always attended branch meetings, 27 per cent that they sometimes did so and 35 per cent that they never did so.[19] The figures for 2010 were quite similar to what was found in 2005.[20] These figures suggest that most members still take part in their workplace or hostel union meetings and that about half of them still participate in branch general meetings on a more or less regular basis – which, of course, also means that half of them do not attend branch meetings.

Mass meetings, which are the seat of local union democracy, involve tense situations in settings where leaders must face hundreds or thousands of members gathered to deal with often volatile situations, as is the case during wage negotiations. In small branches it may be the case that such meetings take place every month as prescribed by the NUM constitution, but it was my impression than in the larger branches they are mostly convened on the basis of arising issues, which means that members are usually called together to deal with contentious items. Workers gather before work (if they are on the night shift) or after (if they are on the morning shift) – that is, either in a state of exhaustion or of relative stress. I observed such a meeting at NUM Impala Platinum mine's South branch. With more than 9 000 members at the end of 2011, it was then the union's largest single branch. The mass meeting was convened at the Impala South hostels' sports arena. The branch leadership was expected to report back about ongoing wage negotiations with Impala management, and to get a mandate on the company's latest offer. But the mass meeting was in fact largely dedicated to another burning issue, the question of the Employee Share Ownership Programme (Esop).[21]

The Impala South hostels are, like other mining hostels, fenced spaces designed in a panopticon-like circle and quite similar in their functioning to what Erving Goffman called 'total institutions' (see Figures 4.2 and 4.3).

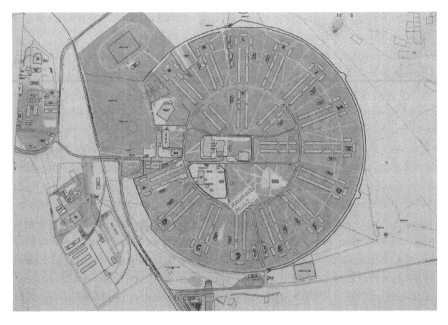

Figure 4.2:   Map showing Impala South hostels layout
Photographer: Raphaël Botiveau

Figure 4.3:   Accommodation at Impala South hostels
Photographer: Raphaël Botiveau

When I arrived at the hostels, the meeting was already underway but the ongoing activity in the hostels showed that many were not attending. A few hundred NUM members were seated in the sports arena, some protecting themselves from a declining but still warm sun with umbrellas. Most participants were men dressed casually, some in their mine work outfits, and only a few displayed NUM tee shirts (Figure 4.4). The branch secretary, speaking in Sesotho, was addressing members through a microphone. The Esop question was at the centre of debates. Since the company had announced Esop dividends two weeks before the mass meeting, employees had been 'angry'. Three years ago, I was later told, employees had 'taken' R8 000 in dividends as opposed to the R3 000 they had now received, their divideneds reduced as a result of the post-2008 economic downturn. A crisis was looming at Impala and a NUM shaft steward told me that about 20 skilled workers (miners) were resigning from their jobs every week. In his shaft alone, six or seven people had done so, arguing that they were badly paid in comparison with what they thought they would get in other companies like Lonmin. This is an important fact if one thinks of the massive strike that took place just a few months later at Impala, after the company had unilaterally awarded a wage increase to its miners. Impala's management argued that the contested increase – which caused a general strike in which workers demanded significant wage increases – was market-related and designed to stop resignations among the company's miners.

Figure 4.4: Mass meeting, Impala South branch, 2011
Photographer: Raphaël Botiveau

The crowd at Impala soon started to disperse after only three members were eventually given a chance to speak. The crowd remained mostly silent, only a few showing reactions of dismay when some of the speakers referred to Impala's profits. At the end of the meeting a circle of about 50 members formed around the branch office bearers in the arena, and two men started to come to blows before they were quickly separated. One of the men next to me told me that 'some of them feel the union has not fulfilled its duties'. The branch deputy chairperson then started to sing the national anthem – virtually on his own – at the very end of the meeting.

A few conclusions about mass meetings in big NUM branches can be drawn from this experience and others. Attendance was poor despite the importance of the meeting (a report-back on wage negotiations) and members who came behaved more as observers than as participants. Taking a decision, which is supposed to be achieved by majority vote, consensus or acclamation, was not even a question here and a mandate on the ongoing wage negotiation was not given to the branch leadership. Mass meetings are typically supposed to reach a collective decision as follows: a few members get to speak and, if they are not contradicted, they are 'seconded' by one or several speakers. Their voice then becomes a collective one that makes the decision or the mandate. In this particular case discussions around the ongoing wage negotiations were very limited. Another member of the NUM negotiation team confirmed that Impala South branch leaders had failed to adequately present management's offer to their members, who did not get a chance to express their views. As a result, the subsequent wage agreement ended up being signed by NUM without the direct assent of members at Impala branch.

NUM mass meetings are, however, not always that tense and many in small branches probably proceed more smoothly. About a year before the Impala meeting described above, I had witnessed another one at Rand Uranium (now Gold One) Cooke 3 shaft. On the agenda that day were health and safety matters, a new bonus system and the Christmas break. Once more, the meeting took place at one of the mine's hostels and was attended by a small audience of about one hundred members, gathered in the local church. Douglas Gininda, the NUM branch secretary in Randfontein, addressed the members in several languages, including isiXhosa, isiZulu and Sesotho. The secretary started speaking about overtime arrangements and the question of bonuses, after which the audience expressed its discontent. Discussion started immediately, some speaking with virulence and receiving applause from others, in agreement. The branch office bearers then started to give detailed explanations, speaking in an open way, calling on members to unite and to consult with their leaders when needed. The meeting ended in a way that suggested the unity of the branch, with everyone saying their own prayer in their own language, guided by one of the branch health and safety stewards. In this case the mass meeting proved to be, for members, an occasion to express grievances, get their leaders' ear and hear his explanations. In other words mass meetings are also designed to 'inform' members, not just to consult them. Despite some members' perception that their leaders who report on company decisions are mere messengers, one should bear in mind that to 'inform' has a number of facets. Apart from simply passing on information, the role of educator is also part of a unionist's job: company processes are often obscure to members and need to be explained time and again. Mass meetings are generally a way to get things clear. 'Informing' members can also mean, as in the case of wage negotiations, 'convincing' them to formulate realistic demands.

Mass meetings such as the two I have described are therefore not democratic insofar as the prescriptions of the NUM constitution are concerned: there was no decision-making process through voting, nor was there any minute-taking at those meetings. But one should not hastily conclude that mass meetings are purely formal gatherings. When well conducted, they are useful for leaders to gauge and stay in touch with their members' views and the general state of mind of their rank and file. In situations such as mass meetings, a leader's value is judged on how well they know their membership and, consequently, on how well respected they are. Moreover, if one links the mass meeting I attended at Impala with the subsequent and animated discussions I also observed among the NUM negotiation team, it clearly appears that 'worker control' – in the sense of having members' fate and interests at heart – is a pressure many local leaders experience. In a negotiating team, discussions among leaders from various branches at the same company therefore bring another layer of internal democracy, in that they have to confront their various perceptions about the state of the union's base and arbitrate between sometimes diverging local aspirations.

INTRA-ORGANISATIONAL NEGOTIATION AS PART OF WORKER CONTROL

One thing that struck me in the wage negotiations I observed was how limited direct interactions between the negotiating parties actually were. When a mediator was involved, as was the case at Murray & Roberts Cementation (MRC), but also at Lonmin or Impala, the NUM team would call him in, give him its position, let him go back to management, and then wait for management's response. Negotiation takes time – a lot of time – but the amount of time dedicated to direct interactions between the two parties is generally very limited: what really consumes time is intra-organisational bargaining – that is, when each team discusses the other's offer. As Ecliff Tantsi, NUM's national education secretary and the union's chief negotiator at MRC, put it: 'I am doing two negotiations: with my team and with them.' This is what Walton and McKersie famously referred to as 'intraorganizational bargaining', a process that is crucial to conflict resolution and that can only happen through the confrontation of one party with its opponent's views and own internal dynamics.[22] This means, in other words, that any given negotiation between two opposing groups is in fact aiming at two agreements: the final agreement reached between the opposing entities, which results from inter-organisational negotiation, but also the parallel agreements within each entity, which are the result of intra-organisational negotiation.

Intra-organisational negotiation 'reflects' the organisation involved in it. In the case of NUM-led negotiations, this involves the consideration of at least two elements: the great disparity of delegations in terms of the size of the branches represented in a given negotiation, and the process of worker-controlled mandating. In the case of the NUM–MRC 2011 bargaining round, which I followed almost in its entirety, the NUM team represented roughly 20 branches of very unequal size, ranging from 30 to 5 149 members. Ecliff Tantsi explained some of the internal dynamics of his team to me. He insisted that 60 per cent of NUM members at MRC came from only a few mining operations. In a delegation like his, two small and two big branches held the balance of forces. 'Small branches may have been more vocal in today's NUM caucus,' he argued at some point, 'but you cannot go on strike with small sites.'

The NUM–Impala negotiation, which I also observed in 2011, was a paradoxical one, in which the union ended with a certificate to strike in hand and a membership that did not want to go on strike. If one thinks of the virtual dissolution of NUM at Impala just a few months later to the benefit of Amcu, what emerged from this negotiation is telling: most branches had failed to reach a mandate. Reporting was apparently badly conducted; leaders had not made it clear to the members that the increase offered by management was linked to a two-year deal and internal political divisions in at least the two largest branches meant that delegates did not have adequate legitimacy to negotiate and convince their rank and file. Another difficulty in the Impala negotiation was that the branches involved were heterogeneous in terms of their workforce and locations. They comprised four underground mining branches, located at Impala's main operation near Rustenburg, including the largest two (Impala North and South); the Services branch, which deals with the workers who provide the mine with essential services mostly above ground; the MinPro branch (Mineral Processes), located at a factory which processes extracted rock; the Refineries branch at Springs, where the extracted rock is treated; and, finally, the Marula branch, another secondary Impala mine, located in Limpopo.

The power of a branch lies not only in its size, but also in the way it relates to its membership, controls it and is able to influence it. In the case of the Refineries branch and as opposed to Impala's four Rustenburg branches, members were not prepared to strike and the mandate received was clear: go and sign. Talking about the mass meeting in which this was at issue, I asked Daniel Sethosa, the deputy chairperson of this branch, how members give their positions and take decisions. His answer shows that the state of local democracy varies from one branch to another. It is dependent on members' participation but also on their leaders' degree of responsibility and commitment to the principle of worker control:

> You know people's opinions because you present issues; they get debated then a majority view is going to prevail. A view is going to prevail. Then we are going to ask them is that so? *Q: How do you know speakers do not speak for themselves?* DS: You will raise the issue and then they will raise their hands. You will say this person is saying this, is there any supporter? And this person is saying the opposite of that – is there any supporter? Then you debate it. But if the issue is supported, the ones who are saying no, you let them debate it up until they convince one another. There will be a point whereby they are going to agree. *Q: Does it happen that you misread the mandate?* DS: No, you can't misread the mandate because you must make sure, if you are writing the mandate you must ask them, 'Comrades, is this what you are saying?'[23]

Figure 4.5. shows shaft stewards deeply engaged in discussion during a meeting at the Impala Refineries branch, with the branch secretary carefully taking the minutes of the meeting (Figure 4.6). It is probably not coincidental that in June 2015, while NUM had lost Impala to Amcu, it still controlled the company's Springs refineries (with 67 to 68 per cent of the workforce belonging to NUM, including 57 per cent in lower employment categories).

Good negotiation therefore starts with a good consultation and mandating process. In the absence of this, the mandate becomes, as I often heard in NUM, a 'leadership mandate' or a 'leadership strike' – in other words, decisions that result from inadequate consultation. Once in the negotiation room, it becomes a back-and-forth process: teammates discuss and persuade one another before reporting back to their respective grassroots constituencies and considering their views on the new position of the negotiating team.

Figure 4.5: Discussions between shaft stewards, branch meeting, NUM Impala Refineries branch, Springs, 2011

Photographer: Raphaël Botiveau

Figure 4.6: Taking minutes of the branch meeting, NUM Impala Refineries branch, Springs, 2011

Photographer: Raphaël Botiveau

Back in the negotiation room, the chief negotiator can convince the minority to join the majority position. In the NUM–MRC 2011 negotiation, one tactic the chief negotiator resorted to was, as he put it, 'isolating the extremists': those identified as the most vocal components of his team, whom he called the 'Abu Sayyaf' in reference to a Philippines-based armed Islamist group. This is what he did when, on several occasions, he put his teammates' backs to the wall, so that the only logical conclusion they were left with was the team's hard line: strike action. His argument was a simple one: if this is what you want, if this is what members want, then even though I disagree with you I will lead you in a strike. Faced with such a prospect, most delegates started considering the deal they were offered in a new light. In other words, a chief negotiator has to arbitrate across a wide range of sometimes very different local situations and interests, between the specific and the universal, while keeping in mind his main goal: to hold his team together.

On the last day of this negotiation, a glitch occurred, raising the question of voting and providing an illustration of the tension between democratic control and leadership in a workers' organisation such as NUM. During the very last minutes of the negotiation, after having reviewed the draft agreement one last time, the chief negotiator asked: 'Comrades, do we sign today or are we going to read it to the masses first?' All answered, 'No' (we sign today). Yet when, just before putting his signature to the agreement in the presence of management, he repeated the question, a far weaker 'no' was heard in reply. Faced with a situation of non-unanimity and a theatrical turnaround, he asked management to exit the room and leave unionists on their own for a last five-minute caucus. He decided that his team was going to vote on the matter. Such a move in an organisation that usually decides by consensus is unusual enough to be noted. The unionists voted by holding their hands up and five hands were raised in support of the 'no' (we will not sign) motion, which implied the need for a report-back to the membership before signing. The chief negotiator then said, 'We're going to have to sign, comrades, … it is a disciplined organisation, we will be bound by it all of us.' One 'no' supporter then motivated his refusal: 'It is about the members, not the leadership.' To this the chief negotiator answered, 'Those who have said yes must motivate their views.' A genuine debate started on an issue that had seemed wrapped up just a few minutes before. The organisation had been about to move forward but its leader stopped it all as he felt disunity. Moreover, the issue here was not only about worker control, since the workers' voice was mediated by their representatives, but also about the control of national leaders by local branch leadership. NUM leaders at all levels are often experienced and politically educated and they do not accept decisions they deem illegitimate. One of the elders in the delegation who favoured the 'no' motion then intervened: 'We are disciplined members and will assume [endorse] whatever decision. There is no reason, however, why we should sign in a hurry.' That is when the chief negotiator decided to end the discussion: 'Comrade, you closed it reminding us that we will stand by the decision whatever it is.' He eventually decided to use his authority (I shall later reflect on this concept as one component of good leadership), which, this time, was backed by an absolute majority, and signed the agreement.

BETWEEN MYTH AND REALITY: ORDINARY MEMBERS' PARTICIPATION

Mass meetings are usually publicised by word of mouth and via posters placed in strategic locations in the hostels and workplaces. They are convened at short notice in cases where time is limited, as in wage negotiations, and members do not always get the information in time if they work in a remote location. Some members come to mass meetings and do not feel sufficiently at ease to speak, which suggests, as in any organisational context, that one must dare or feel comfortable or legitimised enough to take the floor. Some members who participate in mass meetings seem content with the way they are conducted even though they confess to not necessarily actively participating because they do not feel the need to, or because the number of speakers allowed to take the floor is limited. When asked about how they felt about their most recent participation in a mass meeting, two members answered:

> It was a mass meeting for all the shafts because they approached [the union] for retrenchments so that's why we were all together. Q: *Did you speak?* PM: I did not get a chance to speak, because you see in a mass meeting we are many and you can't point twenty people, only three and if somebody seconds that one it's obvious. Q: *How do you state your ideas?* PM: I just want[ed] to speak up about the retrenchment … and propose another system of [part-time] shift instead of retrenchment in wait of platinum prices to go up.[24] Q: *Did you speak in the meeting?* OM2: No. Q: *You did not want to?* OM2: There is nothing who forced me to speak because all of the things spoken were right, there is no need to intervene to repeat.[25]

Another ordinary member, a man in his fifties, was satisfied he had got a chance to express his views:

Q: Last year there was a wage negotiation … before the negotiation did you go to a mass meeting? OM3: Yes … I asked a lot of questions before the negotiations of the increase. I was talking about the ten per cent and said it's smaller than the cost of living, which is very high and the kids need to go to school, pay for fees. It was little.[26]

Beyond speaking out grievances, opinions, demands, in one's own name or in the name of several, mass meetings are usually a place where decisions are taken collectively. An ordinary member at Lonmin described the decision-making process at mass meetings in the following terms:

The last meeting I could recall is the one that was at Wonderkop stadium, a central mass meeting, we were talking about the working arrangement days for Easter. *Q: How do you take decisions in mass meetings?* OM7: What we normally do, we would call five people who will come and support or talk about the issues that we have. Then if we support each other we have got five or six, then we reach the conclusion. What we do is that we would raise the matter to the leadership to send them and go and negotiate for us. After that they come back to have a shaft stewards council, then the mass meeting. What we do there is people raise their hands on the report given by the leadership … and comment on that one. If they support maybe they give only five or six people a chance to talk, if we still have different views we see who supports the others and we come to the conclusion. *Q: How do you see who supports whom?* OM7: What we normally do is that we check the motion around us and then if we all clap our hands after the speakers talk, then it's whereby we see that we are still on the right track.[27]

Such testimonies by ordinary NUM members at a Lonmin and an AngloGold Ashanti branch on how decisions are taken in mass meetings corroborate the description given by the NUM chairperson at the union's Mponeng branch (AngloGold Ashanti):

We call a mass meeting … and all the members go there and we give them reports, we engage on the reports and then we take the resolutions, we decide there. *Q: And how do you reach a resolution in such meetings?* MM: We reach resolutions by majority. Let's say we debate a point and then they agree to that point and then the majority takes a decision, they say we agree and then we take it as a resolution. *And how do you vote in a mass meeting?* MM: You

> raise your hand in and then you check the majority and then the majority
> rules … When we can't reach an agreement we reserve a point for the next
> mass meeting so that we can engage as a branch; we take the point and we
> go back and sit down in a branch executive committee meeting. We look at
> it and then we take it to the shaft steward council who looks at it again and
> then we take it back to the mass meeting.[28]

Decisions taken at mass meetings are therefore also channelled and it is clear that
elected structures, when they prepare for a mass meeting, shape the type of debate
that is to take place. This, however, does not necessarily imply that leaders appropriate power as they also have to 'learn the members' in order to be good leaders.
As a NUM branch office bearer at one of the union's Lonmin branches (a branch
composed mostly of surface workers) explained:

> As a leader you sort of learn the members, you learn their tendencies and
> their behaviours well so you tend with time not to be scared or nervous. Q:
> *What are their behaviours?* BOB: In our branch for instance there aren't any
> negative behaviours so we understand that they prefer engaging on issues
> and debating them. We deliberate. During the mass meeting a person would
> ask a question: can you please explain this … Q: *How do you take decisions
> in mass meetings?* BOB: Decisions are taken like if a person comes up with
> a suggestion we would see whether the suggestion is seconded. If there is a
> 'general feeling' that it's the right way to go then we go that way. Q: *So it's a
> lot about feelings too, feeling the crowd, the people?* BOB: Not necessarily. It
> comes up with the step of checking. We first hold a branch executive com-
> mittee meeting. The decisions will then be taken based on the mass meeting
> but coupled together with the deliberation that have occurred.[29]

In this last testimony, it becomes apparent that the mass meeting is not necessarily
a critical step in the NUM local decision-making process, which, as we will see,
is more decisively informed by a second local structure: the branch that prepares
mass meetings upstream and follows them up downstream. Members are, of course,
not consulted through mass meetings only but also during shaft general meetings
where they address issues directly relevant to their workplaces in smaller groups.
The diversity of mass meetings, the ways in which they are conducted and perceived
from one mine to another and, more decisively, the types of relationship between
leaders and members that develop locally, give one an insight into the complexities
of lived local democracy. It is noteworthy that the process of consultation in mass

meetings used by NUM was quite like that used by Amcu. Here is one description of how Amcu consulted its members during the major 2014 strike, a description that also raises doubts about the reality of democracy in Joseph Mathunjwa's union: 'Amcu's strike ballot, the same one used to canvass the strike in the beginning, involved Mathunjwa carving up the stadium into sections and then asking the crowd "yes or no". It happens so fast that if you blink you could miss it and does not allow for individual expression. It merely fosters group-think.'[30] However, what differs in the two unions is not necessarily related to levels of democracy approached in procedural terms, but rather to attendance at meetings and the quality of the relationship between top leadership and the membership.

THE PHYSICAL PROXIMITY OF LEADERSHIP AS A DEMOCRATIC FACTOR

What was obvious in the 2012 rejection of NUM by its own members was the complaint, expressed by many members, that their leaders had become distant and more at ease with managers than in the company of their own people. At Lonmin, for example, and despite the gravity of the crisis experienced by the union there long before the August 2012 strike started, I asked one NUM shaft steward about how upper leadership helped local NUM branches to deal with the crisis and he complained:

> Q: And the region? HW: Even them since the strike, they only came when they were pressured by head office. They did not come in numbers, they only sent comrade Moloi who made sure the elections happened. the region only comes if they see things are going smooth.[31]

This reference to Rustenburg's deputy regional chairperson Eliott Moloi, an old man viewed as having limited charisma and political influence, expressed my interlocutor's feeling that the calibre of the leaders sent to the branches on the ground reflected a great lack of consideration on the part of national leadership. At Lonmin in August 2012 or at Impala in January the same year, the request of strikers was the same: they rejected local leaders they deemed corrupt and unreliable and agreed to 'be addressed' only either by Amcu or by senior NUM or Tripartite Alliance leaders such as Zwelinzima Vavi or Julius Malema. In other words, they did not trust the local leadership layer and demanded the highest authorities in the organisation to come and listen to them. In August 2012, as in other instances before, however, Senzeni Zokwana, the NUM president, would talk to his members only via a loudspeaker and from within a police vehicle, on the grounds that his security would not be guaranteed were he to address a mass meeting directly. Given the levels of anger prevailing among members at the time and taking into account what had happened in previous cases in which NUM leaders had been attacked, there was indeed a security risk. Mass meetings can become dangerous places for leaders when they turn into a theatre of encounters between rival local political factions that can heat the crowd and turn members into a violent mob. Zokwana's refusal to directly address members, however, brought further discredit to an already weakened NUM in Lonmin and elsewhere in the platinum belt.

Mass meetings sometimes seem like a modern-day embodiment of Athenian democracy in which union members – citizens of the mining compound conceived as city-space – would assemble in an arena-agora and reach decisions after a duly followed deliberation process. Just like the ancient Athenians, however, mineworkers also like tribunes, the tension of debate and discussions; they seek physical proximity with their leaders. They are reluctant to mediate their relationship with leaders through intermediary representative bodies and tend to be suspicious of institutional distance. This suggests that rather than procedural or constitutional compliance with the principle of worker control, members like to see their leaders – that is, to meet with them and to have some influence over them. Mass meetings are thus not unlike indigenous 'traditional' forms of democracy, including community gatherings controlled by elders or chiefs (imbizos or lekgotlas).[32] There is also a tradition of charismatic leaders on the mines and in NUM.[33] Joseph Mathunjwa, Amcu's president, exemplifies this tradition when he makes a point, as he did at Marikana, of coming to the workers in order to hear them, be with them and speak to them. In a famous 16 August 2012 episode, Mathunjwa went to address the Marikana strikers gathered on the mountain, kneeled down and begged them to disperse since he feared for their lives. Shortly after he left, the police killed 34 mineworkers. He broke down and cried together with his general secretary at a press conference held on the following day. Mobilising the religious register as Mathunjwa, the son of a Christian preacher, often does also roots 'his' union in another ground on which NUM rested and sometimes still rests.

The importance of having top leaders address members is not new, as is shown by the following decision of the NUM national executive committee in 1991:

> It was also agreed that the time table of meetings be arranged and regions should furnish us with available date at which the office bearers should attend and address meetings at regional and branch level. The purpose is to

guarantee maximum participation of the national leadership in the affairs of the union. It is the intention of office bearers to try to address as many regional shaft steward council and or mass meetings as well as meetings at branch level.[34]

At the end of a day of negotiations at MRC, Ecliff Tantsi, a national office bearer and NUM chief negotiator for the company, asked his fellow branch leaders when they were planning to hold their mass report-back meetings and said he would attend one and delegate two regional leaders to supervise two others. This suggested that Tantsi was conscious of how important it is to carefully report back during negotiations and that when misconducted, report-backs can easily derail the entire process. Given the historical weakness of local NUM structures, national leaders always played a key role in the resolution of conflicts arising at mine level. One key to understanding what lies beneath NUM's loss of popularity in 2012 is to be found in its leaders' failure, at the local level but even more importantly in the union's upper leadership levels, to fulfil workers' aspirations for direct forms of local democracy. Instead of subscribing to the principle of representation embodied by legal-rational organi-sation, and although, as I have shown, the NUM constitution was never applied to the letter in union branches, workers used mass meetings to express their views and sometimes to elect new workers' committees to represent them. These workers' com-mittees relied on previous experiences in which workers – and rock drill operators in particular – had short-circuited local NUM structures.[35] As Crispen Chinguno wrote about the committees elected at Lonmin, 'there are two contesting narratives on the emergence and independence of the committees and the role of unions in influencing their emergence'. The first one insists that workers joined forces in a common cause and elected a new leadership that was 'across the [Amcu–NUM] union divide'. Another narrative, however, insists on the fact that the workers' com-mittee would have been installed as a result of an Amcu plan.[36] Conversations I had with present and former Impala managers suggest that while workers did resort to old repertoires of action such as the workers' committees, the Impala 2012 strike was sufficiently well organised and the demands management received sufficiently well written to suggest that an organisation such as Amcu played at least a supportive and counselling part in it, with a view to eventually taking over. In any case, the pro-cess of direct democracy and worker control they involved implied that the newly elected leaders were, at least during the strike and its immediate aftermath, directly accountable to the masses. The direct connection between leaders and workers that had been lost under NUM was hence re-established and Mathunjwa came in person from time to time to enact this accountability at the top level of Amcu.

What is crucial here is that workers rejected representative democracy and the detachment between the represented and the representative it had implied under NUM. The gap became too wide. Consultation of members by their elected leaders had become increasingly infrequent since the inception of NUM. In the early 1980s, the national congress generally gathered on an annual basis even if it was punctually convened on a biyearly basis for practical purposes. Since 1994, however, national congresses take place once every three years. Elective conferences at the regional level also became less frequent. At the branch level mandates used to last for two years until their length was extended to three years in 2004. This growing gap between occasions for contact between leaders and members in turn fostered the empowerment of leadership as against that of membership, which entailed a redefinition of the workers' mandate into something closer to a document signed in blank. I will show in the next section that triennial conferences at branch level, which are supposed to produce agendas and resolutions and influence regional conferences and national union policies, are now virtually reduced to elective meetings.

These developments can be usefully read against the backdrop of wider analyses of modern democratic forms, which, as Bernard Manin observed, represent only a parenthesis in the time-honoured traditions of democracy. In a now famous book he notes that it is commonly assumed that representative democracy is just one variant of a wider democratic model. For political thinkers of the eighteenth century, however, be they opposed to representation (Rousseau) or supportive of it (Madison, Sieyes), the 'representative government' was conceived as different in nature from 'democracy'. NUM is, in that sense, a representative organisation that accords with the four principles identified by Manin as constitutive of 'representative government': (i) the rulers are appointed through regular elections; (ii) the rulers retain some independence vis-à-vis the voters' will in their decision-making; (iii) the governed express their views and political will independently of the rulers' control; and (iv) public decisions are submitted to the trial of discussion. As Manin rightly notes, the election is the central institution of this type of government, whereas in Athenian democracy the magistrates in charge of specific tasks were appointed through a mixed system of drawing lots and election. Magistrates were generally closer to administrators than to decision-makers and all decisive political choices lay in the hands of the assembly (*Ekklèsia*) – the 'mass meeting' by another name. This was, of course, an ideal, since only an authorised few actually spoke and since, in practice, most citizens did not actually attend such meetings. The power of the assembly was also restrained insofar as other institutions had decision-making powers in Athens.[37] What the designation of leaders through mass meetings also suggests, as was the case in the workers' committees established in 2012, is therefore that members prefer to choose or elect leaders through acclamation rather than through long NUM processes that involve campaigning, battles for leadership positions and secret ballots. The latter allow for manipulations and enable contenders, who are more versed in politics than their electorate, to reach leadership positions in order to fulfil personal ambitions removed from the shaft floor. The 2012 rejection of the union by its members was therefore also the expression of a more general defiance against the type of representative democracy NUM had set up over time, with the distance between constituency and representatives it involves.

ELECTING LEADERS AND FIGHTING FOR POWER IN THE BRANCHES

The branch is NUM's basic structure: it is located at the interface between the union's upper levels (regional and national) and its general membership at local, grassroots level. (Branches are also divided into 'shafts' or 'shops' that are not directly represented in upper-level decision-making bodies.) According to the NUM constitution, a branch may be formed where there are 100 union members and the regional committee oversees the creation and functioning of the branch. The branch is led by a branch committee composed of the same top five office bearers that are found at each NUM level: the chairperson and deputy chairperson, the secretary and deputy secretary, and the treasurer. The 'top five' are joined on the branch committee by the chairperson and secretaries of each shaft or shop committee and those of the three branch sub-committees dedicated respectively to education, health and safety, and women. Branch office bearers (BOBs) are elected for a three-year term. The role of the branch committee is to manage local affairs at mine level, which includes dealing with labour disputes, attending to members' grievances, ensuring that proper communication takes place downward and upward, and, more generally, promoting the interests of members. In addition to the branch committee, the local level relies on the first union structures with which ordinary members are confronted: the workplace structures. The first act of delegation in the union is when ordinary members elect, under the supervision of the branch committee, their shaft stewards for a three-year mandate.

The struggle for local power is generally viewed as 'new tendencies' that have crept into NUM because of the leaders' lack of commitment and greed. Contrary to what is often thought, the existence of 'cliques' or 'cabals' as they are called – competing groupings that fight for positions in the organisation and particularly at branch level – has historical precedence. In May 1992, the national executive committee noted: 'the ConsMurch branch [at Divisions, Phalaborwa Region] is paralysed by cliques'.[38] Another report in the same year states: 'there is a power struggle within the [F.S.S.] branch leadership [in the Free State]'.[39] In 1998, the first SWOP report on the state of NUM already pointed to 'destructive branch politics', 'cabals', infighting and division among the leadership. Such cases of competition at the local level are, however, far more visible in reports nowadays. As one veteran NUM regional chairperson reported:

> Where the elections are usually disputed in our union, it's mostly at branch level; regional level no, we accept the outcome, at national level we accept the outcome. But it is not the case in the branches, they would write letters and complain that they were not ran fairly, or it was not constitutional, or I was nominated but my nomination was not accepted for that particular position … I suppose at branch level it is because I would say these days there is too much powermongering, everyone wants to hold a particular position.[40]

Interestingly enough, while regional and national leaders often denounce their counterparts at the local level in such terms, the agenda at branch conferences, which take place every three years, is in fact largely reduced to electing leaders. In other words, electoral politics is also the result of the absence of any real space for participation in policy formulation at the local level. Policy formulation actually starts at the level of the region to which branch committee members are delegated and carry members' views. Clearly located at the bottom of the chain in terms of its autonomy, the branch is subjected to top–bottom democratic centralism. This point sounds logical since each union structure is bound by the constitution first, and by its upper counterpart second. But it clearly shows that NUM is supposed to function bottom-up only from time to time (once every three years) and that it usually works the other way around. Regional committees, which include regional leaders as well as the chairperson and secretary of the region's branches, certainly meet six times a year but they do not necessarily provide enough space and time to channel and address local grievances to the upper level.

The branch conference is composed of delegates from each shaft or workplace. Despite its power to make decisions, in practice it often seems to be reduced to an elective operation in which delegates cast their votes instead of providing a genuine arena for contradictory debate on the state and future of any given local NUM structure. Moreover, direct member participation in local union conferences is also reduced to the shaft or workplace level, since branch conferences gather workplace delegates. The tension between election and policy formulation at the branch level was underlined in a report the NUM general secretary presented at the union's 2004 special congress. On the one hand, Mantashe observed that 'union structures at the branch level must continue to emphasise mass participation'. On the other hand, however, mass participation was equated with 'the dual purpose of developing and screening union leadership and future leadership'.[41] In other words, and viewed from the top of the organisation, one main purpose of branches is to grow and provide leaders for the union rather than to inform its policies. Ordinary members' participation was further reduced when, at the same special congress, the stipulated 'annual general meeting of the branch', which had given members the opportunity to express their views on policy, was removed from the constitution. This move was intended to rationalise local union structures but left the triennial branch conference – a mostly elective and generally representational meeting – as the only remaining decision-making body in NUM branches.[42] Before discussions on the matter at the 2004 special congress, the general secretary had pointed to the 'current confusion around annual general meetings and branch conferences' which had ignited problems at the branch level. While noting that the constitution made no provision for branch conferences and prescribed the organisation of annual general meetings, 'a big number of our branches have developed a tradition of holding branch conferences', Mantashe wrote. He further argued for settling this debate 'once for all' and explained:

> The branch annual general meetings are the only structures where members participate directly in the strategic direction of the union and the election of the leadership. We must ensure that such mass participation is not totally eliminated in the structures of the union. On the other hand, branch conferences have proven that they can ensure that processes at branch level can be structured. What normally comes through as shouting of angry insults, can be decoded into communicable messages and demands. The branches can deal with reports in detail. The challenges facing the union is to benefit from both worlds.

Having thus presented the stakes to the congress delegates, Mantashe then proposed two alternatives: (i) to keep holding annual general meetings at branch level before the actual branch conference; or (ii) to do away with the annual general meetings at the branch level with every shaft or workplace structure sending delegates to the branch conference. The second alternative was his preferred option and NUM thus chose, in 2004, to deepen its internal delegation process: branch conferences, gathering delegates in the place of the masses, were to be mainly dedicated to the election of leadership.[43] Concomitantly, the growing number of provisions, rules and codes of conduct for holding elections[44] and for good leadership suggests that competition is always rifer in NUM's local structures. As opposed to previous versions of the union's constitution, the latest (2009) directly tackles the problem of contested results in local elections by giving instructions for cases where there is a tied result or where a position has fallen vacant.

In practice however, local leaders can variously interpret the way a branch conference ought to take place. The ideal process, as described and promoted by national leaders, is a two-step election made up of (i) a nomination process free of campaigning, and (ii) an unopposed election in which only one candidate is nominated through consensus, without the need to hold any further election process. Candidates for election are not supposed to promote themselves, but must first be nominated and seconded by members, before deciding to avail themselves or not. Nominating and seconding members to turn them into a candidate is supposed to be based on ordinary members having detected what they consider to be leadership qualities in one of their fellow comrades and therefore believing that the person should be elevated to a leadership position. Nomination can also take the form of co-option – hidden or not – by a branch leadership in place. Koos Nkotsi, chairperson of the Impala Services branch, falls into the category of leaders who developed leadership skills, before being nominated by their fellow members:

> I was involved as a member, going to the mass meetings and checking what's going on through NUM until I realised I also needed to make more input and to be an activist … I felt I needed to contribute more … that's when I decided I should go forth for leadership. Then I was lobbied [by comrades] a long time ago to join the leadership and I said no because 'I think I have got lots of things to learn' … They said they really need me to be part of the committee, that's what they were suggesting. It was almost five years ago. But I felt I needed to be sure, some things you have to mature. Remember [at] that time I was from school … That's when I applied to health and safety as a rep; I had to engage with the company.

Koos Nkotsi then worked in the company's payroll department under the supervision of the NUM deputy branch secretary, from whom he learned a lot.

> Q: *How does it work concretely (the nomination process)?* KN: Normally they do … when we meet maybe in town, at work, remember I was at payroll department where I used to meet many people … There are lots of issues I

realised from the payroll department when the company was not complying on some things.[45]

An ideal NUM election is supposed to be uncontested. In the ideology of the union, disputed elections are not equated with vigorous democracy but with conflict and disorder. They are nevertheless often the rule, as described by Koos Nkotsi, who recalls the politics behind his own election:

> It was moody, adrenalines were high … You know we still have this thing of the cabals … There is a group of people who group themselves and say let us discuss our leadership. Maybe for example the whole branch committee members they would say let us agree or discuss the leadership before the branch conference. Sometimes there are some who don't want to throw the towel, who did not do their work well; some will say we need Koos, some will say Joseph or whoever. That's where these people will split. So when they split these people they are forming the cabals, you might have heard we have two groups now.

The Impala Services branch conference, in February 2011, was highly disputed and each position was contested by two candidates. The Rustenburg regional chairperson for health and safety scrutinised the process and one of the candidates was dismissed on the grounds that she had been a member in good standing for only two years and 11 months (the rule is three years). Koos Nkotsi beat his opponent by only seven votes (out of about 700). What was even more striking in this case is that the branch had failed to hold a branch conference and had to organise an election via a mass meeting and ballot paper. Koos Nkotsi explained that the situation was so tense in NUM at Impala that 'people were not ready to have delegates, they were all saying we want to be part of the election and the conference. You know I think this culture of the members who are not willing to accept that we should go for a conference, it also affected the situation.'[46]

This situation is not unique and the same actually happened at the nearby Impala MinPro branch, where a shaft steward complained that, in April 2011, the Rustenburg region decided not to hold a conference and to replace it with an electoral process: nomination, verification and voting. Some candidates were disqualified by the regional leadership, which was accused by some of not being 'neutral', on the grounds that their membership did not match the three years normally required: 'In essence they had three years but to make that three years they counted the days as well as the hours … They were three days short,' one shaft steward complained.

The same happened at the Impala South branch, and the following comments by one office bearer in that branch suggest that electoral competition and cliques or cabals have been internalised as a somewhat normal practice in NUM:

> I've been co-opted because the secretary went sick and passed away but they co-opted me to be the deputy secretary after that on the elections, this year around April, then they elected me again as a deputy secretary. *Q: Were there different camps?* MM: Yes, normally as you know in terms of when we go to the elections two camps have been going around, tried to lobby and all those stuff. I belonged to the previous [leadership team] and was the only one left. But for now we are working together.

At Impala South no branch conference was held either and there too it was decided that members would vote directly in breach of the the above-mentioned 2004 revision of the constitution:

> MM: This decision was taken by the mass at the mass meeting. Not by the region. Because the region came here and heard the workers who said they did not want a conference where delegates would be sent to elect a branch committee since Impala South is so big, but rather a mass meeting where all would be part and parcel of the election.

According to this shaft steward, participation in the vote was good and, from six in the morning to half past one in the afternoon, about 8 000 out of about 9 000 branch members voted. In 2008, only 2 500 members had voted and he attributed this remarkable increase in the voters' turnover to campaigning:

> MM: We go to people who we know are influential and try to tell them: 'Comrades look our mission is this and that.' When you lobby in the mining industry you must have a chief lobbyist. You must talk to the shaft steward. It's very easy for them to go underground and talk. Because every week there is a safety meeting underground. The shaft steward says we are going to election and we want to put this guy or that guy because he is having potential.[47]

Campaigning and lobbying for positions, however, do not necessarily always prevail. At the isolated Impala Springs branch, the deputy chairperson, Daniel Sethosa, told a different story in which nomination clearly emanated from the members – that is, at least from the aspiring leader's colleagues at work:

I've been working for Impala since 1985. I started being a shaft steward in NUM since 1989 ... I was then elected to be the secretary of the branch six or eight years ago up until 2007 that's when I took a break for the past three years then members persuaded me to come back. *Q: What about the last branch conference you had here?* DS: In April [2011], it was very good, it was contested by leaders in a good atmosphere and eventually leaders were chosen by the people on the floor and I was one of them that was chosen as a deputy chairperson of the branch. I never thought I would be a deputy chair of a branch one day but workers came to me and approached me and it was difficult for me to resist because there is this thing in the struggle if people are coming to you and requesting to you to avail yourself, that is a call in other words, to come and serve the organisation. So I took it that way.[48]

Daniel Sethosa is a respected leader from the old guard at his branch but younger union representatives sometimes tell stories that are not so distant from his:

BOB: I stood for the position for a number of reasons: firstly because I was nominated by the people from our plant, our immediate plant, as well as by people from other areas. I also stood for the position because I'm passionate about workers' rights, seeing equality. *Q: Were you expecting nomination?* BOB: No, not really. It did not come as a surprise at the branch conference because before it, it was sort of discussed in our plant but it was a surprise to win thereafter.[49]

The process of nomination is an important part of the elective process, which, in line with my previous metaphor, can be matched with Manin's comment that in Athens, nomination played a major part in the process of electing magistrates and that 'it is the judgement of others that opened access to public positions' which was exercised before the election actually took place.[50] The degree of commitment and the weight of the task have therefore not fully disappeared among current NUM leaders even though, given the repressive political environment of apartheid, being a NUM representative was much more of a burden back in the 1980s.

In sum, the reduction of internal debate and the transformation of branch conferences into mainly elective meetings was not only a consequence of the increased local competition for power positions. It was also the result of constitutional reforms that extended the time between such local meetings, turned them into mainly elective moments, and deepened the principle of delegation, which, as I have shown, mineworkers reject.

5

The Regions as Antechambers of National Power

THE BRANCHES VIEWED FROM THE REGIONS

The regions' point of view is a useful one in approaching NUM at the grassroots since it is both panoramic and derives from direct access to the union's branches. However, it is difficult to generalise about NUM branches, their state of affairs and functioning, since they differ from one place to another. They differ in size, ranging from more than 9 000 members in the biggest branch to less than 100 in the smallest. There are also differences between large mining companies where there are several branches, and smaller companies where most staff are subcontracted by external service providers. If one follows the path along which the mining strikes have spread since 2011, what is revealed, apart from the most obvious feature (their location), is that the more recent branches (in platinum) appear to function in a more chaotic way than the older, more established branches. However, gold mines were also affected and it seems that problems involving rebellion against the union in certain branches had already been identified in NUM reports, including as recently as in the reports presented at the various 2011 regional conferences. The branches experiencing governance problems were usually the biggest ones – those sometimes referred to as 'makhulu' (big, strong) branches. A 2005 Carletonville regional report suggests that branches in this gold-rich region are weaker than their counterparts in the Pretoria-Witwatersrand-Vereeniging (PWV) area and Rustenburg. Its leadership, however, is probably harsher than that of Rustenburg in assessing the state of its own structures. If one considers three different regional reports, it seems clear that the union has experienced deep challenges both externally (by employers) and internally (via leadership battles and defiant members) over the last decade. The following section examines, through a regional lens, how NUM assesses the state of its own local structures.

Rustenburg, by far NUM's largest region before the 2012 strikes, had a total of 164 branches and 107 866 members paying subscription fees to the union. Only 113 branches, however, totalling 95 101 members, qualified for participation in the 2011 Rustenburg regional conference. The main branches around Rustenburg were Impala North (8 547 members) and Impala South (9 015 members) where the strikes started at the end of 2011. Not quite as large were the Lonmin Eastern (5 741 members) and Western Plats (5 097 members) branches. Anglo Platinum's Tumela (5 475 members), Union (4 467) and Dishaba (3 400) mines were also among Rustenburg's main membership pools. All three companies (Impala, Lonmin and Anglo Platinum) – the top three platinum producers in the world – suffered major strikes in 2012 and thereafter. Also in this region was the Kroondal-Marikana branch (5 110 members), situated in the operations of mining contractor Murray & Roberts Cementation, where major unrests happened in 2009. Among the larger Rustenburg branches only Northam Platinum (5 862 members) has remained relatively quiet since 2012. In order to understand how this relative stability has come to be, it is useful to look at the way in which wage negotiations were managed and conducted there (see chapter 8). Sydwell Dokolwana, Rustenburg's regional secretary, was generally positive about his team's work during its term in office. He nevertheless pointed to organisational weaknesses, which he connected with the autonomisation of branch leadership:

> When no progress is seen by members, they always report these matters to our head office. We must always take lessons from branches that belong to individuals not the organisation. They begin to be defiant, grow bigger than the union and become law unto themselves. Karee branch in Lonmin is a living example and we must keep a watchful eye on Northam Platinum not to fall into the same situation.[1]

At Lonmin, as opposed to what had happened at Impala, where workers' committees were formed outside of existing trade unions, Amcu and NUM had been fighting for members since May 2011. At the time, about 9 000 Karee employees had embarked on an 'unprotected' work stoppage – the 'RDO (rock drill operator) strike', as managers in Lonmin referred to it. Most of the Karee workforce was subsequently dismissed before it was eventually re-employed (NUM later fought Lonmin on behalf of some of the 872 workers who were not reinstated). The majority of the dismissed workers belonged to NUM and they protested against a union decision to suspend their branch chairperson, Steve Khululekile, for his alleged refusal to hold a scheduled NUM branch conference. According to a NUM Karee shaft steward I met several times, Khululekile – who obviously enjoyed popular support and was a charismatic leader[2] – had refused to hold a branch conference for fear of losing his position after two terms in office. This would, moreover, have prevented him from reaping the benefits of a wage increase, negotiated by NUM for its branch office bearers at Lonmin, as part of a new recognition agreement. Accusations of corruption and preferential award of company housing were also formulated against Khululekile's administration and his supporters allegedly killed one of his declared opponents for the position of branch chairperson in 2011.[3] The 2011 strike clearly paved the way for Amcu's penetration in Lonmin as its leaders, who, as part of the company's mass dismissal, were not re-employed became the backbone of NUM's rival union. Khululekile actually became Amcu's regional organiser in Rustenburg, where he started recruiting for his new union.

As a result of their 2011 dismissal, the strikers lost their union membership and NUM fell under the 50% plus one threshold required for recognition. The union had to sign its members back in order not to be de-recognised by Lonmin, but Amcu also started recruiting and an aggressive campaign for members ensued. There was a violent background in this company, where two local NUM leaders had been killed in 2008. One was shot several times at the Western Plats branch while the other 'was stoned to death during a union mass meeting' at the Karee branch.[4] Most Lonmin shafts are located in these two branches, and although they remained unexplained, such assassinations show how unstable the union environment already was at this mine a few years before the 2012 strike. In 2012, NUM could no longer access the Karee hostels without heavy mine security and police protection. In May that year, I accompanied a delegation of national, regional and local leaders who held a mass meeting at Karee's sports ground. We were escorted by several security vehicles and virtually no workers showed up at the meeting (see Figure 5.1.)

In May 2011, workers assembled for a mass meeting had also attacked NUM's Rustenburg chairperson, the late Lazarus Ditshwene, and his secretary, Sydwell Dokolwana. Some had apparently reported that the two leaders had agreed on Lonmin's decision on a massive dismissal of the strikers, which is unlikely, and which Eliott Moloi, the region's deputy president, contested when I talked to him in May 2012. For him, Dokolwana would in fact have told the strikers that unless they went back to work, they would face dismissal, as the company had threatened. The situation, however, was tense enough for the two to address their fellow workers from the top of a Protea Coin Group Hippo (an armoured police vehicle used by the mine's private security). Some members in the crowd apparently told them to

Figure 5.1:   Jerry Ndamase, NUM's Karee branch secretary, addresses shaft stewards at Lonmin Karee mine hostels, 2012
Photographer: Raphaël Botiveau

come down and had threatened to 'cut their necks'. When I suggested that it was devastating for NUM to show such distance from the strikers and such acquaintance with mine management, Moloi answered that it was too dangerous a situation for the NUM leaders to be unprotected and that the meeting had been stirred up by a group of armed people.

In his 2011 report, after dealing with the situation at Lonmin, Dokolwana went on to discuss the specifics of mining houses with more than one NUM branch. Anglo Platinum, with a workforce of 20 761, had significantly restructured its operations over the previous year, which affected NUM's local organisation. The union used to have only one branch at Anglo Platinum (Rustenburg Platinum Mines), which was then, after the company's restructuring, split into six distinct branches in the place of what used to be, in the union's architecture, a series of shafts. Written in a telegraphic style, the report suggests that this forced change in internal union structures involved a great deal of disturbance for the union:

> Our comrades bought in this idea which carried serious challenges/threats for NUM and employer, benefits for few, disadvantages and advantages …

Application of divide and rule philosophy … No guaranteed tangible benefits for members in these arrangements. Membership is declining from NUM and opponents such as Uasa [the United Association of South Africa] getting a boost … Fight for control of NUM is alive.

According to the report, this forced restructuring was divisive and exacerbated internal fighting for the control of NUM. The multiplication by six of branch committees created new full-time positions (branch chairpersons and secretaries), which necessitated campaigning and elections. In other words, the situation of NUM at Anglo Platinum was weakened on the eve of the 2012 strikes and before Amcu's penetration there. 'No effort to systematically integrate the experienced NUM cadres with the inexperienced' was made and new leaderships were elected. The consequence of this, according to Dokolwana, was that 'fulltime status of all secretaries in these operations [is] not paying back qualitatively' and that because of a decline in servicing (for instance, the bad management of labour disputes), NUM rivals started recruiting.[5] The situation in NUM branches at Impala Platinum and Lonmin was quite similar in terms of the concerns they raised among NUM leaders. The fragility of local structures in the platinum sector, especially in virtually all operations where the situation derailed in 2012, was clearly known to the regional and national NUM leaderships. Other comments on branches in the same report include references to organisational weakness: 'shallow organisational understanding. No leadership depth. Unstable membership. High contestation of union positions. Emergence of undemocratic tendencies' (NUM branches at Murray & Roberts Cementation). A top mine manager who was involved in managing the 2012 strikes concurred with this view on the fragility of NUM branches: 'Retrospectively there were signs of the 2012 strikes coming. In the year or two before, the attendance of NUM mass meetings dropped. Before it used to be "exceptional"; Impala was the flagship branch of NUM.'[6]

It is important to note that Dokolwana's report made references to the hostility of management and its union-bashing strategies (managers can, for instance, prevent NUM officials from attending union activities), which undermined already vulnerable local structures. This dimension is not to be ignored, since management in the platinum sector differs to some extent from management in the gold sector. Because of Bophuthatswana's 'independence', its repression and legislation that prohibited the development of 'foreign' unions (the white Mine Workers' Union, however, was exempted), NUM was established in Rustenburg only about a decade after it had started unionising gold mines in the Free State and Gauteng. Platinum companies had remained hostile to any attempts at developing the union. As Gavin

Capps explained, Bophuthatswana's fictitious autonomy from the apartheid regime also had repercussions on the way platinum houses were organised in a 'distinctly labyrinthine structure of conglomerate control'.[7] Racism was the norm and labour relations were generally horrendous in platinum. When I asked him about his memories of negotiations with companies there, Martin Nicol recollected a still vivid episode:

> The thing I really remember is that at tea time they brought in a tray that was … for me they brought in a tray with silver and pots and cups and things, and for the workers they brought in mugs. So I said 'what is this?' And the workers explained to me it was because I was white, they gave me what white people got … I mean the level of racial discrimination at that mine was absolutely terrible, in that whole area it was completely chronic. I remember, I think it was at the refinery there, a worker was actually killed for drinking tea out of a white person's cup – his name was Jeffrey Njuza.[8]

Mpho Phakedi, secretary of NUM's PWV region, drew quite a similar picture of local union branches in his 2011 report. In June 2011, the PWV region had 53 997 members in all three sectors organised by NUM. The construction sector was its main growth prospect in a gold-declining region. In mining, there were 23 branches. A few local structures were praised for their consistency, efficiency and stability. The leadership at Impala Refinery in Springs, for instance, was congratulated for their 'amazing' level of capacity and for their sustained good service to members. A significant number of branches were affected by external factors such as the appointment of union leaders to management positions and, more importantly, by retrenchments in the workforce (as in the case of Aurora's Grootvlei mine). Tensions were also likely to be fuelled locally by retrenchments in which companies often targeted union leadership, which then leads to the need to hold special branch conferences in which politics outweighs workers' issues. Kloof, a Gold Fields mine, was the PWV region's largest branch (over 8 000 members) and was described as having functioned quite autonomously from the region on the basis of 'leadership preferences'. Phakedi's report noted that following 'complaints that ar[o]se from the branch', 'many members and shop stewards of the union' were suspended and expelled. In 2012, Kloof was one of the hotspots of internal contestation against NUM as soon as the strike movement spread from platinum to gold. It is important to note here that the large size of the Kloof branch also resulted from Gold Fields' decision to merge three of its operations (Kloof, Leeudoorn and Libanon). The situation was thus the opposite of what had happened at Anglo Platinum. The union was left with no choice but to form a 'super-branch'. But in the process of merging, the number of available leadership positions in the branch was divided by three and 'challenges that came out from that process were like dealing with the model of government of national unity', the regional secretary wrote in a reference to the early 1990s transitory political arrangements between the ANC and apartheid's National Party. Given the context, it is not really surprising that the contest for local leadership in 2012 was based in 'cliques' that were already in place. At another branch, Mintek, it was noted that the company had embarked on the task of destroying NUM through a 'deeply entrenched' 'old style of management' despite the nomination of a new CEO who had worked for NUM but was not 'sympathetic to the union'.[9] A few years later at Mintek, tensions persisted in the membership itself, described as 'very much militant', 'impatient sometimes' and divided between 'the white collar and blue collar workers'.[10] Such local tensions around militancy are often quoted in reports and it is interesting to note that NUM leadership often sees the fact that members are 'militant' in a negative light. For leaders, such behaviours mean members' actions are not channelled through union processes or compliant with labour law. Militancy is sometimes also valued in reports, however, as in the case of the Tau Tona branch: 'This branch is known for its militancy. It has been consistent in mourning for those members who died at work. It forced its management to dismiss a racist Mine Overseer through a stay away. The leadership must be encouraged to maintain this militancy. But, it must go with the discipline of the organization.'[11]

Another element about the life of local branches quoted in regional reports is the issue of 'tribal divisions' between leaders. This is a dimension that is difficult to assess in present-day NUM. With regard to the national leadership team headed by Zokwana and Baleni, former leaders such as Archie Palane argued that they had been sidelined because of the 'X factor' (the domination of Xhosa people). Overall, however, 'tribalism' remains a complex item in NUM: first, because the union claims it historically united workers beyond the tribal divisions created by the mining industry and, second, because the 'communist' ideology of national leaders underplays such divides. In South Deep (Gold Fields), for instance, 'this [tribal] division can be seen to the extent that when one regional leader goes to that branch to address shop stewards some will display disrespect and in the instance the other office bearer goes there will be respect [based on tribal affinities]'.[12] However, tensions in that branch were also resource-driven and based on job classifications, as members started to divide themselves between white-collar and blue-collar workers. Such divisions were perceptible during the election of a new leadership when some 'semi-skilled' comrades rejected those elected on the basis of their higher work skills grading. This dimension was certainly at play during the 2012 strikes in which RDOs – through their workers' committees – fought NUM branch leaderships that were mostly controlled by workers in the upper grades.

Mbuyiseli Hibana, secretary of the Carletonville region (Figure 5.2 shows the region's relatively modest office), listed 26 branches during the 2011 regional conference, including six new branches created since 2008, and a total membership of 26 238 in 2010. As in other regions, there were tensions between members and leaders in some branches and the members' militant repertoires of action were sometimes an issue. Organisational problems also arose in Carletonville when branch leadership were dismissed. Since the late 1980s, regular retrenchments in this gold-dependent region had proved a constant sword of Damocles for the union. The 2005 Carletonville report, for instance, announced that 5 400 mining jobs had been shed in Merafong City over the previous 18 months. The introduction of mechanised processes in deep mining posed a challenge to the union in this respect. In 2005 the state of the Savuka branch (AngloGold Ashanti), one of the union's 'stable branches', was described as follows: 'The branch is facing the problem of the closure of the mine. As a result their membership is declining as there are transfers of members to other operations … We might be without Savuka branch when we come to the next conference.'

Figure 5.2: NUM Carletonville regional office, 2011
Photographer: Raphaël Botiveau

Size was also an issue in Carletonville. It was noted that the Driefontein branch (Gold Fields) was the region's biggest, and although it was assessed as 'strong' 'organizationally', the report insisted that 'the leadership must be reminded that when members elect us into positions it is not because they see us as friends but they see potential in each one of us'.[13] It is worth noting, however, that such a comment did not necessarily suggest incompetency on the part of the branch leadership, and could also be an indication of the frequently tense relationships between local leaders and their regional hierarchy. A branch report submitted by the same Driefontein branch to the regional leadership at the end of 2011 hence suggested that local workplace issues, such as the quality of food provided to workers and RDO bonuses, had actually been addressed – from the point of view of the branch leadership.[14] This question of the relationship between branch and regional leadership is a major aspect of regional politics.

FROM GOLD TO PLATINUM

NUM was formed in the gold mines of the Witwatersrand south-west of Johannesburg. All founding branches were on gold mines, of which all but one were operated by Anglo American in either the Orange Free State, Klerksdorp, Carletonville or Westonaria. Four years after its creation, the union counted 13 regions and claimed a paid-up membership of 228 000 and a total membership of 344 000. Figure 5.3 shows the evolution of NUM membership from 1982 to 2017. Most its members at the time were drawn from its three gold-rich regions: Klerksdorp (39 000), Orange Free State (76 000) and Carletonville (36 000). The Witbank region (25 000), located on the Mpumalanga coalfields came next, followed by Westonaria (18 000), where other gold mines were found.[15] This geographic spread in the early years was the result of NUM's strategy to start recruiting at Anglo American mines where its emergence was initially not met with antipathy from the company's head office, although local managers' attitudes were diverse. This initial trend then evolved and, in 1989, 42 per cent of NUM members were employed by Anglo American.[16] It was also strategic for NUM to target South Africa's gold mines first since they were then more labour intensive by far than the country's other extractive industries. In 1987 the gold mines employed a record 554 000 workers out of a total workforce in mining of 829 000 countrywide. Gold was followed by coal (114 000) and platinum (83 000).

The post-1987-strike period marked the beginning of an uninterrupted decline in both South Africa's gold output and its gold mines' workforce.[17] By 1994, the total

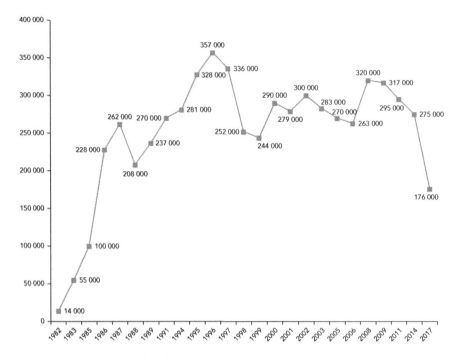

Figure 5.3: NUM membership from 1982 to 2017

Source: Allen (2003), NUM congress reports from 1989 to 2015 and Mahlakoana (2017)[18]

South African workforce in mining had dropped to 611 000, including 392 000 in gold, 98 000 in platinum and 60 000 in coal. Until then, platinum had remained a relatively marginal portion of the total NUM membership. The Rustenburg region, where most of the platinum mines were located, was established only in 1986 and by 1987 it had 2 000 members, all of them employed by Anglo American's Rustenburg Platinum Mines. By 1994, however, while membership in the Klerksdorp, Free State and Carletonville regions had remained steady, Rustenburg had become the second-largest region in the union with 52 000 members. Over the 1994–1997 period, the percentage of subscriptions received from Rustenburg rose from 1 to 13 per cent of the total amount NUM received. In the meantime, the proportion of gold subscriptions decreased from 69 to 57 per cent.[19] The 1997–1999 period was labelled 'disastrous' for the mining industry, which shed about 176 000 jobs and saw the number of NUM members decrease by almost one-third, dropping to about 244 000. This historical trauma remains in the union's collective memory; it has also helped NUM leaders relativise the loss of membership experienced since 2012.

Faced with a declining gold sector, the union identified new areas for growing its membership: the platinum industry, the construction sector (which it organises since the absorption of the Construction and Allied Workers Union – Cawu), and skilled workers in the mining industry.[20] Although construction offered significant growth prospects in former gold regions that are also urban areas, such as PWV,[21] it was, and remains, a precarious, difficult sector to organise. Considering that skilled workers outnumber general workers by far, it soon became clear that the booming platinum sector was to become NUM's lifebelt in a depressed mining industry. The democratisation of South Africa further eased access to platinum mines when the Bophuthatswana bantustan was dismantled in 1994. The other, more decisive dimension of the union's extension in the platinum sector lies in the commodity's boom in the mid-1990s. Platinum has basically replaced gold and, between 1994 and 2009, South Africa experienced a 67 per cent increase in its platinum production as opposed to a simultaneous 63 per cent decrease in its gold output. In 1994 there were 8 platinum mines as against 23 active mines and 25 projects in 2010 (see Figure 5.4).[22] In the rest of this chapter I will look at NUM regions as political units, through focusing on three of the union's 11: Carletonville, PWV and Rustenburg. The first two are historically grounded in the gold industry and can be considered as historical NUM regions, while the third is grounded in platinum and is to be viewed as a recent region, which developed dramatically over the past decade. This allows me to approach the strategic transfer from gold to platinum not mainly in terms of how it impacted on the South African economy, the mining sector or the life and work of mineworkers, but rather as a political shift within NUM's own organisational architecture. At the time of my 2010–2012 fieldwork, Rustenburg had become by far the leading region in NUM, accounting for one-third of the union's total membership.

This shift in the balance of regional power within the architecture of NUM, from gold-rich regions (especially the Free State, PWV and Carletonville) to platinum regions (especially Rustenburg but also the North East region), is not of minor importance. At NUM's 2012 national congress, Rustenburg sent by far the largest contingent of delegates. In 2015, the consequences of its loss of membership did not yet drastically reflect at national level and, at the 15th National Congress, it still had the second-highest number of voting delegates after PWV (respectively 93 and 103). However, being a younger, more recently established region, Rustenburg was also potentially more turbulent, less united and more subject to faction fighting. The 2012 strikes confirmed this to an unprecedented and dramatic extent. As the regional secretary of the Carletonville region Mbuyiseli Hibana put it when I questioned him on the 2011 Rustenburg regional conference we had attended together, and in comparison with his own region's conference held a few months before:

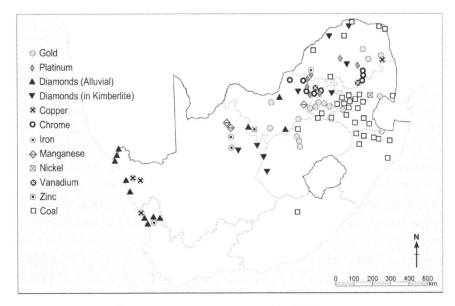

Figure 5.4: Map of main active mining areas in South Africa

Source: Council for Geoscience, South Africa, April 2003

> I think there were big differences between both. One, even if we went to our conference as a region divided in terms of our support to different leaders, as an outsider you would not be able to see that because it was done with organisational discipline. Comrades knew that what was important was NUM. We understood that going there and supporting different people is part of what is going on in our organisation.[23]

This is, of course, a biased statement insofar as Hibana is preaching to his own parish but it suggests, between the lines, that the 'art of politics' is better mastered in older regions. Hibana was nonetheless re-elected 'unopposed' for a third term as Carletonville's regional secretary in 2011. Moreover, while Rustenburg had become the centre of campaigning for national political positions (the many delegates it sent to union conferences were key to securing electoral victories), the top five positions in the union at head office level were still held by leaders from other regions in 2015. Rustenburg had nevertheless produced two national leaders: the national secretaries for health and safety (Eric Gcilitshana, a Lonmin employee) and education (Ecliff Tantsi, an Impala employee). In 2012, however, NUM president Senzeni Zokwana (who left NUM when he was appointed to

Cabinet in 2014) and his general secretary, Frans Baleni, had both been originally employed in Free State gold mines. (David Sipunzi, who replaced Baleni as general secretary in 2015, also came from the Free State.) The union's deputy president used to work on Mpumalanga's coalfields, its deputy general secretary in the Kimberley diamond-rich region, and its treasurer general in the energy parastatal Eskom, just like the national chairperson for education. The balance of forces between regions and industries was therefore well laid out at the national level, although not proportionate to regions' importance in terms of membership numbers. Moreover, the union's top two, Zokwana and Baleni, still embodied, at the time of my investigation, the old guard of NUM leaders bred in a declining gold industry.

Regions can be seen as the antechambers of national power since, before entertaining ambitions of election to national office, aspiring leaders must first rise through the ranks from branch to region. The socialising that takes place after the national executive committee meeting, which gathers national leaders as well as the chairpersons and secretaries of each regional committee, is the occasion when regional leaders network with and learn from national leaders. Moreover, before being 'eligible' to the head office, and even though such training is not formally planned, regional leaders are often either co-opted to intermediary leadership positions that put them in direct contact with the national level. The diverse areas of NUM's activities at the national level are subdivided into sub-committees (on finance, auditing, human resources, economic transformation, health and safety, education and women) which provide such opportunities. These committees are headed by the relevant national office bearer assisted by others, including regional office bearers, who can hence get a foot in the door to national office.

RUSTENBURG: DISCIPLINING A TURBULENT REGION

When they gathered in Bela Bela (Limpopo) in the last days of September 2011, delegates to the Rustenburg regional conference knew that stakes were high. Rustenburg had become by far the largest NUM region. Its growth had been incredibly fast, from 51 000 members in 2006 to 85 000 in 2008 and 97 733 in 2011.[24] Needless to say, with more than one-third of the total NUM membership, Rustenburg was expected to be the decisive factor in the run-up to NUM's 2012 national congress. This political game, however, was also played at the expense of main union priorities such as the good servicing of its membership. Archie Palane, NUM's former deputy general secretary whose main political fief used to be Rustenburg, confirmed this:

'When I left I think the major problem is there was no senior leadership paying attention to the rank and file, they saw Rustenburg as a "voting region" because of the numbers.'[25] In 2006, Gwede Mantashe described Rustenburg in the following terms, providing a good summary of the stakes at play in that key region: 'It is one of our youngest regions and it has taken time to stabilise. It was complicated and we had a number of problems. It grew very fast – faster than our infrastructure … Its membership did not grow up with our democratic, accountable traditions and the result was a lot of infighting and turnover [in] leadership.'[26]

Delegates to the 2011 regional conference met at the three-star Forever Resorts' Warmbaths leisure park about 200 kilometres north-east of Rustenburg. By isolating them from their daily environment for this three-day organisational marathon, the outgoing regional leadership expected to manage tensions that had arisen at previous conferences and, especially, to prevent the possibility that the gathering be disturbed by uninvited branch delegates who may have wished to directly influence the proceedings. In such a fast growing, young region competition for leadership positions was rife, this time particularly since a few months before the conference Lazarus Ditshwene, the region's chairperson, had died in a car accident, leaving the position vacant and stimulating ambitions among local leaders. Hence, at Bela Bela, as at other union conferences, NUM hired security agents to screen entrants to the venue.

Instability in the regional committee was not a new feature and Rustenburg was slowly recovering from a troubled period. In 2005, the regional chairperson, secretary and treasurer had been expelled from NUM in an alleged 'fraud/theft' case in which they were accused of having worked with a hotel to cash donor money intended for union activities.[27] 'For the first time in the history of the union, NUM dismissed serving NEC members.'[28] Such expulsions were no minor event and neither were they accidental. The dismissed chairperson, Dan Balepile, and his secretary, Abram Yende, had jointly run the Rustenburg regional office since 1999 and Balepile had even been in power since 1996, which suggests that it is a 'system' that was brought to an end in 2005. The intervention of national leaders – who are likely to have been aware of problems in Rustenburg before, without necessarily being politically able to intervene in such a volatile environment – and their decision to remove their counterparts in Rustenburg should also be read against the broader context of the extension of Gwede Mantashe's control over NUM (see chapter 9). As soon as the 2011 conference started, it became clear that ensuring leadership stability, unity and the continuity of the organisation were the national office's main concerns.

Delegates – all of them shaft stewards or branch office bearers – started gathering in the Bela Bela conference room during the afternoon of 29 September 2011. The room was large enough to comfortably accommodate the roughly 350 NUM representatives who were attending the conference, hosted in shared bungalows and rooms at the resort (see Figure 5.5). Delegates were virtually all black, mainly males, with only a few females here and there in the crowd. As usual at such gatherings, they received a conference kit containing regional reports and other NUM documents, as well as a NUM bag, cap and three tee shirts – one for each day of the conference.

The hotel, close to the conference venue, accommodated mainly regional and national leaders in single rooms and three meals were served to participants every day in a dining room close to the conference hall. As usual in NUM conferences of this type, singing punctuated the speeches and breaks from day one to day three. One 'freedom song' or mining song usually emerges during events like these, to climb the charts and eventually become the 'anthem' of the conference. In Rustenburg, it was a song dedicated to former ANC president-in-exile Oliver Tambo that shot to the top of the charts. Even if this was partly coincidental – delegates spontaneously pick a song they like and enjoy singing – the fact that this precise song became number one is not fully random in a conference where leadership stability was key. After the ANC had been banned and most of its leaders incarcerated in the early

Figure 5.5: NUM Rustenburg regional conference, 2011
Photographer: Raphaël Botiveau

1960s, Tambo, its future president, became a beacon for the scattered anti-apartheid movement. The song that bears his name enumerates complaints and claims directed at the elder, the guide towards liberation in times of hardship (nowadays the song makes mention of HIV and Aids, retrenchments and other contemporary issues).

NUM president Senzeni Zokwana's opening speech focused on the value of time when it comes to growing leadership. Leadership is responsibility, Zokwana argued, and he reminded his counterparts in other structures that 'your [national] leaders respect you: they make you full-time, they lodge you in 3-star hotels, they make you drive cars for union business. Now pay back through your work.' He then referred to the value of unity and organisation above cliques:

> Our enemies are still strong comrades. Being full-time should not fool you [and make you think] that things have changed, make you lose contact with comrades. In Germany they say 'when Hitler targeted the communists I did not say anything, I was not a communist. When Hitler targeted the Jews I did not say anything, I was not a Jew. When they came for me, I was alone.'

The president's speech enumerated NUM 'values' and the one that he pushed particularly in Rustenburg was 'stability': 'Yes you must judge your leaders. But if you always change of leadership, you agree, you disagree but you don't grow.'

The 2011 Rustenburg secretariat report stated negatively:

> Whilst the national union of mineworkers is having two presidents since its inception in 1982, our region is having seven regional chairpersons from 1986–2011. This is not good at all as it clearly reflects badly on high leadership turnover in the region. The conference should come up with a solution to this challenge. Some might think it is democracy at its best, but we can assure you that from an organisational perspective, this is not assisting at all.[29]

Stability in NUM leadership at the national level is remarkable for a thirty-year-old organisation, but the same stability is generally not reflected at other levels in the union (see Table 5.1 for an overview of NUM's national leadership from 1982 to 2017). The Rustenburg conference was marked by the repeated support of national leaders (all of them attended and addressed delegates) for their outgoing counterparts in the region. Leadership stability is generally praised as a necessary condition for the organisation to grow and to short-circuit internal divisions ('organisations die', the president recalled). Being elected without having to face a contender – that is, by consensus and without needing to vote – is considered to be a panacea for division and instability. It underlines a recurring tension between the right to electoral competition in a democratic organisation on the one hand, and the need for continuity in leadership to build up solid union structures on the other hand.

As a rule, in the regional conferences I witnessed, national leaders are present to make sure the constitution is well enforced and that the union's institutional framework is respected. In doing so, however, they also impose their dominant hierarchical position on less experienced leaders and tend to shape the meeting's outcome in favour of certain ideas and people. Because of their imposing presence, furthermore, delegates may feel intimidated and shy away from talking. National leaders have privileged access to the microphone and when they want to intervene in the conference, the session's chair (one of the regional office bearers in place) generally grants them priority.

	Nat. Congress	Pres.	Dep. Pres.	Gen. Sec.	Dep. Gen. Sec.*	Treas. Gen.
1982	1st	J. Motlatsi	E. Barayi	C. Ramaphosa	/	
1983	2nd				/	
1985	3rd				/	S. Benjamin
1986	4th				/	S. Benjamin
1987	5th				M. Golding	P. Nkuna
1989	6th				M. Golding	P. Nkuna
1991	7th				M. Golding	P. Nkuna
1992	Special			K. Motlanthe**	M. Golding	P. Nkuna
1994	8th		S. Zokwana	K. Motlanthe	G. Mantashe	P. Nkuna
1997	9th		S. Zokwana	K. Motlanthe	G. Mantashe	D. Elbrecht
1998	Special		S. Zokwana	G. Mantashe**	A. Palane	D. Elbrecht
2000	10th	S. Zokwana	C. Moni	G. Mantashe	A. Palane	D. Elbrecht
2003	11th		C. Moni	G. Mantashe	A. Palane	D. Elbrecht
2006	12th		C. Moni	F. Baleni	O. Komane	D. Elbrecht
2009	13th		P. Matosa	F. Baleni	O. Komane	D. Macatha
2012	14th		P. Matosa	F. Baleni	T. Montoedi	D. Macatha
2015	15th	P. Matosa	J. Montisetsi	K.D. Sipunzi	M.W. Mabapa	D. Macatha

Table 5.1:   NUM top five national office bearers from 1982 to 2015

Source: NUM national congress reports from 1982 to 2015

* The position of deputy general secretary was created in 1992 (assistant general secretary until then).

** Acting.

The role of national leaders, however, is not to be viewed exclusively as a form of control designed to prevent dialogue and the expression of opposing views. They are also there to mentor and teach less experienced leaders about the operational side of the organisation. For example, at some stage Ecliff Tantsi, the national secretary for education, took the floor to say how worried he was about the fact that nobody from the regional committee seemed to be taking notes when delegates were speaking. He recalled that resolutions had to be formulated based on such interventions and gave a few examples of how resolutions in this conference could be formulated. National leaders thus also perform as leadership role models.

In a conference like this one, outgoing leaders, as both conveners and organisers of the event, with its agenda in their hands and acting as masters of ceremony standing on the stage for three days with a monopoly on the microphone, clearly have the advantage over their contenders. The latter can only take advantage of the few opportunities they are given to speak from the back of the room. Delegates usually indicate they want to speak by raising a board with the name of their branch written on it, but taking the floor is not that easy. One must first be well positioned in the room to attract the chair's attention. Some delegates in favour of aspiring regional leaders regularly complained about the lack of space for debate during the conference. National leaders were quick to discredit them. Zokwana urged delegates to be suspicious when people call for 'regime change' and, in an allusion to ongoing revolutions in the Arab world, he recalled that in such cases leaders were overturned because they were corrupt (innuendo: in NUM this is not the case, hence contesting leaders is not legitimate). When President Zokwana's speech ended, the session's chair, in a show of good democratic will, insisted on the need to discuss speeches and issues. As soon as he had finished, however, the national secretary for education, Ecliff Tantsi, was prompt to rectify: 'the president's speech is not discussed'.

The second day, the conference began at eight o'clock and some delegates even started singing as early as six o'clock (one reminder that in mining people clock in before dawn). I met a branch secretary wearing a badge with the inscription 'candidate'. He explained to me that he had been 'nominated' by 18 branches and was being pushed by his own branch which, given the quality of his work, thought he should be 'deployed' to the region. He was standing for the position of regional deputy secretary for education. This encounter showed that despite allegations by top union leaders that NUM is eroded by private agendas, politics also remains linked to collective ambitions, as shown by the practice of 'nomination': candidates do not declare themselves; they are nominated by others who feel they have leadership qualities (this, of course, does not exclude the fact that nominations may be part of trade-offs with the possibility of co-option).

Debates on that second day were introduced by Frans Baleni, NUM general secretary, who rhetorically asked, after a short introduction: 'Comrades, do you want to build or destroy?' At this stage, a delegate from the Impala MinPro branch complained that one of his branch's four delegates had not been allowed into the conference room. A conference organiser silenced him: 'We spent a lot of money to hold the conference out of Rustenburg and avoid this. We want to see only people who are delegates here.' This event fuelled subsequent discussions on the 'credentials' that delegates had to approve before the conference could fully start (note that the event was already in its second day). It was expected that 308 'voting delegates' would vote the new regional committee in. The debate on 'credentials', which supposedly consists of a technical validation of the number of voting delegates, was very agitated – another indication that the conference was both primarily focused on electing the new Rustenburg leadership (rather than on dealing with workers' relevant issues) and highly contested. One representative from Union Mine belonging to the contesting faction argued that eight mining house coordinators[30] were included in the list of voting delegates when, according to him, they were not supposed to vote. A few minutes later, and as the atmosphere heated up, Frans Baleni referred to the NUM constitution booklet and quoted from several of its articles. On this particular matter, he pointed out that the regional committee was in charge of organising the conference and decided that they must vote. The meeting's chair eventually declared the credentials adopted even though the debate was not fully exhausted and the atmosphere remained tense for a while.

The Rustenburg regional secretary, Sydwell Dokolwana, then presented his report to the conference. It proudly stressed that his team had managed to employ six regional office bearers full-time, which is not the case in many NUM regions, where most leaders are part-time. He reported that the number of regional committee meetings had been reduced from six to four in order to save resources. Rustenburg is so big a region that regional committee meetings gather more than two hundred delegates and last for two to three days, as opposed, for instance, to similar meetings in a region like Carletonville, where no more than 40 delegates are mobilised for one day only. He was applauded by about half of the delegates upon concluding his report to the conference, in yet another sign that the audience was clearly divided into two camps: the outgoing team supported by head office on the one hand, and its contenders who were also constituted into a relatively homogeneous group on the other hand.

The session broke and I asked Eliott Moloi, the acting Rustenburg regional chairperson, why he had not availed himself for the top position in the region after his chairperson had died, but preferred instead to compete for his former position as deputy chairperson. I understood between the lines that it was safer for him to target a humbler position. He reminded me of the fact that beyond politics, the electoral competition was also a material one since there are 'union benefits' attached to the positions of regional secretary and chairperson. The two get 'union cars' and NUM renegotiates their salaries with their respective companies, which is not the case for their deputies and other regional office bearers. The election seemed well prepared, however, and Moloi seemed confident: 'I don't think they're going to make it.' Another interlocutor, Simon Rasogo, NUM coordinator at Impala Platinum, added another facet to the election, telling me that what was also at stake for big branches like his was to 'have Impala people in the region and at national level'.

Eliott Moloi was chairing the conference as its third and last day began. Representatives from the African Institute for Democratic Elections (Aida), hired to monitor the poll, came on stage to ask that six observers be provided to supervise the voting process. Moloi suggested that three should be nominated from each camp and things went smoothly. Two of the three observers selected from among the contesting motion were among the most turbulent delegates in the conference, from Anglo Platinum's Union Mine. It is worth noting here that Union Mine was to become one of the hotspots of Amcu–NUM clashes in 2012 and was threatened with closure in the aftermath of the strikes.[31] Elections in NUM regional conferences or national congresses generally seem free and fair as far as procedural democracy is concerned and, as a rule, the 'one man, one vote' principle is well entrenched in the culture of South Africa's Charterist organisations (see Figure 5.6).

The conference then hosted Madoda Sambatha, head of NUM's parliamentary pillar and provincial secretary of the SACP. Sambatha, whom I shall introduce later in further depth, is a reputed orator and one of the most vocal communists in NUM. He is regularly called on to deliver tough speeches and, in Rustenburg, he was the last bullet thrown in by the national leadership in support of the incumbent slate. He started off: 'I had not expected to come in a divided conference like Rustenburg Kloof. I am going to tell you about bitter conferences where people do not contest based on leadership quality but because they failed to analyse the situation correctly.' Sambatha did not beat two paths and clearly positioned himself in favour of continuity.

Figure 5.6:   Impala delegates queue to cast their vote, Rustenburg regional conference, 2011

Photographer: Raphaël Botiveau

Delegates were singing as the electoral commission came in to announce the election's results. Simon Rasogo told me it was going to be very tight. Normally there are leaks, he said, yet this time the results were unknown and observers were not allowed to take their phones with them into the voting station. Faces were tense with anticipation as the delegates awaited the results. Pete Matosa went on stage to announce the 'official dissolution' of the regional committee. Following procedures and organisational rituals such as this is, of course, an important component of meetings like this one, where it is the task of the national leaders to make sure they are enforced.[32] Regional conferences are therefore key places where union codes and conduct are learned by junior leaders under the supervision of their more experienced national counterparts. These include, for instance, to learn how to speak in public, how to build an argument and how to engage in constructive debate. In other words, they are key sites for the diffusion and perpetuation of NUM's ethos in crucial areas such as decision-making and organisational discipline. What is problematic, however, is the fact that if such meetings play a role in the organisation's self-perpetuation, they largely leave the ordinary membership aside and feature as power arenas that are almost fully disconnected from the base, without whom the organisation would not exist.

Outgoing Rustenburg leaders vacated the stage and observers declared the election 'free and fair'. Aida announced that 280 delegates out of 308 had voted. Richard Mahoha, a historical 'opponent' (a former regional deputy chairperson and the outgoing deputy chairperson for health and safety), was elected chairperson of the Rustenburg region by one vote, and two of his supporters triumphantly carried him on stage. The Moloi-Dokolwana team was re-elected (out of nine positions opposed, only Mahoha made it to the regional office). No single candidate came in by a lead of more than 19 votes, an indication of how contested the election was. Ultimately, however, Mahoha's victory eventually sounded like 'continuity' since he is himself a professional unionist, and although he had been marginalised during most of the event, his union background spoke for itself; national leaders could be confident that he had enough union experience to be co-opted. He started as a shaft steward in 1986, before he became a branch office bearer in 1990, and was elected as regional deputy chairperson in 1996, 1999 and 2002. He was then re-elected as regional deputy secretary for health and safety in 2008. Talking about the fact that competition between the two opposing camps in the 2011 conference had been tight, he concluded: 'Of course, these things they are there always. There are always two camps.'[33]

In 2012, Frans Baleni would give the following summary of the Rustenburg conference: 'The regional office bearers went to the 2011 regional conference highly divided and as a result the quality of debate was very poor and not objective.'[34] The Rustenburg conference was, overall, an illustration of how removed NUM sometimes is from its members at the grassroots. The latter were physically absent from the regional arena and very little space – if any – was available for debate on the fate of mineworkers. The quest for organisational stability as against leadership change – in other words, self-perpetuation – and the battle for top union positions dominated debate in the conference. That is how union politics functioned in NUM's key region in the first decade of the twenty-first century and on the eve of major upheavals in South Africa's platinum belt.

PWV: A MODEL CONFERENCE

Three weeks after Rustenburg, it was the turn of the PWV region to hold its conference at the Birchwood Conference Centre, near Johannesburg's O.R. Tambo

International Airport. In comparison with what I had witnessed in Rustenburg, it proved a far quieter gathering and the election was disputed in a more cordial atmosphere. PWV was by then a stabilised region with a collective leading its committee, as opposed to what had prevailed three years earlier, when its conference had been highly contested. It was also the last appearance of PWV regional chairperson Thamsanqa Joko as a NUM leader. Joko, a union apparatchik experienced in regional politics, had been leading the region since 2002. Elected a branch chairperson in 1991, he was consistently elected to various positions at the regional level until he successfully led the PWV region for a decade (see Figure 5.7).

Thamsanqa Joko was greeted with a 'revolutionary song' and addressed delegates in his usual contained but firm style. Playing on his social position as an elder and on his historic legitimacy as a NUM leader, he imposed respect. After regaling the conference with PWV's successes, Joko took on a paternalistic tone to add 'but comrades it would not be a proper Joko if I did not put' to the conference 'the negative sides'. In a show of wisdom, he reminded his audience that 'this is my last conference as a bona fide member of this organisation'. He then quoted bestselling

Figure 5.7: Thamsanqa Joko, PWV regional conference, 2011
Photographer: Raphaël Botiveau

American author Robert Greene, in words probably taken from Greene's *48 Laws of Power*: 'being perfectly honest ... is to be free of personal motivation'. Only one nomination for the position of regional chairperson, which Joko was about to leave vacant, had been received ahead of the conference, that of his deputy Kanetso Matabane – an indication that succession had been well planned. Overall, the position of deputy chairperson was to be the only one contested after nominees to other positions declined to stand.

In PWV, just as in Rustenburg, national leaders complained that delegates focused too much on the election and not enough on political matters, but between protocol and speeches – including those of ANC, Cosatu and SACP guests – there was just no time left to talk about ideas. When the floor was opened to delegates to engage with the report, only a dozen delegates got to speak one after the other. Although they tackled a wide spectrum of issues (from the situation in Libya to general political and economic interventions), most of them were irrelevant to the daily life and work of mineworkers. Delegates from an Eskom branch I talked to complained that debates did not address workers' issues and were too political. They worried that 'when we come back from the conference our members will ask us to report back and we'll only be able to say for whom we voted ... but nothing on wage negotiations and they will say we went there to get our packs, tee shirts. They want NUM to review the agreement with Eskom.'[35]

The PWV conference provided an illustration of what a 'good' NUM regional conference ought to look like from the point of view of the union's national leaders who view themselves as custodians of NUM's organisational tradition. The 2011 Carletonville regional conference was also considered a success and, although I did not witness it, I was a guest at the first regional committee meeting that followed it (see Figures 5.8 and 5.9). The meeting was a useful reminder that although debates are, as I have described, limited during conferences, meetings that take place before and after regional conferences can be arenas for robust discussion. During the regional committee I attended, for instance, branch leaders discussed the minutes of the previous meeting, which included important local issues, for one whole hour before agreeing to accept them.

FIGHTING FOR UNION RESOURCES

As in any political organisation, one dimension of the struggle for positions in NUM and between the union's various levels is dictated by strategies to access and control resources. The struggle for resources is one key factor leading to instability.

Figure 5.8: Regional office bearers, Carletonville regional committee meeting, 2011
Photographer: Raphael Botiveau

Figure 5.9: Branch office bearers, Carletonville regional committee meeting, 2011
Photographer: Raphaël Botiveau

Mantashe summarised it in the last report he released as NUM general secretary, in 2006:

> As we develop the resource base we have also been aggressive in implementing organisational programmes. At the same time union structures have tried hard to spend in what we can call luxuries. This can be in the form of the accommodation we stay in when there are activities, the cars we drive (from Corolla, Jettas, not 4x2 bakkies). We can be easily tempted to move to BMW's, Benz or Volvos. It is also evident in cases where comrades are given allowances on international trips but expect the union to buy food where catering is not provided. These are luxuries that can easily alienate the NEC from the base. They constitute the underlying tensions that translate into highly contested regional conferences. We must continue building this resource base without getting tempted into helping ourselves from them. The union leadership should never be contested on the basis of who controls the resources, but on the basis of who manages them best and will protect them from abuse.[36]

As I have shown before, NUM is now a rich organisation.[37] The collection and management of union funds remains a national office monopoly. Funds are centralised in a national NUM bank account before being allocated to the regions. As prescribed in the NUM constitution: 'the funds received for the union by the General Secretary or other agents of the union, must be deposited within 5 days of receipt in a National or Regional banking account'. Branches have virtually no budget and their running costs are covered by companies (wages, cars and transportation, phones, venues for meetings, offices, computers, and so on), and by NUM regions that channel head office money. Things were not always that way, however. One of the main bones of contention in NUM over the past decade finds its origin in the management of 'agency fees'.

Agency fees are part of a labour relations dispensation known as an 'agency shop'. In this system, the employer may hire employees regardless of their affiliation to a union. Employees are not forced to join any union yet non-unionised workers, because they also benefit from agreements passed by unions and management on the improvement of wages and working conditions, must pay an 'agency fee' to cover the costs of bargaining. The Labour Relations Act of 1995 provides for the signing of agency shop agreements between an employer and a majority union. Such agreements are nevertheless not compulsory and are signed based on the stakeholders' free will.[38] In such agreements, the agency fees paid by non-union members are paid into a separate fund and administered by the majority union with a view to advancing the 'socioeconomic welfare' of all employees. Agency fees also apply in the case of a 'closed shop' agreement signed between an employer and a majority union that becomes the only union by virtue of thresholds of representativity at a given workplace.[39] This happened, for instance, at Impala, where NUM had become the only representative union in 2011. The issue of agency fees is therefore supposed to solve the problem of 'free riding', which Mancur Olson underlined in his classic utilitarian analysis of collective action.[40]

The debate around agency shop agreements goes back a long way; the NEC was already discussing it in the early 1990s. In September 1991, the committee observed: 'One of the biggest problems faced by the union is that there are many workers who are not members of our union but who enjoy the benefits of collective bargaining arising out of union activities.' The issue had also been discussed in the national congress, yet at a time when NUM was looking for new members and was still faced with the repressive environment of apartheid, the NEC was 'requested to consider whether the time is appropriate for us to make the demands of Agency Shop'.[41] The first agency funds were subsequently established and the question arose about 'what should be done with the money that is paid by free riders into the various funds'. A resolution adopted at the Eighth National Congress (1994), noting that several mines had created such funds, worth a total amount of R750 000, resolved that a list of charities should be produced by the secretariat and, more generally, that the 'funds should, where possible, be spent in ways that will strengthen NUM's development strategy'. Martin Nicol, head of the NUM collective bargaining department, produced a document entitled 'The Industrial and Human Relations Funds: Ideas on How to Make Good Use of Them'. These funds were to be credited with more than R4 million per annum, a sum Nicol deemed 'considerable'. He suggested that they should be jointly administered by a union/management board of trustees and noted that 'although the money cannot go to the union – it does allow the union to influence how and where the money is spent'.[42]

In many cases, however, companies transferred agency fees at mine level, to accounts opened and directly managed by NUM branches. At the Harmony-Rand Uranium branch near Carletonville, for instance, non-members contributed 0.75 per cent of their wage in agency fees as opposed to the one per cent subscription fee for members.[43] This money was absorbed into union money and used to fund union expenses such as buying a coffee machine and a car for the branch. Later, some money was also donated to retrenched workers in Aurora.[44] This created a situation in which branches now had money of their own to manage even though these funds were supposed to benefit all employees and not only NUM members or, for that matter, branch leaders. The situation was soon out of control and it appears that NUM lost track of many accounts, which were not audited and were mismanaged to the benefit of a few individuals. An accountant at NUM head office, whom I met in 2012, explained to me that many branches did not have good accountancy systems, that cases of corruption and maladministration were reported and that the union decided to transfer the accounts to the regions. There was still R13 million in agency accounts at the regional level, waiting to be centralised at the national level (following a decision the NEC had taken in 2008).

This question of agency shop funds became, as mentioned above, a much-gnawed bone of contention. It is a cause of much heated argument, among members and non-members alike, about the extent of corruption in NUM branches and, as observed in Rustenburg in 2008, 'the agency accounts are a primary source of sustained infightings among the leadership'.[45] Moreover, NUM head office experienced great difficulty in getting hold of the money involved and stumbled across withheld information in several branches. The NEC remained unable to find out how many accounts were concerned and how much money was involved. The process of auditing these accounts started in 2006 and Frans Baleni could only note the extent of the task in 2008:

> The process of collating information and converting that information to be in a state of readiness for auditing, continues to be a monumental challenge. The reason being that the process is entirely dependent on the co-operation of the Regions and branches ... The first phase of collating information about the existence of agency fees accounts resulted in sixty-five agency accounts being reported. Of these, thirty-six accounts have no basic information provided about them i.e. basic account details, contact person etc. Of the remaining twenty-nine agency fee accounts that provided the basic information on their existence, only two agency fees accounts were in a position to be audited.[46]

The deadline for the auditing process had to be postponed several times because branches did not 'co-operate' with national office and the regions. This situation, and the use of a verb like 'co-operate' to describe the relationship between subordinate NUM structures and the union's national office, offered yet another indication of the type of dynamics at play internally in the union. These dynamics are obviously not reduced to a hierarchical chain of command. The troubles related here provide a particularly significant illustration of what happens when what is at stake is money – the sinews of war. In 2011 it was estimated that branches controlled

60 agency fee accounts; only 18 had been accounted for, and 6 audited.[47] The saga of agency funds continued and six years after the process of auditing started, it remains unsolved even though, according to treasurer general David Macatha, the situation is now under better control, with 28 accounts at First National Bank branches. However, as Macatha also explained, the auditing process continues and the reallocation of funds to the head office to date remains incomplete.[48] Some, if not most, of this money belonging to workers will probably never be found, accounted for and invested to benefit them.

PART II

LEADING MINEWORKERS: A CHARTERIST LEADERSHIP SCHOOL

Q: Do you want to add something? BM: Yes. I want to say I am proud to be a union NUM member and a leader of the union because I've learned many things … When I joined the mine I did not know anything about laws, procedures; I was just focusing on my work. Not knowing about the rights. But when I started to join the union I was at least politically aware … As I am speaking right now I am not afraid to stand in front of the majority and talk about the right things … especially the rights of the employees, because of NUM. They trained me in many things. In fact I don't have standard at school but since I've joined the union I've learned many things, I've learned to speak different languages because of NUM.

Bhongo Mvimvi, full-time shaft steward,
Cooke 3, Randfontein branch, interview,
Cooke 3 mining hostels, 1 July 2010

6

The Burden of Leadership

A 'GOOD' LEADER: LEADERSHIP OF A SPECIAL TYPE IN NUM

There is no leadership where there is no power relation. But leadership fails to exercise power effectively if it lacks another asset: authority. If one follows Hanna Arendt,[1] authority is what gets lost in the transition to political modernity, a shift that is well exemplified by NUM's adoption of a Weberian type of collective organisation. This tension was clear, for instance, in August 2012, when NUM leaders kept telling their members on strike to go back to work with no result: they had organisational power (as described in Part I) but lacked the associated authority to exert it effectively. As Richard Sennett wrote, 'The bond of authority is built of images of strength and weakness; it is the emotional expression of power.' The word 'bond' has a double meaning, which expresses at the same time a 'connection' and a 'constraint', because authority is as much needed for one to prosper (as in the case of parental authority) as it is feared since it holds the prospect of enslavement.[2] Leadership and authority are considered necessary to govern human societies and, over the past century, strong leaders were equally needed in communist and in liberal settings. What differed between the two, however, was the definition of how a 'good leader' is expected to behave. 'Authoritarianism' – a negative concept used to point at a deviation from authority – suggests that when exercised with discernment, authority and leadership are often viewed in a good light from an ethical point of view, as positive qualities in the exercise of power. Definitions of what a 'good leader' is or ought to be may vary from one person, group or society to another, yet they always obey a 'moral economy'[3] of leadership that grounds the leader's legitimacy. As Max Weber observed, authority identifies with legitimacy: people do not obey those they deem illegitimate.[4] The rejection by their own members that NUM leaders have experienced since 2012 is decisively rooted in such disaffection, and what is important is not whether NUM leaders are indeed corrupt or bureaucratised, but the fact that they are perceived as such by entire segments of their constituency. This said, however, neither corruption nor bureaucratisation is enough to make a leader illegitimate.

In Durkheim's concept of 'anomy', social disorder was perceived as a consequence of the disturbance of old relationships of authority by industrial society, which, with its growing individualism, calls traditional sources of legitimacy into question. Where the 2012 strikers resorted to grassroots and indigenous forms of organisation to replace NUM in an environment that put traditions in jeopardy, the union viewed the lack of leadership as a cause of disorder and generally equated it with a lack of leader education. At the 2011 Rustenburg regional conference NUM head of production, Eddie Majadibodu, reacted to one delegate's intervention on the growth of the union. He argued that 'we' cannot recruit members without servicing them and that, in order to do so, leaders should be trained at all levels and that no elected shaft steward should be in office for more than six months without being inducted and trained. He then concluded, referring to the competition of rival unions: 'We have thousands of shaft stewards, hundreds are full-time, tens of bearers with cars and resources. How can we have competition from unions who have an office in the boot of their car?'

The authority exercised by a prince or an emperor is, of course, not the same as that of a workers' leader. However, and as Arendt rightly noted, 'authority precludes the use of external means of coercion; where force is used, authority itself has failed'.[5] In other words, when NUM leaders from the Karee branch allegedly opened fire on their angry members on 11 August 2012,[6] or when the union's national leaders called for police intervention in order to curb violence during the 2012 strike, they lacked authority, not necessarily power. This issue is rooted in the tension between views about legitimacy and social order based on competence, as advocated by the union and its leaders on the one hand (in short, political modernity), and by its own members' attachment to previous bonds of authority and holistic solidarity on the other hand. This caesura is, of course, not clear-cut and one needs to address the following questions in depth to better understand how power and domination are exercised in the union: how do NUM unionists and cadres conceive leadership and the exercise of authority in the organisation? How, then, are authority and power defined in NUM? And more crucially, if one thinks of the type of legitimacy that is attached to authority and leadership, how is a 'good' NUM leader defined in terms of social and educational competences? One can also question, as I have already argued, whether NUM members are looking for a service union – that is, for leaders who view them as individual customers – or have another conception of how they should be led.

Observers of the 2012 wildcat strikes in mining were quick to describe sponta-neous, self-managed and quasi-acephalous workers' mobilisations.[7] There was clear evidence, however, that the strikers were well organised locally, had leaders (drawn from the RDO corps) and received the support of an established organisation – Amcu. Not only did Amcu successfully try to take over these mobilisations, it also played a part in igniting some of them in places such as Lonmin-Marikana where its leadership had been at work, recruiting members for more than a year before the 2012 strike started. Rather than rejecting traditional forms of domination or a hypothetical ancient leadership order embodied by NUM, it is arguable that the workers in fact rejected the modern type of a more distant and technocratic lead-ership (described in chapter 3 as linked to neoliberal forms of legal-rational dom-ination) proposed by the majority of NUM leaders. What they supported, rather, was a type of leadership that Amcu leader Joseph Mathunjwa well embodied, char-acterised by a mixture of paternal and religious authority (or, in Weberian terms, of tradition and charisma). Mathunjwa went to the mineworkers and preached; he assured them of his empathy and compassion and showed that he cared for them as if they were his own children.

This type of leadership was not mobilised randomly. The mines, the minework-ers' environment and their stories at times seem almost like a biblical epic and the archetypal NUM leader[8] is sometimes described in quasi-messianic terms as in the following words of Ecliff Tantsi, NUM national secretary for education, in October 2011. Tantsi, who was acting as the union's chief negotiator at Murray & Roberts Cementation, was talking to branch leaders in his delegation and, during a break in the negotiations, he congratulated one of his team members who had recently been elected as a regional treasurer:

> If you read the Bible, comrades, in Exodus when Moses is given the respon-sibility to conduct the Israelites out of Egypt, first he communicates with God. Leadership does not happen naturally. God first puts something on you then people see it … I like to read the Bible because it was written in those times and for times to come. What is interesting about Moses is that he did not know he was a leader; he did not want to lead in the first place. He told God of his weaknesses: now that's the first thing you have to be aware of, your weaknesses.

His words sacralise leadership by identifying the skills associated with it as a gift. Behind the idea of election lies that of a calling, in biblical terms, or – if one translates it in NUM terms and norms – that of 'nomination'. In other words, as previously explained, NUM leaders are not supposed to stand for election based on their own will. Instead, they attract their fellow members' attention through displaying skills based on which they are subsequently nominated and seconded to a leadership position. This sometimes happens against their own will, which suggests that leadership is ideally conceived as a mission or a burden. There is also in Tantsi's words a call for humility: leaders are fallible and they should not wander from the straight path dictated by their leadership role. He insisted on this point based on another biblical analogy when, after taking the example of Elijah, he explained that 'the essence of the analogy is when you are given something and you become pompous. You see my strength [is that] when I talk I go to Cape Town before I go to Polokwane.' Through using geography Ecliff Tantsi meant that to achieve one's personal ambitions (represented here by Polokwane, the capital of Limpopo, remembered as the site of the highly contested 2007 ANC National Conference in which Jacob Zuma defeated Thabo Mbeki), one must use a roundabout way, a collective one. In his sermon-like speech, the national leader thus called upon his local counterparts to follow Moses' example and assume their own leadership role in the organisation but also to limit their personal ambitions:

> God was trying to show him that you have to know about power. When the Amalekites were fighting, he had to lift his hands but he got tired and his people supported … [him] and it worked. What it taught me is that you cannot take someone else's responsibility and role. Do you understand the analogy, comrades, the importance of the role you are playing in the organization?

He then made his remark more explicit by alluding to upcoming local elections and rejecting the possibility of one 'comrade' supporting another based on motives other than the members' best interests:

> The point I'm trying to explain is … we have done a good job. There's always a tension in our organisation that … would [make you] push a comrade for the wrong reason … You are matured enough comrades … My leadership style is to educate and lead. I hate chaos, I hate instability, I hate tensions. The process of election, my perception is you will handle it as mature leaders. I am very clear in my mind that I'm not anarchist.

The ideal NUM leader therefore has charisma – a form of charisma sometimes inspired by religion but above all by great forebears from the struggle – that makes him able to preach/talk 'to the masses' gathered in the hardship of the mines and in the cold nights and blazing days of the veld. The ideal NUM leader is also a chosen one, if not by God then by his fellow mineworkers whom he leads with no personal ambition, as their teacher and guide. The analogy between the leader and the teacher – or a preacher when the teaching is also a moral one – is a common one, and as a NUM shaft steward at a gold mine told me: 'My role is to represent the members, teach members their wrongs and their rights ... and negotiate for members for better benefits and give guidance to the members of the organisation, and interpret laws and procedures to members.'[9] The teacher in the NUM sense of the term, however, is never an absolute master and he derives his authority from his capacity to explain the reasons for a given situation and to persuade his members to opt for an appropriate course of action, based on sound arguments and advice.

The leader is also legitimate, from the viewpoint of NUM, because he 'knows', as opposed to members, who do not know. He must understand the workings of the organisation but also the wider mining and political environment. This technical knowledge, acquired over time, is precisely what Amcu would lack, according to NUM. It was therefore a reason why the rival union would be doomed to fail in the long run. In other words, the leader can educate because he himself is educated:

> He must understand the culture and the norms of the union in which he is leading. He must understand the environment in which the union is operating. You must at least be familiar with the government laws. Because when you lead you will find situations in which some employees get killed underground so you must have a certain understanding of what the law says.[10]

The leader is expected to teach but his teaching is also dependent on his capacity to listen – good NUM leaders are often described as 'good listeners' (that is, also as good interpreters). In the words of a NUM Lonmin branch office bearer I interviewed in 2011:

> [A good leader] would be somebody who is a good listener because you would have to get an understanding of what the members want; a person who is able to engage with other people and share ideas with them so that you can have a bigger picture when discussing things; and somebody who is also decisive, a person who can take a decision.[11]

In ideal NUM leaders, one therefore finds a combination of qualities, which include some degree of selflessness and the abilities to teach and to guide, as well as the more standard items that Sennett described as components of authority: 'assurance, superior judgement, the ability to impose discipline, the capacity to inspire fear: these are the qualities of an authority'.[12]

Discipline and fear, however, are fragile: they can easily be subverted, which I will show in chapter 9. But let me first address what abilities top NUM leaders probably lacked in the face of the 2012 strike movement, according to former NUM deputy general secretary Archie Palane. In his analysis of how leaders are expected to handle volatile local situations, leadership is a complex, alchemical process that moves back and forth from imposing authority and organising, to listening and convincing members. We were talking about a wildcat strike that had occurred at the Impala Platinum mine in 2005. According to Palane, the strike had been fomented by a group of shaft stewards who wanted to take control of the branch and promised mineworkers they could get a wage increase. Palane exposed how good leadership was applied to solve the crisis:

> From head office you go there. The starting point is not the mass meeting, the starting point is with that leadership. You have to organise those 40, 50 at some point 100 shaft stewards. They will throw whatever word, insult, but at the end of the day you go out there unified as the leadership. By the time you go to the masses you are not divided. If you are not providing that leadership, you are in the office … [and] you are creating a vacuum that is not filled. I think that's the current leadership problem. When they go there they don't go there to listen, they've already concluded that workers are wrong. In our own days we've learned that when workers go on strike there must be something and it is that something that we have to find out before you can conclude that workers are wrong. If you send a junior official they don't know how to handle conflict. But if you realise that we have a problem here, you take yourself and go in there whether the fire is burning or not and understand the situation, mineworkers will respect you because during bad times you are with them. It's not only during good times that they see you around and say thank God we have our leader. In all the strike actions I've been involved when mineworkers mobilise legally, you mobilise, you are with them. When they were involved in an illegal strike you were with them when they were fired and when they were reinstated. I think it is something today's leadership needs to address.[13]

Figure 6.1 shows NUM deputy president Pete Matosa addressing assembled shaft stewards in 2012 at the union's Karee branch. In what is reminiscent of the strategy

Figure 6.1: NUM deputy president Pete Matosa addresses local leaders, Lonmin Karee branch, 2012

Photographer: Raphaël Botiveau

described by Palane above, regional and national leadership tried, unsuccessfully, to organise and mobilise the local leadership to reconquer the union's lost position at this Lonmin branch where Amcu had started recruiting former NUM members.

A crucial quality in the NUM conception of a good leader involves the capacity to 'give' leadership on the one hand, and to 'feel' the members on the other hand. A good NUM leader is typically one who exercises his authority through guiding members in a complex environment, who is frank about how good or how bad a situation is, and shows presence if not charisma in front of the masses. This ultimately implies that there is some distance between leaders and members but that this distance needs to be carefully presented as something positive, reasssuring. A good leader must always, for instance, carefully listen to members' grievances and express empathy with their feelings. Nowadays this basic definition of what a good union leader is matches more closely the profile of Joseph Mathunjwa, whose presence beside the strikers in 2012 was key to the rise of Amcu. For their part, contemporary NUM leaders were only able to display contempt for a movement they deemed both unlawful and illegitimate. Crucial to their rejection of it and their subsequent loss of authority was the idea that the strikers were wrong and misled. This was most coldly expressed by Frans Baleni, who, only four days after the Marikana massacre, stated:

> We are deeply saddened by the recent events in Impala a few months ago as well as recently in Lonmin where about 44 workers have been killed. It is something which is regrettable, it is something that could have been avoided. It does suggest that things must be done in a particular manner, that we need to be vigilant. There are those dark forces who can mislead our members.[14]

To describe members as too easily influenced rather than influential, as unconscious (which in the communist jargon means uneducated) rather than responsible, cannot but sound contemptuous and, even more crucially, insensitive to pain and suffering. What lies behind this quote is the decisive question of education, which, as far as leadership and authority are concerned, is where the shoe pinches. As I have argued and will further show, from its inception NUM was orientated towards organising mineworkers and producing skilled and educated leaders. One of the unintended consequences of this endeavour has been the growing gap between 'ordinary members', as they are often called among unionists, and those whom I will later refer to as their 'distinguished leaders'.

Baleni's conception of leadership stresses the underlying tension in current NUM leaders between a certain moral economy of leadership, which is supposed to bind the leadership together and the leaders to their base, and the managerial conception of the union that the former general secretary embodied. This tension was well illustrated in a union leadership development course I attended at the Elijah Barayi Memorial Training Centre in October 2011. The fourth activity proposed to participants was entitled 'Union Leaders and Managers'.[15] Participants were asked to 'reflect on our roles as leaders and managers in our trade unions' and Mercy Sekano, the course convener, asked them: 'Do you agree with the statement in page 15: there are no managers in unions – only leaders?' This question, from a NUM point of view, was meant to underline at least three dimensions of leadership: (i) union leaders are expected to not just 'manage' a situation but to inform it, to give guidance; (ii) union leaders are not the same as managers in a company since they fit into a democratic process of decision-making rather than into a top-down chain of command; and (iii) there is an irreconcilably different class interest between a workers' leader and a capitalist manager. If several participants in the leadership course agreed on the fact that there was indeed a difference between leaders and managers, one of them disagreed, arguing that 'even Frans Baleni is our manager'. Such confusion between the union leader and the manager is also linked to the fact that NUM leaders are now increasingly employed in managerial positions in the companies they work for. This became clear in Activity 7, on the values and traditions of the trade union organisation. Sekano introduced it in these words: 'When you wear a suit – I am sure some of you are managers – or a tee shirt to address a mass-meeting, it is not the same thing.' 'The values of the labour movement is what make us different from government or the corporate sector,' he added. These values, which one often finds in various union documents and on NUM posters, were listed by participants as 'loyalty, integrity, honesty, respect, commitment, unity, quality service, organise … ' and, as if it were a recitation they knew by heart,

Sekano concluded this exercise by saying 'and so forth and so on … '. The model answer provided in the course pack read: 'Some of these values include: non-sexism, non-racism, democracy, worker control, collectivity, independence, international solidarity.' The clash between these two lists, the first one spontaneously given by trainee leaders and the second one, which refers to the traditions of the union, reveals a confusion that has a lot to do with the transformation of union leaders into managers.

As a result of the NUM organisation-building process, the distinction between union leadership and company management is thus no longer so clear-cut. Managers have become an example that, on the one hand, differs from the union's historical ethos of leadership while, on the other, also matches its ever-evolving definition of a good leader. The course pack distributed to participants included some reading material that was particularly illustrative of this. The first lines of a Frans Baleni article, written when he headed NUM's training centre, referred to the Enron scandal and read: 'The unions should endorse good corporate governance principles, including the checks and balances that ensure those who steer the ship are accountable.' The article also made extensive reference to the ideas of international consultant Bob Garratt on what a 'learning organisation' is.[16] Baleni then argued that the relevance of combining union and company approaches to organisation 'lies in the fact that unions have various structures and processes that are supposed to be accountable to the membership'.[17] The view of NUM's former general secretary, focused on the widespread notion of 'accountability', was balanced in the leadership development course pack by the more conventional activist approach of Suraya Jawoodeen, former deputy general secretary of the National Education, Health and Allied Workers' Union, who later lost her position because of her critical stance towards the ANC. She recalled that 'the trade union movement is not like journalism, accounts, nursing or the teaching professions. It is not a career but a struggle to improve the living and working conditions of the working class. Therefore elected leaders do not bring about change as individuals but they work as a team.'[18] The course pack also included a piece by former Harvard Business School professor John P. Kotter on the difference between leaders and managers. Kotter's argument is that management and leadership – in the corporate sector – differ but are complementary. In a nutshell, 'managers promote stability while leaders press for change' in a fast-evolving environment – a tension that is clearly found in the current NUM.[19]

All in all, one could say that the definition of 'a good leader' refers to tangible and shared elements that one often encounters in NUM leaders. Good leaders are teachers and guides who, based on their knowledge, can help members to take the right direction, can 'give leadership' even when this involves going against the flow of common sense. Guidance, however, implies a dynamic relationship based on direct physical proximity, empathy and good listening. It is only once the leader has felt for the members' concerns and understood where their issues come from that he or she can either follow them or try to persuade them, appealing to both emotions and reason, to see their issues in a different light. The good leader is also, of course, a good organiser and a disciplined member of their organisation.

Behind these leadership qualities lies another set of tensions, which is at the heart of the crisis the union currently faces in its relationship not only to its membership, but also to some of its own core leadership. It is a tension between the expectations the people who are led have of those who lead them, on the one hand, and the conception that leadership has of the former, on the other hand. It is a clash between short-term and long-term visions of the organisation and the mining industry. It is also sometimes a clash between recklessness and caution. For the member, the emotional warmth of direct contact is often the most important aspect of the relationship (a paternalistic or religious one) whereas for the leader, it is the opposite: rational knowledge must lead and authority be exercised in a challenging economic environment. Both can find embodiments of their conceptions in the forebears who led the struggle. In one of the many speeches coloured by morality that Mercy Sekano gave participants in his leadership course, he summed up this clash well: 'You don't declare a strike from one day to another, you don't lead members based on emotions. If you do this they are dismissed. You lead based on facts, which is why you have to read.' The question of emotions has long featured as some kind of taboo in the social sciences, as if social actors were led only by rational calculations.[20] It is nonetheless a crucial component of mobilisations, which aim to generate sympathy for the cause in the general public, and to inspire solidarity among those who mobilise. The mineworkers who regularly went on strike after 2012, either fully or partially mobilised by Amcu, rejected NUM on the basis of what the union had shown them in the past: leadership. The 'leadership of a special type' had been based on the adroit balancing of emotion and reason, adjustment to concrete local situations and union rules. This tension between managerial forms of leadership – which, as I will show in chapter 9, went very well with communist discipline in Gwede Mantashe's NUM – and more traditional representations of the leader, based on a direct face-to-face confrontation with the masses, is a constant in NUM. Yet management and discipline have now arguably got the better of relational leadership. The leadership NUM mineworkers long for is one in which leaders were close – not necessarily similar – to them; when leaders cared for mineworkers and, in that sense, were regarded as selfless. That is why many mineworkers turned back to values of solidarity and repertoires of action they knew because these had guided them and their union in the past. What recent mobilisations have shown quite clearly is that mineworkers do not reject and possibly even enjoy leadership and leaders, orators and champions of their cause. However, they like to see (almost touch) those who lead them. Back in 2012, at Lonmin and Impala, it was striking that only those leaders identified as caring and uncompromised were allowed to address the mineworkers, including Zwelinzima Vavi, Julius Malema and Joseph Mathunjwa. For different reasons (leftist and anti-Zuma tendencies, populist indiscipline and/or charismatic and militant leadership) all three have been banned from the ANC and its aligned union movement. Two of them, it is worth noting, openly display their material wealth and, in doing so, do not demonstrate much affinity with the workers' condition. The 2012 strike movement was thus also an expression of disenchantment and ultimately, a movement attempting to create re-enchantment in mining and the organisation of mineworkers.

THE WORK OF ORDINARY LEADERS IN UNION BRANCHES

After considering the values attached to leadership, it is now time to look at what branch leaders actually do. This is necessary in order to address the simplistic yet well-entrenched idea that NUM failed because it is a generally corrupt organisation, out of touch with its members' concerns. A close look at local social situations in which leadership (shaft stewards at workplace level and branch office bearers in union branches on mines) and membership come into daily interaction suggests a more complex picture. A NUM intermediate steward manual explains: 'The steward is a vital link between the members and the Union leadership and its structures. The steward is also a vital link between the membership at the workplace and the management.' The manual continues:

> As an elected worker leader you have many roles. You can be an advisor to workers with problems. You can be a trouble-shooter if anything happens at work. You can be a good and trusted friend to a worker who is facing difficulties. You can be an advocate and speak up for gender equality. You can be someone with ideas, about how to make the Union more effective. You can play a role in your community to help make links between people in the community and the workers you represent.[21]

In the manual, written by South African former unionist and academic Kally Forrest, which NUM uses to induct its newly elected shaft stewards, the steward is described in succession as 'an organiser' ('the main duty of a steward is to build up and maintain a strong membership at the workplace'); 'a representative' (in the face of management, as well as in union structures and political forums); 'a watchdog' (make sure employers stick to agreements); and an 'educator' ('educate workers about the workers' movement').[22] At a gold mine like AngloGold Ashanti's Mponeng, NUM had over 4 700 members – or 82 per cent of the total workforce, including 400 Swazi, 500 Mozambican and 1 000 Lesotho nationals – who were represented by 40 shaft stewards when I visited the operation in 2010, 2011 and 2012. On Thursday 8 July 2010 I attended a NUM Mponeng branch committee meeting. It gathered ten branch office bearers and started late, after local and regional union representatives had had a 'difficult discussion' with management. The situation was tense at the mine after an accident, on Monday 5 July, had left one mineworker paraplegic. (Figure 6.2 shows the dangerous work environment of RDOs in South Africa's underground and deep-level mining.) Before the meeting started, a delegation of eight managers and unionists from other workers' organisations entered the room and, before indicating that another version of

Figure 6.2: Rock drill operator at work, Impala Platinum mine, October 2011
Photographer: Raphaël Botiveau

the document unsuccessfully discussed with NUM in the morning would soon be resubmitted for review, they insisted that health and safety was their 'absolute priority'. The NUM meeting then proceeded and it somehow struck me – I was still new to such meetings at the time – that rather than dealing with how to address issues such as safety at work in concrete terms and in close touch with the workers, the proceedings consisted mainly of general statements denouncing the unacceptable. This, for me, suggested, at worst, some sort of disconnection from the workers underground or, at best, some degree of powerlessness in the face of management. The way NUM meetings are often conducted, usually in an urbane and disciplined way, with representatives unrolling arguments to deal with a given situation or making statements of good intention, is a hint that the union is more at ease with orderly negotiations with management through institutionalised channels, than with the militant type of approach adopted by Amcu during and after the 2012 platinum strikes.

These strikes may be analysed as a renewal of a more militant stance towards the union–management relationship, and as a shift in the balance of union power at mine level. In the strikes, it is the underground – the shafts – that regain power, literally and figuratively, over the surface. At Impala Platinum South and North branches, virtually all local Amcu leadership positions in 2015 were filled by RDOs, whereas they had been almost absent from branch committees under NUM. This resulted in the revival of a more direct, action-orientated stance in the face of management. Labour relations were thus affected not only by national Amcu leaders, who do not hesitate to demand major wage increases or to threaten management with strikes, but also by a change of attitude on the ground in daily managerial interactions. RDOs are not accustomed to dialogue and negotiation; they have little knowledge of labour law and local managers sometimes described them as 'brutal' in their practice of labour relations:

> With NUM when we had a problem, we could solve it through meetings, through the leadership, we had a good relationship. When Amcu came into power it was a different situation; they operated totally differently; they don't go into meetings, they don't negotiate, they bring the whole operation to a standstill, they make demands; if you don't listen to the demands they become violent.

This approach to communicating with management is also rooted, as I have suggested, in an institutional reorganisation of union branches, in which the shafts regained power over the surface. Amcu is often described as a copycat, institutionally, of NUM, yet this is not all that obvious if one considers the same Impala manager's description of new local union structures:

> With NUM we only had a full-time health and safety rep and a full-time shaft steward on each shaft that was permanently on surface. When Amcu came in you had now five full-time Amcu shaft stewards and five full-time health and safety stewards. Basically you have ten guys on the shafts permanently. That also means you will sit in your office, then all ten of them will come. Like I would be sitting here then all ten would come and then they've got a certain issue on which you have said no and they put pressure on you, start bad-mouthing you, try for you to give in and give them the answer that they want. So you had to be very strong because these ten guys although it is five health and safety and five Amcu they stood together.[23]

The difference between Amcu and NUM is also in the types of demand they formulated. Where Amcu mainly focused on the battle for wage increases, NUM submitted more integrated sets of demands on issues as diverse as housing, safety or dignity. During the Mponeng meeting I started describing earlier, local leaders also argued for the implementation of mass education (decided in a previous encounter some three months earlier) but without further details on how this should be done. The lack of safety at work was denounced, but NUM leaders sounded powerless as to how they could counter the production targets imposed by AngloGold Ashanti on its workers, which the union generally saw as playing against safety at work. (See, for example, Figure 6.3, which shows an underground mine overseer pointing to the stope to be mined as the production target for the month at Impala Platinum mine 1 shaft and Figure 6.4, showing the dangerous-looking gallery leading to that stope.)

The possibility of adding a few full-time health and safety stewards was mentioned, along with salary incentives based on the safety record of the workers. A few concrete points presented as feedback from the base were raised, such as the need for union representatives to attend the company's induction training, and the request of some women workers to be accommodated in the mine's hostels. None of this is to dismiss the work or the degree of commitment of local NUM leaders at Mponeng. Rather, it questions the strategy adopted by the union, which may have been too conciliatory to challenge managerial power effectively. Historically, NUM has undoubtedly achieved a great deal through this strategy of reasoned engagement; certainly the reports of local-level union–management discussions that I was given to consult showed that engagements were sometimes robust. There are

Figure 6.3: The production target for October 2011, Impala Platinum mine shaft 1

Photographer: Raphaël Botiveau

Figure 6.4: The gallery leading to the stope to be mined in October 2011

Photographer: Raphaël Botiveau

nevertheless indications that NUM's stance in many mines and at national level has become one of institutionalised engagements with management, which in the short term probably yield fewer gains than more confrontational strategies might do.

During my fieldwork, between interviews, I used to wander around the large properties of South African mines, from the diverse sites of operations to the mining hostels. It is in such moments that I often witnessed ordinary scenes of local union life that gave me a sense of what local leaders do daily. As visual examples of what I typically saw, Figure 6.5 shows a NUM shaft steward at work in his office and Figure 6.6 shows the modest accommodation of a NUM local office.

One hot afternoon of November 2011, for instance, I walked past NUM Impala South branch office, where it was rush hour. This was one of the most problematic branches in the union in terms of discipline and leadership rivalries, and it disintegrated a few months later, in January 2012. Most NUM office bearers were out of office that day, at a joint union–management branch meeting dedicated to the company's provident fund, but the local secretary was there attending to members' queries and grievances. It was a revealing moment; a moment that gave me insight into precisely how important it was for the union to have literate and skilled representatives. That day, many queuing members were holding letters from their employers that they could not read or with administrative content they did not understand. In other words, the role of a shaft steward is sometimes that of a public letter writer. A little later, I came across the local NUM secretary for health and safety, who was rushing to a disciplinary hearing: a member had been accused of stealing a bag of copper – which was true, the union representative confessed. He told me that

Figure 6.5: Impala MinPro shaft committee office, October 2011

Photographer: Raphaël Botiveau

Figure 6.6: AngloGold Mponeng branch office, November 2011

Photographer: Raphaël Botiveau

he had to represent his member and spoke proudly about his achievements in defending employees. At the level of the Commission for Conciliation, Mediation and Arbitration (CCMA) he had won 100 per cent of his cases. At company level, he counted fewer victories, but he thought this case was 'winnable'. Representing employees is one of the most common duties performed by union leaders at local level.

In 2010, when I arrived at the mining hostels where I was to meet the NUM Randfontein branch secretary, I found him at work with an ordinary member, preparing his 'case' after he had been dismissed in 2009. Douglas Gininda explained to me that they had to prepare answers to questions that he would be asked. Branch office bearers or shaft stewards generally represent members when they appear before the CCMA and the union does not usually hire lawyers unless a case goes to the Labour Court. Most cases are therefore prepared locally, yet when unsure of how to act, local leaders can refer a case to the full-time NUM legal advisors at head office. Douglas Gininda told me, for instance, that he did not know whether a case he was dealing with qualified as 'discrimination' or 'unfair labour treatment'.[24] However, the representation of members is not always conducted adequately. During one of my visits at Mponeng, for instance, I walked to the mine gate with the local branch secretary to exchange information with a lawyer representing dismissed workers (see Figure 6.6, the Mponeng branch office). Goodwell Tshitshiba told me that these members had had to privately hire a lawyer to represent them because the union representative at their workplace had not done the job properly.[25]

At another NUM Impala branch, the local treasurer told me about his morning that day. He was dealing with the case of a deceased member and explained:

> When someone passes away, the first step is the family coming to our NUM office. I personally took them to the hospital to identify the corpse. Then the doctor makes the … application form for the death certificate. Then we send it to the Home Affairs where the legitimate person in relation to the deceased takes his or her fingerprints and stamps it. After this we go to IWPF [Impala Workers Provident Fund] to claim the amount of R15 000. That money is only to assist the family in relation to the burial and transport. After a year we assist them again … They stamp the last payslip of the deceased. We then go to apply for UIF and then the Esops … I forgot something. If there is a funeral like now the one who will arrange for transport is me. I have to get the quotation from two or three companies and submit it to Impala.[26]

Dealing with paperwork in preparation for the funeral of a deceased member is surely not the most spectacular type of duty performed by local NUM leaders, but it reflects the kind of administrative task union officials perform daily. At Impala, the union had also negotiated that the company would provide transport for union representatives and mineworkers to attend funerals following fatalities on the mine: two buses if the death occurred underground and one bus if it took place at the hospital. It is also around the question of death, however, that one comes across cases of corruption or misappropriation. Cases were reported to me in which NUM shaft stewards took advantage of a fatality to get hold of the attached benefits in cash, sometimes with the complicity of the mine's local human resources manager.

When one looks at the daily occupation of local NUM leaders, however, the other side of the coin is that their work is also largely dedicated to organising union logistics. The same Impala Services branch treasurer told me that he was required to deal with stationery for the union, to find sponsors for its conferences, to organise transport for unionists to attend union meetings, and to sit with management in job interviews. The latter duty is surely important: from a NUM point of view it is intended to make sure that a company complies with employment equity regulations, yet from an ordinary member's point of view – especially in companies like Impala where a situation of de facto closed shop prevailed until 2012 – it also gives NUM great power in the hiring process, with concomitant risks of co-option (and indeed former unionists are regularly hired in management positions) and corruption (selling jobs).

Beyond accusations about conflicts of interest, a major reason for the mistrust of NUM officials is the pay increase branch leaders allegedly receive when they become union representatives. The recognition agreements signed between NUM and mining companies, however, suggest that such allegations of collusion or corruption are rumours, which, spread by rival organisations, become formidable propaganda tools. First, wage increases in fact apply to only a minority of local union officials – when it is the case at all, it is usually only the chairperson and secretary of a branch who are promoted to a C1 position on the Paterson Job Grading System and thus receive a wage increase (note that a branch committee is composed of a minimum of 11 branch office bearers).[27] Second, these two officials are often the only ones among their peers to be deployed on a full-time basis, apart from a few shaft stewards. And third, if increased, their pay is brought back to its previous level within six months after they have stopped acting as union representatives. However, this obviously can put pressure on them to retain their union position. Some unionists also have access to benefits in kind – including the use of company cars, stationery, computers and offices provided by the company, but usually on a collective basis and with clear limitations (on telephone or cellphone bills, for instance). Nevertheless, most elected unionists in fact do not experience any substantial socioeconomic change but – and this is important – they are given time off work to perform union duties if they have not been released on a part-time basis. Some unionists I met actually argued that their personal interests, money and career-wise, would be best served by focusing only on their career rather than election as a shaft steward, since activism is not necessarily a career booster and can in fact prove counterproductive if one annoys management in the process of one's involvement. Being elected as a union representative, however, means training opportunities and it regularly leads to promotion within mining companies in search of skills to meet their Black Economic Empowerment targets. Shaft stewards also have a better knowledge of their company's workings, and when it comes to subsidised company housing, for instance, it is likely, as I was told by some local leaders in Lonmin, that they will consider their own interests and apply for themselves and their political 'clients'. This said, it is worth remembering that much of what some now consider as privileges attached to elected union positions were hard-won union rights in the 1980s and 1990s, designed to make sure that union representatives had the necessary skills, time and freedom to fulfil their mandates. Hence, if the fact that full-time union leaders remain employees of their companies may be contested in the case of top national leaders,[28] one should not forget that the principle of having time off work to represent workers has historically and universally been regarded as social progress. To date, having a company agree to release union representatives on a full-time or even part-time basis is still very hard for NUM to achieve and it remains a recurring union demand in order, for instance, to improve safety standards. With time, of course, the number of full-time positions did indeed increase in NUM, which the union itself also approached as having bad side effects on levels of leadership commitment. The 2003 secretariat report reads:

> **Warning**: There is an emerging worrying trend where every structure demands to have full-time office-bearers. Although this can be seen logically as being about capacity, we must be aware that the rush for almost everybody to be full-time will result in a backlash, wherein the industry will begin to resist. In this way we may destroy the concept. This approach has the inherent risk of destroying the shaft/shop stewards movement of part-time committed stewards. We are beginning to see signs of over-dependence on full-time positions. There is a growing reluctance on the part of part-time comrades to work hard because there is nothing in it for them. If we are not careful we are going to end up with very weak structures and very strong individuals.[29]

The remuneration of full-time local NUM leaders was described to me as one source of discord between Steve Khululekile, the former NUM Karee branch chairperson at Lonmin – where the 2012 strike started – and his union region. The NUM's Rustenburg leadership excluded Khululekile in 2011 after he allegedly refused to hold the local election. A major wildcat strike in his support followed. One alleged reason why he refused to hold branch elections was that a new recognition agreement was being negotiated at the time, which would have increased his wage as NUM branch chairperson from R7 000 to R14 000. The election, however, was due to take place before the actual signing of the agreement and he was afraid of losing the poll and, with it, the benefits attached to the new agreement.[30]

'ORDINARY MEMBERS' AND 'DISTINGUISHED LEADERS'

In this section I return to what I earlier called the 'SWOP hypothesis', yet from another perspective. The three already quoted longitudinal surveys conducted by the SWOP Institute at the University of the Witwatersrand for NUM between 1998 and 2010 constitute the main available primary source on the membership of NUM. This data is, of course, of great interest for anyone concerned with this union and others within the South African labour movement. The three reports were firstly produced for internal use and designed to inform NUM leaders on the state of their rank and file. As such the SWOP reports constitute neither a neutral nor a scientific knowledge. They are indeed regarded as expertise by their producers, as well as by their commissioners. The former, a group of sociologists, resorted to their scientific skills but acted as experts in that they complied with the requirements set by NUM's head office. The data collected by the surveyors then partially filtered into the academic field through the Bezuidenhout and Buhlungu articles cited in chapter 2. As already mentioned, the SWOP 2005 and 2010 reports essentially concluded that the NUM membership base was changing, an idea that has become common sense among NUM leaders. From what I was given to observe, and as the 2012 strikes showed, however, the transition experienced by NUM and its gradual transformation, for instance, into a 'white collar' union[31] have been much slower than suggested. What did change faster and to a more dramatic extent than the union's members and their aspirations over the past twenty years is, I argue, its leaders' profile and *habitus*.[32] This in turn widened the gap between 'ordinary members' and leaders along the lines of what I will refer to here, after Pierre Bourdieu, as a process of 'distinction'. As the sociologist argued, 'Whereas the ideology of charisma regards taste in legitimate culture as a gift of nature, scientific observation shows that cultural needs are the product of upbringing and education …'[33] In the case of NUM, 'culture' is to be considered in its broadest sense, rather than reduced to high cultural products (fine arts). Another deviation from the Bourdieusian argument here is that what is at play in the case of NUM is not a definition of 'legitimate culture' as something earned outside the school environment through family education. 'Culture' relies, rather, on a broad opposition between the educated and the uneducated,[34] between the literate and illiterate and, eventually, between the compound or squatter camp mineworker – that is, the ordinary NUM member – and the union leaders who are engaged in a process of upward social and cultural mobility. I find the concept of distinction particularly heuristic in the South African context, in which social mobility is often reduced to its classist and socioeconomic dimensions, and not sufficiently analysed in terms of the cultural effect and representations it produces. Bourdieu further differentiated between 'popular' and 'distinguished' cultures and argued that 'the pure [distinguished] implies a break with the ordinary attitude towards the world, which, given the conditions in which it is accomplished, is a social break'. The sociologist extended his argument beyond the world of art: distinction is about submitting all primary urges to sophistication in domains as diverse as cooking, clothing and decoration, but also, of course, one could argue, political representation(s).[35] The example of Senzeni Zokwana, NUM president until mid-2014, is illustrative of such a process of distinction because he embodies both the emancipation of black mineworkers through and thanks to NUM, and the sophistication of its top leadership, who are arguably now more at ease socially in urbane settings than in mass meetings on the mines. After starting to work as a mineworker at President Steyn Gold mine, he rose through the ranks and became the first black person to earn a blasting certificate and be elevated to the position of 'miner', one that until 1989 had been barred to non-whites. The former NUM president is now a refined man whom I personally heard several times quoting the verses of William Shakespeare.[36] Here the concept of 'distinction' is closely linked to that of 'cultural capital', which accompanies economic and social capitals, and fits into a broader economy of symbolic violence that sets leaders in opposition to their members.[37]

The concept of distinction is also politically linked to the history of representative government. The inventors of this new form of government made sure that those elected to representative positions were of a higher social rank than those who voted them in. This mechanism was initially ensured via a poll tax (*cens* in French) and it was 'instituted with the clear conscience that elected representatives would and should be distinguished citizens, socially distinct from those who elected them'.[38] In NUM, the principle of distinction is essentially achieved through education. Those who become leaders are either more educated than ordinary members in the first place (having attended or completed high school) or they benefited from union-sponsored education as soon as they were elected. In both cases leaders gradually distance themselves from the ordinary mineworker. The principle in which a representative government is not founded on resemblance between the represented and their representatives is at the basis of both this political regime and its critique. As Manin also recalled, however, ideals of proximity and resemblance are always put forward politically and formal obstacles such as the poll tax soon vanished when it became clear that the same result could be achieved by the simple game of the electoral process.[39] In short, and as I will show in the following section, leaders are not only socially distinct from their constituency, they also legitimate their domination based on the skills and competence they presumingly own as opposed to their members.[40]

Scholarly analyses of NUM, while insisting on its changing membership base, have, of course, not fully missed that point and they have shown that NUM leaders became increasingly professionalised, socially mobile and materially at ease.[41] One crucial dimension of these changes, however, which authors like Buhlungu tend to miss or underestimate, is that they have also had a crucial impact on the way NUM leaders see their own members. Thus the top level of the organisation tends to represent the base level by opposing what I am calling 'distinguished leaders' to what they refer to as 'ordinary members'. This dimension is crucial if one is to understand the distance and contempt – that is, essentially, an absence of empathy due to the absence of identification – often expressed by top NUM leaders towards striking mineworkers since 2012. Education here proves crucial in a broader process of distinction and in representations of the membership as unsophisticated and eventually as unfit for fully participating in the life of the organisation. NUM leaders often quote their members' lack of education as a problem and they regularly insist on the need for the union to enforce efficient education strategies to make sure members 'raise' their 'class-consciousness' and 'deepen the understanding' of what their 'class interests' are.[42] In Marxist terms, a class has indeed to become self-conscious of its own systemic exploitation before it can identify its real interests. The members' alleged lack of class consciousness, however, is here mirrored by a change in the class interests – and therefore in the class consciousness – of their union leaders. This process of distinction is the result of changes in the leaders' material condition, such as, Buhlungu succinctly notes:

> the adoption of a more formal dress code, the ownership of expensive consumer items such as cars, the use of luxuriously furnished offices and the

hiring of specialised staff ... These do not apply to all leaders, nor do they apply in similar ways to leaders at different levels of the unions ... What is important [however] is that many union leaders and full-time officials give the impression that they would like to be seen as important people with an elevated social status.[43]

The SWOP reports discussed above represent what is to date the most comprehensive set of quantitative data on NUM members. Over a period of more than ten years, they surveyed union members' expectations of their union and their level of (dis)satisfaction with its service. These surveys were designed to help the union improve the quality of its services to members. NUM leaders, especially at national and regional levels but also regularly at branch level, commonly refer to SWOP's expertise. At the eighth Rustenburg regional conference in 2011, for instance, the regional secretary quoted from the 2010 SWOP report and noted, based on its findings, that union members were not familiar with NUM values. At some point during the conference, the national secretary for education suggested that one of the conference's resolutions could tackle the question of service delivery and be framed as: 'noting Swop results the conference resolves not to let new branches without assistance'. When I visited NUM's Karee Branch at Lonmin in May 2012, Jerry Ndamase, its secretary, mentioned the SWOP report in support of the observation he was making that most of the mineworkers came from the Eastern Cape. The latest SWOP 'Research Report' was handed to delegates at the 14th National Congress in May 2012, and my observations led me to conclude that expert views now permeated the union's representation of and discourse on its membership, while also serving as a point of departure for policies aimed at improving its services. Thus Frans Baleni, for instance, emphasising how democratic NUM was, told me: 'We get the University of Wits to conduct a survey, interact with our members, and our members give us feedback: what they like, what they don't like, why they are not happy. We respond to that.'[44]

The power of such data lies in the fact that it is scientifically grounded and, as such, at least partly performative. Branch office bearers may be distant from 'ordinary members' because they are generally not or are no longer underground workers, yet they are still based at mines. When it comes to their counterparts at regional and national levels, however, greater value is attached to the research reports, and one can venture that these have now become one of the primary sources of knowledge and information on members for senior union leaders. Representations of the lived realities of NUM members presented in SWOP reports are mostly quantitative, which had the unintended consequence of further feeding NUM's technocratic organisational culture described earlier as a mimicry of the corporate sector's managerial culture. The latter is indeed typically expressed through numbers, percentages, tables and graphs. In other words, there are similarities between the type of expertise SWOP reports produced on NUM and opinion polls, consumer satisfaction indexes, or the reports NGO consultants produce for government and international agencies. Another problem in commissioned surveys lies in the fact that the very questions asked – on servicing levels and quality especially – do not necessarily match the actual preoccupations of those being surveyed. They also participate in the process of producing opinions and views. In the case of NUM, the data have become authoritative because they are accepted as representing the diversity of the membership and because they are consistent with the type of professional organisation that general secretaries like Mantashe and Baleni wanted to build. As a result, approaches to union membership were based increasingly on second-hand data, which also then penetrated the organisation's official discourse on itself and, in so doing, arguably contrasted with first-hand sociological data gathered by leaders during field visits. There are, of course, many reasons why senior leaders now go less often to the field, but one of them is that they do not feel the need to do so, which is probably more comfortable for people who have achieved a certain level of distinction and distance. A consequence of this is that, for increasingly distanced leaders, the 'members' increasingly become an abstract entity to which they attach a set of stable qualities. This is clear, for instance, when they are represented as customers of an organisation that provides them with services.

Members are generally portrayed – not necessarily in negative terms – as gregarious and uneducated by their leadership. This justifies the basic role of the union, which must defend the ill-educated and isolated worker against a stronger employer. As a head-office-based legal officer told me:

> I represent members against abusive employers like in unfair dismissal, unfair labour practice … For me it appears that there is no law because if I don't know about that law then you can't tell a poor … I mean in the mining industry when you look at most of our members their level of education is very, very, very, very, very, very low, I mean you might find matric and downwards.[45]

A second dimension of the members' lack of school or union education is that it makes them difficult to lead; their particular levels of literacy, training and maturity is often what comes to differentiate ordinary members from local leaders. Leaders also view linguistic skills as decisive and English is considered to be the vernacular of modernity, as opposed to Fanakalo, South African mines' pidgin, or any other (South) African languages. English – written English one could add – is indeed the language of South Africa's labour relations. When questioned about what it meant to be a NUM leader, one branch representative told me:

> We are trained as branch members, office bearers. It is easy for us to understand through the explanation. But for us to explain to a mass it becomes a challenge. Of course some have a literacy problem, some they did not even go to school, it becomes more challenging for us to lead at branch level. Regional, national it is easy because you lead other leaders. *Q: How is it difficult to lead someone who does not know how to read and write?* MG: Of course he will insist on asking you questions that you have already explained, and you must explain it into his language other than [that of] the leadership, we use the common language being English. When it comes to members we need to use multi languages to explain things and it's time-consuming.[46]

This lack of linguistic and literary skills can even be used to justify a departure from constitutional prescriptions. An Impala Platinum South branch office bearer told me the following, which, among other elements, sheds light on the malfunctioning of the union's largest branch and its virtual implosion during and after the 2011–2012 mining strikes: 'At Impala South, the constitution says you must have the branch conference but in terms of the situation: lack of literacy of our comrades and all those stuff, we decided look it's very early to go to the conference.' What eventually happened is that a decision was taken by the region – according to my interlocutor – after it had heard the workers say at a mass meeting that they did not want a full branch conference where they would be represented by delegates – to reduce the conference to a poll in which they could all cast their ballot. I then asked:

> *Q: Okay, so they did not want delegates but themselves, they did not say they were illiterate …* MM: No it's us [the leaders] because we know, we've been in the mines, almost I'm having ten years in the mining industry, this is the eleventh year you see, so I know, I have been working with them underground, I know.[47]

Sometimes leaders argue that the low level of ordinary members' education is a problem since it prevents them from understanding the labour relations process as dictated by the law. One NUM branch leader in the platinum sector recalled an episode in which the union had declared a dispute with his employer and was about to go on strike. The process leading to the strike was suddenly interrupted when the mine made a new offer to workers which, according to the law, means that industrial actions must be postponed. Not understanding this, the workers disobeyed their leaders and went on strike. When asked why the workers did not understand the process, he answered:

> I can give you the background of the mines. The mining industry is comprised mostly of employees who are at a low level of literacy so for one to explain and for them to ... understand, it's a serious challenge. So it was explained, I was part of the meeting although I was [just] a member [at the time], even myself I can ... say we advised our colleagues our fellow comrades ... to listen to the leaders that we have elected, but some chose to say no they want to go for a strike and there was a high level of intimidation to say how we must go for a strike.[48]

Referring to the same strike during a wage negotiation process in 2011, Ecliff Tantsi, the union's national secretary for education, told his teammates: 'You know, if you are rude to me I take no offence because I am dealing with rude members.' He then looked at me before stating: 'You are leading mineworkers and the only person they trust is themselves. When you lead mineworkers you are insulted, aren't you?' The audience approved. 'You must tell them what they don't want to hear. There is nothing more painful than to face the revolt of your own members.'

THE MEMBER AS A 'BASIC' OTHER AT THE GRASSROOTS

NUM leaders often express deep respect for mineworkers, who work hard and embody the struggle for liberation they fought for throughout the years of apartheid. However, for leaders who have gone a long way since they were first employed on the mines, the figure of the 'poor' mineworker has become almost disembodied through a process of detachment that has turned the ordinary member into a 'basic' Other at the grassroots. In other words, the leaders' reference to the 'popular' has in some way become a 'populist' one that places the life and work of mineworkers on a mythical pedestal, isolated in historical time and space.[49] Moreover, by creating the image of the poor mineworker, the 'heroic mineworker' – or one could say, for that matter, the 'noble mineworker' – a distanced leadership also clashes with daily representations of ordinary members who are depicted as unsophisticated and guided by their stomachs rather than by rationality and vision. This 'distanced' leadership originates historically in the fact that NUM was formed by a group of workers who had never or were no longer working underground. This raised concerns from the union's very start in 1982, and one member of the Council of Unions of South Africa, which had been instrumental in establishing NUM, was reported to have said to the university-educated Ramaphosa: 'The trouble with you … is that you are an intellectual and you intellectuals always want to have positions so that you can have power. We uneducated people don't want power. We serve the masses in their struggle.'[50] Stories and jokes echoing this tension are commonly heard in union conferences and congresses. At the 14th National Congress in 2012, in an address Ramaphosa was invited to give in celebration of NUM's thirtieth anniversary, he told the following story:

> So today this union is able to hold a conference over five days, stay in a hotel, it's wonderful. And I always tell this story. When we had a little bit of money … we decided that we are going to give mineworkers a treat, we are going to get them to come to their first conference in Johannesburg … So we brought them to Johannesburg and when they came … we booked them in hotels. And one comrade later said to some of us: 'You know comrades this was my first time in a hotel and the very first time in a hotel bedroom.' And he said he got into the room, he looked at the bed and he saw how the bed had been made and it was nicely laid out … you know the pillow case was nice, he just looked at this and [thought]: 'I will never be able to make up this bed.' [laughter in the audience] Because he thought that once he sleeps he must make it out in the morning [laughter in the audience]. So what did your poor comrade do? He slept on the floor – and in the morning he walked out and told somebody: 'My back is sour.' So, comrades, I hope you are able to sleep peacefully in your beds!

One should not conclude hastily that all NUM leaders view their members with contempt because they deem them uneducated. The asymmetry of capitals (cultural, economic or social) between leaders and members also has concrete impacts on their respective perceptions of social situations that make up the life of the union. In 2010, during a recruitment campaign that I observed at a worksite in Centurion, some 40 kilometres north of Johannesburg, a small team of NUM leaders and officials from the PWV region met about 40 construction workers. When the NUM team arrived with bags, tee shirts and other union merchandise as well as subscription forms, the workers were taking their thirty-minute lunch break in the middle of a squalid environment of shacks (where they slept at night), tins, ladders and machines. There were no toilets on site; there was no separation between the place of work and the place of living; and most of the workers, who looked unkempt, were seated on the ground. Several lamented that they had worked for the company for six years before being formally recognised as employees and hired on a full-time basis. As soon as the NUM delegation arrived and after some of its members had introduced the recruiting campaign in isiZulu and Sesotho, an animated discussion started. The workers were angry because they were not expecting a recruitment campaign and had thought that NUM would come the day before. They were, rather, expecting a report-back on wage negotiations which, obviously, NUM could not conduct without first having members to represent in that company. This is but one of many situations I have come across or been told about in which two vastly different worlds meet: that of the organised and trained unionists on the one hand, and that of the isolated and often deprived workers on the other. A mass meeting I attended at a gold mine in 2010 gives another glimpse of how didactic NUM leaders must be when they explain complex administrative procedures to their membership in tense contexts in which money is at stake. On that day, local NUM leaders gave the following explanation to the assembled mineworkers:

> When you remember last year, there was a white man who was in charge of bonuses, who was on leave at the time, who left a lady in charge, and it was found that at that time she had to go for maternity leave. Then the office was closed and then we took a decision that the issue of bonuses had to be revisited and a decision was taken that all documents of all workers should be kept in one place in order for whoever in charge to be able to access so that workers would not complain they did not get their bonuses because of missing documents. They took the decision to put these bonuses in classified groups so that there would not be an issue that others did not get a bonus because of too many overlapping documents.

The explanation then went on. This summary is meant just to give an idea of the complexity of the issues dealt with by NUM at local mines and of how hard it is for the union to report back to its membership in clear and comprehensible terms.

This said, however, NUM leaders' levels of education should also be seen in perspective since they are not always higher than those of many ordinary union members.[51] Moreover, if the difficulties caused by the educational gap in NUM are real, as I have shown, the use of such explanations on the part of leaders to justify their sometimes difficult relationship with the base ultimately downplays the workers' intelligence and their capacity to deal with complex work-based issues, as well as, more generally, their agency and their expectations of the union. When joining NUM, many members know what they are doing and harbour expectations in terms of what they are to receive in exchange for their subscription. In the 1980s NUM did not have much to offer to its members beyond collective mobilisation and activism, which, in the context of the struggle for basic rights, dignity at work and against apartheid, was already a lot. In the context of political freedom in which the prospect of social mobility becomes more feasible, members are increasingly conscious of what they can reasonably expect from their union. Some of them thus turn into 'rational members', as one could call them by analogy with political theory.[52] This is another way to read massive NUM defections in the platinum sector since 2012. Dissatisfied members did not join another union – Amcu – only by conviction or because they were intimidated; they also consciously decided to punish NUM. This understanding of membership behaviour can be offered as one explanation for Amcu's success. Their success, however, was not as fast-spreading as the wildfire depicted by many observers. When the strike started at Lonmin on 9 August 2012, rivalry between NUM and Amcu was almost a year old and it was restricted to the Karee section of the company's operations. Karee is, of course, strategic since it includes most of the mine's shafts and the largest chunk of its underground workforce. A few months before the strike, however, out of a workforce of roughly 10 000 in Karee, 2 000 belonged to NUM, 3 000 to Amcu and 5 000 to no union. This suggests, as some workers also reported, that many initially adopted a wait-and-see stance regarding the conflict between the two unions before eventually choosing one side.[53] This situation prevailed until after the strike and NUM still had an overall membership of 53 per cent at Lonmin in September 2012, as against Amcu's 21 per cent (note that 18.5 per cent of the workforce belonged to no union).[54] Even seven months after the strike, NUM still represented about 30 per cent of Lonmin's workforce, with Amcu representing more than 50 per cent, while 20 per cent were not unionised.[55]

Workers are not simply hostages of a fight between two blocs, as suggested by NUM's argument that Amcu is a dark force behind defections. Mineworkers are capable of sophistication in their understanding of work-related situations, of complex processes and of whether it is in their best interests to join a trade union or not. What follows are some of the answers given by ordinary NUM members employed by Lonmin and AngloGold Ashanti in May 2012, when I asked them why they had joined NUM in the first place. Those among them who had joined in the 1980s or in the early 1990s tended to give answers linked to workers' solidarity, whereas more recent members seemed slightly more utilitarian in their choice. What also emerges out of their views, and in a way also supports the way leaders see their members and some of the findings relayed in SWOP reports, is that by joining the union, they acknowledge their need for a skilled intermediary to mediate their relationship with mining companies and to 'translate' the language of mine management in terms they understand. Although they phrase it in their own words, some also clearly state the 'class' difference that exists between employee and employer. Finally, all the interviewees had good, precise reasons for joining NUM, while only one had joined in a pure 'follow-my-leader' fashion.

> My intention was to, when I have a problem, for NUM to speak on behalf of me; it's just like a lawyer, it was my intention, and to advise me on a certain thing that I don't understand (joined NUM in 1999).

> I joined it because I'm here by now and NUM assisted me to get in the space of my husband [in a family unit]. Because many years ago some females did not get in mining but when there is NUM, NUM fights to have females here. So I like NUM about those things and when you have a child, NUM can help you with your child when you have no money to push the child to get in university, NUM can assist you. And many things, when we are underground, you work free because you have the rights, because of NUM, you don't work with the stress, you are free. So I say we have the rights because of NUM, NUM fights in the mining for us (joined NUM in 2009).

> I joined this NUM because I could see there is a difference between the employer and the employee so I just wanted someone to be my representative and then someone who could talk for me in fact if I want to practise my right (joined NUM in 1985).[56]

> I think it's part of the company's policy or even the Labour Relations Act that I've got the right to be a member of an association I'm willing to be; then I was not forced but I decided to join NUM (joined NUM in 2004).[57]

The views expressed in this sample of 'ordinary members' give an insight into the complexity of motives – albeit briefly expressed and involving some reconstruction of faded memories – that make one join an organisation. As Dhiraj Nite and Paul Stewart remarked in their introduction to the volume they edited on the social biographies of mineworkers, 'These then are the stories of "ordinary" people. Yet what comes to the fore challenges the very idea that there is any such thing as an "ordinary" person.'[58] Another element that impacts on the relationship between mineworkers and the union is also connected, as we shall see below, to the fact that younger generations of workers tend to be more educated, which in turn generates a split among the membership itself (as noted in SWOP reports too). A NUM shaft steward described their possibly different behaviour in the following terms:

> The young guys are not recognizing the union either. They believe that NUM is only for the older people. They regard us, those people working in the coal industry, as less educated people. They assume that they know all company procedures. I had a case. One young guy was charged with negligence. He did not want me to represent him. He hired his own lawyer. The lawyer thought to see the case at the CCMA, whereas the case was still at the mine level.[59]

Many NUM leaders, with their modernising agendas, still subscribe to old paternalistic representations of their workforce. This was suggested by a former NUM shaft steward at Impala, who became a local Amcu leader post-2012. Recalling the 2009 strike meeting in which NUM deputy president Pete Matosa was wounded in a clash with angry workers, the shaft steward explained how he answered the national leader after the latter had tried to press workers towards accepting management's offer and dropping their demands. He took the microphone: 'I told Matosa: we are not kids. Don't speak to us as our grandparents. There is new blood in the mining industry now.' He then further told me: 'My father was a mineworker and NUM was telling our parents: if you do this and that you'll lose your jobs. We are not like them anymore, we are new blood coming with the transformation of the industry.'[60]

7

The Learning Organisation

LEADERSHIP DEVELOPMENT VS WORKER CONTROL

NUM is and has always been conceived as a school. Referring to 'pastoral power', in the footsteps of Michel Foucault, as one type of leadership that is 'formative' and 'redemptive' because it seeks to involve those it leads through a display of empathy and selflessness, Moodie explained:

> Marcel Golding, who joined Cyril Ramaphosa as deputy general secretary, talked about how important it was for the union to deliver in redemptive terms as well as in practical terms. The union led by producing new 'selves' (in Foucault's terms), forming trade unionists. This involved intense educational work on the meaning of unionism and productive leadership with tactical skills. It was crucially important to listen to what the workers themselves had to say. Golding told me: 'Never, ever, just take the liberty of deciding for them. They must decide what to do on their own and I think that was one of the good things we learned. That mine-workers were not fools. They knew what they wanted despite [low] levels of education.'[1]

Eddie Majadibodu, head of the union's production pillar, expressed this very well when I asked him what he thought of the trajectory of renowned past NUM leaders:

> First of all and I am proud about NUM is that it has become the school of [the] working class but also the school of prosperity. Because these people you are talking about all come from NUM. Now one of the key decisions of NUM was leadership development, was to build leadership. Somewhere in

1986, 1987, 1988, NUM sent a number of people to Cuba to study as engineers because they did not have those opportunities here … And they came back and some of them are in the mines. But on the other side we also built people politically … In NUM we have got a particular way of nurturing the talent in leadership skills and I think so far we have done very well.[2]

This view of the union as a school was also put to me by former general secretary Frans Baleni:

NUM can develop a person; when I joined NUM I had no matric but through the exposure in the union, I completed matric through correspondence; I went to university through correspondence; I have got a degree today through NUM … I did Social Development Studies at the University of Johannesburg. I have done lots of international training programmes and so on … So the union gives you full training and also it gives exposure, you know you are tested; I've been given things that I had never done and we've been told: that's your job do it … and you start from scratch and you end up knowing how to do these things. So I have been an organiser, I have been a health and safety person, I have been an educator, I have been a chief negotiator and I'm still doing that. I have been marketing the union, so that's a good training background. You also obviously get exposed and people can get attracted to you, be it politics, be it boards [of directors]. I mean I serve in the board of the Development Bank of South Africa. I serve in the Council of the University of Johannesburg, I serve in the Rand Mutual Assurance which deals with compensation of mineworkers, I serve … [as a] trustee of the Mineworkers Investment Company.[3]

It was the ambition of the NUM leadership school to empower mineworkers, who had been used as cannon fodder by the mines for a century, through giving them access to education, knowledge and, therefore, to social mobility. In front of an audience of young NUM leaders gathered at the Elijah Barayi Memorial Training Centre (EBMTC), the union's president declared in October 2011: 'NUM's dream is to build doctors and engineers out of mineworkers' children, people who have PhDs in mining engineering. Being a shaft steward is not the end of the road; you have to study … My dream is to see you say: "I came to the mine with a grade 10, I left with a PhD"'.[4]

Such an endeavour to educate the masses and produce new emancipated selves as part of South Africa's struggle against apartheid is, of course, unique neither to NUM nor to South Africa. The union was born as a late offshoot of the black consciousness movement, whose iconic figure, Steve Biko, had been a decisive inspiration for the 1976 Soweto uprising against Bantu Education (of which Biko, who attended university, had been one victim), as well as generally for the youth that continued fighting apartheid throughout the 1980s. Far more popular at the time than the old guard of imprisoned ANC leaders, Biko had established the all-black South African Students Organisation (Saso) in 1968 and developed his 'black consciousness' doctrine. The heir of a long tradition of Africanism, he was influenced by, among others, the thought of Franz Fanon. Opposing apartheid's negative discrimination between 'white' and 'non-white', Biko turned the stigmata upside down and prescribed the use of the positively connoted term 'black'. Central to Biko's thought was his idea that 'the most potent weapon in the hands of the oppressor is the mind of the oppressed'. Hence black people firstly had to redefine and reinvest in their own value systems and educate themselves to fight apartheid. Political and civil society organisations were regarded as instruments of mass education for the oppressed black majority in South Africa or, one would say in another echo to Foucault, as institutions of 'counter-dressage'.[5]

Another important influence felt in South Africa as elsewhere in the decolonising world has been that of Brazilian educator and pedagogue Paulo Freire. After fleeing his native Brazil in 1964, Freire developed and practised a pedagogy of 'critical education'. Critical pedagogy, a 'pedagogy of knowing' in which educators and learners are part of a process of mutual empowerment, was born out of Freire's experience of the oppressive educational system in Brazil, and it was designed to teach learners how to think, with a view to challenging cultural and ideological domination. According to Freire, 'education is always a political act … educators have to make political choices because it is impossible to remain neutral in education'.[6] The People's Education movement in South Africa, which was created in 1986, walked in Freire's footsteps and influenced both the struggle against apartheid education and thought on the production of a new education system after its demise.[7] Literacy and the participation of learners in the learning process are central to Freire's theory of education. The black consciousness movement, including Steve Biko himself, was involved in literacy programmes,[8] and a Paulo Freire Institute of South Africa was established in 2004 at the University of KwaZulu-Natal.[9]

Despite its ambitions, mass education in NUM turned into, I argue, mostly cadreship development. Rather than benefiting from training opportunities, the majority of mineworkers saw their educational status relatively unchanged, while a minority of more fortunate unionists were being developed thanks to and through their organisation. NUM can therefore be regarded as a school with an ambiguously conceived role, right from the start, in its joint endeavour to develop worker control – that is, internal democracy – through leadership development. In a 1990 NEC meeting report, a paragraph dedicated to worker control read: 'One of the founding principles of the union and our federation is worker control, but this has not been placed in the forefront of our organisational work.' Interestingly, this subsection of the meeting's minutes is entitled 'Development of Worker Leadership', which shows that in the minds of the union leaders of the time, there was a confusion between worker control and the development of skilled leaders at the grassroots. In the same meeting, it was decided to hold an annual 'week of education' in order 'to remedy the trade union "illiteracy"'. Out of the 30 000 shaft stewards listed by NUM at the time, the union was planning to reach out to at least 1 000 during that week.[10] The same idea of leadership development as a prerequisite for worker control appears in a 2003 report by general secretary Gwede Mantashe, where section 2.5 on leadership development reads:

> Our union was founded on the principle of worker control. Worker control is about workers being able to run their organisation. It is this principle that makes our organisation bias towards recruiting workers when vacancies occur in the operational structures. We always had problems in getting workers filling technical positions. We are beginning to reap the fruits of our long-term strategy of investing in skilling our cadres. We can fill any position today. Our investment remains intensive.

And indeed, in the three years prior to this report, 1 081 stewards had been inducted by NUM. In 2002, 172 stewards from four regions had gone through the intermediate course, 139 through the advanced course and 55 branch educators had been trained, while 41 women had completed a course on 'women and the law' and 121 stewards had done a labour law course. Within three years, 394 'comrades' had received a computer course and 300 cadres had been through the Labour Studies programme offered by the Technikon Natal. In 2000, 23 NUM members went through the Effective Leadership Programme at the Kagiso Leadership School; and in 2002, 24 'comrades enrolled in a certificate programme in the Sociology of Work with RAU [Rand Afrikaans University, now the University of Johannesburg]'.[11]

But producing skilled leaders as the apartheid regime and the colour bar were collapsing also meant deepening the gap between ordinary members, who were confined to the mines and the hardship of underground labour, and NUM leaders who were now spoilt for choice with the number of career opportunities opening up. In other words, the dual task NUM had assigned to itself since its foundation – (i) training a skilled and numerous cadreship to maintain the union organisation, conscientise its rank and file and withstand the mining industry's fire power; and (ii) 'broadening access to effective education to the mass of our membership; and ensuring that education becomes an instrument of changing the oppressive and exploitative situation that mineworkers find themselves in' – clashed with reality on the ground.[12] While NUM could indeed achieve the first task based on its own will, the second was intertwined with the structural foundations of South Africa's mining industry and depended on the joint involvement of the union, the State and mining bosses. NUM's two educational goals therefore also played against each other. The production of a stratum of competent unionists is but one of the factors that led to the crisis the union now faces. Authors such as Michels have observed such conflicting dynamics:

> It is undeniable that all these educational institutions for the officials of the party and of the labor organizations tend, above all, towards the artificial creation of an élite of the working class, of a caste of cadets composed of persons who aspire to the command of the proletarian rank and file. Without wishing it, there is thus effected a continuous enlargement of the gulf which divides the leaders from the masses.[13]

This historical observation, however, should not lead one to conclude that NUM's attention to membership education has been just wishful thinking; the facts suggest otherwise. It nevertheless implies that when it came to educating ordinary mineworkers, the union was dependent on the mining industry as well; it could not rely solely on its own programmes of action. In short, the union's aim to provide its members – and more generally mineworkers – with elementary education must be viewed in the context of apartheid and its immediate aftermath, the 'transformation' era. At the time, black people had long been deprived of equal access to education and held back, through the Bantu Education system, in the second row of a two-tier educational system. NUM always showed concern for providing its members with education opportunities: in 1993, for instance, it had negotiated with mining houses to have voter education sessions conducted at mines during the first democratic election campaign.[14] In October 1994, the same year as South Africa's first democratic government introduced legislation about Adult Basic Education and Training (Abet) as part of its Reconstruction and Development Programme (RDP), NUM and the Chamber of Mines signed an agreement on Abet.[15] NUM had for its part held its first Abet workshop in July 1993, and the drive for Abet spread from the top in Cosatu and NUM, before spreading to all union structures via dedicated training sessions for shaft stewards.[16] In the mid-1990s, the question of the involvement of the union in the planning and provision of basic education to mine-workers became one of the main problems in implementing Abet programmes. As Menzi Mthwecu wrote:

'Management are doing their own thing. They do not involve workers when making decisions about the classes.' This simple statement by a union shaft steward summarizes the problem-focus of this study. Historically, in South Africa, black workers have mostly not been involved in the planning, implementation and evaluation of their education and training programs. The non-participatory nature of programs has been a factor in program loss of legitimacy and poor participation.[17]

Mthwecu also pointed out that 'the quality of education provided to mineworkers is suspect, to put it mildly'. Needs in the mining industry were immense, if one considers that out of 679 000 workers employed on the mines in 1994, 422 000 or 62 per cent would then have been 'illiterate', which here is taken to mean 'people who need ABET'.[18] Mthwecu put these figures against the wider context:

Among South Africans in formal employment, the lack of basic education is reflected in a National Manpower Commission Report (NMC, 1986) which states that: 30% of the labour force had no formal education, 36% had primary education or below, 31% had secondary education, and only 3% had diplomas and degrees. These figures mean that about 66 percent of adults in formal employment need ABET.[19]

Mthwecu further observed that, in addition to the limited numbers that accessed Abet courses, the quality of what was provided was also problematic:

According to my own experience as an Adult Education Officer in the mines, qualitative problems in Adult Basic Education Programs can be summarized in the following manner: The curriculum is mostly irrelevant to the needs of adults; is biased in terms of class, race and gender; and poorly imparts knowledge and skills needed on the job. There is also a lack of competent educators. ABET programs do not lead to qualifications which are recognized industry wide or nation wide. Teaching and learning facilities are inadequate. Other stakeholders, like unions, educators, and learners, are not involved in decision making. It is now obvious to say that apartheid policies and practices are the root causes for this situation.[20]

The union's involvement or will to get involved in Abet was, of course, linked to 'educational' motives, like 'getting rid of illiteracy in the mines', or to broader ambitions, such as 'to enable workers to change the country'. But Mthwecu also points out that NUM's involvement in Abet was largely reactive: 'To some extent, some unions became involved in education and training issues as a response to management initiated programs ... In early discussions with the union general secretary, before I even arrived at NUM, he informed me that there were "management initiatives that were awaiting" union response.'[21]

All in all, education and training in NUM, beyond nationally designed leadership and staff courses, seems to have faded into very little in the structures dedicated to educating members at local level. The 2004 special congress report noted:

> Over the years, these structures have developed life of their own and have shifted away from the centre ... The adverse effect of this is that the main structures do not see education as being central to the work of the union. It has been shifted to the periphery. Every year our education campaigns are a disaster. No one wants to take full responsibility.[22]

A 2008 Kimberley region report further added:

> Although we have signed ABET agreements in many branches, little has been done in terms of implementation of these agreements. There is no programme in place, no monitories of classes, no full-time attendance with full pay by our members. This programme ... is relegated to the periphery. We need stocktaking and revisit this area of work. ABET classes should be viewed as a necessary basic education that provides access to further Education and Training.[23]

According to the latest SWOP report, even if education and training were provided by NUM in branches, a high level of dissatisfaction among members remained. Members regularly complained, for instance, that it 'is not recognised as formal education', or that 'NUM organizes limited training and education for us – for example we are currently doing ABET which ends at level 4 – what happens after that?' Another worker stated that 'they provide training to NUM officials only'. The lack of professional mobility resulting from the lack of training opportunities for members thus remained problematic and, indeed, even if training was provided it was not seen as linked to any improvement in workers' circumstances: 'People go for internal training but they are not being paid according to their knowledge gained,' one worker argued. There were also several mentions of the fact that mine-workers were striving for more than just Abet in terms of educational standards or that NUM did not pay enough attention to the upward mobility that should logi-cally follow members' training and education.[24] This is a crucial reminder that even where Abet is in place it remains 'basic' education, not professional development. This said, however, a full assessment of Abet policies in mining would require an exploration of the ways in which ordinary members and mineworkers take advan-tage (or not) of the programmes on offer in order to advance their careers, and whether professional mobility results mainly for NUM leaders or whether it also results in career mobility for ordinary union members.

Twenty years into South Africa's democratic regime, progress in terms of skills development in the mining industry proves unsatisfactory. According to the 2004 Mining Charter as well as the Skills Development Act (No. 97 of 1998), the mining industry, together with government[25] and trade unions, is required to 'expand the skills base of HDSAs [Historically Disadvantaged South Africans] in order to serve the community'.[26] Stakeholders in the mining industry had ten years to reach the goals set by the Mining Charter, and the Department of Mineral Resources con-ducted a mid-term assessment of their achievements. The report submitted to the minister concluded the following on skills development:

> The assessment of this Charter element further indicates innate inhibitions against progress on skills development, which include, albeit not limited to, lack of management support for staff participating in Adult Basic Education and Training (ABET), as evidenced by recalling of staff from classes to accel-erate production, loss of bonuses for ABET attendees and classes arranged after working hours, typically non-proximal to employees residences. Con-sequently, the prevailing conditions are less attractive for employees to enrol on the programs of skills development.[27]

Susan Shabangu, minister of mineral resources at the time, further added that 'the bulk of mining companies continue to harbour illiterate workers'.[28]

JB MARKS: A TOOL OF EXCELLENCE IN THE HANDS OF A FEW

'Turning tragedy into triumph – that's the inspirational story of comrade Ntsane Monaheng of the Free State; the former mine store worker at Beatrix mine was fired four times, and each time he was reinstated through the National Union of

Mineworkers (NUM) intervention.' Those are the first words of a mineworker's success story reported in one issue of *NUM News*, the union's official newsletter. His testimony, as reported in the publication, is worth quoting at length:

'I wanted to go to school so that I can be empowered,' he said ... Monaheng graduated with an MBA qualification from Mancosa with distinction in May 2012. He came top of his class and he was also awarded the best dissertation trophy for his MBA by Mancosa.

'I only had matric when I started working in the mine in 1988, but now I have an MBA ... *ke rata ho leboha* [I would like to thank] NUM,' said Monaheng with a grin on his face. 'If it was not for the NUM, I wouldn't be where I am today,' he added. 'I want to thank the NUM for being with me. The union has been with me through rough patches; at times when steward bashing tactics were rife, NUM was with us,' said the former branch chairperson at Orix Mine.

In 1999, Monaheng approached his employer, then Orix Mine, asking for financial help to study further but he was snubbed. 'I approached the company and said that I want to go to school and they refused, but NUM allowed me to go and study further ... this union paid for my studies,' he said. The NUM paid for Monaheng's tuition fees through the JB Marks Education Trust, established by the NUM in 1997 to advance its members and dependents educational interest ...

The MBA was not the first and only qualification he obtained through NUM; the former Free State regional deputy secretary is armed with four qualifications paid for by the union. Monaheng holds a Bachelor of Business Administration degree from the University of Wales in the United Kingdom. In 2005 he graduated with a postgraduate diploma in labour law from the University of Johannesburg. He also has a qualification in employee relations from Unisa under his belt. Monaheng aims to use the skills he has acquired through the MBA to help bridge the gap between the mining houses and the union. 'The relationship is sour because of the missing link. We need to improve relations between employers and the union at the branch level.'[29]

On the website of the Mineworkers Investment Company one can access another such testimony from a female NUM member:

My mother is a single parent, she used to take care of me and my brother and I have made her aware that I am not going to make it if I am not studying.

> I wasn't ready to go away and work … She was not in a position to fund my university fee … or … my tuition. So I actually applied for a student loan, which was going to be the only way I was going to survive. I was sponsored by JB Marks when I was at the University of Natal, that is when my mother was a mine worker.

In the video from which it is extracted, the above testimony is complemented by the words of Jako Mokgosi, principal officer of NUM's JB Marks Education Trust Fund: 'The JB Marks Education Trust Fund was established for the benefit of the members of NUM, their spouses and their dependents. NUM realised that there was high illiteracy levels amongst its members and that it wanted to do something about it.'[30]

The above success stories are paradigmatic of the paradox illustrated in the previous section of this chapter. The success of Monaheng is marketed in the article's title ('Mineworker Graduates with an MBA') as that of a mineworker – an ordinary mineworker, one reads – when Monaheng in fact worked above ground and had already completed secondary education when he joined Gold Fields. Moreover, the article suggests that Monaheng had been a union shaft steward for some time, including at the regional level. Finally, his last statement indicates that his development can be instrumental in bridging the gap between 'the mining houses and the union'. One might have expected him to say something closer to 'empower mineworkers in their class struggle against capitalist employers' or, at least, something like 'paving the way for mineworkers to rise in their companies'. In other words, through such a story one is faced with a sore point in the type of workers' education proposed by NUM. Rather than in membership development (opening new professional opportunities up to union members), it is in leadership development that NUM has proven successful over the years.

In the history of the development of black independent trade unions in South Africa, Buhlungu recalls, most black leaders had no university education (exceptions such as that of Cyril Ramaphosa can be counted on the fingers of one hand) and, although some had education to matric, many such as Mantashe slowly developed into organic intellectuals thanks to the education they gained via their organisation. He then argues, based on available data, that 'since 1994 there has been a remarkable improvement in the educational levels of Cosatu members'. Buhlungu explains this change in several ways: first, younger Cosatu shop stewards tended to be better educated; second, retrenchments in the workforce reduced the number of the least educated and skilled workers; third, Cosatu comprises a significant number of public sector and white-collar workers; fourth, the structure of the labour market has evolved and a higher education standard is now expected from new recruits; and 'finally, there is a growing trend for union members, particularly those in leadership positions, to enrol for part-time and distance-education courses'. He then predicts the consequences of such trends:

> These findings have far-reaching implications for the future of Cosatu … While workers with little or no formal education led the mobilisation of the struggle period, the period of democratic consolidation seems to rely on those with higher levels of educational attainment … Thus in the long term unions are going to increasingly represent the winners – namely, those workers who by virtue of their education stand to gain materially from the unfolding processes of transition in South African society. This will accentuate contradictions between these workers and the new losers – those workers inside and outside the workplace who by virtue of their limited education and skill stand to lose from current processes of work restructuring and its associated retrenchments.[31]

However, Buhlungu fails to draw full conclusions from his analysis. First, his argument mixes up the results of surveys concerning ordinary union members and union leaders, which maintains the confusion between these two very different categories of individual. Second, he does not connect high levels in the training of union personnel with much lower levels in membership education. This contradiction is nevertheless central to the argument I put forward here regarding NUM: the union never fully had the education and training of its membership in hand; most relied on general education provided by the State, as well as on the initiatives that mining houses undertook to train their workforce. NUM may have professed mass education to be its central mission, yet it remained focused on cadreship development, which, in turn, boosted the career opportunities of elected leaders rather than those of ordinary members. The RDOs who have waged major strikes since 2012 can thus be seen as the 'losers' Buhlungu describes. Under apartheid the educational gap between union leaders and members hardly showed since both categories followed their careers under the glass ceiling of the colour bar – despite its relative porosity in the last decade of apartheid. Changes in the post-apartheid workplace were crucial in deepening the educational and career gap in NUM, a process in which the increasing professionalisation of the union also played a part. As I showed in chapters 2 and 3, this was no accidental evolution; the making of a centralised organisation went hand in hand with the production of a top-down elitist structure, based on a skilled leadership. In other words, in practice, NUM was never really shaped into a university for mineworkers but into a leadership school.

NUM created the JB Marks Education Trust Fund in 1997, overseen by the MIT, to which the main financial contributor is the MIC. The fund is central to the union's self-assigned educational mission; on its home page one reads: 'NUM has always been an advocate for the advancement of its members in terms of health and safety, collective bargaining, legal issues and education. When the union was formed in 1982, a huge number of its members were totally illiterate. Furthermore, NUM has also been a strong advocate for the establishment of the Adult Basic Education programs in the workplace.'[32] 'Education is power', one also reads on the MIT's presentation of its beneficiary, the JB Marks Education Trust Fund, whose logo pictures John Beaver Marks, a communist leader and ANC member in the 1940s and 1950s, and the founding president of the African Mineworkers' Union (Amwu).[33]

The mission of the JB Marks Education Trust Fund is to be a 'fountain of hope and inspiration to fill future career opportunities'. Its 'main objectives' are 'to provide funding to members of NUM and their dependants; to provide funding to dependants of NUM officials …; ensure that NUM members and their dependants gain competitive advantage in the labour market; … make a contribution towards transformation of the mining, energy and construction industries; ensure that graduates identify with NUM and its working class orientation'. Applications for funding can be made by 'a paid up NUM member/official or a former NUM member/official who has retired, become retrenched or disabled'; 'a deceased NUM member/official's dependants'; 'the immediate family i.e. spouse or dependent children of [a] NUM member/official'. The bursaries awarded by the JB Marks Education Trust Fund are for studies beyond compulsory education. It can support individuals towards completion of high school (grades 10 to 12), but the fund is more specifically designed for tertiary education leading to the award of a degree (postgraduate studies are not covered). Applications are channelled through NUM's regional offices, which are supposed to dispatch forms to aspiring applicants. The mere fact that the administrative process involved in applying is – as is common in such cases – a complex one already limits the reach of the fund when it comes to the mass of ordinary NUM members. Prospective applicants must provide an official payslip to prove membership of NUM, copies of the student's latest results, an acceptance letter or a letter showing that the student has applied for study at an institution, as well as copies of identity documents and so on. Another major limitation is that while the fund covers registration, tuition, textbooks and accommodation, it does not include a stipend.[34] This means that workers would either have to work while they study or be released by their companies on full or partial pay in order to do so.

Ordinary members' access to the NUM education fund appears to be highly problematic. In one of the panels at the 9th International Mining History Congress that took place in Johannesburg from 17 to 20 April 2012, a few NUM members whose life histories had been compiled in the book *Mining Faces*[35] recounted their stories. At one stage, Luke Mathebula, whose story is told in chapter 13 of the book, unexpectedly declared: 'I am not a big fan of NUM.' He explained that he had joined the union in 1986 and was later retrenched and left with only R5 000, which was why he was 'bitter', he said.[36] A moment later, one of the panel organisers asked Richard Xati, NUM Carletonville deputy secretary for education, to answer. Xati launched into a legitimist tirade: 'I joined the industry in 1991. [A] mineworker is a well-respected person now thanks to NUM. There is no union of choice in this industry except NUM, which is also a leader in Cosatu. We are now far better than workers in other sectors.'

One of the academics present in the room contended that the hostels were still problematic (Paul Stewart), and another that the union's action was also limited by the decline in gold mining, which now only allows it to negotiate the best possible retrenchment packages (Dunbar Moodie). Richard Xati then summarised the actions the JB Marks Education Trust Fund undertook to promote the tertiary education of former mineworkers' children – if they could prove they were members – and he vehemently added: 'I am a beneficiary of that … my child is'. This last point precisely reveals some of the problems linked to beneficiation from the JB Marks Education Trust Fund. One problem is the contentious issue of publicising the fund and bringing it to members' attention. Instead of doing so, it seems that some union officials and leaders have been taking advantage of the opportunity to advance their own skills or to give their relatives access to higher education. This is a complaint that I heard throughout NUM meetings and conferences. Access to bursaries, which are significant but also limited in number if one considers the total number of potential applicants,[37] has therefore primarily remained the privilege of a few leaders. One can venture that it is probably not in the best personal interests of local leaders to fully publicise the opportunity that the fund represents. This is clear in the confusions around the target of the fund, which were exposed in a 2008 regional report:

> It is crucial to report that our fund administration is superb. However at branch level not got up to standard, we need leaders who had passion for development through Mass participation and activism, formal and informal education. JB Marks Education Trust produced 425 graduates since 2000 and 220 new graduates in 2006 … NUM has capacity to take ordinary worker with no formal Education and transform him/her into an organic intellectual. Today any leader, any union official can go to school. The union pro-

vides us with good bursaries for members and their dependants. We must
release ourselves from chains of poverty through Education and Training
e.g. Rock Drill Operator must be able to give birth to Mine Engineer.[38]

Clearly, behind its claimed commitment to mineworkers' education, there is confusion in the union as to what the JB Marks Education Trust Fund is really for.
This reflects in the alternative and undifferentiated use of terms such as 'ordinary
worker', 'organic intellectual', 'member' or 'leader' to talk about potential beneficiaries of the fund. Yet in the organisational architecture of NUM, the mission of the
fund is clearly not that of cadreship development: that is the role of the EBMTC,
discussed in the next section.

And indeed, figures on the dispatch and return of application forms tend to confirm the lack of involvement in distribution and follow-up by leaders at regional
and local levels. In 2007, for instance, 2 439 application forms were distributed in 12
NUM regions; only 806 were returned (32.3 per cent). Return rates were as low as
4 per cent in the Eastern Cape, 10 per cent in Natal and 19 per cent in Rustenburg.
Carletonville was the best-performing region with a 68 per cent return rate and
51 applications approved (21 per cent). Approval rates were 27.2 per cent union-
wide and reached up to 47 per cent in Natal. These already high acceptance rates
increase if one excludes those forms that were incomplete (99 union-wide). Return
and approval rates were even lower in 2008. Records about incomplete application
forms strongly suggest that the poor quality of many applications might explain
records about the fund not being able to grant all its available bursaries every year.
Nonetheless, to nuance the idea that leaders take advantage of the fund one should
stress that top union leadership do not seem to do so. In 2007, the fund received
three applications from head office and only one was approved, just as in the following year when Rissik Street submitted four forms and only one bursary was
granted.[39] Moreover, return rates have now dramatically increased and 1 780 forms
(59.3 per cent) out of 3 000 distributed were returned nationally in 2012.[40]

In Rustenburg, however, the situation proved particularly bad. In 2009, only 20
forms out of 400 allocated to the region were returned (5 per cent). This figure was
164 out of 800 (20.5 per cent) in 2010 and 80 out of 600 (13.3 per cent) in 2011.
According to the region's 2011 secretariat report, 'most of the branches are not
bringing the application forms back; some are submitting forms that are clean showing that they never issued none to needy members at branches'. 'Forms not reaching
real people we need them [to reach]', the report continued, before highlighting yet
another limitation: the fact that many mineworkers live far away from their families
makes it even more difficult for them to potentially benefit from the fund.[41]

Faculty	Qualification	Number
Finance	Accountants	84
	Commerce and economists	61
		145
Health Science	Doctors	14
	Nurses	9
	Chemistry	10
	Zoologist	2
	Veterinary surgeons	4
	Genetics	3
		42
Engineering	Civil Engineering	15
	Mining Engineering	5
	Geology and Extraction Metallurgy	10
	Electrical Engineering	55
	Chemical Engineering	9
	Mechanical/Motor Engineering	22
	Quantity Surveying and Architectural Science	7
		123
Agricultural Science	Environmental Health/Science	13
	Food Management	4
	Analytical Chemistry	20
		37
Information Technology	IT technicians	65
	PC Engineering	3
	Computer System/Science	7
		75
Law	Lawyers	15
	Political Science	1
	International Studies	2
		18
Education	Teaching	15
		15
Humanities	Human Resources (HR)	49
	Psychology	10
	Public Management	11
	Public Relations	6
	Social Work	15
		91
General	Business Management, Journalism, Drama	127
	Marketing, Receptionist, etc.	
		127
Total		**673**

Table 7.1:   JB Marks Education Trust Fund graduates, 1997–2011
Source: MIT Annual Report, 2012

A second problem of major importance in the failure of the fund to benefit mostly ordinary NUM members is that it remains focused on tertiary education. However, before 'a machine driller gives birth to a mining engineer' or 'a "DAKA BOY" gives birth to an architect' or 'a general worker gives birth to an electrical engineer',[42] they must have either completed high school or have children who did so. In other words, it seems that the way in which the fund was framed was not adapted to the more basic needs of many ordinary workers who do not have the necessary cultural capital to even think about studying, and would first have to complete their primary education, or secondary education in the case of their children (education is now compulsory for all South Africans from the age of 7 to 15). Table 7.1 shows the distribution of JB Marks graduates since the inception of the fund, by branch of tertiary education. In 2011, out of 36 graduates supported by the fund, not one had completed a secondary education qualification. The JB Marks Education Trust Fund had paid close to R13 million in bursaries that year, and more than half of this amount was allocated to the payment of tuition fees.[43]

THE ELIJAH BARAYI MEMORIAL TRAINING CENTRE

In October 2011, I attended a one-week NUM leadership training course at the Johannesburg-based and NUM-owned Elijah Barayi Memorial Training Centre. NUM's 'leadership school', the centre was named after the late Elijah Barayi, a founding father of NUM, its first deputy president and the first president of Cosatu. During the same week, the EBMTC also hosted training on HIV and Aids for unionists from South Africa and other African countries, with one guest from the Fédération Générale du Travail de Belgique. The training was organised by Mercy Sekano, a union employee and the EBMTC's executive director. When I met him, Sekano was still new in his position and he was to embark on a Master's in Business Administration in the following year. A professional union educator and a former regional secretary of the South African Democratic Teachers Union (Sadtu), Sekano had gone through a rigorous recruiting process before being appointed.

Attending the course were 23 trainees – 9 women and 14 men – all of them NUM leaders of diverse ages, leadership levels and experience in the union, and from various regions and branches. Most of them had never been trained in Johannesburg and their respective regions had selected them for this training. When asked for how many years they had been involved with NUM, their answers varied from 2 to 17 years, although 14 of the participants had been in the union for less than eight years. Sekano calculated that their added years of union experience made for a total of 202 years, and he reminded them that they were attending NUM's 'university'. This university, he added, was not based on the typical knowledge dispensed in universities through books, as, for example, with sociology, but was more interactive and participatory. Harking back to Paulo Freire's pedagogy, this also had a specific meaning in the context of union education in South Africa's mining industry. This was strikingly revealed to me in an interview I once had with a NUM regional coordinator. Referring to a political school course we had attended together at EBMTC, I questioned him on the role played by the course 'instructor' in it. In his answer it appeared that the word I had picked was inappropriate to describe the person who acted as 'teacher' and that my choice was wrong because it suggested a top-down dynamic:

> My view on the thing would be the same as that of the [seeking the right word] the facilitator … *Q: The facilitator?* JM: [laughter] That is what you call the instructor … *Q: Oh yes, sorry, and I made a mistake by calling him instructor?* JM: The instructor yes ah ah [laughter] … *Q: What is the difference … Why does it make you laugh that I called him instructor?* JM: It's because the word or term or designation instructor is used in the mines where you have Raphaël as an instructor and what he says is the end of story, you only have to follow what he says. He is management, it's like a supervisor of the people who are undergoing training, now he instructs you to do this and that in order to comply and you just have to do this and that for you to comply. It is not contested, it is not debated and the facilitator is somebody that is going to introduce to you and say this book has got a hundred pages and when looking at this book it stands like this and this. His work is to do a, b, c, d, now if you would have then to use this kind of arrangements, what else can you come up with in relation to this book? It then opens a discussion for these people to participate and come to some kind of a conclusion. That is the facilitation.[44]

The EBMTC[45] was opened on 4 December 1993 as a non-profit organisation designed for 'training and development of steward and leadership'.[46] The 'college' is located in Johannesburg's historic Yeoville neighbourhood and it is yet another subsidiary of the Mineworkers Investment Trust that 'services' NUM. In other words, NUM uses the EBMTC and deploys some of its education and training staff members to it. Its mandate within the NUM galaxy 'is to facilitate the logistics and other related requirements of the National Union of Mineworkers members to participate in Educational Courses'.[47] The college counts four conference rooms named after prominent figures from the union movement and the struggle against racial discrimination (Sam Tambani, Moses Kotane, Sol Plaatjie and Jeffrey Njuza), as well as offices, accommodation and food facilities. It is used by the NUM education department to hold courses relevant to union work in subjects such as Skills Development and Employment Equity, Labour Law, Women and the Law, Job Grading, Basic Economics, Political School, Minutes Writing and Report Writing, Leadership Development, and Arbitration. Other courses include induction for shop stewards, introductory and intermediate computer training, workshops on topics such as negotiation and health and safety, and workshops for specific roles such as that of treasurer or trustee.

The EBMTC is an independent entity – although its board consists mostly of NUM national office bearers and officials – entitled to host meetings with clients others than NUM, in conference rooms that can accommodate groups of 15 to 200. It is fully equipped with conference facilities to event management market standards and is also available for events other than training.[48] In addition to its Yeoville training centre, NUM made a crucial step in advancing its educational enterprise when it invested R45 million,[49] via its real estate subsidiary Numprop, and opened, as of 2012/2013, a second and much larger training centre in Midrand, about 20 kilometres north of Yeoville and within walking distance of the Midrand Gautrain station.

In 2011, the EBMTC had 25 permanent or temporary staff, including its director and four national educators, and it was running about 20 national courses per annum in addition to decentralised courses at the regional level.[50] When I spoke to Mercy Sekano in 2011, the target of the NUM education and training unit was to train, through the college, 553 shaft stewards per year. The role of national educators is to teach courses, help induct branch staff and support the regions since the position of full-time regional educator was frozen. Each one of them is given three regions to support (out of 11 regions and 900 NUM branches). Its executive director described the centre as 'a strategic unit' since many leaders such as former NUM general secretary Frans Baleni had come from it, and because 'most of the educators are used on negotiations to help the shop stewards and give them ammunitions'. NUM dedicates significant resources to its education and training unit – more than any other union in South Africa. At the time of my fieldwork it was investing around R4 million per annum just for training, excluding operating costs. As an example of these costs, Sekano mentioned a one-week intermediate computer training course in which NUM had invested R200 000.[51]

The NUM Education Strategic Plan 2005–2010 summarises the union's goals in terms of education. Once again it reflects the paradoxical tension between members' and cadres' education that I have been outlining throughout this chapter. While it conceives 'education as a tool to help liberate our members and the working class', as a way for members to engage more effectively with 'the Union' and regard it 'as their own property', and while education 'has to be universal [which] … means it has to be available to everyone in the union irrespective of where they work, their sector or how big their branches are', education is principally designed for leaders. And indeed the 'Key Features of the Strategic Plan' included mainly induction, intermediate and advanced courses for shaft stewards, and national courses for staff members, with a view to solving the 'basic problem … of the high turnover of stewards, compounded by the practice or perception that management will promote the most active stewards and thereby reduce the union's human resource base'. In the plan, the tension between the fact that as a result of union education 'individuals will, of course, grow and develop' and the need for NUM to benefit from and retain the skills it produces is palpable.[52] Another important orientation in NUM's education plan is connected to the union's will 'to build a 'holistic approach' to education that is coordinated with and fits into 'public education, the work of SETA's [Sector Education and Training Authorities] and the educational implications of the Skills Development terrain'.[53] The involvement of NUM in the Seta framework, a system of sector-based vocational skills development organisations established by the Skills Development Act (No. 97 of 1998), is channelled through the Mining Qualifications Authority (MQA), which 'is responsible for driving transformation in the Mining and Minerals Sector through the facilitation of skills'.[54] The MQA gathers stakeholders in the mining sector, including NUM, the EBMTC and some mining houses.

NUM has therefore undertaken, with the EBMTC, to align NUM education with South Africa's formal education system, including the Setas, through which the EBMTC was accredited in 2011. Behind this endeavour, as Mercy Sekano noted, is the idea that 'currently we don't have union skills dispensed in universities. We want companies to recognise skills based on what people actually know … A boilermaker may not have matric but he may have the right skills so he must be elevated.' There is hence an assumption that the type of education NUM is able to provide is a particular one: 'our methodology is participatory, people learn from one another and are recognised in their experience. We also believe in worker control, respect [for] each other. We believe in the bottom-up and not the contrary, as in companies'.[55] But the union's ambition even goes beyond training its own people. Initially designed for union cadres, the EBMTC is now seeking to gain accreditation to award degrees recognised by the State and to turn into a fully fledged Further Education and Training (FET) institution.[56]

8

Trajectories of Union Leaders and NUM Leadership Ideals

OF PERSONAL SUCCESS AND WORKING-CLASS LEADERSHIP

What is common to the NUM leadership ideals considered in this chapter is a tension between, on the one hand, the union's aspiration to the type of organisational modernity epitomised by neoliberal forms of management and, on the other hand, the organisation's aim to remain a class-conscious union committed to fighting for mineworkers' rights. This was well captured in Gwede Mantashe's 2002 report to the central committee in which he prescribed:

> In the Year 2002 every national leader of any structure must go through a political school. Every Regional leader and Branch leader must go through a political school … This will be a blitz on political education. We must reinstate our confidence in working-class tools of analysis. This will require us to cut on resources allocated to management courses and redirect such resources to political education … Although these management programmes assist us [to] improve our efficiency level they equally temper with our ideological outlook. With many of the former leaders of the NUM being in business, and being our role models, going into business becomes an option without any morality crisis. This imposes a duty on us to intensify our political education.[1]

This tension is also found in two ideals of NUM leadership that I shall call the 'trade union executive' and the 'communist cadre' – two ideals that have, I argue, become complementary in the contemporary NUM. Another tension, which partly overlaps with the former, is linked to the age or generational factor, opposing the figure of the 'legitimist elder' to that of the 'young leader'. As mentioned in the above quote, NUM people who made it into business after apartheid have become 'role models' for many, given the rapid transformation of the job market, which has seen black and white elites converge at the top.

Aspirations to success, both symbolic and material, are palpable among local NUM leaders and they recall the fact that only a happy few among the union leadership have made their way out of their former socioeconomic condition. In May 2012, I spent time with NUM in and around Lonmin's Marikana operations. At one NUM shaft committee office, I met a local union leader. This office was shared and was rather typical of South African mines, furnished with tables and chairs and equipped with a PC and a telephone. On the computer screen behind him, one could see the picture of a two-storey house similar to those found in low-rise housing areas in the US or in South Africa's richest suburbs. One could guess that it had a garden at the back and that two cars – a saloon car and an SUV – were parked in front of the house. At some point I asked him about the picture:

> Q: *Did you put this picture on the screen?* NUM shaft steward: No, it's just a house. Q: *It's your house?* NUM shaft steward: [laughter] No, I'm earning very little; just a screen saver, a picture that I like, one day I wish to have a house like that but I cannot afford it.[2]

The story of this ordinary NUM shaft steward was that of a 'normal' union leader, who dismissed the idea that NUM leaders would now be gentrified and cut off from reality. When I met him he was 32 years old and he told me he had joined the company on 10 October 2006 (in South Africa, mine employees often know their exact engagement date by heart). Before that he had been working in the kitchen of Lonmin's Karee mine on a catering contract. He explained: 'Then I searched for a job at the mine, I started at the lowest grade; early this year I got a promotion to winch driver; it's a promotion by name but not something you can be proud of.' When I met him he appeared to me to be a smart, young and disillusioned man. His basic salary, he told me, was R5 200, a figure consistent with, if not lower than, the wages of the 2012 Marikana strikers, and he stressed his desire to study. He would first have to pass the matric exam but confessed it would be difficult since he would have to look after his family in the meantime. He then explained that 'with the end of the job reservation, people discovered what they could reach with a proper degree', before adding that he would like to do mining engineering. I later visited his house, not far from the mine. He lived in a 'company house', a 'rent to buy' in his own words.

The modest housing development I visited, slightly superior in standard to a typical Reconstruction and Development Programme (RDP) house,[3] was sponsored by Lonmin as part of a programme designed to turn some of its employees into homeowners. The shaft steward's house comprised three rooms hosting him, his wife and their three children. The house was equipped with a TV, a fridge and a washing machine, and his old VW Golf was parked in the street outside the small front yard. It is difficult to conclude based on his relatively modest way of life that this shaft steward was a privileged person among his peers – privilege for which NUM shaft stewards were often disparaged by their opponents in the 2012 strikes. He is certainly better off than those mineworkers staying in informal settlements, where they rent a piece of land and build their own shacks. Among those, however, many with similar wages choose to save on rentals in order to send money back to their rural homes. It is likely, of course, that those unionists who benefit from company housing do so partly because they manage to make their way onto the list of potential beneficiaries. One of my interviewees, in fact, accused the previous NUM Karee branch chairperson, who was suspended by the union for allegedly refusing to submit himself to the local election, of having rewarded his supporters with housing opportunities. When I asked how he could be sure that his accusation was true, he answered: 'I know because I was here. It's company housing but the issue is the list must come from the NUM branch. Even the registration for a house, you come and give your name here. If I give you a house, you come to me and tell me what's going on around, what people say on me … '[4] This, of course, is just one individual's view on the matter but the very fact that the list of beneficiaries is compiled by NUM makes for a conflict of interests and the establishment of patron–client relationships. What this example also brings to light, however, is that while they may from time to time gain materially from their leadership positions – be it in the form of housing or training opportunities – most NUM leaders do not experience any dramatic improvement in their socioeconomic status after achieving leadership status. The material life of a NUM leader is only decisively altered when one is elected full-time at local, regional or national level. From the regional level upwards, leaders start to receive benefits such as union cars and, most importantly, their salary is renegotiated by the union. It is therefore not difficult to imagine how high electoral stakes are for leaders, and to understand that it is because a union career path may be unpredictable that one must keep other doors open, including a move into business.

Another way to read individual success is against the backdrop of the broader community to which the individual belongs. What is often condemned socially as well as politically is the fact that personal development and career opportunities for black South Africans have so far been conceived in narrow practical terms or, in moral terms, left to greed and selfishness. Cosatu and NUM are always prompt to denounce revenue-based inequalities, 'which have made us the most unequal society in the world'. Unions often publicise CEO salaries, comparing them to the wages of ordinary workers, in an effort to heap opprobrium on individual managers on the eve of wage negotiations. Cosatu, for instance, declared in 2010: 'As [we] prepare for next year's living wage conference, we shall keep these figures in mind and use them to convince workers that they have every right to mobilise their members to fight for big increases, so that we can start to narrow the chasm between rich and poor in South Africa.'[5] Anglo American Platinum CEO Chris Griffith was once quoted as declaring, nearly four months into South Africa's longest mining strike at the time: 'Am I getting paid on a fair basis for what I'm having to deal with in this company? Must I run this company and deal with all this nonsense for nothing? I'm at work. I'm not on strike. I'm not demanding to be paid what I'm not worth.'[6] Opulence may logically be condemned from a union's point of view when it comes to a mining boss such as Griffith, but wealth and ownership are not always looked at with suspicion. If top NUM leaders were regularly shouted down and booed off the stage in recent times because of their perceived detachment from the plight of mineworkers – allegedly in part because of the material comfort they now enjoy – others, like Amcu president Joseph Mathunjwa, are still popular despite a far more conspicuous display of wealth. In a 2014 news article, Mathunjwa was described as arriving 'at meetings in luxury vehicles, surrounded by bodyguards and wearing expensive suits. At Wonderkop Stadium in Marikana last Wednesday, Mathunjwa received a hero's welcome as he arrived in a convoy of sleek vehicles, including two BMWs, to address the workers'. Mathunjwa was the registered owner of three BMWs and three houses, the article continued, including a four-star guesthouse, and his wife, Nokuthula, was the director of several businesses.[7] Whatever the relevance of such information, it was dismissed by the 'incriminated' with the following assurance: 'Mathunjwa is working. Did I steal to anyone? … Mathunjwa comes from a background of poverty and now it's a sin to have one, two, and three without stealing anything.' In the same interview he added:

> The minerals have to benefit South Africans first before it benefits people in London or wherever they are … You can have all this democracy but if you cannot feed your family it means nothing. So therefore after 20 years of democracy there's no person that can say 'I've benefited from the minerals of this country' … The pay of mineworkers from 1652 was made by British colonialists … it was continued by the National Party. We hoped in 1994 it would change … in 20 years, the status quo still remains.[8]

The above quote echoes the Freedom Charter, which, in 1955, stated: 'the mineral wealth beneath the soil, the Banks and monopoly industry shall be transferred to the ownership of the people as a whole'. Mathunjwa's words, just like his assumed lifestyle, also recall that of self-proclaimed Economic Freedom Fighter Julius Malema.[9] Known for his 'lavish lifestyle', his tenderpreneurship and many financial scandals, the former president of the ANC Youth League made the nationalisation of mines his hobbyhorse. After expulsion from the ANC he created a new political party, the Economic Freedom Fighters (EFF), which secured 6.35 per cent of the vote in South Africa's 2014 general election (1 169 259 votes), thus winning 25 seats in Parliament.[10]

Reasons for the popularity of leaders like Mathunjwa and Malema – who are typical illustrations of the 'new figures of success' described elsewhere in Africa[11] – are many, but one is no doubt their show of activism and compassion for those who suffer. As opposed to most contemporary top NUM leaders, Mathunjwa and Malema's presence by the sides of those who suffered, such as the 2012 and 2014 strikers, was a physical one: they were there, on the ground, and listened to the strikers before addressing them. The way these two post-apartheid 'self-made men' opposed the political domination and agenda of the ANC and its allies, their display of empathy with those who suffer, and their promises of a more equal society are a way to honour the social call to 'give back to the community' and 'consider success not so much as a personal advantage but as a collective issue'. Based on an ethnographic research project she conducted with young South Africans in Daveyton, a former black township east of Johannesburg, anthropologist Judith Hayem approached the issue of 'success' in such terms. One of her aims was to challenge the stereotype of a post-apartheid generation portrayed as materialist and thirsty for selfish success. Among other conclusions, she found that 'while envisaging themselves successful, many young people I talked to consider that it would then be their duty to take care of others at large in the community by giving back; either financially or in the form of advice, employment or initiatives which would profit to what they see as their community'.[12]

APPROACHING NUM LEADERSHIP IDEALS

Relying on Max Weber's analytical category of 'ideal type', I have identified four distinct types of leadership style in today's NUM: the 'trade union executive', the 'legitimist elder', the 'young leader' and the 'communist cadre'. These are neither exhaustive nor exclusive categories since they often overlap. The interest of this gallery of portraits is that it connects social interactions and collective organisational dynamics to the trajectories of individuals, be they notorious or not.[13] In other words, the ideals I have identified here will allow me, first, to provide embodied answers to the question, 'what types of leader does NUM produce?' and second, to give more flesh to dynamics I describe elsewhere, such as the neoliberalisation of NUM's administration, the opposition between generations, or the political workings of a union that has also been impacted by its 'communist' identity.

In their classic study of the International Typographical Union (ITU), Lipset et al. 'examine the careers of two typical union leaders' from the internal opposition of the ITU's two-party leadership system. Their findings are useful and to some extent illustrative of career paths in many organisational settings beyond the ITU and NUM. The first leader, 'Mr. M', relies on both his knowledge and his skills 'in the use of union law' to lead a career based on 'a strong motivation toward achievement and advancement, and a political ideology which, on the one hand, defined the union as an appropriate channel for achievement and mobility and, on the other hand, allowed him to use one of the major local political groups as the vehicle for his aspirations'. The second leader, 'N', is 'a very different kind of man, although his union career does not look very different from that of M'. However, 'his entrance into union political activity was much more the result of social relations and personal pulls than of any strong ideological commitment to union work'. Furthermore, the authors observe, 'the union careers of these two men cover the range of personal and organizational activities which, in different combinations and sequences, constitute the career lines of almost all of the active leaders in the union'. The latter involve aspects of a union's life that are also found in NUM, such as 'early and regular attendance at local union meetings'; 'speeches from the floor at local meetings'; 'appointment to minor local union committees or posts'; 'membership and activity in a union political group or party'; 'appointment to paid full-time local office … and election as delegate to International conventions'; and 'election to the local executive committee or higher local office'.[14] As I have shown in Part I, continuous involvement over time and participation in many different types of union activity at various levels are key to one's internal ascent in NUM.

If one looks back in history, the NUM of the 1980s and early 1990s rested on a combination of different leadership types that rarely conflicted openly, having one concern in common – namely, organisational building and stability. This is still palpable among contemporary national leaders of NUM. Cyril Ramaphosa, the union's founding general secretary, was in charge of administration and negotiation, whereas James Motlatsi, its first president, would 'talk to people' and, where necessary, address the masses to whom he was closer given his background as a mineworker.[15]

In his study of 'ungovernability' at Anglo American Vaal Reefs mine in 1985, Moodie insists that the NUM of the early years, while promoting organisational modernity and denying 'any claim to prophetic charisma', also relied on 'charismatic power with supernatural assistance'. This happened, for instance, when Lira Setona, a local leader, challenged the authority of management, and organised unauthorised meetings and a boycott of mine-sponsored stores and leisure activities, and of the local branches of Teba (The Employment Bureau of Africa), from which workers withdrew R1.2 million in savings in the course of one week. Motlatsi admired Setona's leadership skills but also criticised him from an organisational point of view for destroying NUM branches, in a way that is somehow reminiscent of contemporary leaders' criticisms of Amcu. Motlatsi argued that Setona

> started to fight not only against management; he also destroyed all union structures there. No branch committee, no shaft committees, no shaft stewards committees, it was he and four other guys who commanded Vaal Reefs. He was saying he doesn't report to anybody. He reports directly to the president or the general secretary. All others in between are sell-outs.[16]

This personalisation of power and the consequent disempowerment of legitimate union structures recalls the situation that developed at Lonmin's NUM Karee branch from 2011 on, after the then NUM chairperson of the branch, Steve Khululekile, had rejected union procedures and stopped reporting to upper union structures.

Although the leadership style of Khululekile or Setona conflicted with the type of leadership promoted and inducted by head office, leaders like them were also instrumental in the development of NUM at branch level. Ramaphosa's own trajectory was that of 'a lawyer' who 'possessed ... extraordinary energy and organisational skills and [was] determined to found a union with deep local roots and a professional and incorruptible central administration'. Yet the early NUM sometimes found great symbolic and organisational resources in 'millenarian' leaders such as Setona, who could frame both the militancy and the demands of the workers in terms that were consistent with their own 'structure of feelings'.[17] Moodie argues that the 'style of leadership' that characterised Cyril Ramaphosa was in fact quite close to what Michel Foucault defined as 'pastoral' leadership. To some extent, Joseph Mathunjwa, the president of Amcu, matches this description of legitimacy, a Foucaultian conception of power as not only 'repressive' but also 'formative'.[18]

In his work on Cosatu, Sakhela Buhlungu looks at the transformation of full-time union leadership. Central to his argument is the idea of 'the disappearance of the activist organiser and the emergence of new types of union officials. This change coincides with a process of generational change within the ranks of these officials'. The 'activist organiser' embodied two roles: 'that of political activist as well as that of full-time official of the union'. At the time rewards for union involvement were found in the solidarity values of the struggle – a risky enterprise – rather than in any financial reward. 'The dissolution of the link between the role of political activist on the one hand and that of full-time union official on the other' marked the end of the 'activist organiser'. According to Buhlungu, 'the old generation' comprises those officials who joined the unions in the 1970s and 1980s and are committed to the idea of building a 'trained worker leadership at all levels of the union movement'. On the other hand, he continues, 'the new generation … are those officials who joined unions when both the assumptions and practices associated with the activist organiser were changing'. Buhlungu identifies three types of leadership attached to three distinct agendas of organisational modernisation: (i) 'ideological unionists represent a diminishing layer of strong defenders of worker control'; (ii) 'career unionists (…) are technocrats who are committed to building an efficient union movement. Some of them could even be union bureaucrats in the making'; and (iii) 'the entrepreneur whose emergence as a category may be a function of the accelerated processes of class formation spawned by the deracialisation of South African society … which has created vast opportunities for a few entrepreneurial individuals'. There is, as often in Buhlungu's take on the transformation of trade unionism after apartheid, a tendency to reify the past. He concludes, for instance, 'that the age of altruistic innocence of union leadership is over … '.[19] In my own observations, however, I noticed that the age distinction between leadership types was not so clear-cut. NUM leaders such as Gwede Mantashe and his heir-in-office Frans Baleni, who both belong to the older generation, can in fact fit into all three categories listed by Buhlungu. They are first committed communists and claim their allegiance to 'worker control'. But they also have well-drawn career agendas and thus do not hesitate to be 'individualistic and manipulative "empire builders"'. Conversely, some younger-generation leaders whom I met during my fieldwork are ideologically committed and not necessarily guided by a sense of personal interest stronger than that of their elders. In other words, building ideal types of NUM leadership without cutting across generations of unionists seems difficult. Union 'entrepreneurs', a category that Buhlungu associates predominantly with the new generation, for instance, are embodied in his classification by former unionists of the likes of Marcel Golding and Johnny Copelyn who, in fact, are prominent members of the older generation.[20]

In the following sections, rather than drawing conclusions about the type of organisational project or approach to unionism that a given type of leadership entails, I prefer to use NUM's notion of 'leadership style'. The latter is more fluid; it is non-normative; and above all, it is aimed at describing the behaviour of a given leader without judging the consequences in advance, since all leaders may be presumed to strive for a common goal – namely the advancement of NUM's project and of the mineworkers' welfare. During the leadership development workshop I attended with a group of NUM leaders (discussed in chapter 7), participants were asked to 'reflect on different leadership styles' in order 'to understand and appreciate different approaches to leading and managing' and to 'begin understanding our own leadership styles and the importance of adapting these for a particular purpose'. In other words, and even though it can be assumed from a sociological point of view that different types of leadership style will have different impacts on how the union is managed, the purpose of a leader's action is expected to fit into the broad framework of NUM's democratic agenda within and outside of the union. I therefore also assume that different leadership styles will not necessarily involve unequal levels of commitment to union democracy or to NUM's project since these, I argue, are not contradictory with the pursuit of one's individual career agenda. Workshop participants were also asked to imagine they were going to 'prepare to vote for the new General Secretary / President of a Union'. Three candidates were standing for election: 'The Coach of Bafana Bafana [South Africa's national football team]', 'A Nun in a Community' and 'The General in an Army'. They were asked to discuss these 'in detail' and 'focus on the style of leadership required from each rather than on the individual'.[21] They listed the qualities of each type of leadership. The 'coach' was a 'motivator, counsellor, analyser, knowledgeable, guide, mentor, tactician, listener' and a 'decision maker'. The 'nun' was 'community-caring, supportive, humble, noble, a people's person, mediator', had 'patience' and was a 'counsellor, communicator', 'compassionate and generous'. Finally, the 'general' was 'disciplinary', had 'command', 'observes', was 'brave, fit, well-trained, sensitive' and a 'strategist'. The result of the vote was the following: the 'coach' earned the support of 15 participants, the 'general' of 10 and the 'nun' of only three. If one considers the list of qualities NUM trainee leaders attached to the three 'types' they were presented with in this activity, one finds that there is a great deal of overlap, as there is also in the ideal types of leadership I have identified. This overlapping is due to the fact that NUM produces a generic type of leadership that attaches more importance to organisational and administrative skills, as well as to the transferability of such assets, than to a form of leadership narrowly conceived as a set of command skills.

In the following two sections, I start by taking the example of Frans Baleni, who in my view embodies the ideal type of the 'trade union executive'. Baleni's organisational skills have gradually incorporated private sector ideas and practices, which he conjugated, just like his mentor Gwede Mantashe before him, with a version of communist ideology that is characterised by the exercise of tight control over the organisation. I then contrast Baleni's career, one that took him far away from his membership base, to that of another national leader of NUM, Ecliff Tantsi. His path may seem comparable to Baleni's at first glance, yet he differs greatly in his leadership style and, when it comes to dealing with the membership, he gives up the ethos[22] of the young union executive that he may exhibit in other settings. This borderline case is interesting because it shows that one can be ambitious from one's individual career point of view, while acting as a good leader in the 'old NUM' sense of dedication to the union and its historic values. The example of Tantsi confirms, as argued before, that what workers strive for is not necessarily to have top leaders who resemble them but, more importantly, leaders who care for and listen to them.

THE TRADE UNION EXECUTIVE

The notion of 'executive' is used here in the sense of the French socioeconomic category of 'cadre' as studied by Luc Boltanski.[23] The sociologist historicises this notion: the 'cadres' category appeared in the 1930s in the corporate sector, around a common base of engineers and a *habitus* formed in the French Republic's 'grandes écoles' (a network of State-funded, elite, tertiary education institutions aimed at producing cadres for the nation's upper administration). It is only in the post-war period, however, that many others joined these first 'cadres' to form a coherent although non-homogeneous social group. This 'social group' is obviously diverse since the category includes people as remote from one another as a CEO is from a shop foreman or an aerospace engineer. The fact that the borders of this group are 'blurred' does not invalidate the idea of a distinct 'social group' and it can hardly be denied that the category 'cadre' has sociological content: 'despite differences, cohesion remains because all find in it, in a way or another, their own interest, be it only a symbolic one'. The existence of this group was also forged via its institutionalisation through, for instance, dedicated trade unions and pension funds.[24] In the context of my analysis of NUM leadership, the notion of 'executive' therefore proves a useful one since it allows me to bring together the figures of the mine manager, that of the State official in high public administration, and that of the trade unionist in the mining industry. They are, of course, not the same types of people and do not have the same interests, but they share habits as well as, increasingly, degrees, skills and career paths.[25] Also crucial to Boltanski's analysis is the fact that the ascent of cadreship was fostered, historically, by the 1930s economic crisis, as well as by a new corporate socio-professional environment consolidated around new technologies, and following the spread of US-devised management techniques – along with the implementation of the post-World War II Marshall Plan – in France and Western Europe. In post-apartheid South Africa, black executives are new figures of success and they embody a desirable conversion for trade unionists. Moreover, the importation of managerial techniques from the corporate sector into trade unionism and the State features as a major trend in post-apartheid South Africa.

Former NUM general secretary Frans Baleni epitomises the ideal type of the trade union executive. As I have shown earlier, he conceives his role in the union as that of a manager, has been instrumental in implementing 'performance management' throughout the union, has increased his salary to match the market or can be seen leading a NUM march in Johannesburg, taking pictures of the crowd with his iPhone, an iconic material token of success. A 2013 *City Press* article on Baleni's participation in the African Mining Indaba in Cape Town provocatively asked: 'Where does Baleni's loyalty lie?' The article reported that despite his union's decline, Baleni 'continues to rub shoulders with the big mining bosses'. After noting that the presence of a union official among mining bosses was, 'in its own right', a 'good thing', the article went on: 'When it does become problematic though is when it serves as an umpteenth example of the notion that NUM and Baleni in particular are seemingly more comfortable in the company of business than the workers they represent.'[26] When I met him, Baleni told me he 'came to the mining industry by mistake'. Born in the Free State, he was attending high school in the Eastern Cape when he became politically involved:

> We were then sort of hunted by the police, those who were seen as the leaders of the action. My colleagues then suggested that [I]'ll be easily arrested by the police in my small town. [They said] 'you'd better go to Johannesburg or Welkom'. So I went to Welkom … that was in 1979, in the Free State. It was quite clear that I would not be able to come back and that I couldn't write the exam at year-end. I had a bursary and the condition was that if you don't write the exam unless you are sick then you lose the bursary … So I lost the bursary and my friends suggested that [I should] join the mines because in the mining industry you stay in the hostels, there are lots of people there, the police won't find you again … And then I joined the mining industry in December 1979; I worked in a gold mine owned by Anglo, AngloGold at the time, for nine years … The mine was called Welkom Gold Mine.
>
> Obviously … in the mining industry there was no union so coming with a little bit of political mind, the issue of the union was very keen to us … We

then learned later that there is a union to be formed for the mineworkers, that there is a person called Cyril Ramaphosa who is organising … and I was one of those first people who joined the union [in January 1983] … I started as an ordinary member, I then became a shaft steward, I then became a branch secretary, I then became a regional health and safety secretary. Then I went back to the branch, I became a branch chairperson, then I was dismissed in 1988 for calling workers to demonstrate and not to go to work against the Labour Relations Amendment Act, which was being proposed at the time by the apartheid government.[27]

Frans Baleni's trajectory resembles that of many top NUM leaders: among the first of them to join the union, he had more formal education than the average mineworker and this fostered his career. Frans Baleni was the 'top employee' of the union and, as such, had a managerial conception of authority and organisation. This is apparent in an article he published in the *South African Labour Bulletin*:

The high-profile collapse of Enron illustrates clearly what happens when the leaders of an organisation don't have the interests of the organisation's future at heart. Although there seems to have been a multiple of factors contributing to the downfall of this empire, the overriding factor was greed … and power of the CEO. This coupled with weak governance structures ensured that shareholders were misled … A clear lesson here is that corporate governance is not just a list of procedures. It is also a state of mind … It is not only the CEO who is responsible for ensuring good corporate governance, but the entire board.[28]

This extract is illustrative of Baleni's conception of the organisation he led, as well as of his role in it. The implied comparisons between a CEO and a labour leader, shareholders and union members, the board of a company and NUM's national executive committee are all the more revealing in that they are sustained throughout the rest of the article. It is no coincidence then if NUM, whose leaders including Baleni, a former educator who sits on the board of trustees of several union-related structures,[29] offers training inspired by the corporate sector, such as one on 'trustees' which I attended in 2010. Conceived as a workshop at the end of which participants were expected to 'demonstrate knowledge and understanding of the role and responsibilities of Trustees of retirement funds', the training was provided by a former Standard Bank employee acting as a freelance consultant. The rationale behind the workshop was, of course, to empower unionists who, since the Pension Funds

Amendment Act had been passed in 1996, were responsible for administering pension funds jointly with employers. In the way things were formulated during the training, however, it was also clear that this new responsibility implied a particular relationship to members. And indeed, at one stage, the course facilitator reminded his audience: 'Your guys are clients there'. On the back of the NUM education and training 2010 brochure is a poem on trade union education that is inspired by the commercial slogans of famous South African and foreign multinationals. It is, of course, humorous but it says much about the tension between union and corporate approaches to NUM:

Trade Union Education is like ABSA [Bank]

It prepares workers Today,

for Tomorrow and Unite Workers Together

Trade Union Education is like BP

It keeps you moving around the world

Trade Union Education is like Coke

It is real Education …

Trade Union Education is like FNB [First National Bank]

It puts workers first

Trade Union Education is like DSTV [digital satellite television]

It's all in one

Trade Union Education is like Mastercard

It is available worldwide[30]

At another training course, the NUM facilitator had nevertheless insisted that 'we don't expect you to bring your corporate experience into the union, we want you to bring your union experience into the corporate'. These days in NUM, however, with its leaders I define as 'trade union executives', it has become harder to be clear-cut about who has more influence on the other: the union or the private sector. Of course, Baleni's embrace of corporate rhetoric and practices does not prevent him from proclaiming himself a communist (he is a member of the SACP's central committee) and he grew organisationally in the shadow of his mentor, Gwede

Mantashe, a dedicated communist whose vision of organisation will be detailed later. I now turn to the leadership style of of Ecliff Tantsi, who, in contrast to Baleni, and despite good administrative skills and his ethos of trade union executive, remained in touch with grassroots members.

'MY LEADERSHIP STYLE': THE TRAJECTORY OF A YOUNG, OLD-SCHOOL NUM LEADER

A NUM national education secretary since 2006, Zwelitsha Ecliff Tantsi was most comfortably re-elected at the union's national congress in 2012 (Tantsi won by 705 votes against his opponent's 389), and his nomination was uncontested at the NUM 2015 congress. When I first met him in 2010, he described his involvement in NUM in 1992, when he was an Impala Platinum employee, as well as his role as a national leader:

> I worked underground for a period of twelve months … I was not specialised in anything but I realised that I'm good in reading, in reporting that information to the members, in interpreting the policies, the agreements, then I was made the branch educator … Let me put it like this: the organisation is having a training department, I am having five educators with the pillar head who is in charge, who is the manager, and also the unit head, they are reporting to me, I am reporting to the general secretary. The organisation will take a policy position with regards to education and training, whether in terms of what we must pursue in the country, or what we must implement for the organisation. So my responsibility is to head that department and to make sure the policies of the organisation are implemented organisationally and otherwise.

His career in NUM followed a very logical path – reminiscent of what Lipset et al. called 'career lines' in the ITU – from the Impala North branch to the Rustenburg region and to the national office: 'In order to be elected to the national office … you must move [in] the hierarchy, you must have been the branch leader for a period of three years, you must have serviced [at region level] for a period of six years consecutively, then you can be considered to be elected to the national level.' Tantsi's involvement in NUM's apparatus was instantaneous and based on competence, hard work and accountability. He also developed a leadership style mixing negotiation, communication skills and grassroots militancy:[31]

When I joined Impala I was fresh from high school. I would always clash with the employer, with my supervisors underground. I was told that I'm politically minded, I didn't know that. I would be changed from one gang to another because nobody wanted to work with me because I'm questioning lots of things … There was this NUM full-time shaft steward who would come to the offices, he would find me having problems, charges and one day he asked me, 'What is the problem every time you are here … you are going to be dismissed, come and join NUM.' I went there and joined NUM. Every day when I come from underground I would go to the union offices, I would find something to do, I would help the shop steward. He recommended me to the branch; I was still young by then, probably 22. They gave me to deal with the provident fund issues. I was not interested …

During those times remember Impala was part of the old Bophuthatswana [bantustan] … The laws were not the same, the unions were not allowed but because of the militancy of NUM they couldn't contain, they had to work with NUM … There was no formal relationship between the employer and NUM because it would appear to the government that the company was recognising NUM. And shop stewards were not properly trained … Now the challenge was that the company was forced to create a platform with the union, the problem was the question of the capacity. What would happen is that every time the branches were going to meet the management, they would call all the shop stewards who would strategise as to what must be the approach. I think that is where I have distinguished myself from the rest of the leadership. I would come up with positions [and] I realised that they appreciated my input. Every time they were going to meet management they would come to me and say: 'What do you think must be the approach?' I was also not trained; I would give them the approach and sometimes I would say, 'I don't think that in terms of the approach the management will [inaudible word] [give in]. We need to come out with a political approach, we need to involve the public, we need to get the public's sympathy, how do you do that? We need to mobilise the masses.' Impala by then, that branch Impala North employed about fourteen thousand employees. We would say let's march, everybody must see that we are on the street while you are negotiating. I would publicise on the radio, the media will catch that, the company was feeling uncomfortable about that. I would always stay with the branch, I was not part of the negotiating team but I was a backroom strategist and in terms of gathering information I was quite good. So that is why I am saying I was not an ordinary member; I became active you know. And to me it was not about the leadership in order for me to participate. I realised that I became respected by the leadership and also by the members and I really enjoyed it; I was humbled by the request which was accorded to me by the organisation.[32]

When I first met him, Ecliff Tantsi was in his late thirties and breathing success. Tall, fit, confident, good-looking and wearing smart clothes, he looked like a young, talented and ambitious man, what one would term, in French, a 'jeune cadre dynamique' or, in English, a 'young urban professional'. An assiduous NUM leader, he sat on the board of trustees of the JB Marks Education Trust Fund and he was also the union's chief negotiator in several companies, including Murray & Roberts Cementation, Samancor and Northam Platinum (Figure 8.1 shows Tantsi leading the 2011 NUM–MRC wage negotiations). Tantsi is a good union organiser, as he revealed during a break at a wage negotiation meeting in 2011:

> Before [I] was regional education secretary, in 2005, and some wanted me to go to national [level], others to stay. I was very powerful at the time because I [had] successfully organised Murray & Roberts and my name was raised by big branches. 'When you have done your work you relax, comrades.' Now people started to wonder how I would be more useful. Some wanted me as mining house coordinator for Murray & Roberts, and wanted to keep me in the region.

The second time I visited his office, I noted a book displayed on his desk: Peter D. Johnston, *Negotiating with Giants*. Later on, during our interview, he showed me the book and explained:

> Read this book about negotiating with the giants ... I was on the plane from North America, somebody was reading it, I borrowed it. I read this book and I found it very interesting. What I've learned about this book is it's quite me and I did not know that. You don't go to university to learn about these things. It's just embedded within you. And as you rise within the level of the organisation you realise ... wow ... I cannot describe but I found this book describing me.[33]

Ecliff Tantsi's reference to this book in the above quote gives an indication of the array of references from the North American business environment that shape his thinking and his actions. In another conversation we shared he confessed: 'Before the "union discovered me" I was on Impala's junior management programme. I

Figure 8.1: Ecliff Tantsi (standing) explains NUM demands to MRC management, 2011

Photographer: Raphaël Botiveau

could have become part of management but I did not want to betray the union and the money it had invested on me.' Clearly, the skills Ecliff Tantsi had developed in NUM were transferrable to the corporate sector and my description of him as a young professional[34] is indeed based on his competence, fine knowledge and management of complex negotiation processes, which I witnessed on several occasions. But Tantsi decided to remain loyal to an organisation – NUM – that had changed his life: when he joined the union, he did not have a driver's licence and had never boarded an aeroplane.

All this, however, does not imply that Ecliff Tantsi's leadership style is restricted to the limits of his office and to the meetings he attends. He is indeed always eager to swap his smart, urbane clothes for a NUM tee shirt (Figure 8.2).

In the aftermath of NUM's debacle on the platinum belt, one of the only bastions where the union was still resisting Amcu's breakthrough was Northam Platinum, the world's fifth-largest platinum producer.[35] The company, in which Tantsi had been acting as NUM chief negotiator, experienced two major industrial actions reminiscent of the militant stance adopted by Amcu, especially of the strike it led at the three top world platinum producers in 2014. At the end of 2013, starting

Figure 8.2: Ecliff Tantsi reviews the NUM–MRC 2011–2013 wage and conditions of employment agreement with his team

Photographer: Raphaël Botiveau

on 3 November, NUM conducted a 77-day strike at Northam's Zondereinde mine, which 'has been as far as many industrial relations practitioners and unionists can recount [and before the 2014 Amcu-led strike], the longest wage strike in post-apartheid labour history'. NUM was demanding an 'incredibly high' pay hike of about 23 per cent above the basic pay rate. The two parties eventually settled at 9.5 per cent (with a R3 000 'ex gratia payment to help workers get back on their feet') and the strike was described as 'long and largely fruitless' since workers had lost 'nearly 25% of their yearly wages' in the meantime. 'Industrial relations at Northam have been fraught,' Tantsi described, before adding: 'Northam is a war zone. The attitude of workers is: "We don't care how much we get as long as we fight. We will fight because we are angry"'. Northam was one of the only mines where NUM was able to display intransigent militancy[36] in the face of Amcu, who by then had secured 20 per cent of the Northam workforce and was threatening NUM's dominant position.[37] In the first weeks of the strike, Tantsi led a march on Northam Platinum's offices in Dunkeld West in Johannesburg where, wearing a red NUM tee shirt, he read a speech from the stage: 'We call upon management to be sensitive and treat us as human beings. Even animals are treated better than the way you are treating us.'

He was then interviewed and added: 'Almost all if not 99.9% of our wage negotiations they are resolved through the strike action. And the strike actions, normally their range is between four weeks up to six weeks and you don't need to be a rocket scientist to realise that there is a lack of leadership [at Northam].'[38]

Northam provides an example of resilience for NUM, based on at least two elements. First, it is a union branch that the CEO of Northam Platinum himself, Paul Dunne, who had previously been a top manager at Impala Platinum, where he dealt with the 2012 strike, described to me as 'solid' in terms of its local leadership. Dunne's role in the strike at Impala was praised, including by one Amcu striker I met. (NUM, for its part, considers that Impala management was responsible for letting Amcu in.) Dunne was one of the people in charge who had possibly prevented the situation at Impala from fully degenerating, by keeping the police at bay, as opposed to what happened in Lonmin, where the police were called in by management, with the disastrous consequences we all know. According to Dunne, Joseph Moloko, NUM's branch chairperson at Northam, had been working in the company from the start and had been a leader in the union for a long time. Stability, good consultation with the membership, legitimacy, but also militancy are therefore ingredients that kept the local NUM branch united. Northam's NUM leadership, which in a 1996 report was criticised as 'maverick NUM leadership' because of its history of resorting to violence and intimidation and its unwise initiatives, was nonetheless kept in place. In 1996 it had promoted the massive eviction of Zulu workers from the hostels in clashes that caused several deaths. This incident is reminiscent of other, similar local situations in which the national leadership of NUM preferred to keep an irresponsible branch leadership in power rather than face disorder and lose ground.[39]

Second, Dunne praised Ecliff Tantsi's national leadership as a source of strength for NUM, although Tantsi's leadership had been exercised at the expense of the company in various strikes.[40] It is, in fact, as a result of NUM's 2013–2014 strike that the union defeated Paul Dunne's predecessor. As Tantsi put it, 'We were fighting the CEO there and we managed to have him out shortly after.' NUM's chief negotiator at Northam Platinum told me about how he led strikes and negotiations there in words that, in today's national NUM leadership, probably make him the last national leader able to combine the qualities of a good organiser, administrator and negotiator, with the needed physical proximity and empathy with workers, based on which a leader can then guide the membership. He first described Northam's branch leadership as follows: 'I think … we have a consistent leadership that has been there for a long time. It is a leadership that starts focusing on the mass meeting – you don't alter the demands, NUM norms are respected.' Tantsi, too, attends mass meetings and, as we saw earlier, his leadership style is based on being a good listener first. He explained how he deals with crisis situations, such as when he has to lead a strike. He does not delegate but gets directly involved on the ground: 'When I declare a dispute, I clear my diary, I switch off my phone and I go to the ground. You see me well dressed now but I don't dress like that. I go to the ground, I must see, not get reports. I go with the workers, in the hostels, I drink mageu with them, without bodyguards.'[41] In addition to several strike actions he led at Northam Platinum, in early 2012 Tantsi had also conducted another successful strike at Samancor Chrome, which yielded significant gains.[42]

There is a sharp contrast between the strikes I have just described, led by Ecliff Tantsi, and those led by NUM general secretary Frans Baleni, at the Chamber of Mines in 2011 and 2013, which can be seen as 'leadership strikes' since they were barely militant and lasted no longer than a couple of days.[43] What Tantsi's leadership style proves is the fact that having the professional ethos of a 'trade union executive' is not necessarily incompatible with retaining the degree of militancy necessary to lead workers and keep the union alive – a decisive combination at a time when it is challenged for its bureaucratisation and a certain degree of gentrification in its leadership.

THE YOUNG LEADER AND THE LEGITIMIST ELDER

As soon as one connects age to leadership, one is faced with the question of 'generation', which translates into relationships – often revolving around power – between the youngsters and the elders.[44] As others[45] and I have pointed out elsewhere, issues of youth and involvement in South Africa – be it in political or labour organisations – are generally viewed through an anti-apartheid and a post-apartheid lens. In short, several 'classes' of young people who shaped the anti-apartheid movement in the 1940s and 1950s and in the 1970s and 1980s were often turned into ahistorical struggle icons and compared with a presumably depoliticised post-apartheid or 'born-free' youth. Such oversimplifications are, of course, not unique to South Africa and they often reflect the older generation's endeavour to control the youth. 'Youth', however, is merely a word that masks a plurality of situations, signifying not just a biological reality but also a social construct. In other words, elders often claim wisdom in the face of allegedly ardent, violent and immature youth.[46] As Pierre Bourdieu once noted, 'every field ... has its *specific ageing laws*: to know how *generations* are outlined, one must know the specific laws presiding over a field's workings, its stakes and the divisions that such a struggle operates'.[47] The ideal type of the 'young leader' in NUM is to a large extent the result of such oversimplifications, which see young people as a monolithic category. It is thus by challenging older leaders that young union leaders often find ways to distinguish themselves. On the other hand, those who choose to follow in the footsteps of their elders become legit-imist. Young people are generally perceived by their elders as both a source of hope for the future and a source of despair about incipient social degeneration as soon as they challenge authority and tradition.[48] In his 2012 report to the national congress, the NUM general secretary wrote:

> The young people today have characteristics that have to be managed maturely. They include the following:
> I. High impatience and intolerance of other people's views;
> II. Demand for quick results on their demands without appreciating difficult and at times complex processes including strategies and tactics of engage-ments;
> III. Claims of knowledge based on levels of literacy but which have not been practically tested;
> IV. High levels of aspirations for power and leadership, or moving to other rival unions if they are not elected into leadership positions;
> V. Quick to make allegations and accusations without proper communica-tion and understanding of issues.[49]

It is by considering the age factor,[50] as well as interactions between generations in an organisation – which are based on preconceptions such as those expressed above – that one may be able to unveil internal struggles around legitimacy and power. The balance of forces between gerontocracy and 'vanguardism' depends on the degree of autonomy that older leaders are ready to grant to their younger counterparts and on whether the latter are, conversely, ready to fight for their independence. In other words, one can wonder whether the involvement of young people in NUM is a means of emancipation, which would aim at promoting organisational change, or whether it is merely a way for the organisation to reproduce itself through control of the youth.

Faced with an increasing tendency of its younger members to short-circuit older local leaders they deemed too slow, and to take over leadership positions in the union, NUM decided to amend its constitution in 2006. A clause was added, which now imposes a three-year consecutive period of employment within a sin-gle company before a member can stand for an elective position.[51] This desire among the old guard to protect their position from the threat of their younger counterparts was clear in an interview I had with Richard Mahoha, a veteran NUM leader and, at the time, newly elected as Rustenburg regional chairperson. In answer to my questions about a stormy regional conference we had attended together, he said:

> The problem I experienced is the same thing of saying this young generation that is coming in the industry and the union we must be sure they understand the background of the union because a number of these people also demand time for us to educate them. It tends to be translated to people who want to occupy positions, not understanding [that] there is a challenge in these positions.[52]

I was personally often stunned by the maturity of young leaders I met in NUM. One branch office bearer, who had joined NUM in 2004 when she was recruited by Lonmin as a plant attendant (one of the lowest levels in the company), described her involvement as follows:

> Usually when you are a new recruit then the stewards in that area would come with the stop-order book and give you the option of filling it in. I joined immediately or maybe a month or two after [I was] hired. I joined NUM for a number of reasons. I knew that it's quite a large organisation. It has a number of good principles, because it is the largest organisation it means that as an employee you are covered you know.

Hers is one example that suggests no reluctance at all towards involvement. Just like her counterparts from the 1980s or early 1990s, she perceived joining NUM as a 'natural' step. Despite her young age (when I met her she was 27), this local NUM leader seemed able to cope with the pressure of the job, including when it came to addressing mass meetings. In her description of decision-making processes at branch level, she also proved more cautious and respectful of processes than many other, more senior leaders. From a political point of view, she also showed involvement even though she was not versed in ideology. In addition to NUM, she belonged to the ANC and to the Young Communist League of South Africa (YCL). Interestingly, she was not a member of Julius Malema's ANC Youth League, which both the ANC and the YCL strongly criticised at the time. However, she did not disapprove of Malema's actions and, about the ANC Youth League's Economic Freedom march, which was due to take place the day after in Johannesburg, she cautiously stated: 'I think it's a good initiative, that we should push such ideas forward. It might only be a problem if there could be aspects of vandalism. I hope not.'[53]

Young people also play an important role in the development of the union, as shown by the example of Sibusiso Mhlala, the chairperson of NUM's Murray & Roberts Kroondal-Marikana branch. Aged 34, he joined the mining industry in 2004 and helped mobilise and organise workers at the company where NUM, which had approximately 5 000 members in the branch at the time of our interview, was not recognised until 2006.[54] Such was also the case of one of Sibusiso's teammates at Kroondal-Marikana, who, after starting to work in mining in 2001, joined NUM in 2002 even though the union was still unrecognised at the company:

> There was no union, I was just a member paying subscription to the union. *Q: Why did you join?* BOB: I had read many articles about NUM and how they help the mining employees so I started to join because I could see the conditions in which we were working, were not satisfying. *Q: What type of articles?* BOB: Because my uncle was a mineworker, he was also a member of the NUM and he would come with articles from NUM, books from NUM that I would read.

He then took part in organising the workers as early as 2003 and remembers: 'It was difficult then. We continued and it was not working … In 2005 we started mobilising again and people started to see the necessity of joining NUM.' The description of his semi-clandestine involvement in the initial recruitment campaign is reminiscent of that of his elders during the 1980s, who had to hide for fear of being victimised by management:

> *Q: Were you one of the main recruiters?* BOB: Yes, I played a part. Normally we would request stop orders from the region, there was an organiser[55] who was organising our branch. When we knocked off, at the hostels we would start recruiting people. We would hide them [the stop order forms] at the workplace. When one book was full we would take it to the organiser, who would bring it to the employer to sign. Up until the time when you get an access now. When we had an access we were able to take stop orders directly to the employer. *Q: Was it difficult to get the employer to recognise the union?* BOB: Yes, it was difficult. Sometimes we would actually embark on illegal strikes, make it difficult for the employer. Mobilising workers, when there was a Cosatu stayaway then we would encourage workers to participate and there would be a total work stoppage. We would also march to the employer

to take him to the CCMA to push him to recognise us. If the employer would call in a meeting we would not attend, make it difficult.

A non-South African citizen, he was also politically active in the country's ruling party. When I met him he was considering joining the SACP.[56] Transmission of the NUM tradition from one generation to another is also a factor of involvement for younger members, as shown in the following words by a 29-year-old local NUM leader:

> The reason why I became a member [at] the time when I was hired [nine years ago], yes I did not have … [much] clue about the mining industry and unions in the mining industry but I got that opportunity when somebody took me and explained everything about the mining industry situation. My father, he is still a miner at Anglo Platinum. I joined NUM a few weeks after I was hired through a comrade who told me about the different unions and their differences. I chose NUM because of the history, the struggle … I did not know much about NUM but I knew much about ANC and politics.[57]

What these examples suggest is that young union leaders do not shy away from activism and political involvement. This, however, does not guarantee any improvement of their position in the organisation since there are constant attempts to keep younger members in subaltern organisational positions. Typically, elders not only try to reduce their younger counterparts to a subaltern status, but they generally do so under the veil of political education.

The older NUM generation largely consider their younger counterparts to be a threat to organisational instability. One of the most significant manifestations of this tension in the last few years occurred around the question of launching a new NUM 'forum' dedicated to organising the youth. In October 2011, I attended a two-day seminar in Johannesburg, in which the question was cautiously discussed. The first day started at eight in the morning and attendees opened the proceedings by singing: 'My mother was a kitchen girl, my father was a garden boy, that's why I'm a communist, I'm a communist, I am a communist!' Forty-one young NUM leaders from all 11 of the union's regions, including 18 young women, took part in the seminar. The young people all seemed quite fashion-conscious and many exhibited trendy South African and international brands: Diesel, Soviet, Puma, Adidas, Uzzi, Levi's, Liverpool F.C. and Orlando Pirates (the latter two are football teams). Majadibodu then opened the floor to Senzeni Zokwana, then NUM president and an embodiment of the ideal of the 'legitimist elder'.[58]

Senzeni Zokwana, who had been president of NUM since 2000, when the historical president of the union James Motlatsi stepped down, was 'deployed' to Parliament and appointed South Africa's minister of agriculture, forestry and fisheries by Jacob Zuma after the 2014 general election. Zokwana, who was also the national chairperson of the SACP and an ANC NEC member,[59] joined NUM in 1983, as an employee of President Steyn Gold mine in the Free State, before rising through the ranks to reach the union's top position. During his years in office, Zokwana – a white-haired man who naturally commands respect – was revered as a 'patriarch', a figure of stability, a living embodiment of tradition, of the hardship of mineworkers and of the prospect of successful transformation in mining (see Figure 8.3).[60]

It is against this background that contentious issues such as the inclusion of women in mining, the demise of mining hostels or the fight against Fanakalo (the pidgin used in South African mines), which, for NUM, are also part of a broader process of decolonisation, must be addressed. As opposed to many top NUM leaders, Zokwana rose from the depths of the pit. In the early 1990s, he recounted his life in a touching testimony before the Leon Commission, which was submitted to Parliament in 1995. Appearing before the Commission, Zokwana told the story of the 14 years he had spent at President Steyn Gold mine. He 'described

Figure 8.3: NUM president Senzeni Zokwana addresses the 2011 Rustenburg regional conference

Photographer: Raphaël Botiveau

his humiliation at the procedures that he was subjected to when he first became a miner'. Part of Zokwana's myth comes from the fact that he was the first black person in South Africa to be officially promoted to the position of 'miner', which until 1989 was reserved for white people only, under the Mines and Works Regulations Act of 1912. According to the report of the Commission, Zokwana had

> now risen through the ranks to be a trainee shift boss, but was now required to join another Union dominated by white miners, although still a leading member of the NUM. When he first joined the NUM his relationship with his superiors became sour. Indeed he was dismissed in 1986 without a hearing and was out of work for two months. Later he was found not guilty but was demoted from August 1986 to February 1991 to the position of station marshal.

Zokwana's testimony included a poignant description of life on a mining compound and of the hostel system, in which he emphasised the importance of age:

> There was no recognition of people of differing ages nor was there any privacy. He had lived in a hostel room shared by sixteen with one person above another. This created many problems. Someone might arrive drunk and late and go out in the middle of the night to relieve a call of nature, and on returning step on his neighbour in a lower bunk. If one person in the room suffers from a contagious disease the whole room is affected [the hostel system contributed and still contributes to spreading the HIV and Aids pandemic]. The lack of privacy meant that if a wife came to stay there was very limited accommodation for her. Hostel life estranges the husband from his family. Allocation of rooms and bunks is without reference to the age of the individual, which may lead to a man of 60 having to use an upper bunk, and having great difficulty in getting in and out of bed.

Zokwana's own experience of racist humiliation and segregation included the obligation to use Fanakalo: 'Although he spoke English and Afrikaans he was required and obliged to speak in Fanagalo when he took up work at the mines. Instead of addressing persons or mine officials as Mr or Meneer, he was required to use the Fanagalo expression "Baas" [Boss].'[61] Because of this, Zokwana and other top NUM leaders insisted that Fanakalo be banned and the use of English promoted since it is the only language that holds the prospect of developing individuals from an educational and career point of view.

Senzeni Zokwana was always quick to present himself as a moral figure. In his speech to NUM's 14th National Congress, he quoted twice from the Bible (including the story of Saul who consulted God 'because he lost his compass'), and he was one of several leaders who denounced the Johannesburg-based Goodman Gallery for exhibiting Cape Town artist Brett Murray's painting *The Spear*. The painting portrayed President Zuma, genitals exposed, in a re-versioning of a famous propaganda poster of Lenin. For Zokwana, this painting was 'nothing more than the way in which white people see black people'. He called on Cosatu to organise a march on the gallery and stated in his characteristic traditionalist tone that 'only men should march because we will march naked'. In his references to women in public meetings where I heard him speak, Zokwana was at pains to appear progressively feminist, but the references generally kept a humorous nuance of sexism, so typical of the enduring, essentialised conceptions of women that are well entrenched in South Africa as elsewhere. During the same national congress he answered a question in the following words: 'I won't respond on sex workers because if you read the Bible you will find them defined as as old as the Bible. You cannot deny they exist, only that you visit them at night you can deny'. At the 2011 Rustenburg regional conference, Zokwana risked the following joke: 'My sister was scared because I respected women and did not exert my right on her.' Later, while insisting on the need to nominate women for inclusion into the union's leadership, he cautioned delegates: 'Don't propose to the first woman you meet ... We [men] are clumsy; when a woman says yes she means it.' He also told delegates that they needed to display high moral standards: 'You can't be a leader of this organisation and be seen with a girlfriend in a park or drunk.' It is worth noting that during the first day of the NUM national congress, the president had received the praises of a Xhosa *imbongi* (praise-poet) dressed in traditional clothes. Zokwana was thus elevated to the position of *madoda* (man), an elder, the leader of the organisation in the steps of its founding fathers. Only President Zuma would later receive the honour of a similar introduction before he addressed NUM delegates.

It is against such a background of tradition and patriarchy that NUM president Zokwana, an eloquent man, addressed the young delegates gathered at the NUM Youth Forum seminar. As he started telling his own story, the stance he adopted was clearly that of an elder who has gone through history and hardship: 'When I joined the mining industry they were not looking at your mental ability but at your body; at 23 years of age I was examined naked. It was made clear that it was not your industry. The battle for transformation is big. You must read and study to change the industry.' He recalled the darkest times of the mining industry: 'You signed a quote of nine months and you did not see home for nine months, if your mum died it was bad luck. Some have numbers on their graves; those times have gone.' He laid great emphasis on the educational role of NUM: 'Why is NUM important in the country? Why is it that NUM produced three ANC SGs [secretaries general] in succession? When Mantashe came to NUM he did not have grade 12 [matric], when he left he was doing his Master's. To be equal you have to study.' He then moved on to the actual purpose of the meeting: the establishment of a NUM Youth Forum. The words used to refer to the forum varied throughout the seminar and Zokwana insisted that it was to remain a 'desk'. He made his point by recalling that there was already a Youth League in the ANC and hence there was no need to have another one.

This, as was to become obvious in the rest of this two-day meeting, was central to senior NUM leaders' apprehensions and fears about the launch of this new youth 'structure'. On the one hand, it was needed in order to tackle the specific needs of the union's younger members, yet, on the other hand, it bore the threat of seeing another Malema scenario unfold. At the end of 2011, the ANC galaxy was greatly agitated by clashes between the mother body, led by Jacob Zuma, and its youth wing, headed by the turbulent and ill-disciplined Julius Malema. Zokwana therefore quoted the example of the early 1940s ANC Youth League, which, headed by leaders of the likes of Nelson Mandela, Walter Sisulu and Oliver Tambo, 'changed the ANC'. 'But they were very disciplined comrades. They engaged with the ANC but they did not run around and insult people. Sisulu was elected the youngest SG of the ANC. Today things have changed; it is the time of tenderpreneurs.'[62] The 'discipline' of the ANC Youth League's founding fathers might be discussed here since the dialectics of 'autonomy' and 'independence'[63] is a recurring feature in the League's history, but referring to this golden struggle era is classic rhetoric among the ANC and its allies. The contemporary Youth League started to reassert its independence in the mid-2000s, when it successfully supported Jacob Zuma in his fierce power battle with outgoing South African and ANC president Thabo Mbeki. Julius Malema became president of the Youth League in 2008. The young and ambitious leader soon became vocal and called for the nationalisation of South African mines, without first consulting NUM. This incursion into the union's reserved terrain was perceived, especially by its old guard, as a great affront and met with grave suspicion.

The NUM Youth Forum seminar was therefore held against the backdrop of an intense struggle about the position of the youth in the organisation, which was not unique to NUM but present also in Tripartite Alliance structures. The meeting was cautiously moderated by Eddie Majadibodu, head of the NUM production pillar, who recalled several times that the Youth Forum was only at discussion stage: 'Comrades, remember you are not a constitutional structure.' Majadibodu told participants that they would need to elect an interim leadership for the youth 'forum' (naming the new institution once again proved difficult and awkward) and again recalled that such a forum was not a constitutional structure: 'I say this because sometimes we became victims of our own initiatives.' The process was expected to function as follows: participants would give four names from four regions for the interim positions of chairperson, deputy chairperson, secretary and deputy secretary, as well as one name per region for 'comrades' who were to form the interim steering committee of the Youth Forum. Playing on words once more, Majadibodu explained that a youth 'summit' would then be held in the following year, 'not a conference'.

Majadibodu then introduced Buti Manamela, national secretary of the YCL, and explained that NUM had not invited the ANC Youth League to take part in the seminar. The reason for that, he explained, was that the SACP is the 'vanguard of the working class'. Majadibodu also recalled that there was tension between the Youth League and NUM and that Malema had accused the union of being opposed to nationalisation and had threatened 'to go and organise mineworkers'. At that point, one participant wearing a green beret (a military-like fashion accessory in the style of the ANC's armed wing, which Malema added to the material culture of the ANC Youth League), who had also introduced himself as an ANC Youth League branch chairperson, asked to speak. He recalled that the idea of creating a NUM Youth Forum had emerged out of a Highveld region resolution before it went to the NUM national congress. As such, he insisted, it had not been imposed from the top but had come from the base and he added: 'When I introduced myself I said I was from the ANC Youth League and I think we should not undermine other Alliance structures and you said Malema said this and that; I don't feel good that you criticise "my leader".' Madoda Sambatha, head of the NUM parliamentary pillar and one of the most vocal communist ideologues in the union, took this opportunity to poin out that the establishment of a NUM 'Women Structure', which was initially just intended to feminise the leadership, proved a 'mistake' when it became a constitutional structure and permanently differentiated between men and women in NUM. Debates heated up and a participant declared: 'You are trying to intimidate us.' Another one added: 'We are here for no reason but to debate … we are not here to be told what to do.' Things settled down for a moment and Sambatha was able to start a long address on socialism and nationalisation: 'we don't define a class by how much they have on their bank account, but in terms of [their] relationship to the means of production … Malema is not a capitalist, he does not own means of production.' Majadibodu then gave the floor to Manamela, secretary of the YCL. His speech generally repeated what his elders had said and he strongly denounced Malema's circle:

> I don't understand why university professors should earn R400 000 per annum while people who don't have matric are millionaires. How do we value our education? In Limpopo, young people before they are born learn the word CC [close corporation]. They want tenders. Instead we celebrate people who steal from the community. I am young and I remember that when I was a kid our social models were lawyers, nurses, teachers, not hustlers or corrupt people.

Majadibodu congratulated Manamela, who 'talks like a teacher', and, as a 'token of appreciation', gave him Victor Allen's trilogy on the 'history of mineworkers in South Africa' (see Figure 8.4).

Manamela's intervention was illustrative of the fluidity of ideals of leadership. A typical 'communist cadre', he also proves to be a young 'legitimist', in alliance with those I have called the 'legitimist elders'.[64] One participant then recalled that there were tensions in the 1940s ANC and, arguing that Marx would have deemed the young and the old irreconcilable, he asked Manamela: 'How can we coexist with the old?' In his response, Manamela recalled that in Marxist dialectical materialism, the

Figure 8.4: Buti Manamela receives Victor Allen's trilogy from the hands of Eddie Majadibodu

Photographer: Raphaël Botiveau

law of the 'negation of the negation' does not refer to age, but to the idea that the old is what has existed, whereas the young refers to what is in the making, the new order. 'But being young does not make you progressive,' he argued, based on the example of former Democratic Alliance parliamentary leader Lindiwe Mazibuko, who may be 'young' but is 'very reactionary', he said. 'Secondly, it is not because you are young that you can be rude and disrespectful. Mandela wrote [that] he used to disrupt meetings of the communist party. It was in the 1940s and he wrote that to show it was wrong. It is no argument to do it today and say Mandela did it. In fact he was also many other things, a lawyer ...' Manamela got a round of applause for this last sentence, intended to show that the opposition between the young and the old is not merely one of age but one of political positions, and he added in a show of irony that 'my counterpart in China is about 60 years old'.

Eddie Majadibodu finally opened the floor to debate, yet not without recalling that the decision to establish a Youth Forum was not a congress resolution, but one taken by the 2010 central committee following a NUM presidential proposition. In other words, it was to remain a process closely managed by the top of the organisation and, in the mind of NUM's national executive, the Youth Forum was to be administered by a permanent employee based at head office.[65] And indeed, in Frans Baleni's secretariat report to the NUM 14th National Congress in 2012, the section dedicated to the Youth Forum was entitled 'Youth Desk'.

The initiative to establish a Youth Forum in NUM was also an acknowledgement by the union that a large chunk of its membership, despite ageing trends outlined in several SWOP surveys, was now located in the 20–39 age group – a segment of membership which required special attention for the union to keep growing.[66] Interestingly, in the minds of NUM leaders, what motivated the idea to launch a youth structure seems to have been somewhat elitist. While noting that NUM was now to 'assume' its place 'as a champion of youth emancipation and development', the programme insisted that the forum was meant to respond to a new trend in the industry, where 'there is a fast-rising sector of youth that belong to what we may refer to as a "middle" and upper-middle strata who traditionally ... [because of job reservation] were never found within the workplaces ... We need to tap on this group's intellectual capital and expertise by engaging with them.'[67] In other words, the Youth Forum was also designed in the minds of NUM leaders to address what they perceived as new needs among a younger section of their membership perceived as more educated, more mobile professionally and more sophisticated.

After two days of proceedings, the NUM executive had reached its objective and the launch of a union Youth Forum had been closely monitored, shaped and in a way co-opted by the elders. As a final tribute to the struggle heritage, forum participants were taken on a tour to Liliesleaf Farm, north of Johannesburg, a site from where the armed wing of the ANC, Umkhonto we Sizwe (MK), had been piloted in the early 1960s until it was raided by the police and core ANC, MK and SACP leadership were arrested. Young NUM leaders were very excited by the visit and humbled by this reminder of their elders' sacrifice. The NUM Youth Forum seminar was therefore concluded with an acknowledgement of the historical sacrifice of the older generation, who managed to maintain control of the younger generation, keeping at bay the spectrum of degeneration embodied by Julius Malema. The clash of generations had been avoided but their difference was also acknowledged, as eloquently – but also ambiguously – put by then president Senzeni Zokwana in his concluding remarks:

> Your fears cannot be my fear. When I was your age I was scared of impregnating a woman and have to pay for her and the kid. Your fear is to transmit disease … People think I'm old but I can google, send messages, go to the bank without going out of home … You are representing an organisation. Just like Jesus said through you we have seen the Lord and me, people should see NUM through you.

The NUM Youth Forum was officially launched on 9 May 2013[68] and it has so far presented itself as a way to contain and co-opt young leaders internally rather than to transform the union.

9

Taking Control of NUM: The Rise of the Communist Faction

THE COMMUNIST CADRE

The ideal type of leadership I now address is closely linked to the type of organisation NUM became as it was increasingly controlled and shaped by Gwede Mantashe, its general secretary from 1998 to 2006. Mantashe was then elected secretary general of the ANC in 2007. This internal reconfiguration is closely related to a changing balance of forces in the union, which started in the early 2000s when, after Kgalema Motlanthe, James Motlatsi left NUM. A former NUM head office employee once described Mantashe to me as a 'hard-core communist', a national leader in the SACP – a party my interlocutor described as the 'most Stalinist in the world', recalling that when Mantashe heard about the coup d'état against Gorbachev, in 1991, he 'was so happy when he arrived at work'. With this in mind, I will first consider the question: what does it mean to be a communist cadre in twenty-first century South Africa? This will then allow me to consider NUM's departure from the type of leadership described earlier, which combined administrative and organisational skills with some form of involvement and proximity with the membership base. In this configuration of the leader–member relationship, the top-down dynamic that structured NUM over time was tempered by mechanisms that allowed the base to retain some degree of worker control, which corrected the union's centralising tendency. In Mantashe's ideal of organisation, 'discipline' became the preferred type of allegiance, which was mechanically imposed on the union in line with the principle of 'democratic centralism'. While Ramaphosa and most of his fellow historical NUM leaders had never been convinced communists,[1] Mantashe was, and under his leadership NUM was brought closer to and almost 'infiltrated' by the SACP at its top level.[2] This, along with discipline and a critical reduction in internal debate, endowed NUM leadership with an increasingly legitimist character. The increase in the influence of the SACP on union structures was also experienced politically in the ANC with the rise of Jacob Zuma to power. After years of marginalisation and even victimisation under Thabo Mbeki's two terms as president, those he used to pejoratively label 'ultra left' – as if it were an insult – were back in business.[3]

When reflecting on the ideal type of the 'communist cadre' in NUM, it is useful to start by portraying 'young communist' leaders, to keep an eye on the type of power relationships produced by age, as well as to see how these communist cadres are being politically nurtured and how they make sense of their own political involvement. Such an involvement in communism remains a choice for a minority in NUM and, more generally, in today's South Africa. Yet being a communist in twenty-first century South Africa is not perceived as old-fashioned, which significantly differs from post-communist Europe, where communist parties have virtually disappeared. Younger and older South African communists are generally more versed in politics and politically more educated than their counterparts outside of the SACP or the YCL. They generally like debating ideas, although this regularly clashes with the ethos of an organisation that tends towards discipline and submission of the younger to the elder.

An initial striking feature in their involvement is that young communists tend to see themselves as 'initiates', as communists in the making rather than as genuine cadres of the Party. Such was the case of Peterson Siyaya, a 26-year-old NUM leader who also belonged to the YCL, the ANC Youth League and the ANC. At a lunch break during the eighth Rustenburg regional conference in 2011, Peterson started a long tirade on the meaning of politics. In a typical Marxist posture, he insisted on the difference between trade unions and political organisations such as the ANC and the SACP. He explained that he was a member of the YCL but did not yet belong to the SACP as he was still a 'student of politics': 'I am not yet a communist,' he insisted. A young female leader, who was seated at our table and had been quite vocal in the plenary session the day before, asked Siyaya if he could spell 'Karl Marx' for her. At that point, the young man started to lecture his fellow comrade with a good dose of paternalism and in mimicry of his elders: 'you have to elevate your mind to the political level'. As another young female delegate at our table started lamenting that she was not going to get anything out of the conference because delegates were just 'fighting', Peterson gave her a taste of political correctness, in the style of South African communists who always strive to avoid any display of internal conflict: 'don't say they were fighting, defend the organisation, don't talk to the media like that'. This idea that one does not become a communist just by carrying an SACP card, but that one has to mature first, applies not only to the younger generation. After he had told me that he also belonged to the ANC and the SACP, I asked a NUM branch leader in his early forties if he was a communist. He answered:

> Yes, I am learning to be because [laughter] you see one needs to have a proper definition of a communist and it is a very big title that one can claim. *Q: And what is the definition for you?* GT: Well it's ... I will have to go back to my notes.[4]

A similar answer was given to me by a senior Rustenburg region official: 'I am a member of the Communist Party, not yet a communist [laughter]. My understanding is that a communist is a very well advanced cadre of the revolution. I aspire to be a communist but it requires a lot of commitment and dedication. Communism is the higher stage of the socialist order we aspire to bring on.'[5]

In both cases, while a discourse is clearly being spelled out, there is some irony in the discrepancy between the actual reality of being a communist and a South African context in which the prospects of a communist 'revolution' now seem so distant. This idea of initiation, a transition from one state to another before one can claim to belong to the group, is reminiscent of what Arnold van Gennep once analysed as 'rites of passage'. Just like initiation rites in the transition from teenagehood to adulthood in societies such as the Xhosa, or in secret societies such as the freemasonry, the SACP imposes several steps before one can be co-opted by elders and claim to belong. But not all young communist cadres I met in NUM seemed to have gone through such a process of political maturing; indeed, clause 5.1 of the Party's constitution makes every South African over the age of 16 eligible for membership (before becoming a full member one nonetheless has to be an 'interim member' for one year). Different meanings are also attached to the fact of being a communist in South Africa today. When asked if she would say she was a 'communist', a young NUM leader told me: 'I think that yes, I am a communist because I believe in communist values. Communism in that there should be equal access of people to the wealth of the country, opportunities.'[6] When asked if he was a communist, another local NUM leader who belonged both to the ANC and the SACP answered:

> I am a communist! *Q: What does it mean?* MM: To be a communist it's very nice because we are socialising, talk politics ... we are not hiding anything. Like when I am having a problem, or maybe I am having an issue against another comrade, we must cough it out.[7]

If members of the SACP often seem to have been co-opted after a period of political maturing and education, becoming a member does not always depend on an individual's level of conscientisation.[8] One NUM regional leader whom I never saw publicly display any sign of adhesion to the communist ideology explained to me that one could sign up for membership for one year or more. He had himself subscribed for five years and told me that when joining one had to pay R25. Afterwards, the monthly subscription ranged from R45 to thousands of rands, since one could decide what amount one wished to give to the Party (unemployed members pay an annual membership fee of R12). He also told me that he had joined the ANC for five years and paid a one-off subscription of R80. The degree of 'political consciousness' that one is usually required to possess before joining the SACP is thus doubled by a higher subscription fee that further reinforces the Party's specificity as a relatively elitist structure of cadres who claim to be the vanguard of the revolution. As opposed to the SACP, the ANC, in which subscription starts at R1, has always strived to be a mass party and, when this book was written, it claimed over one million members, almost ten times more than the former.[9]

There is no uniform way to be a communist cadre in South Africa's NUM and in the trade union movement. For some, such as shaft steward Bhongo Mvimvi, belonging to the SACP meant having an understanding of 'politics' and being 'between the two groups of people, the rich and the poor. I'll regard the demands if maybe the poor demand something from the rich people, the rich people will refuse … And also the issue of discrimination it is also politics to me. Also the issue of the economy, land.'[10] Belonging to the SACP for unionists was therefore also seen as being part of the class struggle. Another way to be a communist while leading in NUM was put forward to me by an Impala shaft steward who was very critical of the SACP and the ANC:

> Q: *Do you belong to another organisation?* TM: Hence I said you know Karl Marx, I am a communist, I have a political organisation, which is not recognised but it's a leftist communist organisation in South Africa. We used to call ourselves Bolsheviks, now it's called Revolutionary Marxist Group. It is in Brazil and the USA as well. Q: *What does it mean for you to be a communist today in South Africa?* TM: For me as a communist in South Africa it's helping a lot, the decisions … prior to 1994, we had a belief that … pre-1994 we had programmes that would elevate black people primarily because they were the oppressed people during the apartheid era and giving them land, I mean nationalise some of the industries in South Africa. But unfortunately it did not happen; a new policy was introduced, [which included] privati-

sations. Currently we are fighting with an organisation that is in power ... which is implementing capitalist policy, the ANC. It has moved right. At that stage workers are not represented. Now South Africa is the biggest country in terms of disparities. *Q: Do you also belong to the SACP?* TM: We don't believe in the SACP because SACP has adopted a philosophy of Stalin [the Revolutionary Marxist Group is a Trotskyist organisation] ... SACP is in Tripartite Alliance with the ANC. We cannot be Tripartite Alliance with a capitalist organisation. They advocated for Nedlac [the National Economic Development and Labour Council]; it is not working for us. They are pseudo communists; they become communists when it suits them. The current general secretary of the SACP is now a minister and an MP [member of Parliament]; he is given all these benefits which workers don't get.[11]

As I mentioned earlier, Buhlungu distinguishes between 'ideological unionists' and 'career trade unionists'. On the one hand, the former would be more 'political', 'collectivist', attached to the tradition of 'worker control', willing to 'achieve socialism' and, from the point of view of organisational modernisation, 'ambivalent' insofar as they would tend both towards 'minimalism' and some degree of 'professionalism to achieve efficiency'. On the other hand, 'career unionists' would be willing 'to make unionism a lifetime career', be 'apolitical' and 'technocratic', 'reformist' and organisationally 'bureaucratic' while leaving decisions to professional 'experts' and 'top leaders'.[12] This typology is problematic, as I argued earlier, since the frontier between these two types is highly porous and because a convinced communist such as Gwede Mantashe perfectly fits the two: he led a successful trade union and political career, is committed to socialism and worked hard to build a bureaucratic NUM.

Mantashe started his career in the gold industry as an Anglo American Western Deep recreation officer before he was fired in 1975. He was then employed at Prieska Copper Mines as a welfare officer, where he worked for seven years before joining Matla Coal and NUM in 1983. With others, he recruited 400 members or 80 per cent of the workforce and became a branch chairperson in Matla. From there Mantashe rose to the leadership of NUM's Witbank region: 'I became the Witbank regional secretary – in NUM secretaries are workers'. His insistence on having NUM led by worker-leaders is an important aspect to bear in mind, a position on which Mantashe always proved inflexible. Mantashe never stopped rising through the ranks: he became Cosatu's Highveld regional chairperson and, after leaving Matla in 1988, was employed by NUM as an organiser until he was appointed a regional coordinator in 1993. In 1994 he was elected as Kgalema Motlanthe's assistant general secretary. He became general secretary in 1998, a position he left in

2006 only to become the ANC's secretary general.[13] Based on his career trajectory one can question whether to be a 'worker' in the words of Mantashe actually means 'working' or 'having been a worker'. Since 1988, he has himself de facto become a professional unionist and a career politician. In the last NUM national congress he attended, Mantashe gave the following description of a strong union:

> One's biggest excitement, as I step down from being the General Secretary of the union, is that a strong organisation is left behind. A strong leadership permeates the organisation, coupled with a strong team of functionaries that provides a professional support to our leadership. We have built a strong and healthy asset base … We must also acknowledge that we are leaving behind a highly contested organisation, and central to this contestation is the desire to access this healthy resource base.[14]

Mantashe – an ideal communist cadre – may be committed to achieving socialism but this did not prevent him from embracing and advancing ties between the worlds of unionism and the mining business. In 1995, he was appointed to the board of directors of JSE-listed chrome producer Samancor. This was no random choice since, at the time, such a move of a trade unionist onto the board of a company was not yet the norm in South Africa or in Cosatu (Numsa, who also represented workers at Samancor, decided not to join its board of directors). At the time, Mantashe justified his move by arguing that it was marking a shift in industrial relations from a 'confrontation' to 'meaningful influence' and to 'worker involvement in decision-making from the time a change is identified – to be part of developing a strategy and not only being called upon at the implementation stage'.[15] The idea was to move towards 'co-determination', which gives some insight into how Mantashe was also embracing orientations usually associated with social democracy.

It is impossible to know precisely how many NUM leaders also belong to the SACP. At a Carletonville regional committee meeting I attended in 2011, the regional chairperson asked his comrades who had attended the recent SACP regional conference. Three-quarters out of about thirty participants raised their hands and he told them 'being a communist is tangible comrades'. Later on that day it was recalled that a 2009 NUM resolution states: 'Eligibility for election in a Shop steward's position and office bearer at all levels of the union **has political obligations** and therefore any nominee for elections should be a **member of the ANC and SACP or accept to join** after successful election'.[16] Being a communist cadre in a trade union in twenty-first century South Africa therefore means being politicised and politically involved. This also often goes hand in hand with the pursuit of a career in unions and/or in political organisations, based on the organisational skills, degree of political acumen and administrative capacity characteristic of South African communists.

HOW CONSCIOUSNESS RULES OVER UNCONSCIOUSNESS

When I asked him about the ideology of NUM, Mercy Sekano, executive director of the Elijah Barayi Memorial Training Centre, answered straightforwardly: 'We are very clear: we are socialists.'[17] The NUM general secretary's answer was as unambiguous:

> Look, we are a left-thinking union, we embrace Marxist theory, we fully understand that trade unions are formative in character, we back the SACP and we also support the ANC which is a left-lining organisation as well. *Q: Would NUM be closer to the SACP or the ANC?* We are close to both but in terms of the final destination we are much closer to the SACP than the ANC.[18]

NUM's socialist ideology, as imposed on the organisation by its leadership, is spread via what Antonio Gramsci famously identified throughout his *Prison Notebooks* (and especially in the twelfth) as 'organic intellectuals'. 'Intellectual' here refers to the social function of an individual rather than to one's particular intellectual capacity. In his own interpretation of the term, Gramsci indeed considered that 'all men are intellectuals' and he did not distinguish between manual or intellectual work. In Gramsci's mind, the importance of intellectuals lies in the part they play in diffusing 'hegemony'. 'Organic intellectuals' are 'organically' linked to a dominant or rising social class to which they belong ('traditional intellectuals' are considered the opposite and identified with a formerly dominant class). Gramsci often uses 'intellectual' and 'leader' as synonyms and all the members of a party are eventually, for him, 'intellectuals'. He decisively linked the 'cultural' function of intellectuals to their 'technical' skills, which, in the complexity of the modern world, had become intertwined (he referred to the 'social democratico-bureaucratic system'). While lamenting this evolution, he nonetheless insisted that the organic intellectuals of the working class had to acquire at least the basics of the 'technical general knowledge' needed to exercise command in a capitalist society. Gramsci concluded that

> the mode of being of the new intellectual ... consists of an active involve-
> ment in practical life, as builder, organiser, 'permanent persuader,' because
> he is not just an orator – and goes beyond the abstract mathematical mind;
> based on techno-work, the intellectual accesses the techno-science and the
> humanistic and historical conception without which one remains a 'special-
> ist' and does not become a 'leader' (specialist + politician).[19]

This last quote shows that Gramsci had isolated one crucial social trend in the
rise of organisational expertise, which decisively brings together the techniques of
administration I described in Part I with the political skills I am referring to here.

The role of white intellectuals (who were not organic intellectuals from the
working class) in the birth and development of the independent trade union movement was at the heart of a controversy between Sakhela Buhlungu and Johann
Maree.[20] This issue of the contribution of intellectuals to the trade union movement
was also addressed when organic intellectuals left the unions en masse, in 1994, to
be deployed to Parliament or government in the aftermath of South Africa's first
democratic election. In a debate with Mike Murphy, a white student activist who
became part of the union movement before he was exiled, Jabu Gwala, the general
secretary of the Southern African Clothing and Textile Workers' Union (Sactwu),
who started work as a 'garden boy' before he became a textile worker and rose
through union ranks, foresaw a 'decline' in the union movement after the departure
of 'intellectuals' to Parliament:

> Look at my situation: As General Secretary I have now to take on tasks pre-
> viously done by intellectuals (eg lawyers) as to what to do, by exercising my
> discretion across a range of factors: If a course of action is taken, will the
> union gain or lose, will it establish a precedent, will it undermine the rela-
> tionship with the employer? The professional intellectuals I instruct do not
> have to exercise the same discretion, and they can disagree with me on the
> course of action I recommend.

Picking up on the word 'professional', Mike Murphy averred:

> In my view the key intellectual capacity we are talking about here, is the
> ability to see the big picture, to weigh up a broad range of factors, and to plan
> and strategise from there. Although it *helps* to have gone to university and
> to have picked up technical skills (accounting, law, etc), it is not essential.
> Unions can hire people with these skills, and obviously it will help you to

supervise them if you have these skills yourself, but it is not essential. What is essential in my view is a practice, gained through experience, of thinking broadly and systematically about matters, weighing pros and cons, and making rational decisions as a consequence. But if you have worked in a team that *follows* this practice, then you *become* an 'intellectual' (in my sense of the word) over time.[21]

This issue of growing intellectuals–leaders as opposed to hiring professionals was partly solved in NUM through what I will later refer to as the '2004 coup'. Communist leaders and organic working-class intellectuals have now taken the lead in the union, as embodied by the examples of Gwede Mantashe and Madoda Sambatha. Mantashe is a self-made organic intellectual, a former mine-surface worker who became a top leader in NUM and in the ANC. The links between NUM and the Wits-based SWOP research institute were deepened when he became a sociology student and worked with the academics who had conducted surveys for the union. In 2008, Mantashe graduated from Wits with a Master of Arts. Madoda Sambatha, head of the NUM parliamentary pillar and provincial secretary of the SACP in the North West, described his background as follows:

I got employed in 1996 in a mine, underground, as a general worker at AngloGold Ashanti Mponeng mine in Carletonville. I worked there until 1997 when I became a NUM full-time shaft steward, then a branch secretary, then education deputy secretary in the region in 1997. I was already a branch secretary of the ANC from 1996 to 1999 and then in 1999 I was released during the local government election to go and stand as ANC local counsellor. I served from 2000 to 2005. I then became employed by NUM in 2006 as national educator, then regional coordinator and now pillar head.

Sambatha was very clear on the role of NUM and the SACP in national politics:

Q: *Why did you insist on the fact that NUM seems to be a good school for training cadres?* MS: The history would prove me correct. First ANC conference in the country in 1991, Cyril [Ramaphosa] was elected as [ANC] secretary general. When he left in 1997, Kgalema Motlanthe was elected as well. When the latter left in 2007 Mantashe was elected as secretary general of the ANC. It may also be one element while some individuals particularly led by the president of the ANC Youth League are very angry with the fact that comrade Gwede Mantashe is the secretary general of the ANC. It is not purely on the basis of inefficiency, he has never been inefficient even in the ANC. He is the best secretary general that the ANC has ever had in this period, but he is the most contested one by the Youth League. You have never heard in any organisation a person told that three years before the end of the term that we are going to remove you … *Q: And why is it so?* MS: It is not as they say because he is the national chair of the SACP: they want to use the office of the secretary general as a distribution agent for tenders. And it is difficult for them to have that access to the current secretary general.[22]

Madoda Sambatha became a prime communist ideologue in NUM or, in other words, a working-class intellectual. In many meetings I attended, he was called in to speak to delegates and, almost like a preacher, to give them a lesson in ideology with a view to disciplining them. This was clear, for instance, in the 2011 Rustenburg regional conference, when he gave a speech in the name of the SACP. The situation there was tense because of stiff competition between two camps aiming at the regional leadership. National leaders clearly showed they wanted the outgoing faction to win the election and the main incoming contender, Richard Mahoha, who was running for the regional chairmanship, was regularly chastised for being divisive. Sambatha told delegates that they were not 'communists' since their conference was not 'ideological'. Such a view seems to suggest that ideology requires the kind of debate that excludes contradictions and the discussion of opposing views. Mahoha was clearly targeted: 'The problem is all of you think you have a right to stand based on the constitution. It is a right given by members, it is a privilege … Leadership should be based on continuity and stability.' Taking the example of controversial ANC leader Supra Mahumapelo who had successfully come back after having been expelled from the union,[23] Sambatha recalled, threatening: 'In the communist party we don't charge you we expel you without a hearing.'

One key characteristic of communist intellectuals and leaders in NUM is that they usually belong to a small elite whose domination originates not only in their capacity as administrator but also in their mastery of a quasi-esoteric form of knowledge, which they use as symbolic power. As soon as one listens and talks to lower levels of leadership, ideological references to socialism are generally quite vague. In a NUM branch committee meeting I attended in 2010, shaft stewards started with a review of the minutes of their previous meeting. On point 12 of the minutes, the local education secretary, a communist, submitted a correction. The minutes stated that there were 'other working class' in other companies and he pointed out that there is only one 'working class'. He looked to me for support – a 'political student' who would, of course, disagree with the existence of several working classes, he argued. He then went on to discuss the issue of xenophobia (the minutes read, 'Non existence of solidarity leads to this zoophobias' and nobody noted the mistake). Such approximations are common in NUM. One day, as we were having breakfast during the 2011 Rustenburg regional conference, Peterson Siyaya made a remark about the hotel's employees, noting that the bosses seemed to be whites. He was immediately corrected by his elder in communism, Sithethi Mxhasi, who reframed his words in classist terms: 'Those are employees, they are white workers, not stake-holders.' Such a gap between the political culture of top leaders and that of their more ordinary counterparts is often expressed through humour, which also indicates that ideology and reality are two different things in the mind of NUM leaders. However, as I will soon show, this does not preclude the use of an ideology such as symbolic violence. During a NUM political school I attended in 2010, the last day was dedicated to the issue of 'nationalisation'. At some stage, Sambatha, who was teaching that day, introduced the arguments weighing against nationalisation and emphasised that those were arguments that 'as revolutionaries we cannot have'. Later, one participant proudly recalled that the role of the State was to help suppress the bourgeoisie. Madoda Sambatha then answered that if he wished to learn more on that he could just go to www.marxists.org and check Lenin's writing *The State and Revolution*. And he jokingly added that 'my worry if you go on www.marxists. org is that after that you will no longer be willing to vote for the ANC' because what this website says is that the State is a tool of class oppression.

One distinctive feature of the SACP and of communism in NUM is that their structure and ideology are largely elitist. In 1998, 55.6 per cent of NUM members surveyed by SWOP reported that they were active members of political organisations. Among those, 79.4 per cent said they were members of the ANC, as against only 5.6 per cent for the SACP. In 2005, a Carletonville report noted with regard to the building of SACP structures: 'we have taken a number of resolutions in this regard but there is nothing concrete happening. There are no structures in place.'[24] This suggests another split between NUM leaders and mineworkers who, as a component of the working class, may be conceived as a 'reference group' by communist cadres in the union, but do not necessarily see themselves as such. While NUM managed to tie workers' identities to the struggle against apartheid embodied in the ANC in the 1980s and 1990s, socialism remained a distant reality for most union members and for a majority of unionists.[25] This, of course, is not to say that South 'African workers' did not develop, beyond other forms of identity such as ethnicity or profession, a distinct 'consciousness' based on their shared experience as mineworkers, which they regularly expressed through acts of resistance to exploitation.[26] What I wish to emphasise, rather, is the fact that most mineworkers do not primarily view themselves as part of a 'working class', a definition that South African communists have applied to them for a long time. From a Marxist point of view, however, the collective mobilisation of mineworkers, and their sustained solidarity in defence of interests that go beyond merely the material demands they put forward, are also illustrative of the durability of class consciousness.[27] NUM thus perceives political education as key in developing workers' and cadres' class-consciousness and discipline. In the Rustenburg region 2011 secretariat report, one reads: 'Only members equipped with theory and ideological tools of analysis from a class perspective … are able to drive the national democratic revolution. This class consciousness can only be cultivated through involvement and participation in SACP structures.'[28] Political education in the communist sense is therefore a way not only to train people as part of NUM's commitment to education, but also to develop their political consciousness before deploying them to strategic positions. As a union branch leader told me:

> We always say we are a political school, where we develop members and then allow them and deploy them to go outside and service the entire community. Get a conscious understanding of the situation of the working class, working people. I am a member of the ANC, the SACP and a district secretary of the SACP in this area.[29]

Political education is also seen as a remedy for the poor state of many NUM local structures:

> There is an emerging trend where members in our respective branches are increasingly unsure of their identity. There's a sense of not knowing who we really are, where we come from, what we stand for … It is because of this state of affairs that there are fights and dirty campaigns for positions at all levels. Comrades are not concerned about acquiring knowledge and understanding of the organization, but more concerned about being leaders of the organization … We may sound controversial, but it is sometimes important to ask much questions whether shop steward's induction courses, advance courses, political schools should be a prerequisite for the elections.[30]

NUM therefore regularly convenes political schools and it often does so jointly with the SACP. Despite statements on the need to educate the membership, participants in political schools are usually limited to a handful of local and regional union leaders. In September 2009, one such school comprised a number of 'cross-cutting activities' centred on the question of 'The Role of Trade Unions in the Working Class Struggle'. More specifically, it aimed to examine 'how classes are formed', to analyse 'the source of the conflict between the two main classes in society' and to explore the nature, purpose and history of trade unions.[31] In 2012, Madoda Sambatha and Malesela Maleka produced, respectively for NUM and the SACP, a joint NUM/SACP political education programme. A 320-page volume, it gives an idea of the type of theory proposed for political training, as well as an idea of its elitist dimension. In addition to classical Marxist texts and programmes of action of the ANC and the SACP, they proposed summarised and full versions of writings from Lenin, Stalin, Mick Brooks, Rob Sewell and others on questions such as historical and dialectical materialism, the State and other adaptations of Marxist–Leninist theory to the South African and African contexts.[32]

Communist ideology, as conceived in and applied to NUM, turns into an implacable disciplinary machine as soon as it identifies enemies to fight not only outside but also within the organisation. In the latter case, the divide between political friends and foes is masked behind the opposing labels of 'conscious' and 'unconscious' members and leaders. This hint at enmity rarely targets enemies by name but instead refers to them as a vague and unidentified threat, which in practice makes the Schmittian label 'enemy' extendable to any form of internal or external opposition.[33] Faced with rejection by their own members in the platinum belt from 2012 on, NUM leaders did not respond with self-criticism. Rather, they denounced a plot by enemies within and without NUM. Four days into the Marikana massacre, NUM general secretary Frans Baleni stated the following:

> There are those dark forces who can mislead our members, make them to believe that they've got extra power to make their life to be different and overloud. An unconscious member is as dangerous as an enemy. We call our members to develop their class consciousness. In this journey without a sharpened class consciousness we will trip and fall.[34]

In a later radio interview, when questioned on his call for 'decisive' police action during the August 2012 Lonmin strike, Baleni coldly responded: 'Decisive action only means to ask law enforcement and prevention of loss of life. Any loss of life is regrettable, our country, our Constitution does not permit anybody to take lives be it the police or be it individual workers.'[35] Figure 9.1 provides a good illustration of how NUM leadership responded to the strike of its former members at Impala (this document was also translated into isiXhosa). This reduction of the strikers and ultimately of Amcu, a registered trade union whose new members had been NUM

RDO STRIKE LEADERS REFUSE TO CO-OPERATE WITH NUM

After NUM brought to an end an illegal six weeks strike at Impala Platinum Mines and it has committed to represent the striking employees to realize their demand. Unfortunately silly games by strike leaders are frustrating the process. Subject to the level of violence introduced to the union and the workplace, it has become difficult to carry the work of the union at Implats. All NUM Offices across Impala operations are closed down because the RDO reps have confiscated office keys. Without access to fax machines, e-mails and telephone calls.

This has hampered the work of the union, cases at the CCMA and the workplace have stalled and people are dismissed.

NUM meetings are consistently disrupted and often not allowed to take place. NUM leaders are undermined, assaulted and injured in mass meetings of the NUM.

While NUM is negotiating with Impala on their behalf, they have displayed a tendency — foreign to NUM and those they claim to represent — of violence, intimidation and false demands.

We have no option but to conclude that the strike leaders are paid agents of a third force and sooner or later it will come up into the open. We took liberty to invite them in negotiation with management and they display caricature like behaviour that management will never listen to.

NUMs view to negotiate for everybody on the salary adjustment issue is rejected by strike leaders. We strongly believe that Implats has reopened negotiation process. NUM maintains that adjustment must benefit every employee working for Impala Mines.

NUM POSITION

- We call for RDOs to appeal to the guys who claim to represent them to return the keys of NUM branch offices to elected NUM Shop Stewards.

- NUM operations be allowed and members continue to enjoy services rendered by the Union such as case representation, conducting accidents inquiries, collective bargaining etc. **The actions of the strike leaders will result in people not being compensated for injuries.**

- We call on our members to defend the NUM and its constitution against forces of darkness, who are geared to destroy the workers parliament and its achievements.

- We call on RDOs strike leaders to stop intimidating and assaulting NUM leaders and members. Workers must be allowed to continue holding their normal mass meetings without fear and intimidation or any form of disruption.

- Memorandum of understanding entered into between NUM and Implats on wage discussion must be observed, and that restoration of stability and normalization should be of priority to the process.

NB: Therefore, until the above have been adhered to, NUM suspends the discussions with immediate effect. Workers across Impala Operations must be aware that we are trying by all means to carry on their mandate despite the current state of anarchy at Impala Mines that has reached a highest stage. The NUM does not and would never condone lawlessness in whatever manner it is exercised.

RDOs should be aware that the work of the NUM is not only salary negotiations. We are responsible to oversee that government legislation that we have fought for is followed by the mine i.e the mining charter, pension benefits, housing, health and safety, education, employee shared schemes.

The RDOs must be aware that their actions are closely monitored by the police and sooner or later they will be prosecuted. The NUM appeals to its members not to participate in any criminal activities, but assist police investigations, as the police are closing on those who killed innocent people at Impala.

Poor demands will never be achieved and management will never give in on poor demands. Don't be fooled.

Figure 9.1: NUM flyer to Impala rock drill operators on strike, 2012

Source: Pamphlet collected by the author at Impala Platinum mine, Phokeng, 26 April 2012 . Reproduced with permission.

members, to criminality was also supported by the SACP, whose general secretary, Blade Nzimande, declared: 'Comrades, we need to distinguish between a trade union and a group of vigilantes. Amcu is not a union and has never been a union. The best way to describe it is a vigilante union.'[36] NUM leaders eventually targeted enemies within their own ranks when, referring to Cosatu's internal divide between supporters of its president and its general secretary, Baleni declared after a union central committee meeting: 'The CC concurred that the NUM did have enemies within … Once you eliminate the enemy within, you are left in a stronger position to deal with external forces.'[37] As I have shown in this section, internal enemies are generally first disqualified and labelled 'unconscious' from a communist perspective, before becoming the target of implacable administrative discipline.

MANTASHE'S IDEAL ORGANISATION: A DISCIPLINED NUM

The combination of elitism and communist infiltration of NUM described in the previous section was ironically illustrated in a union press release responding to alleged accusations by Amcu president Joseph Mathunjwa against NUM president Senzeni Zokwana. According to the press release, the 'ill-informed and professional liar Association of Mineworkers and Construction Union (Amcu) president Joseph Mathunjwa' had declared that 'NUM President Senzeni Zokwana serves in an entity called SAPS Bureau'. It is not clear whether Mathunjwa meant that Zokwana was indeed serving the 'SAPS' (the South African Police Service) or whether it was a slip of the tongue, but NUM nonetheless decided to correct it thus: 'NUM President Senzeni Zokwana is the National Chairperson of the South African Communist Party (SACP) and a member of the SACP Politburo. We think that Mr Mathunjwa was referring to the SACP Politburo.'[38] Such an exchange provides an ironical reminder that NUM was organised, disciplined and one could indeed say 'policed' by its communist cadres under Gwede Mantashe's secretariat.

The wish to build a disciplined organisation led and organised by a limited pool of leaders is as old as Marxism–Leninism. It lies at the heart of the opposition between Marxists and anarchists, which materialised in the conflict between Karl Marx and Mikhail Bakunin during the First International. While acknowledging the former's 'immense' contribution to socialism, the latter, and other European 'revolutionary socialists', had identified and condemned Marx's political views, which tended towards subjecting the 'proletarian masses' to the leadership of the Party hierarchy and to an 'aristocracy of intelligence'.[39] Lenin later confirmed this last trend through insisting on the need for leaders.[40] This need for leaders with technical skills and leaders with authority was later reasserted by Stalin, who, in 1934, wrote: 'we have accumulated a lot of authority, we now need leaders'. The distinction between cadres and leaders was an important one since cadres' submission to class-conscious leaders with a political view was conceived as a means to short-circuit the peril of bureaucratisation.[41] Once the leaders are ideologically established as legitimate, the rest of the organisation is expected to be disciplined and unconditionally agree to their vigilant leadership. The organisation – the revolutionary Party or, in the case of a NUM with a communist leadership, the trade union – was seen by Lenin as a new form of centralised organisation adapted to the psychology of factory-trained workers. The Party was conceived as a weapon rather than as an arena for debate, which would have jeopardised its action. In 1905, Lenin hardly accepted the existence of the soviets and he made sure they were controlled by the Party: in the Communist Party, the principle of 'democratic centralism', which Rosa Luxemburg condemned as a 'regime of barracks', then became the key organisational principle. Through it, leaders were centrally elected and subsequently enjoyed virtually full power over the organisation. This top-down principle is still alive in organisations such as the SACP and NUM, as well as in other South African trade unions and in the ANC. It was inherited from the years of exile in which the SACP had a major influence on the top structures of the liberation movement and when underground activity imposed tight organisational and secret decision-making mechanisms. Democratic centralism implies that upper structures make decisions that are then automatically applied to the lower level in a military-like fashion. In NUM, discipline is thus equated with order and the orderly functioning of the union. The crucial evolution here insofar as the internal functioning of NUM is concerned is that its bureaucratic tendency, which was aimed at building a functional organisation (as discussed in Part I), was intensified by the political understanding of bureaucracy and discipline and its consequent practice under the leadership of Gwede Mantashe.

'Discipline' is a well-entrenched organisational principle and practice in NUM. When asked whether he thought his was a disciplined organisation, Baleni explained:

> We are a very disciplined organisation of the left. *Q: And how is discipline achieved, what does it mean?* FB: We have priorities; every year we've got a Central Committee and then we have a Congress; we've got our National Executive Committee so we have common structures to run, it must run very effectively and … we must interact with our members to an extent that we do a survey every three years.[42]

Discipline also becomes a verb when the organisation 'disciplines' those it deems to have stepped out of line. The NUM constitution is often quoted as the source of discipline in the union, as if the rule of law were a self-fulfilling process. As I will soon show, however, the constitution and its amendment are at the heart of political conflict in the union and it has also become a tool for disciplining reluctant leaders. Organisational discipline and respect for rules are recurring features in structures of the Tripartite Alliance. In 2010, Cosatu's general secretary, Zwelinzima Vavi, had publicly denounced the erring ways of Zuma's first presidency, including the presence of allegedly corrupt ministers in the Cabinet. The former NUM general secretary and now ANC secretary general, Gwede Mantashe, had then pressed charges against Vavi on the grounds that he had publicly criticised the president and undermined structures of the Tripartite Alliance. Charges were eventually dropped but, despite his trade union background, Mantashe proved particularly intransigent. Key to understanding his behaviour was the fact that Vavi, who was expelled from Cosatu in 2015, had publicised his views in the media – in violation of the principle according to which organisational matters should be dealt with internally. If Vavi had gone public, however, it was because internalising contention had proven vain and remaining silent would also have meant accepting that secrecy prevailed on an issue relevant to all citizens. I questioned Baleni at the time and his answer provides a taste of how democratic centralism operated in the union and, more generally, in Tripartite Alliance structures:

> Any disciplined cadre is bound by a collective decision so if a decision of my NEC [National Executive Committee] is taken, I might not like it but I have to implement that decision and I must not pronounce on that decision. So if you would move with your emotions then you're not disciplined, you must make a case there before the decision is taken. Once a decision is taken you must implement it.[43]

Discipline is therefore a difficult issue in an organisation such as NUM: it is supposedly an objective principle, but in practice it is generally enforced by those who have more power against those who have less. Moreover, it sometimes proves difficult to know whether internal tensions are the result of interpersonal relationships or based on political and programmatic divergences. The principle of debate was officially promoted in NUM:

> It is always tempting for leaders in a revolutionary organization to characterize all [op]position to their program as acts of counter-revolution. In general

terms, we should be tolerant of members' opposing views, as long as they pay allegiance to the constitution, principle, vision and seek to modify the program of transformation or even express a retrogressive school of thought shared by a given constituency that should be treated as a legitimate expression of the organizational social or political contradiction. One basic principle of collective leadership is cultivating the culture of open debate within an organization … If we suppress the spirit of open debates within an organization, and then we shall continuously treat each other with the suspicion to an extent that when a group of comrades gather and chat to each other then an immediate conclusion that occupies our mind constitute a clique.[44]

However, in Rustenburg, a notoriously ill-disciplined region where corruption cases are regularly exposed, the secretariat report to the 2008 regional conference warned:

Lack of discipline is a hindrance to the progress of an organization. Comrades elected to constitutional structures who misbehave should be handled in a structured way in accordance with the provisions of our constitution. There are comrades who are engaging in sinister activities pushing their own agendas and we must warn them that their time is running up. They will be isolated and dealt with aggressively.[45]

The problem, as we shall see, lies in the definition of legitimate and illegitimate behaviours and opinions. The definition usually belongs to those in power, with the union administration at hand to enforce their decision. It is important to understand here that the ascent of communists in the NUM and in the Tripartite Alliance structures was based on their unmatched administrative skills, grounded in a mastery of organisational processes. These are then easily turned into political assets. In the course pack distributed to participants in the leadership development course I attended in 2011, Baleni listed what the qualities of a general secretary and his deputy should include:

Must have the ability to read and write.

A good political administrator.

Result orientated, honest and a visionary.

Ability to detect weaknesses and alert the team in order to rise to the challenge.

Must be knowledgeable about the union and educational expectations.

Skilful, patient, passionate, tactful and self-motivated.

Good in compiling records and presenting reports to the appropriate forums and structures.

Must have financial and budget monitoring ability.

Ability to analyse various situations.

Must have a clear political stance, which is not contradictory to the union profile.[46]

In possession of such skills, the 'communist cadre' with political consciousness ends up having full control of the organisation and finds himself in an ideal position to rise through its ranks. This, of course, is not exclusive to NUM: in political or non-political organisations, administrative positions may appear less political than others that are more exposed to public attention. However, the supposedly neutral activity of a bureaucrat – organising – is often turned into a strong foundation for a political career, as illustrated by Mantashe's trajectory. This is discussed, as I have already mentioned, by Weber and Michels in their classical works, and the fact that NUM produces formidable organisers was instrumental in its gaining importance within the ANC and in the Tripartite Alliance. Moreover, in 2004, Gwede Mantashe fostered reform of the NUM constitution, officially to combat bureaucratic tendencies. From a political perspective, however, he wanted to secure the position of his heir. As his successor, he had chosen Frans Baleni, a leader who, just like him, had started work in mining and had experienced all levels and types of responsibility in the union. Baleni was, for instance, in charge of the organising department in 1993 and an extract from his activity report shows how versatile he was at the time, attending meetings in various mining companies, in Eskom, as well as in NUM.[47] Under Mantashe, the orderly functioning of the organisation was technicised a great deal as shown by his description of his own achievements, which interestingly intertwines political and bureaucratic loyalties:

In the past three years we built and improved the capacity. We have built a secretariat team based on the network of regional secretaries. Our success in building regional secretaries into a secretariat team led to what we witnessed in the regional conferences, that is, these comrades being attacked as 'LOYALISTS' of the General Secretary. We can confidently submit to this congress that we have not built a team of loyalists, but an effective machinery that is hands-on … Among these regional secretaries we have a team of worker-leaders who have political leadership, administration skills and managerial capacity … In 2000, we were grappling with the tensions of full-time office-bearers and regional coordinators in the administration of regions. We can confidently submit that we have overcome these tensions. We are now dealing with operational politics. We cleared the operational relationship. The regional chairperson is the political leader of the region. The regional secretary is the operational and administrative leader of the region.[48]

THE '2004 COUP'

A few years before Mantashe stepped down as NUM general secretary to join the ANC leadership, the union was more organised and disciplined than it had ever been. It was not necessarily working better, but Mantashe had turned it into a powerful machine and had successfully managed the transition to a new generation of NUM leaders:

The 2000 National Congress marked the total change of guard … The Motlatsi/Ramaphosa team ultimately handed over the leadership baton to the second generation of leadership. This in itself posed new challenges, wherein a number of comrades did not believe that there could be a National Union of Mineworkers beyond the original team of leadership. Many, consciously or unconsciously, worked for the new team to fail. There was commitment and drive to succeed. Swimming against the tide translated into determination. We worked hard to put up monuments of success.[49]

The 2003 national congress was the last in which Mantashe was elected to head up NUM's administration. After three terms in office, he considered his re-election to be a vote of confidence:

Our members recognized the hard work of the NEC [National Executive Committee] and re-elected them as they were in the past term. This choice of continuity is good for the organisation. The organisation continues to invest in developing capacity amongst these national leaders of our organisation. There were few changes that were effected by the regions … The outcome of the regional conferences is a vote of confidence in the NEC by delegates and representatives of the members.[50]

Approaching retirement as a trade unionist, Mantashe was in control of NUM but in open conflict with his deputy, Archie Palane, who was also re-elected in 2003 and whom he wanted to substitute with his protégé Frans Baleni, then the union's education officer. Although Mantashe claimed 'the union is not a monarch', he carefully planned his own succession, as point 2 of his report to the 2004 special congress, entitled 'succession planning', shows. It is worth quoting this document at length:

We would like to remind the delegates that in 1994 the current General Secretary [Gwede Mantashe], who was the National Organiser at the time, committed himself to dedicating 10 years – after the 1994 elections – to the labour movement. That 10 years ends in 2004. On the strength of the pledge he declined going into parliamentary politics in 1994, 1999 and 2004.

In 1997, as a way of taking this approach forward, we had a detailed debate on what the succession plan of the union would be. We concluded that the union is not a monarch and, therefore, cannot have a list of names indicating successors to the current leader at the time. The best approach, we concurred, would be to invest in a pool of cadreship from which leadership would then emerge. The democratic processes would continue to be used as a tool of electing leadership.

We took this debate forward in 1999 by reminding ourselves that in our succession planning we must always seek to strengthen the principle of 'Worker Control'. This principle is about workers in the sectors we are organising in, members of the union taking control of the organisation and determining their destiny. The election of the first worker general secretary in 1998 [Gwede Mantashe], on the 16th year of our existence as a union, was acknowledged as a positive development and a breakthrough. We opened the sensitive debate of the role of intellectuals in a trade union, an organisation of workers. We made a distinction between a trade union, an organisation of workers and a working class organisation like a communist party. We highlighted the danger of intellectuals using their intellectual capacity as a source of power. In such a situation workers get relegated into being mere ballot papers. Ideally, members must develop to a point where they can occupy strategic and technical positions. This debate must be allowed to continue openly within the structures of the union. It must be elevated above rumour and whispering.

This raises the question of whether we have not reached a stage where our constitution should expressly stipulate that, only members and former members of the union can stand for elected office – including the Secretariat … This debate must help deal with the reality of the current General Secretary [Mantashe] being unavailable for elections in 2006 … The culture of debating succession openly in the organization must be inculcated. It will help our organisation arrest the trend of succession being a pure function of cliques and groupings.[51]

The question of succession was therefore framed by Mantashe in such a way that he could claim to be putting democracy and the sacrosanct principle of worker control at its centre, while at the same time relegating electoral politics and political debate backstage. His suggested amendment to the NUM constitution was a carefully planned move aimed at depoliticising the leadership transition, as if a 'pool' of leadership could naturally 'emerge' to fill positions left vacant, or as if worker leaders were less capable of influencing the vote of NUM members than 'intellectuals'. Mantashe's argument also went against another major NUM principle pertaining to leadership: that of 'continuity', by which deputies are expected to be elevated to the positions they were assisting when their respective incumbents step down.[52] In the normal course of affairs, Archie Palane would be next in line, just like Motlanthe and Mantashe had been before him.

The 1997 national congress had resolved:

1. That a shaft steward candidate must have been an active member of the union or active in progressive organisations; …

3. That to be eligible for a position of National Office Bearer one should have served the union for a period of no less than thirty-six months or have a quality record in the working class struggle;

4. Any candidate who avails himself/herself for an elected position shall be compelled to divulge his/her life history.[53]

An 'active member' is de facto synonymous with a (former) 'worker', for one cannot belong to NUM without being employed by a mining, energy or construction company. In 1997, however, the terms were ambiguous enough to suit re-elected secretary general Kgalema Motlanthe, who himself had never worked in mining and had joined NUM as a union employee. Gwede Mantashe brought up the issue of the role of 'intellectuals' in the trade union movement in relation to worker control because of his personal and bitter experience with them. In 1987, Mantashe had stood for election as assistant general secretary against Marcel Golding, the then NUM press and publicity officer. 'I lost by 20 votes. Marcel got 572 and I got 552,' he told a journalist, who concluded: 'it took place more than 27 [*sic*] years ago, but Mantashe tells it as if it happened yesterday'.[54] It was the first time that a staff member recruited by the union had successfully defeated a former worker for an elected position and it was a frustrating personal experience that Mantashe was not to forget. A few years later, when, after his re-election as NUM general secretary in 1991, Cyril Ramaphosa was deployed to the same position in the ANC, his deputy, Marcel Golding, became NUM's acting general secretary. There was no constitutional provision in place for the appointment of a new deputy, and since the next national congress was scheduled for 1994, some in the union asked for an extraordinary election to be held. 'By January 1992, the political animosities in the union had coalesced around the personality of Golding who was perceived as a leading member amongst those opposed to the SACP.' A 1992 central committee meeting was convened and the question of electing a new secretariat was on the agenda. President James Motlatsi opposed the option of electing a new general secretary at this meeting, arguing that the constitution did not provide for this, but Ramaphosa, who attended the meeting, said that since it had been convened to address precisely this issue, the central committee should solve the matter. After many tribulations the election was eventually held and Golding lost it to Kgalema Motlanthe, head of the education department. Golding was subsequently returned to his previous position as assistant general secretary.[55] The election of Motlanthe, however, did not solve the question of worker control, narrowly and technically understood as having been employed in the mining industry, since he himself had initially been recruited by NUM as a staff member. A City Council of Johannesburg employee in the 1970s, he had joined the ANC's armed wing and, in 1977, was sentenced to ten years' imprisonment on Robben Island. On his release in 1987, he had joined NUM as national educator, and after five years as general secretary of NUM, he was deployed to the ANC, also as general secretary.

The issue of worker control is, as I have already discussed, a difficult one to address. Can one claim that Mantashe, who, before becoming NUM general secretary, had served for 12 years as a national office bearer and 23 years in various union structures (he came to the national office after the 1987 strike) – a career trade unionist in other words – was still a worker? Can Baleni – who joined the mining industry in 1979 and NUM in 1983 and, ever since, had held either elected office or worked for the union – be considered a 'worker'? The two certainly qualify as 'organic intellectuals' but cannot be considered, by any definition, as anything but former workers turned professional activists and unionists. Questions about how 'worker' is defined and on the basis of what criteria one can claim to be a worker are not limited to NUM. In 2010, Irvin Jim, general secretary of the more workerist Numsa, had called for 100 per cent representation of workers within top ranks of the ANC.[56] In a 1994 conversation quoted earlier, Mike Murphy asked grassroots trade unionist Jabu Gwala: 'Many unions – in South Africa and elsewhere – are today led by people who came into the unions as a "professional" (for example as a lawyer) and stayed on, gained experience and finally became general secretaries, etc. Do you accept that this could now take place in Cosatu unions?' Gwala's answer was a short and unambiguous one: 'The issue is commitment. A leader does not have to have been a worker on a shopfloor. I see no problem with this.'[57]

The control that career trade unionists and communist cadres, who claim to be workers, have over NUM is hence primarily exercised at the expense of others who may not qualify as workers by some relatively arbitrary standards, but are nonetheless competent and popular among the membership. More generally, this control has to be related to the attitude of leaders such as Mantashe and Baleni towards their opponents. A leader such as Joseph Mathunjwa, president-founder of Amcu, was, for instance, expelled from NUM in the early 2000s despite the popularity he enjoyed. One could also venture that he was dismissed because of his growing popularity in the Witbank region. After his dismissal, Douglas Colliery's 3 000-strong workforce held a ten-day underground sit-in to support its leader.[58] Interestingly, when Archie Palane, the then NUM deputy general secretary, was sent to the coal mine, he found that Mathunjwa had done nothing wrong, but his judgement was later allegedly overruled by Mantashe. Similarly, Mantashe subsequently sidelined Palane in NUM, on the grounds that he had never been a worker. This took place notwithstanding the fact that Palane enjoyed significant popularity among workers in the platinum belt. The issue is therefore not who, among the above-mentioned names, was more legitimate in NUM at the time, but rather the fact that the criteria according to which one can claim leadership are not decided by the union's rank and file but by those in power. If the former were to speak, it is not clear that all workers would prefer to be led by former workers, and as one NUM shop steward at Eskom, interviewed by Alexander Beresford in 2007, put it: 'Frans [Baleni] is not a comrade because his background in terms of the union is not clear … This guy is dicey; we don't know where this guy comes from. It is their union now; we are no longer the union because I believe the union starts from the ground upwards, not upwards downwards.'[59]

It is against this background that NUM held its 2004 central committee meeting, which, following the 2003 national congress recommendation, was converted into a special congress. Carefully planned by the general secretary, its purpose was mainly to turn Mantashe's political agenda into constitutional amendments, although several important organisational changes were also scheduled for discussion.[60] In his organisational report, Mantashe pointed to 'the entrenchment of cliques in our structures' without, however, naming those he was talking about. The 2004 special congress made one key amendment to the NUM constitution, effectively preventing 'non-workers' from being elected to leadership positions in the union. Thus the new constitution soberly specified: 'Only workers who have been members in good standing for an unbroken period of five years or who have been stewards before are eligible to stand for a position of a branch office bearer.' The same provision was applied to election at regional and national levels (at the latter level it was added that 'workers who have been members in good standing for an unbroken period of seven years may be nominated and elected into all positions of a National office bearer').[61] Other constitutional changes comprised the inclusion of the chairperson and secretary of the structures dedicated to education, health and safety, and women on branch, regional and national committees. Except for the women structure, these structures were to be incorporated into NUM's main structure at the regional level too. They nevertheless continued to exist at branch level, where they are critical in addressing day-to-day issues.[62]

From Mantashe's point of view, the 2004 special congress was more than successful: he went as far as to call it a 'revolutionary congress'. For him, this revolutionary character was 'clearly illustrated in the resolution adopted that if you want to be elected to any official position in the union such as an office bearer you have to have been a member of the union. This resolution is critical as it reflects the union's commitment to worker leaders.'[63]

At the subsequent 2006 national congress, the coast was thus clear for former NUM general secretary Frans Baleni to take over his mentor's office. Mantashe's succession was perfectly managed from the vantage point of organisational expertise but, for all that, it did not go smoothly. Before the congress, Palane, who had been deputy general secretary for the previous eight years, declared: 'Yes, the union must be led by workers, but the liberation struggle should be fought in other ways. If someone has leadership qualities, why deprive that person? Many in the liberation movement have led the union without a background as workers.'[64] He was criticised, however, by his detractors among NUM leadership for being a 'businessman', for being 'managerial', for undermining democracy,[65] and for having 'no passion for workers'. On the eve of the congress, Palane was said to have the support of four regions against six to Baleni. Some also pointed to 'tribal' divisions as Palane was not, in contrast to most of his fellow national office bearers, an isi Xhosa speaker, as well as to political divergences since he was perceived as an Mbekite (pro-Thabo Mbeki) whereas Baleni's supporters were in favour of Jacob Zuma.[66] Palane ended up in the minority at the congress and, after having been disqualified from standing based on the new constitution, he was left with no choice but to resign from NUM. After the congress, about one hundred NUM members protested in front of the union's Rustenburg office.[67]

I met Palane a few days before NUM's thirtieth anniversary national congress, where he was one of the only former NUM leaders – if not the only one – whose name was not on the guest list. Palane, who had remained publicly silent on his trade union background since his 2006 eviction, was now head of corporate affairs and transformation at Samancor Chrome, the world's second-largest producer of the metal. He told me the story of his entry into mining, which, in several ways, disproves his alleged distance from both the industry and its workers, and makes his career trajectory consistent with those of well-known NUM leaders:

> I belonged to the Young Christian Workers Movement and we linked up to many unions, including NUM. Then there was a position at NUM and I was asked to apply for it. But when I look in retrospect, my grandfather, uncles, worked in [asbestos] mines, and in ERPM [East Rand Proprietary Mines] gold mine. I would later recall their talking about mining, the technology and so forth. [After having organised NUM in Phalaborwa, Lydenburg, Rustenburg and Witbank, a] … crisis emerged in Carletonville where I was sent. There it was a challenge because one would deal with real mining: depth, heat, numbers. Even though Rustenburg was big, Carletonville posed a challenge because one branch there was equivalent to two or three mines in Rustenburg. It was the time when we dealt with tribalism, workers were kept in hostels, there were faction fights. So you were not only just mobilising workers to join the union but you were also mobilising workers to orientate them that blacks cannot be fighting amongst themselves especially when we are workers. Because you had a hostel separately but when you go underground there is no underground for Zulus, or Xhosas or Sothos, you're all there together. One of my campaigns was to demolish tribalism in the hostels in Carletonville. That created in me an understanding of what NUM is. It also informed my understanding of the mineworkers. Also, politically the mining industry was seen as a pillar of the government, and if we were able to bring down the mining industry, there was no reason why we cannot bring down the government.

His political career in the union started in 1998:

> You may have heard that the current deputy president of the ANC [Kgalema Motlanthe], when he was a GS [general secretary] of NUM was asked by the ANC in 1998 to come back to the ANC as SG [secretary general]. That created a vacuum in NUM and a special congress was then called and many of the regions lobbied me to contest the position of the DGS [deputy general secretary]. That's how I came back to NUM.

Palane may not have been a former worker per se but this did not necessarily mean that the principle of worker control was foreign to him. His words are reminiscent of those of Ecliff Tantsi, whose leadership style, as I have shown, made him a resilient leader in the crisis NUM has been facing at the grassroots since 2012:

> Within the union I've learned one principle: when we say workers are in control, it means before you meet with management you need to know what workers want. Before you go public on what you have achieved with management, you first go to the membership and say 'you said we must get a cup of coffee, we have got half a cup of coffee and we believe it's better off than nothing'. You don't go and address the public before your members know about it. We appreciate technology but we are not dealing with a sophisticated workforce. It respects leadership and expects respect from it.

At the 2004 special congress and the 2006 national congress, Palane presented himself as a responsible leader who preserved the unity of NUM. He also insisted on the fact that as opposed to others, he was not an easy leader to manipulate. Finally, he argued that the 2004 amendment of the constitution and its 2006 enforcement were illegal moves:

> I did not insist. If I wanted to insist the union would have gone either way but I wanted to save the union because what it would have meant, the constitution is quite clear. If the congress is not happy about a particular clause in the constitution, it will go to a vote, if there is no consensus. Now there it was clear that the interpretation by the president and Gwede was wrong. And all I would have insisted is we need to go to a vote. But then you would have divided the organisation. And I said I am not above the organisation, I don't want to lead people who would point a finger to say: 'You divided the organisation.' Unfortunately what I thought was to the benefit of the organi-

sation it went the other way round because then people started paging those who were supporting me and dismissing them from the union … I realised, if I am going to sit with the same team again … maybe this is time for me to move on because the division would have been expressed and have remained. *Q: What was the division about?* AP: As I say you sit with your colleagues, you think that you are serving mineworkers based on the congress agenda. But people are having their career path: where I want to be five, ten years from now.[68]

Palane was skilfully outmanoeuvred by Mantashe and Baleni and was left with no choice but to exit NUM. For most of the following decade, Baleni ruled NUM along with President Zokwana and, pursuing the work of his mentor Mantashe, he kept disciplining NUM at the expense of internal debate. Behind Baleni's hand, however, some still saw 'Gwede's unseen hand', as one former NUM official and SACP member once put it to me.

10

Conclusion: From Bureaucratic Organisation to Bureaucratic Politics

Former NUM general secretary Frans Baleni defined NUM as a democratic organisation in the following terms: 'We normally have very robust debates in all our structures, even mass meetings, members can disagree with you, with the President, they can shout at the President, they can walk away sometimes, so we are a very democratic organisation.'[1] A national congress such as the NUM 14th National Congress, which I attended at the end of May 2012, was cautiously prepared for the outgoing leadership to be re-elected and for the gathering to quietly celebrate the union's thirtieth anniversary. Stakes are always high for an incumbent leadership in office and, from a career point of view, one cannot leave one's re-election in the hands of delegates only. This was made clear in a conversation I overheard a few days before the congress. One national NUM leader was chatting on the phone with his human resources manager at the mining company that employed him. The two were seemingly intimate. The leader gave his manager news of his family and asked the manager about his. He then referred to the congress and said he was confident things were going to go well as his team had been nominated by seven regions out of NUM's eleven. He added that it was 'a very critical congress at a personal level', and said he had a bond to pay off and an expensive family car to buy.

At the NUM 14th National Congress and during other union meetings I witnessed, it had become common to refer to internal competition between opposed motions by stating, 'It's Mangaung', a reference to the big leadership battle that was expected to be waged at the ANC National Conference in Mangaung (Free State), in December 2012, where it was feared that the 'mother body' would be divided. It was therefore not coincidental that the theme song of the 2012 NUM congress was a song called 'Kodoa Ena' ('Disaster Here'). One Free State delegate told me that her region wanted the outgoing leadership to remain. She said they sang 'Koda Ena' together with other regions who wanted it the same way and that only the PWV region wanted to remove NUM president Zokwana. She said that among candidates there were 'two skeletons' (slates): namely, that of Oupa Komane and Joseph Montisetsi's (respectively NUM deputy general secretary and Matlosana region secretary), and the incumbent Zokwana–Baleni motion (see Figures 10.1 and 10.2). The song warned against a forthcoming disaster, against contestation, which was seen as a threat to the unity and integrity of the organisation. Based on this view and as argued earlier, leadership contest is seen, not as an expression of democracy, but as an anomaly that puts the collective at jeopardy.

President Zokwana's speech included a veiled accusation to those internal enemies who were fighting for positions:

> I was told a story when I was young that the only way of feeding a baboon is with your hand so that at all times it can depend on you for food. If you can sign a deal with an employer that if you succeed to win there will be no strikes, you are not different to a baboon.

Such accusations were regularly uttered by outgoing leaders and, in the written version of Zokwana's speech, his allegations were more precise:

IN DEFENCE OF THE REVOLUTION

1. President : Senzeni Zokwana
2. Dep President : Piet Thamsanqa Matosa
3. General Secretary : Frans Msokoli Baleni
4. Dep General Secretary : Tshimane Montoedi
5. Chair : Health & Safety : Peter Bailey
6. Chair : Education: Essop Mokgonyana
7. Sec : Education: Eclif Tantsi

Figure 10.1: 'Slate' in support of the outgoing national leadership, NUM 14th National Congress, 2012

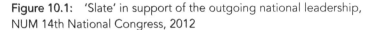

Source: Collected by the author at the national congress. Reproduced with permission.

Figure 10.2: *NUM News*, Congress Special, 26 May 2012

Source: Author's copy; distributed to all attending the national congress. Reproduced with permission.

> We are all aware that some mining companies are involved in the internal
> campaign trail on union affairs. Companies like Shiva Uranium and Impala
> are alleged to be typical in this malice … A company called Umvuzo pro-
> viding medical aid services to our members is also alleged to be involved in
> our internal contestations. Hoping to capture and corrupt union leadership
> after the congress.[2]

Be this true or false, such allegations are often uttered and they also comprise an
electoral trick. It must be recalled here that outgoing leaders generally rely on the
union's apparatus and resources for their own campaign needs. In addition, incumbent leaderships also rely on corporate sponsors to fund union meetings such as
the national congress or regional conferences (sponsors include mining houses and

private companies like Ubank, Capitec or Bonitas Medical Aid). During a congress interlude, Baleni recalled once again that there were enemies within:

> There was a comrade in the MK [Umkhonto we Sizwe] camps whose combat name was Mangaung and he had the ability to whip his comrades' emotions. He would make them sing and they would cross the border to fight. Then it was found that he was a police graduate and a sell-out. We are hoping comrades that we don't have a Mangaung.

Just like Gwede Mantashe's rule before his, Baleni's tenure as NUM general secretary had been characterised by constant denunciations of internal enemies and of the personal ambitions of his contenders. The latter were contrasted with the presumably more altruistic and professional ones of his team in power. And indeed, at the 2012 congress, Frans Baleni was at the height of his art as twenty-first-century NUM administrator. He presented his secretariat report in his usual corporate style, walking around the stage with a small microphone fixed on a headset and bombarding his audience with figures; on the second day of the congress, he also used a laser pointer to draw attention to parts of his PowerPoint presentation and even boasted that he had attended the Davos World Economic Forum. Such a display of corporate management style, in Mantashe's and even more in Baleni's NUM, went hand in hand with a systematic call for unity and an equally systematic downplaying of debate and internal opposition, if necessary by resorting to communist ideology to muzzle opponents. The 'cult of unity' is an integral part of political and workers' organisations. It is often criticised as intrinsically anti-democratic by promoters of pluralism, yet it is not as simple as that. In a hostile environment such as South Africa's 1980s, the unity of the oppressed was key to successful resistance against the joint attacks of the apartheid State and of its allied mining industry. In 2012 South Africa, the mining industry was arguably not more worker-friendly and it still had strong ties with the State and the ruling ANC. However, it was now bound by the rule of law and the conditions under which trade unionism could be practised had been structurally altered. Moreover, NUM could now count on the support of the country's ruling party, in alliance with the SACP and Cosatu. The union had strong teams in Cabinet and in the Presidency to which it had deployed many cadres over the years. The aim of dismissing internal opposition, as Baleni had done for the nine years of his NUM secretariat, with the support of his mentor Gwede Mantashe, who thereafter imposed the same conception of politics on the ANC, seemed to be simply to perpetuate the power of one camp over another one.

In this book, I have shown how NUM, which had been built into a highly competent centralised organisation (through what I have called strategic bureaucratisation), was turned, from 1998 onwards, into a union ruled by a form of bureaucratic politics. This manifested an extension of the type of organisational governance that had been developed underground in, among others, the SACP – a political formation in which most top NUM leaders after 2000 had also held leadership positions. The shift from bureaucratic organisation to bureaucratic politics is one of the factors that has brought NUM to near collapse in the platinum belt and beyond since 2012. Under the organisation's founding fathers, the bureaucratic and disciplined national structure – the 'professional' structure that they had identified as key to advancing their emancipatory project – was complemented by a relatively loose approach to rules in subnational structures, especially at local union branches. In the meantime, NUM produced leaders who could deal with vastly contrasting situations: they could operate in a complex professional environment and they could go to the grassroots and listen to their membership's basic grievances. These leaders managed often volatile situations at branch level, sometimes dealing with maverick leaders, through a display of both distance from and closeness with their membership. In other words, there was a sense of what being a 'good leader' involved on both a material and a moral basis – namely, a balance between competence and empathetic presence by the members' side. This type of leadership has not disappeared; there are still trade unionists of this calibre in NUM today. What changed under Gwede Mantashe was that discipline became understood and imposed, no longer as an instrument of organisational efficiency but literally, as a form of authoritarian control that is otherwise known as democratic centralism. This not only caused tensions in the relationship between members and their leaders, it also fuelled tensions in the relationships between leaders themselves, as shown by the results of the 2015 NUM congress, in which Frans Baleni was defeated. The result of this congress does not, however, suggest that the old NUM is back on track. There is still the vivid memory of how, in 2007, the left of the ANC had made Zuma its champion against Mbeki. It was a choice 'against', not one 'in favour of'. This said, Baleni's orderly acceptance of his electoral defeat in 2015 and the fact that the 'one man, one vote' principle ruled the conference show the persistence of a shared culture of democracy in the former liberation movement, understood as the possibility for the masses to remove leaders in power. The debates that took place during the congress, against the will of the outgoing leadership, which tried to reduce the opposition's space to a minimum, offered yet another illustration – widespread in NUM – that members and local or regional leaders display no excessive deference towards leadership: when they disagree, they speak.

In the 1980s and 1990s, the marriage between Ramaphosa's administrative skills and Motlatsi's appeal to the masses worked well and the two relied on the work of many others. Second- and third-generation leaders such as Zokwana, Matosa and Baleni lost this ethos, these skills and abilities, and, arguably, the commitment required to wage the fight of the weaker against the stronger. This was clearly evident in the post-congress report-back rally held at AngloGold Ashanti Savuka gold mine following the climax of their rule in 2012. The distance they had put between the arcane head office national power and the mundane mines' compounds could no longer be bridged. At Savuka, on 27 May 2012, those I have described as 'distinguished leaders' had become physically unreachable to the grassroots. The mass rally was held the day after the NUM 2012 national congress ended at the mine's stadium – one of those leisure facilities conceived by mine owners to entertain their workforce within the boundaries of the mine's grounds. In the 1980s, such sport facilities had been used by organisers like Gwede Mantashe to recruit and mobilise mineworkers. This meeting, some thirty years later, featured as a very important moment in the NUM 'liturgy': it was the time when the union's newly elected leaders would report back to their constituency, return to their mandate-givers, to where they came from, to the mine as the foundational unit of NUM – in a nutshell, to the grassroots.

A few hundred delegates from branches (including Bambanani, Tshepong, South Deep, Vaal Reefs, Tau Tona, as well as the local Savuka) had been bussed to the venue and gathered in the stadium's two lateral terraces, one of which, unroofed and unprotected from the sun, remained almost empty. Most of those present, however, were not ordinary members but union representatives. In other words, and as I have already observed in other instances, it was a mass meeting that involved shaft stewards – leaders, not members. As was often the case in NUM mass meetings at the beginning of this decade, the disproportion between the venue's capacity and the actual crowd it lodged was striking. A sound system and a giant screen had been erected next to the covered stage that was to welcome speakers. It would have taken nothing more than a megaphone to address such a small crowd. On that day, however, the space between the speakers' voices and the crowd's ears was vast. The physical distance separating the leaders on the stage from the members or local union representatives on the field was no less than fifty metres. In addition, an iron fence prevented anyone from crossing the VIP perimeter and the two covered tents it accommodated. About two dozen union marshals in yellow tee shirts or black military or scout-like attire protected the VIP perimeter and allowed invited guests in. The latter probably made up at least a fourth if not a third of the total number of delegates. Striking in that picture was the empty field at the centre of the play.

Facing the stage, behind the iron fence and unprotected from the blazing sun, were about two dozen men in wheelchairs. They were former mineworkers who had been permanently disabled in mining accidents (see Figures 10.3 and 10.4). Their position, cut off from the stage and at the same time central to the field, turned them into unevenly 'privileged' spectators (they were given the best 'seats', close to the stage, but had to remain behind the fence and were directly exposed to the sun). From a different perspective, they were also part of a spectacle, the objects of a somehow disturbing show in which they were exhibited as embodiments of NUM's heroic struggle for the health and safety of mineworkers.

The vast majority of the members Amcu has recruited in mining since 2012 used to belong to NUM. Although most of them neither viewed themselves nor behaved as activists involved in the life of their union beyond occasional participation, their decision to withdraw their allegiance to NUM was based on their rejection of the type of organisation and leadership they now associated with it. A former NUM shaft steward who became Amcu's organiser at Impala Platinum, where the 2012 strike movement started, said that workers had formed an autonomous committee to 'challenge the NUM of Zokwana and Baleni'. He also insisted

Figure 10.3: NUM 14th National Congress report-back rally, Savuka gold mine, 2012

Photographer: Raphaël Botiveau

Figure 10.4: Disabled union members at the rally, seated close to the stage

Photographer: Raphaël Botiveau

that 'Mr Mathunjwa' had 'approached' them only later to 'present his labour movement'. When asked about the difference between NUM and Amcu, he was adamant
and answered without a second's hesitation:

> One, the president himself came to the members, there is no gap between
> him and the members. Before you would see the NUM president once every
> two years. Two, Mathunjwa works with the mandate of the members and he
> comes back to report to the workers. Three, by the time of the NUM there
> was only one full-time shaft steward on surface per shaft, now we have five.[3]

These three points are key to understanding why NUM lost ground at Impala first,
then at Lonmin, Anglo Platinum and in other mining operations after 2012. First,
union members expect to have regular and direct contact with their top leaders,
which they view as the only way to make sure they remain accountable. Second, the
mass meetings in which leaders report back on the progress of negotiations with
mining houses is the place and level where workers expect such accountability to
materialise. Third, the RDOs, who led the 2012 strikes, want power in the shafts to
be stronger than power on the surface. In other words, the 2012 strike movement,

which later manifested itself through the rise of Amcu, was primarily rooted in a rejection of representational democracy, as embodied by NUM, and it affirmed that union power must come from the miners underground. The need to go back to the grassroots was, at times, identified as key among the NUM top leadership, including in Baleni's 2012 report to the 14th National Congress: 'There are serious lessons to be learnt from this experience. Branch leaders must report regularly and honestly to members at least every month as dictated by the constitution. The region must monitor branches and where branches fail to report to members, the region must intervene.'[4]

Such important comments, however, have so far remained merely declarations of good intentions. In the mind of many NUM leaders, indeed, the strength of their organisation lay principally in the machinery they had managed to build from scratch since 1982. It was built by and around a relatively large body of leaders who became workers' representatives – most were not underground workers and certainly not RDOs. NUM was also built, over time, by the carefully strategised succession of three generations of leaders. Removing some of these leaders, as happened at the 2015 national congress, is a democratic prerogative, but it is also viewed as putting the organisation and its good functioning at risk. That is one reason, beyond the reproduction of their own power, why established cadres push for continuity. A good organisation relies on quality leadership and good leadership can only be produced over time. NUM put an impressive training and education infrastructure in place to fulfil such a mission. Today, leaders still view the strength of their organisation as a key to overcome the current crisis. There is no doubt that NUM is a very strong organisation and, even if only from a financial point of view, it can buy itself time to recover. However, the union will have to start thinking about whether it wishes to include all mineworkers in its ranks or to turn into an intermediary union, representing a category between blue- and white-collar workers. The RDOs have led popular struggles over the past few years. However, they are also a minority within the total mining workforce and their domination over workers' committees and Amcu structures at mines such as Impala may soon be interpreted as a new form of corporatism by other segments of the workforce. Only time will tell if the strategies that enabled this historic union of mineworkers to recover after the 1987 strike, or in the mid-1990s when it was challenged by maverick unions in the platinum sector, will prove enough for it to come back into the limelight. To do so, NUM will have to recruit outside the organisation; go back to the grassroots; patiently and stubbornly organise, organise or die!

NOTES

1   NUM has produced all three secretary generals and two deputy presidents of the ANC since 1991 – Cyril Ramaphosa, Kgalema Motlanthe and Gwede Mantashe. Kgalema Motlanthe also became South Africa's third post-apartheid head of State in the interregnum between Thabo Mbeki and Jacob Zuma (2008–2009).

2   In his presentation, Frans Baleni opportunely gave membership figures only in percentages. He concluded by stating: 'We remain a majority union in mining energy and construction', representing 51 to 56% of workers in these economic sectors. In 2012 the union's claimed membership reached a historic high of more than 300 000. In 2015, NUM leadership acknowledged a net loss of 40 000 members. This number, however, was probably underestimated and internal sources claimed that the union's largest region, Rustenburg, had lost at least 50 000 members in the interim. Carletonville, a relatively small region, had also lost more than half of its approximately 25 000 members. All in all, it is likely that NUM had lost around 100 000 members between 2012 and 2015. As of June 2017, the union officially counted 176 000 members. Theto Mahlakoana, 'NUM Report Details Its Many Failures', *Business Day*, 8 June 2017.

3   'The formations of the Workers Committees and their links with the yellow union, WASP [Workers and Socialists Party] and later the EFF [Economic Freedom Fighters] demonstrated a Master Plan which seemed to have been coordinated by properly organized forces beyond the ordinary mineworkers' capacity' – a statement made in NUM, 'Back to basics – members first', Secretariat Report, 15th National Congress, 2015, p. 21.

4   Desmond Mfuloane, regional secretary, NUM Rustenburg region, interview, 9 June 2015.

5   I have shown elsewhere that the SACP's influence in the Tripartite Alliance has been at its height, after the 'exile years', under Jacob Zuma's leadership. See Raphaël Botiveau, 'Longevity of the Tripartite Alliance: The Post-Mangaung Sequence', *Review of African Political Economy* 40 (2013). This influence of the SACP went largely unnoticed. See Carol Paton, 'The Meteoric Rise and the Compromises of the SACP', *Business Day Live*, 16 April 2013.

6   The French speak of 'alternance'; that is, literally, 'alternation' – a regular and ordered succession in space and time. From a political point of view, it means that while there is no interruption in the actual exercise of power, incumbents and their opponents have a chance to rule alternately.

7 This relationship between the individual leader and the organisation is well summed up in the nine-page letter disavowed ANC leader Thabo Mbeki wrote to ANC president Jacob Zuma on 9 October 2008. Putting ANC leadership into historical perspective, he criticised what he viewed as a mounting 'personality cult' in the movement. Yet he also recalled several times that, having been defeated politically, he behaved as a disciplined member of the organisation and submitted himself to the ruling of the collective, including by conforming to the humiliating decision that he should resign from the presidency of the Republic 'a mere 6/7 months before the end of our term, as mandated by the masses of our people!'. It is significant here that while Mbeki uses the personal pronoun 'I' throughout his letter, he turns to the third person to imply that his position in the State was only exercised on behalf of the ANC. Accessed 12 September 2017, https://cdn.mg.co.za/uploads/mbekiletter.pdf.

8 Raphaël Botiveau, 'Negotiating Union: South Africa's National Union of Mineworkers and the End of the Post-apartheid Consensus' (PhD thesis, Université Paris 1 Panthéon-Sorbonne, La Sapienza Università di Roma, 2014).

9 Complementary fieldwork was also conducted in May and June 2015.

10 In that spirit, see Peter Alexander et al., *Marikana: A View from the Mountain and a Case to Answer* (Johannesburg: Jacana, 2012).

11 Franco Barchiesi's annotated bibliography is of great value to start exploring the dense literature: Franco Barchiesi, *I Sindicati Indipendenti Sudafricani: Bibliografia* (Centro Amilcar Cabral, Bologna: Il Nove, 1994).

12 Both their doctoral dissertations remain as landmarks in the field: Ari Sitas, 'African Worker Responses on the East Rand to Changes in the Metal Industry, 1960–1980' (PhD thesis, University of the Witwatersrand, 1983); Edward Webster, *Cast in a Racial Mould: Labour Process and Trade Unionism in the Foundries* (Johannesburg: Ravan Press, 1985).

13 Assassinated in 1978, Turner has had an enduring influence on South Africa's radical left. See Rick Turner, *The Eye of the Needle: Towards Participatory Democracy in South Africa* (Johannesburg: Ravan Press, 1978).

14 In addition to its scientific mission, SWOP has been a provider of quantitative and qualitative investigations on Cosatu and its affiliates, with a focus on the mineworkers' union. The SALB self-describes as 'the only alternative anti-apartheid publication which survived into South Africa's new democracy'. As such it offers a unique historiographical insight into forty years of debates, contributions to and analyses of South Africa's labour movement. Cutting across academia and the trade union movement, it is designed for a broad audience of readers interested in labour and socioeconomic-related issues.

15 The question of the contribution of white intellectuals to black trade unions was at the centre of a controversy between Sakhela Buhlungu and Johann Maree in two articles and two responses published in *Current Sociology* 54:3 (2006).

16 Gwede Mantashe, 'The Decline of the Mining Industry and the Response of the Mining Unions' (MA thesis, University of the Witwatersrand, 2008).

17 Buhlungu describes the intellectual engagement of labour scholars as an instance of what Burawoy called 'public sociology': Sakhela Buhlungu, 'The Decline of Labor Studies and the Democratic Transition', *Work and Occupations* 36 (2009).

18 Edward Webster, 'South African Labour Studies in a Global Perspective, 1973–2006', *Labour, Capital and Society* 37 (2004). See also the excellent textbook produced by SWOP scholars: Edward Webster, Sakhela Buhlungu and Andries Bezuidenhout, *Work and Organizations* (Oxford: Oxford University Press, 2003).

19 The work of Leo Panitch is often quoted by South African scholars: Leo Panitch, *Social Democracy and Industrial Militancy* (Cambridge: Cambridge University Press, 1976).

20 On workers' subjectivities after apartheid and for a critique of what she considers to be classist pitfalls in Websterian analysis, see Judith Hayem, *La Figure Ouvrière en Afrique du Sud* (Johannesburg, Paris: IFAS, Karthala, 2008).

21 Edward Webster, 'The Rise of Social-Movement Unionism: The Two Faces of the Black Trade Union Movement in South Africa', in *State, Resistance and Change in South Africa*, ed. Philip Frankel et al. (London: Croom Helm, 1988). For a discussion of the concept, see Karl von Holdt, 'Social Movement Unionism: The Case of South Africa', *Work, Employment & Society* 16 (2002). See also Michael Schiavone, 'Social Movement Unions and Political Parties (in South Africa and the Philippines): A Win-Win Situation?', *African and Asian Studies* 6 (2007); Geoffrey Wood, 'Organizing Unionism and the Possibilities for Perpetuating a Social Movement Role: Representivity, Politics, and the Congress of South African Trade Unions', *Labor Studies Journal* 26 (2002); and Philip Hirschsohn, 'From Grassroots Democracy to National Mobilization: Cosatu as a Model of Social Movement Unionism', *Economic and Industrial Democracy* 19 (1998). On NUM, see T. Dunbar Moodie, 'Becoming a Social Movement Union: Cyril Ramaphosa and the National Union of Mineworkers', *Transformation* 72/73 (2010). For a critique of the loose understanding of social movement unionism when applied to trade unions, see Gay Seidman, 'Social Movement Unionism: From Description to Exhortation', *South African Review of Sociology* 42 (2011). See Moodie's response, which further insists on the usefulness of this concept to address the early development of NUM: T. Dunbar Moodie, 'Social Movement Unionism: From Enthusiasm to Delivery – A Response to Gay Seidman', *South African Review of Sociology* 43 (2012).

22 On mining, see Jonathan Crush et al., 'Undermining Labour: The Rise of Sub-contracting in South African Gold Mines', *Journal of Southern African Studies* 27 (2001), and Andries Bezuidenhout, 'New Patterns of Exclusion in the South African Mining Industry', in *Racial Redress and Citizenship in South Africa*, ed. Kristina Bentley and Adam Habib (Cape Town: HSRC Press, 2008).

23 Sakhela Buhlungu, 'The Building of the Democratic Tradition in South Africa's Trade Unions after 1973', *Democratization* 11 (2004). See also Franco Barchiesi, 'Orientamenti Metodologici e Bibliografici per lo Studio del Sindacalismo Indipendente Sudafricano', *Africa* 48 (1993).

24 Edward Feit, *Workers without Weapons: The South African Congress of Trade Unions and the Organization of the African Workers* (Hamden: Archon Books, 1975). There were earlier attempts at organising black workers, which included the Industrial Workers of Africa (1918), the first African trade union in South Africa; Clements Kadalie's Industrial and Commercial Union (1919); and, later on, the South African Trades and Labour Council, which, in the 1930s, had attempted to organise workers of all races before splitting on the issue of the inclusion of black people with, on the one hand, the non-political and skilled-workers-only Trade Union Council of South Africa (Tucsa, 1954) and, on the other hand, Sactu.

25 Tom Lodge, *Black Politics in South Africa since 1945* (Johannesburg: Ravan Press, 1990), p. 198.

26 See the very well-documented work by Michelle Friedman, *'The Future Is in the Hands of the Workers': A History of Fosatu* (Johannesburg: University of the Witwatersrand Historical Papers Labour Archive Project, 2011).

27 Robert Lambert and Edward Webster, 'The Re-emergence of Political Unionism in Contemporary South Africa', in *Popular Struggles in South Africa*, ed. William Cobbett and Robin Cohen (London: James Currey, 1988).

28 Glenn Adler and Eddie Webster, 'Challenging Transition Theory: The Labor Movement, Radical Reform, and Transition to Democracy in South Africa', *Politics & Society* 23 (1995), p. 76. See also Glenn Adler and Eddie Webster (eds), *Trade Unions and Democratization in South Africa, 1985–1997* (Johannesburg: Wits University Press, 2000). Interestingly, the concept of strategic unionism was also investigated by trade unions like NUM: see Frans Baleni, 'Strategic Unionism in the New South Africa', *South African Labour Bulletin* 20 (1996): 79–81.

29 Karl von Holdt, 'Strategic Unionism: The Debate', *Southern Africa Report* 8 (1993), p. 36, and Neeta Misra, 'Strategic Unionism: The Political Role of the Congress of South African Trade Unions (Cosatu) in South Africa and What it Means for Black Workers' (PhD thesis, Massachusetts Institute of Technology, 2008).

30 Eddie Webster and Glenn Adler, 'Towards a Class Compromise in South Africa's "Double Transition": Bargained Liberalization and the Consolidation of Democracy', *Politics & Society* 27 (1999). See also Edward Webster and Sakhela Buhlungu, 'Between Marginalisation and Revitalisation? The State of Trade Unionism in South Africa', *Review of African Political Economy* 100 (2004). Webster and Von Holdt later talked about a 'triple transition' when they added the postcolonial transformation of the 'workplace order' to regime change and economic internationalisation. See Edward Webster and Karl von Holdt (eds), *Beyond the Apartheid Workplace: Studies in Transition* (Pietermaritzburg: University of KwaZulu-Natal Press, 2005).

31 Cosatu, *The Report of the September Commission on the Future of the Unions to the Congress of South African Trade Unions* (Johannesburg: Cosatu, 1997).

32 Sakhela Buhlungu, *A Paradox of Victory: Cosatu and the Democratic Transformation in South Africa* (Pietermaritzburg: University of KwaZulu-Natal Press, 2010); Sakhela Buhlungu, 'Gaining Influence but Losing Power? Cosatu Members and the Democratic Transformation of South Africa', *Social Movement Studies* 7 (2008).

33 Sakhela Buhlungu (ed.), *Trade Unions and Democracy: Cosatu Workers' Political Attitudes in South Africa* (Cape Town: HSRC Press, 2006); Sakhela Buhlungu, Mick Brookes and Geoffrey Wood, 'Trade Unions and Democracy in South Africa: Union Organizational Challenges and Solidarities in a Time of Transformation', *British Journal of Industrial Relations* 46 (2008). The 1994 survey also served as a basis for Johann Maree, 'The Cosatu Participatory Democratic Tradition and South Africa's New Parliament: Are They Reconcilable?', *African Affairs* 97 (1998).

34 Sakhela Buhlungu and Malehoko Tshoaedi (eds), *Cosatu's Contested Legacy* (Cape Town: HSRC Press, 2012).

35 This raises epistemological and sociological questions on the 'performativity' of science. In the case of economics, see, for instance, the very stimulating article by Timothy Mitchell, 'The Work of Economics: How a Discipline Makes its World', *European Journal of Sociology* 46 (2005). I am also referring here to what Ian Hacking has called 'dynamic nominalism'. See Ian Hacking, 'Making Up People', *London Review of Books* 28 (2006); Ian Hacking, *The Social Construction of What?* (Cambridge, MA: Harvard University Press, 1999).

36 Mahmood Mamdani, *Citizen and Subject: Contemporary Africa and the Legacy of Late Colonialism* (Princeton, NJ: Princeton University Press, 1996).

37 See for instance, William Mervin Gumede, *Thabo Mbeki and the Battle for the Soul of the ANC* (Cape Town: Zebra Press, 2005); or Marianne Séverin and Pierre Aycard,

'Who Is Governing the "New" South Africa? Elites, Networks and Governing Styles (1985–2003)', in *Ten Years of Democratic South Africa Transition Accomplished?*, ed. P. Guillaume et al. (Johannesburg: IFAS, 2006).

38   T. Dunbar Moodie suggests, in reference to Sakhela Buhlungu, that contemporary analyses of trade unions are sometimes in part blinded by a tendency to deplore 'what has been lost'. Moodie, 'Social Movement Unionism', pp. 81–86.

39   Buhlungu, *Paradox of Victory*, p. 172.

40   Andries Bezuidenhout and Sakhela Buhlungu, 'Old Victories, New Struggles: The State of the National Union of Mineworkers', in *State of the Nation: South Africa 2007*, ed. Sakhela Buhlungu et al. (Cape Town: HSRC Press, 2007); Sakhela Buhlungu and Andries Bezuidenhout, 'Union Solidarity under Stress: The Case of the National Union of Mineworkers in South Africa', *Labor Studies Journal* 33 (2008).

41   Buhlungu, *Paradox of Victory*, p. 18.

42   Buhlungu, *Paradox of Victory*, p. 119.

43   Buhlungu and Bezuidenhout, 'Union Solidarity', p. 268.

44   This view was historically that of anarcho-syndicalism. See Rudolf Rocker, *Anarcho-Syndicalism* (Edinburgh, Oakland, CA: AK Press, 2004).

45   On Marxist conceptions of trade unionism, see Richard Hyman, *Marxism and the Sociology of Trade Unionism* (London: Pluto Press, 1971).

46   In this regard, NUM is opposed to the National Union of Metalworkers of South Africa. See Kally Forrest, *Metal That Will Not Bend: National Union of Metalworkers of South Africa 1980–1995* (Johannesburg: Wits University Press, 2011).

47   For a recent and full overview of debates around the question of organisational democracy, see Kim Voss and Rachel Sherman, 'Breaking the Iron Law of Oligarchy: Union Revitalization in the American Labor Movement', *American Journal of Sociology* 106 (2000).

48   This English translation was re-edited several times, including in 1962 with an introduction by Seymour Martin Lipset: Robert Michels, *Political Parties: A Sociological Study of the Oligarchical Tendencies of Modern Democracy* (New Brunswick, London: Transaction Publishers, 1999).

49   I have relied mostly on this latest edition (although when excerpts are also available in the English translation of the book I quote from the latter). It is a translation by Jean-Christophe Angaut of the second German edition of Michels's book as reviewed by its author (1925): Robert Michels, *Sociologie du Parti dans la Démocratie Moderne: Enquête sur les Tendances Oligarchiques de la Vie des Groupes* (Paris: Gallimard, 2015).

50   Webster, Buhlungu and Bezuidenhout, *Work*, p. 46.

51   The 'iron law of oligarchy' reads as follows: 'It is organization which gives birth to the domination of the elected over the electors, of the mandataries over the mandators, of the delegates over the delegators. Who says organization says oligarchy.' Michels, *Political Parties*, p. 15.

52   Michels, *Political Parties*, p. 61.

53   Michels, *Political Parties*, p. 371.

54   Hyman, *Marxism and the Sociology of Trade Unionism*.

55   The question of what type of organisation is suitable is, of course, relevant here. Trapped in a face-to-face with Marxism-Leninism, Michels dismissed too quickly other forms of contemporary organisation such as anarcho-syndicalism.

56   Michels, *Political Parties*, pp. 337–338; and Michels, *Sociologie du Parti*, pp. 489–490.

57   Quoted in Andries Bezuidenhout et al., *Research Report on NUM Servicing* (Johannesburg: SWOP Institute, September 2005), p. 7.

58   Michel Crozier, *Le Phénomène Bureaucratique: Essai sur les Tendances Bureaucratiques des Systèmes d'Organisation Modernes et sur Leurs Relations en France avec le Système Social et Culturel* (Paris: Seuil, 1971). Crozier suggests starting by describing an organisation's goals, the different categories of its personnel, its internal division of labour and office routines.

59   Max Weber, *Économie et Société, Tome I*, 'Les catégories de la sociologie, (Paris: Pocket, 1995).

60   Michel Crozier and Erhard Friedberg, *L'Acteur et le Système: Les Contraintes de l'Action Collective* (Paris: Seuil, 1977), p. 25.

61   Erhard Freidberg, 'La Dynamique de l'Action Organisée: Entretien avec Erhard Friedberg', interviewed by Philippe Cabin in *Les Organisations: État des Savoirs*, ed. Philippe Cabin (Auxerre: Sciences Humaines Éditions, 1999), pp. 51–56.

62   Antonio Gramsci, 'Disciplina' and 'La Confederazione Generale del Lavoro', in *Scritti sul Sindacato* (Milano-Roma: Sapere Edizioni, 1975).

63   I borrowed the title of this section from Dunbar Moodie, 'Leadership of a Special Type: NUM at Vaal Reefs', *South African Labour Bulletin* 34 (2010). I take the occasion of this footnote to acknowledge Moodie's work, which, as far as my own intellectual journey is concerned, was a life-changing discovery. I wish to thank Professor Moodie for our past discussions and for being part of my doctoral committee.

64   Hyman, *Marxism and the Sociology of Trade Unionism*.

65   Peter Kallaway, ed., *The History of Education under Apartheid, 1948–1994: The Doors of Learning and Culture Shall Be Opened* (Cape Town: Pearson Education South Africa, 2002).

66   Mez Ramatena, treasurer, NUM Impala Services branch, interview, Impala Platinum mine, 20 October 2011.

67   The sociology of communism analysed in depth this sense of owing to the organisation. See Bernard Pudal, *Prendre Parti: Pour une Sociologie Historique du PCF* (Paris: Presses de la FNSP, 1989).

68   Douglas Gininda, secretary, NUM Randfontein branch, interview, 30 June 2010.

69   Daniel Sethosa, deputy chairperson, NUM Impala Refineries branch, interview, Springs, 24 November 2011.

70   Buhlungu, *Paradox of Victory*, pp. 62–63.

71   Seymour Martin Lipset, Martin A. Trow and James S. Coleman, *Union Democracy: The Internal Politics of the International Typographical Union* (New York, London: The Free Press, Collier-Macmillan Limited, 1968), p. ix. For a discussion of the ITU's patterns of internal democracy, see J. David Edelstein and Malcolm Warner, 'Research Areas in National Union Democracy', *Industrial Relations* 16 (1977), pp. 194–195.

72   For a history of South African trade unions' focus on education, see Linda Cooper et al., '"Schools of Labour" and "Labour's Schools": Worker Education under Apartheid', in *History of Education*, ed. Kallaway. See also Salim Vally, Mphutlane wa Bofelo and John Treat, 'Worker Education in South Africa: Lessons and Contradictions', *McGill Journal of Education* 48 (2013). See also Linda Cooper, 'The Trade Union as a "Learning Organisation"? A Case Study of Informal Learning in a Collective, Social-Action Organisational Context', *Journal of Education* 39 (2006).

73   Sakhela Buhlungu, 'The Big Brain Drain: Union Officials in the 1990s', *South African Labour Bulletin* 18 (1994).

74   Janet Smith and Tromp Beauregard, *Hani: A Life Too Short* (Johannesburg and Cape Town: Jonathan Ball Publishers, 2009).

75 Anthony Butler, *Cyril Ramaphosa* (Johannesburg, Oxford: Jacana, James Currey, 2007).

76 Gumede, *Thabo Mbeki*.

77 Yves Cohen, *Le Siècle des Chefs: Une Histoire Transnationale du Commandement et de l'Autorité (1890–1940)* (Paris: Éditions Amsterdam, 2013), pp. 9–10.

78 It is not coincidental here that the first chapter of economist Thomas Piketty's recent book, which was inspirational for these mobilisations, started by telling the story of the 2012 Lonmin-Marikana strike. Thomas Piketty, *Capital in the Twenty-first Century* (Cambridge, MA: The Belknap Press of Harvard University Press, 2014).

79 Cohen, *Siècle des Chefs*, p. 12.

80 Andries Bezuidenhout and Sakhela Buhlungu, 'From Compounded to Fragmented Labour: Mineworkers and the Demise of Compounds in South Africa', *Antipode* 43 (2010).

81 Cohen, *Siècle des Chefs*, pp. 14–15.

82 Everett Cherrington Hughes, *Men and Their Work* (London: The Free Press of Glencoe, Collier-Macmillan Limited, 1964), p. 63. Of interest in Hughes's study, and relevant to the South African context, is the distinction between career paths in more 'rigid' or 'freer' societies in terms of the fluidity of their social structures. Hughes also links careers to an individual's biological and social age in relation to the transformation of work organisation and social systems.

83 At the end of each formal interview (all formal interviews were digitally recorded), I asked the interviewee if I could quote him/her by name. When the answer was 'no' I removed the interviewee's name, which I also did when the person specified that a section of the interview was 'off the record'. On a few rare occasions, when I judged that a section of the interview could be sensitive for the interviewee, I removed their name on my own initiative. Only once did a branch office bearer ask to listen to his interview, which he did, seemingly content with his own oral 'performance'.

84 During my observations of union activities or interactions with other actors, I always remained a silent observer. I mostly talked to participants during breaks or after the activity was over. Only twice was I asked by NUM unionists to assist them: in minute-taking at the 8th Rustenburg regional conference, which took place in Bela Bela, Limpopo, from 29 September to 1 October 2011. The second time was when I helped head office officials to transport posters and pamphlets in preparation for a NUM march that took place in Johannesburg on 4 October 2011. I think my mostly 'non-participant' posture was key in making sure that my presence would be forgotten; I could clearly see that, after a short while in a given situation (which often lasted for several hours or days), people were 'bored' with me – I was just there taking notes and they forgot or saw me as part of the furniture.

CHAPTER 2

1 Bezuidenhout and Buhlungu, 'Old Victories'; Buhlungu and Bezuidenhout, 'Union Solidarity'; Bezuidenhout and Buhlungu, 'From Compounded to Fragmented Labour'.

2 Andries Bezuidenhout et al., *Servicing the NUM: A Report of Surveys Conducted with NUM Branches in the PWV, Highveld and Rustenburg Regions.* (Johannesburg: SWOP Institute, 1998), first page, unpaginated.

3 Bezuidenhout et al., *Servicing the NUM*, p. 1.

4 Bezuidenhout et al., *Servicing the NUM*, first page, unpaginated.

5   Bezuidenhout et al., *Servicing the NUM*, pp. 30–33, 36, 38, 44, 48, 59.

6   Bezuidenhout et al., *Research Report on NUM Servicing*, pp. 44, 51, 52, 65, 66.

7   Andries Bezuidenhout, Christine Bischoff and Themba Masondo, *Meeting Expectations? A Research Report on the State of Servicing in the National Union of Mineworkers* (Johannesburg: SWOP Institute, 2010), pp. 105–109, 112, 120–131, 150.

8   NUM, National Executive Committee Meeting, 'Minutes of previous NEC meeting', 23 March 1991, pp. 6–7.

9   NUM, National Executive Committee Meeting, 'Consolidated regional reports', 9 May 9 1992, pp. 36–37.

10   NUM, National Executive Committee Meeting, 'Minutes of previous NEC meeting', 23 March 1991, p. 8; NUM, National Executive Committee Meeting, 'Congress preparations', 23 March 1991, p. 50.

11   In October 2011 I observed a tense informal meeting involving NUM and Impala Platinum's management at the mine's MinPro section. Contentious on that day was an impromptu work stoppage by some employees after one local union leader had allegedly told them they could leave work to attend a NUM meeting.

12   P.A. Noble, general manager of Grootvlei Mine, 'Letter to NUM general secretary', in NUM, National Executive Committee Meeting, 12–14 June 1992, pp. 25–27.

13   NUM, National Executive Committee Meeting, 'Consolidated regional reports', 8 August 1992, pp. 52, 63–76.

14   NUM, National Executive Committee Meeting, 'Consolidated regional reports', 9 October 1993, p. 36.

15   NUM, National Executive Committee Meeting, 'PWV regional report to the regional committee meeting on 16 and 17 April 1994', 30 April 1994, p. 78.

16   NUM, National Executive Committee Meeting, 'Regional report for Carletonville', 9 October 1993, p. 32.

17   NUM, 'Members first – today and forever', Secretariat Report, Central Committee, 2002, p. 5.

18   NUM, National Executive Committee Meeting, 'PWV regional report: September 1993', 9 October 1993, pp. 38–40.

19   NUM, National Executive Committee Meeting, 'Monthly report for July 1993, organising department', 21 August 1993, pp. 40–42.

20   Micah Reddy, 'Tswana Mineworkers, Industrial Unrest and "Worker Consciousness" on the Platinum Mines of Bophuthatswana in the Early 1990s', paper presented at the International Mining History Congress, Johannesburg, 19 April 2012.

21   Snuki Zikalala, 'Impala Platinum: No Easy Road to Collective Bargaining', *South African Labour Bulletin* 16 (1992), p. 27.

22   When management failed to attend to their grievances (on wages, working conditions and NUM access), some 30 000 workers went on strike in January 1986, after which Impala dismissed over 20 000 miners: it was the largest mass dismissal at a single company in southern African labour history. SALB correspondent, 'Impala: Gencor Strikes Again', *South African Labour Bulletin* 11 (1986). Before the 1986 mass dismissal, 70% of Impala's black workers were non-Bophuthatswanans, and a large percentage of these were Lesotho nationals. Subsequently, Impala embarked on a programme of replacing 'foreign' workers with local labour. This first attempt to establish NUM at Impala failed.

23   NUM, National Executive Committee Meeting, 7 September 1991, p. 55.

24   Zikalala, 'Impala Platinum'.

25   NUM, National Executive Committee Meeting, 7 September 1991, pp. 9, 55.

26   'Diary of Impala Conflict in 1991', *NUM News*, special edition, September 1992, p. 11.

27   Zikalala, 'Impala Platinum', pp. 29–31.

28   A similar arrangement by which a 'shop stewards' committee' was recognised – but not NUM – had earlier been found at UCAR Minerals. SALB correspondent, 'UCAR Minerals in Bophuthatswana', *South African Labour Bulletin* 9 (1984). Amcu faced the same problem in 2012 before it gained recognition.

29   Victor Leonard Allen, *The History of Black Mineworkers in South Africa*, Vol. III, 'Organise or die, 1982–1994' (Keighley: The Moor Press, 2003), pp. 537–538.

30   'Report of the Commission of Enquiry into Events at the Bafokeng North Mine during March 1992', p. 19. Appointed at the request of Impala Platinum and NUM, the commission comprised Advocate Paul Pretorius (who also acted as chairperson), Mr Edwin Molahlehi and Professor Clive Thompson.

31   Zikalala, 'Impala Platinum', p. 33.

32   Impala Platinum's official history reduces the 1991–1992 events to a clash between NUM, 'representing the "legal" face of the ANC', and Bophuthatswana (via its aligned Bonume). It also insists on violence as a tool NUM would systematically have used in an uneven reference to 1789: 'If you were not for them 100 percent, then you were considered an enemy and dealt with accordingly. Deliberate rumours of collaboration were spread to cause further dissent and anger in the mob – all very reminiscent of the French Revolution.' See John K. Bannon, *Who the Hell Wants to be in Platinum? An Illustrated History of Impala Platinum Holdings Limited* (Johannesburg: Impala Platinum, 2012), pp. 66–67.

33   NUM, Secretariat Report, Rustenburg Regional Conference, 2011.

34   After decreasing from 310 596 in 1994 to 279 099 in 2003, NUM membership started growing anew until 2012 and, in 2005, Frans Baleni deemed the union's goal of '400 000 members in three years' 'a realistic and achievable task'. The platinum sector was key to this strategy, which, it is needless to observe, has so far proven a failure. Dinga Sikwebu, 'NUM Aims to Remain "Champ of Champs"', *South African Labour Bulletin* 29 (2005/2006), pp. 26–27.

35   NUM, Draft Report for the Rustenburg Regional Conference, 2008, pp. 18–19.

36   NUM, Secretariat Report, Rustenburg Regional Conference, 2006, unpaginated, p. 6 from first page.

37   Archie Palane, former NUM deputy general secretary, interview, Johannesburg, 21 May 2012.

38   NUM, Secretariat Report, Kimberley Regional Conference, 2008, p. 58.

39   Allen, *History of Black Mineworkers*, p. 98.

40   Allen, *History of Black Mineworkers*, p. 423.

41   Sithethi Mxhasi, regional coordinator, NUM Rustenburg region, interview, Rustenburg, 25 October 2011.

42   Sithethi Mxhasi, regional coordinator, NUM Rustenburg region, interview, Rustenburg, 25 October 2011.

43   Sithethi Mxhasi, regional coordinator, NUM Rustenburg region, interview, Rustenburg, 20 September 2011.

44   Joseph Morallana, regional coordinator, NUM PWV region, interview, Johannesburg, 29 June 2010. In 2011, the PWV region had 54 000 members. Its regional office was composed of 15 employees including ten organisers, three administrators, one paralegal officer and the regional coordinator, in addition to its two full-time elected office bearers.

45   Archie Palane, former NUM deputy general secretary, interview, Johannesburg, 21 May 2012.

46   Collin Mohala, regional coordinator, NUM Carletonville region, interview, Carletonville, 21 June 2010.

47   Sakhela Buhlungu, 'The Rise and Decline of the Democratic Organizational Culture in the South African Labor Movement, 1973 to 2000', *Labor Studies Journal* 34 (2009), pp. 102–103.

48   Buhlungu, *Paradox of Victory*, pp. 125–129.

49   Daniel Gaxie, 'Économie des Partis et Rétributions du Militantisme', *Revue Française de Science Politique* 27 (1977). Daniel Gaxie, 'Rétributions du Militantisme et Paradoxes de l'Action Collective', *Swiss Political Science Review* 11 (2005).

50   Moodie recalls that Anglo American, as opposed to its other counterparts in the gold sector, initially had a rather favourable attitude to the establishment of NUM. T. Dunbar Moodie, *Going for Gold: Men, Mines and Migration* (Berkeley: University of California Press, 1994); T. Dunbar Moodie, 'Comprehending Class Compromise in the History of Class Struggle on the South African Gold Mines: Variations and Vicissitudes of Class Power', *South African Review of Sociology* 41 (2010).

51   Jean Leger and Phillip van Niekerk, 'Organisation on the Mines: NUM Phenomenon', *South African Review III* (Johannesburg: Ravan Press, 1986).

52   Between January 1986 and January 1987, the union, for instance, reported ten cases of violence between mineworkers leading to the death of 133 workers. NUM, Annual Report, 5th National Congress, 1987.

53   Jonathan Crush, 'Migrancy and Militance: The Case of the National Union of Mineworkers of South Africa', *African Affairs* 88 (1989).

54   Ingrid Oberry, 'NUM Tests Legal Strategies', *Work in Progress* 33 (1984).

55   Phillip van Niekerk, 'NUM First Legal Mine Strike', *South African Labour Bulletin* 10 (1984).

56   Allen, *History of Black Mineworkers*, pp. 116–124, 158–161.

57   T. Dunbar Moodie, 'Outraged Feelings Burst Forth: Mineworkers at Vaal Reefs', *South African Labour Bulletin* 33 (2009/2010).

58   It was, for instance, the case in the mine Donald Donham names 'Cinderella' (an East Rand Proprietary Mines gold mine), where NUM used the Amabutho (the 'regiment'), a Xhosa secret society allied to the ANC, to fight the Zulu and Inkatha Freedom Party–aligned United People's Union of South Africa (Upusa). Donald L. Donham, *Violence in a Time of Liberation: Murder and Ethnicity at a South African Gold Mine, 1994* (Durham, NC: Duke University Press, 2011).

59   NUM, National Executive Committee Meeting, 'National Union of Mineworkers NEC-staff joint workshop, 10–11 September 1992', 10 October 1992, p. 31.

60   Allen, *History of Black Mineworkers in South Africa*, pp. 114–116.

61   Allen, *History of Black Mineworkers in South Africa*, pp. 169–171.

62   See T. Dunbar Moodie's review of Allen in *African Studies Review* 50 (2007).

63   The genesis of trade union formation, which, historically, consisted of either the merger of several unions or locals or of a process of top-down organisation building, has been regarded as key to the ulterior development of internal union democracy. See Lipset, Trow and Coleman, *Union Democracy*.

64   Forrest, *Metal That Will Not Bend*.

65   Barry Streek, 'Organizing the Struggle: Cyril Ramaphosa, General Secretary, National Union of Mineworkers', *Africa Report* 31 (1986), p. 12.

66 Coletane Markham and Monyaola Mothibeli, 'The 1987 Mineworkers Strike', *South African Labour Bulletin* 13 (1987), p. 62.

67 T. Dunbar Moodie, 'Managing the 1987 Mine Workers' Strike', *Journal of Southern African Studies* 35 (2009), p. 46.

68 NUM, Annual Report, 5th National Congress, 1987.

69 Allen, *History of Black Mineworkers*, pp. 422–423.

70 One must bear in mind this episode to understand why Mantashe, who later became general secretary, decided to change the NUM constitution (2004) so that it confined access to elected positions to 'workers' only. This constitutional reform allowed his protégé Frans Baleni's victory against Mantashe's deputy, Archie Palane.

71 Allen, *History of Black Mineworkers*, pp. 435, 604–607.

CHAPTER 3

1   NUM, Biennial Report, 6th National Congress, 1989, pp. 27–44.

2   Buhlungu, *Paradox of Victory*, pp. 122–123.

3   NUM, National Executive Committee Meeting, 9 May 1992, pp. 43–44.

4   NUM, National Executive Committee Meeting, 5 February 1994, p. 2.

5   NUM, National Executive Committee Meeting, 2–3 February 1991, pp. 23–24.

6   NUM, National Executive Committee Meeting, 'Office bearer's report', 7 September 1991, p. 9.

7   NUM, 1991 National Staff Seminar Report, Alpha Training Centre, Broederstroom, 7–8 February 1991, pp. 7–8.

8   NUM, 1991 National Staff Seminar Report, Alpha Training Centre, Broederstroom, 7–8 February 1991, pp. 9–20.

9   NUM, National Executive Committee Meeting, 9 May 1992, p. 46.

10 NUM, National Executive Committee Meeting, 'Decisions of the national executive committee', 12–14 June 1992, p. 9.

11 NUM, National Executive Committee Meeting, 12 September 1992, p. 9.

12 'NUM staff: Contract employment', letter from Frans Baleni to Kenny Mosime, 2 September 1992.

13 NUM, National Executive Committee Meeting, 'NUM staff response to the "Staff salary structure" document addressed to the national office bearers and national executive committee of the NUM', 10 October 1992, p. 60.

14 NUM, Staff Seminar, 3–5 June 1994.

15 NUM, National Executive Committee Meeting, 30 April 1994, pp. 13–14.

16 NUM, Staff Seminar, 3–5 June 1994, pp. 15–16.

17 NUM, National Executive Committee Meeting, 'Grievance procedure', 30 April 1994, pp. 15–24.

18 Letter from D. Woodhouse for Deneys Reitz to Kgalema Motlanthe, 21 September 1993. NUM, National Executive Committee Meeting, 'Staff matters', 9 October 1993, pp. 103–104.

19 NUM's head office used to be located in Lekton House, Wanderers Street, Johannesburg. The current head office building is owned by the NUM via its real estate subsidiary, Numprop. It was bought by the union in 1993 for R4.95 million (NUM, National Executive Committee Meeting, 21 August 1993). The decision to refurbish it was taken under Frans Baleni's secretariat, for approximately R6 million (NUM, Secretariat Report, Central Committee, 2008, p. 35). Allegations of fraud in the awarding of two renovation tenders for the Rissik Street building were made by Baleni's opponents ahead of the

2012 national congress. Matuma Letsoalo, 'Gloves Off as Union Heads for Elections', *Mail & Guardian*, 11 May 2012, http://mg.co.za/article/2012-05-11-gloves-off-as-union-heads-for-elections.

20 At the time of this research, NUM still lacked space to accommodate all its national employees and was in the process of expanding to an adjacent building overlooking the ground-floor parking lot and garden.

21 NUM, Secretariat Report, 9th National Congress, 1997.

22 NUM, Secretariat Report, 11th National Congress, 2003.

23 NUM, 'Members first today and forever!', Secretariat Report, Central Committee, 2005, p. 15.

24 NUM, Secretariat Report, 12th National Congress, 2006, pp. 30–31.

25 Matuma Letsoalo, 'Uproar over Unionist's Huge Salary Hike Just "a Campaign"', *Mail & Guardian*, 18 May 2005, accessed 15 June 2017, http://mg.co.za/article/2012-05-18-uproar-over-unionists-huge-salary-hike-just-a-campaign.

26 NUM, Secretariat Report, Special Congress, Johannesburg, 2004, p. 29.

27 Mercy Sekano, executive director of the Elijah Barayi Memorial Training Centre, interview, Johannesburg, 3 October 2011.

28 NUM, Secretariat Report, 11th National Congress, 2003, p. 48.

29 NUM, Secretariat Report, Special Congress, Johannesburg, 2004, p. 30.

30 NUM, Secretariat Report, 13th National Congress, 2009, pp. 46–47.

31 NUM, Secretariat Report, Central Committee, 2011, p. 47.

32 NUM, 'A revolutionary union for a conscious membership', Secretariat Report, Central Committee, 2010, p. 55.

33 See the Aubrey Daniels International website, where a biography of its founder is available as well as a list of his publications on performance management: accessed 27 November 2013, http://aubreydaniels.com/.

34 'New public management' is based on the neoliberal assumption that market-orientated management techniques would be cost-efficient and lead to better organisational performance. See Christopher Hood, 'A Public Management for All Seasons?', *Public Administration* 69 (1991). On the penetration of managerial knowledge and practices in the French trade union movement, see Baptiste Giraud, '"Le Syndicalisme Saisi par le Management": Les Conditions de Production d'une Expertise Managériale de l'Action Syndicale au Prisme de Ses Investissements Diversifiés', *Politix* 79 (2007). See also Cécile Guillaume and Sophie Pochic, 'La Professionnalisation de l'Activité Syndicale: Talon d'Achille de la Politique de Syndicalisation à la CFDT?', *Politix* 85 (2009).

35 See, for instance, a three-page brief entitled 'Change Management … Involve Everyone', excerpted from a larger piece on strategic management originally published by the Harvard Business School in 2004. Collected at the NUM Elijah Barayi Memorial Training Centre in Yeoville, Johannesburg, 17 October 2010. On the ambiguities of participatory management, see Frank Heller et al., *Organizational Participation: Myth and Reality* (Oxford: Oxford University Press, 1998).

36 Anglo Platinum, 'Careers in Anglo American Platinum Limited', accessed 18 June 2013, http://www.angloplatinum.com/careers/careers_ang/human_resources.asp.

37 If one follows Gramsci's observations on 'Funzionarismo' – that is, on the full-time employees and representatives of the organisation – one conclusion is that the very way in which they work daily, and relate to organisational matters internally, gradually leads to a change in their interactions with employees and representatives from the other side (in this case mining companies). Antonio Gramsci, 'Il Controllo Operaio al Consiglio del Lavoro', in *Scritti sul Sindacato*, pp. 101–103.

38   Lonmin, 'Developing Our People: Training, Development and Transformation', accessed 18 June 2013, http://sd-report.lonmin.com/2012/people-planet-profit/people/developing-our-people.

39   Allen, *History of Black Mineworkers*, pp. 423–424.

40   NUM, Secretariat Report, Central Committee, 2008, p. 7.

41   'Tough Wage Talks But New Wage Policy Advanced', *NUM News*, 1989.

42   See Frans Baleni's already quoted secretariat report to the 2008 central committee, as well as to the 2009, 2012 and 2015 national congresses.

43   To take only an example of these trends, the use of PowerPoint has been analysed in Franck Frommer, *How PowerPoint Makes You Stupid: The Faulty Causality, Sloppy Logic, Decontextualized Data, and Seductive Showmanship that Have Taken Over Our Thinking* (New York: New Press, 2012).

44   NUM, Secretariat Report, Central Committee, 2008, pp. 23–24.

45   NUM, '30 years of unbroken revolutionary trade unionism struggle', Secretariat Report, 14th National Congress, 2012, p. 58.

46   NUM, Secretariat Report, 12th National Congress, 2006, p. 7; NUM, Annual Financial Statements, 1994, 2006, 2011.

47   Newly recruited members are requested to fill in an 'application for membership' and a 'stop order authorisation form' to authorise their employer to deduct their union membership fee and transfer it to NUM on a monthly basis.

48   NUM, Biennial Report, 7th National Congress, 1991, p. 21.

49   NUM, National Executive Committee Meeting, 7 September 1991, pp. 9–10, 41–44.

50   Address by NUM president, James Motlatsi, at the 10th NUM National Congress, Pretoria, 26 April 2000. NUM Resource Centre, Johannesburg.

51   NUM, Biennial Report, 6th National Congress, 1989, pp. 46–47.

52   NUM, Biennial Report, 7th National Congress, 1991, p. 52.

53   NUM, Resolutions adopted by the 7th Biennial Congress, 1991, p. 33.

54   NUM, Secretariat Report, National Congress, 2009, pp. 66–71.

55   Mineworkers Provident Fund, Member Booklet, 2008, p. 5.

56   NUM, '30 years of unbroken revolutionary trade unionism struggle', Secretariat Report, 14th National Congress, 2012.

57   'Mineworkers Provident Fund', accessed 20 June 2013, http://www.mineworkers.co.za.

58   'Shape your future', Report: NUM Retirement Fund Summit, 3–5 March 2005.

59   Mr S. Wall, Chairman of the Mineworkers Provident Fund, letter to all stakeholders of the MWPF, 3 November 2008.

60   It seems that workers from the West Driefontein gold mine demanded the repayment of their provident fund contributions. Renee Grawitzky, 'South Africa: Provident Fund Officials Receive Death Threats', *Business Day*, 18 May 1999. The NUM branch chairperson at the same mine was shot dead in 2006, just like Mayise's former deputy a few years before him. The NUM, however, did not seem to connect these two alleged assassinations with Mayise's murder. 'Assassination Suspected as Mine Leader Dies', *Sapa*, 5 July 2006.

61   Mbuyiseli Hibana, regional secretary, NUM Carletonville region, interview, Carletonville, 2 December 2011.

62   Thabang Sefalafala, 'Union Splits on the Mines: A Case Study of Legal Voice at Driefontein East Gold Mine, Carletonville, Gauteng (2010)' (Honours thesis, University of the Witwatersrand, 2010). The NUM discussed Sefalafala's findings in Eddie Majadibodu,

'Progressive and Dynamic: NUM Always Improving Service to Members', *South African Labour Bulletin* 36 (2012).

63   Eva-Lotta Jansson, 'Migrant Workers Owed Billions in "Unclaimed" Social Security Funds', *Mail & Guardian*, 22 February 2013, accessed 15 June 2017, http://mg.co.za/article/2013–02–22–00-migrant-workers-owed-billions-in-unclaimed-social-security-funds; Moyagabo Maake, 'Custodians "Cannot Trace Many Beneficiaries"', *Business Day Live*, 26 May 2013, accessed 15 June 2017, http://www.bdlive.co.za/national/2013/05/26/custodians-cannot-trace-many-beneficiaries.

64   K. Nkosi, N. Erasmus and J. Winson, 'Report from the Mines 1970's Provident Fund to the Ad Hoc Parliamentary Committee on Matters Related to ex-Mineworkers', 15 February 2008. Accessed 8 August 2017, http://pmg-assets.s3-website-eu-west-1.amazonaws.com/docs/080215mines1970sfund.htm.

65   Rebecca Davis, 'The Disgraced Fidentia Boss and His Unlikely Friends', *Daily Maverick*, 21 May 2013, accessed 15 June 2017, http://www.dailymaverick.co.za/article/2013–05–21-the-disgraced-fidentia-boss-and-his-unlikely-friends/. Charlotte Matthews, 'Mineworkers Provident Fund – Disharmony Among Trustees?', *Financial Mail*, 9 February 2012.

66   She later wrote a PhD dissertation on the MDA and co-ops. Teresa Kate Philip, 'Enterprise Development on the Margins: Making Markets Work for the Poor?' (PhD thesis, University of the Witwatersrand, 2006).

67   MDA, 'Creating Livelihoods in Communities', Information flyer (undated).

68   NUM, 'Members first – today and forever', Secretariat Report, Central Committee, 2002, p. 28.

69   The MIC's portfolio included participation in FirstRand (finance), Primedia (media), Tracker (technology), Eastvaal Motors (automotive), BP (petroleum), Peermont (hotels and casinos) and Set Point (industry). For a full list, see http://www.mic.co.za, accessed 21 June 2013.

70   MIC, 'The Dawn of a New Era', Annual Review, 2012.

71   MIT, 'Celebrating 15 Years of Looking After Our Own 1995–2010', MIT Annual Report, 2010.

72   MIC, '1995–2010: 15 Years of Changing Lives, Altering Perceptions and Making a Difference: We Are Only Getting Started', Annual Business Review, 2010, pp. 12–14.

73   NUM, Resolutions adopted at the 9th National Congress, 1997, p. 9.

74   MIC, '1995–2010: 15 Years of Changing Lives, Altering Perceptions and Making a Difference We Are Only Getting Started', Annual Business Review, 2010, pp. 24–26.

75   NUM, Biennial Report, 6th National Congress, 1989, p. 28; NUM, Biennial Report, 7th National Congress, 1991, p. 21.

76   NUM, National Executive Committee Meeting, 7 September 1991, pp. 21–27.

77   SALB correspondent, 'Union Investment, New Opportunities, New Threats', *South African Labour Bulletin* 20 (1996), p. 33.

78   Robert Oakeshott, Job Ownership Ltd, fax to John Copelyn, London, 22 September 1993. In NUM, National Executive Committee Meeting, 'Cosatu matters', 9 October 1993, pp. 174–187. Job Ownership Ltd has now become the Employee Ownership Association: see http://employeeownership.co.uk/, accessed 21 June 2013.

79   Deanne Collins, 'An Open Letter to Johnny Copelyn and Marcel Golding', *South African Labour Bulletin* 21 (1997).

80   John Copelyn, 'Seizing the Moment: Union Investment Companies', *South African Labour Bulletin* 21 (1997), p. 77.

81 Marcel Golding, 'Pioneers or Sellouts? Exploring New Lands', *South African Labour Bulletin* 21 (1997), p. 90.

82 Okechukwu C. Iheduru, 'Organised Labour, Globalisation and Economic Reform: Union Investment Companies in South Africa', *Transformation* 46 (2001), p.13.

83 'Not an Ordinary Man', *Mail & Guardian*, 23 April 2007, accessed 21 June 2017, http://mg.co.za/article/2007-04-23-not-an-ordinary-man/ >.

84 Philip Dexter, 'Union Investment towards a Political Strategy', *South African Labour Bulletin* 21 (1997), p. 72.

85 MIT, 'Celebrating 15 Years of Looking After Our Own 1995–2010', MIT Annual Report, 2010.

86 Address by NUM president, James Motlatsi, at the 10th NUM National Congress, Pretoria, 26 April 2000. NUM Resource Centre, Johannesburg.

87 Bill Fletcher and Richard W. Hurd, 'Beyond the Organizing Model: The Transformation Process in Local Unions', in *Organizing to Win: New Research on Union Strategies*, ed. K. Bronfenbrenner et al. (Ithaca, NY: ILR Press, 1998); Jack Fiorito, 'Union Renewal and the Organizing Model in the United Kingdom', *Labor Studies Journal* 29 (2004).

88 On the work of expertise, see, for instance, Timothy Mitchell, *Rule of Experts: Egypt, Techno-politics, Modernity* (Berkeley: University of California Press, 2002); see also Mitchell, 'Work of Economics'.

89 Bezuidenhout et al., *Meeting Expectations?*

90 This is the key argument of one convincing piece on Marikana: Gavin Hartford, *The Mining Industry Strike Wave: What Are the Causes and What Are the Solutions?*, 3 October 2012, accessed 4 August 2017, http://us-cdn.creamermedia.co.za/assets/articles/attachments/41878_2012_10_03_mining_strike_wave_analysis.pdf.

91 Crispen Chinguno, 'Continuities and Discontinuities in Repertoires of Strike Violence in Post-apartheid South Africa: Cases from Rustenburg Platinum Mines', paper presented at the International Mining History Congress, Johannesburg, 19 April 2012.

92 NUM, 'Members first today and forever!', Secretariat Report, Central Committee, 2005, p. 3.

93 NUM, Secretariat Report, 12th National Congress, 2006, p. 3.

94 NUM, Secretariat Report, Central Committee, 2011, p. 4.

95 Bezuidenhout et al., *Meeting Expectations?*, p. 3.

96 NUM, Regional Secretariat Report, Carletonville Regional Conference, 2005, p. 22.

97 On Fanakalo as a revealer of tensions between ordinary NUM members and their leaders, see Raphaël Botiveau, 'La Langue de Ceux d'en Dessous: Les Bases Morales des Mobilisations de Mineurs dans la Platinum Belt Sud-Africaine', in *Quand l'Industrie Proteste: Fondements Moraux des (In)Soumissions Ouvrières*, ed. Amin Allal, Myriam Catusse and M. Emperador Badimon (Rennes: PUR, forthcoming).

98 Eddie Majadibodu, 'Implementing the Ten Dimensions for Quality Service to Members', NUM, 2001. Report prepared by the union's production pillar. This report is in itself illustrative of NUM's shift from militancy to servicing, which led the union to consider its members more as customers than as activists involved in defence of a cause.

99 NUM, Secretariat Report, 11th National Congress, 2003, p. 48.

100 NUM, 1991 National Staff Seminar Report, Alpha Training Centre, Broederstroom, 7–8 February 1991, pp. 7–8.

CHAPTER 4

1   NUM, Discussion document for NUM Central Committee, Central Committee, 1999, pp. 34–35.
2   Bezuidenhout et al., *Servicing NUM*, p. 1.
3   Allen, *History of Black Mineworkers*, pp. 173–176.
4   Allen, *History of Black Mineworkers*, pp. 173–176.
5   Sizwe Timothy Phakathi, 'Membership–Leadership Conflict within a Trade Union on a South African Gold Mine: A Worker Perspective and Reflection on Marikana', *Global Labour Column* 140 (2013), unpaginated. Similar arguments appear in Alexander et al., *Marikana*.
6   Buhlungu, *Paradox of Victory*, pp. 52–53.
7   Buhlungu, 'Rise and Decline', pp. 92–93.
8   Buhlungu, 'Rise and Decline', pp. 95–96.
9   Buhlungu, 'Rise and Decline', pp. 98–99.
10   Buhlungu, 'Rise and Decline', pp. 100–101.
11   Buhlungu and Bezuidenhout, 'Union Solidarity under Stress', pp. 267 and 268.
12   Allen, *History of Black Mineworkers*, p. 117.
13   NUM, National Executive Committee Meeting, 'Consolidated regional report', 8–9 December 1990, pp. 102–105.
14   NUM, National Executive Committee Meeting, 2–3 February 1991, p. 10.
15   NUM, Special Central Committee Meeting, 'Proposed resolutions', 4–5 October 1986, pp. 1–4.
16   NUM, Secretariat Report, Carletonville Regional Conference, 2005, pp. 22–23.
17   This an indication that NUM is now trapped in its role as an 'intermediary organisation' – that is, an actor of labour relations institutionalisation which induces clashes between increasingly distinct organisational and membership interests. Walther Muiiler-Jentsch, 'Trade Unions as Intermediary Organizations', *Economic and Industrial Democracy* 6 (1985).
18   A branch general meeting is scheduled to take place at least once every month. It consists of an assembly of members and their leaders where the latter typically seek a 'mandate' from their rank and file. But mass meetings are not always convened on such a regular basis and they are often called only when issues arise. NUM, Constitution of the National Union of Mineworkers, as amended by 2009 National Congress, p. 15. Further references to the constitution of NUM will be based on this document.
19   Bezuidenhout et al., *Research Report on NUM Servicing*, pp. 63–64.
20   Bezuidenhout et al., *Meeting Expectations?*, pp. 130–131.
21   The Employee Share Ownership Programme is agreed upon between company and union. The programme is intended to award employees participation in the profits of their company, in the form of a contingent of shares. Employees are thus supposed to be financially 'interested' in the success of their employer. Moreover, in South Africa, Esop also enhances the Black Economic Empowerment profile of companies that are now supposed to reach targets in terms of black shareholding. For mineworkers who battle to make ends meet, however, Esop involves deferred and fluctuating payments since shares cannot be exchanged for cash before an agreed period of time has passed.
22   Richard E. Walton and Robert B. McKersie, *A Behavioural Theory of Labor Negotiations: An Analysis of a Social Interaction System* (New York: McGraw-Hill, 1965).

23 Informal conversation with Daniel Sethosa, 15th National Congress, 5 June 2015.

24 Pete Manamela, loader drill operator (category 4 worker), ordinary NUM member, interview, Mponeng branch, 18 May 2012. Note that this member refers to a mass meeting he attended when he was still working for Lonmin in Rustenburg, where he was subsequently retrenched.

25 Ordinary NUM member 2, winch operator, interview, Mponeng branch, 18 May 2012.

26 Ordinary NUM member 3, team leader, interview, Mponeng branch, 18 May 2012.

27 Ordinary NUM member 7, construction team leader, interview, Lonmin 4 Belt 1B Shaft, Karee branch, Marikana, 16 May 2012.

28 Musa Mnisi, chairperson, interview, NUM Mponeng branch, 13 July 2010.

29 NUM branch office bearer (BOB) at Lonmin, interview, 26 October 2011.

30 Kwanele Sosibo, 'Mathunjwa Pats Self on Back after Amcu Strike Ends', *Mail & Guardian*, 23 June 2014, accessed 8 July 2017, http://mg.co.za/article/2014-06-23-mathunjwa-pats-self-on-back-after-amcu-strike-ends. It is important to note that a repeated suggestion by some labour specialists is that mandatory strike balloting, which is prescribed in many unions' constitutions, including NUM's, be enforced in order to curb strike violence.

31 NUM shaft stewards committee member, interview, Lonmin Karee branch, Marikana, 16 May 2012.

32 Buhlungu, 'Democratic Tradition'.

33 T. Dunbar Moodie, 'Becoming a Social Movement Union', pp. 152–179.

34 NUM, National Executive Committee Meeting, 7 September 1991, p. 8.

35 According to Paul Stewart, the Mouthpeace Workers Union was born at Amplats out of informal 'machine operator committees' dissatisfaction with NUM, which then gave birth to the 5M. Paul Stewart, 'Labour Time, Worker's Control and Exploitation: A Moment in the Practical Production Politics of a Group of Rock Drill Operators on a South African Platinum Mine', paper presented at the 7th Global Labour University Conference, University of the Witwatersrand, Johannesburg, 28–30 September 2011. Paul Stewart, 'The 2012 Strike Wave, Marikana and the History of Rock Drillers in South African Mines', *Global Labour Column* 121 (2013).

36 Crispen Chinguno, 'Marikana and the Postapartheid Workplace Order', Working Paper 1. Johannesburg: SWOP Institute, 2013, pp. 20–21.

37 Bernard Manin, *Principes du Gouvernement Représentatif* (Paris: Flammarion, 2012), pp. 11–18, 26–28, 39, 61.

38 NUM, National Executive Committee Meeting, 'Consolidated regional report', 9 May 1992, p. 36.

39 NUM, National Executive Committee Meeting, 'Consolidated regional report', 12–14 June 1992, p. 17.

40 Thamsanqa Joko, chairperson, NUM PWV region, interview, Johannesburg, 12 July 2010.

41 NUM, Secretariat Report, Special Congress, 2004, p. 6.

42 NUM, Constitutional Amendments, Special Congress, 2004, p. 11.

43 NUM, Secretariat Report, Special Congress, 2004, pp. 6–7.

44 See for instance NUM, 'Leadership code of conduct and guidelines for elections and shopsteward councils', 2012, a document that was distributed widely in NUM structures and can be accessed at the union's Resource Centre in Johannesburg.

45 Koos Nkotsi, chairperson, NUM Impala Services branch, interview, Johannesburg, 11 October 2011.

46 Koos Nkotsi, chairperson, NUM Impala Services branch, interview, Johannesburg, 11 October 2011.

47 Meshack Moeng, deputy secretary, NUM Impala South branch, interview, Impala Platinum mine, 20 October 2011.

48 Daniel Sethosa, deputy chairperson, NUM Impala Refineries branch, interview, Springs, 24 November 2011.

49 NUM branch office bearer at Lonmin, interview, 26 October 2011.

50 Manin, *Principes*, p. 26.

CHAPTER 5

1 NUM, Secretariat Report, Rustenburg Regional Conference, 2011, p. 12.

2 Characters like Khululekile recall popular local leaders of the 1980s such as Lira Setona, whose charisma was useful to mobilise workers but whose personalisation of power was also detrimental to organisation building. T. Dunbar Moodie, 'Who was Lira Setona? Why Should We Care?', *South African Labour Bulletin* 33 (2009).

3 Khululekile was shot dead less than a year after the 2012 Lonmin strike. Greg Marinovich and Thapelo Lekgowa, 'Marikana: Fear and Terror at the Unions' Battlefield', *Daily Maverick*, 14 May 2013, accessed 13 August 2017, http://www.dailymaverick.co.za/article/2013–05–14-marikana-fear-and-terror-at-the-unions-battlefield/. NUM itself was either directly or indirectly a party in such incidents of violence, and Joseph Mathunjwa, Amcu's president, declared a few days after Khululekile's death: 'You'll remember that the President of Cosatu in their meeting in Boksburg he once said that they will employ the skills of MK [Umkhonto we Sizwe, the ANC's former armed wing] to deal with Amcu. This killing is it the result of his call? He must be called and be questioned by the authorities: what he meant by that he will employ the MK skills to deal with Amcu?' Joseph Mathunjwa, 'We Believe in Peace, Not Violence', *Mail & Guardian*, 13 May 2012, accessed 28 June 2017, http://mg.co.za/multimedia/2013–05–13-amcu-we-believe-in-peace-not-violence-1.

4 NUM, Draft Report, Rustenburg Regional Conference, 2008, p. 23.

5 NUM, Secretariat Report, Rustenburg Regional Conference, 2011, p. 18.

6 Paul Dunne, CEO of Northam Platinum and former manager of Impala Platinum's operations in Rustenburg, interview, Johannesburg, 18 June 2015.

7 Gavin Capps, 'Victim of Its Own Success? The Platinum Mining Industry and the Apartheid Mineral Property System in South Africa's Political Transition', *Review of African Political Economy* 39 (2012), pp. 65–66.

8 Martin Nicol, former head of the NUM collective bargaining department, interview, Cape Town, 9 May 2012. Jeffrey Nzimene Njuza, 26, was shot dead by a white co-worker at the Rustenburg Refineries in the then Transvaal, allegedly because he drank from a cup reserved for white workers. 'Comrade Njuza' was the first victim of NUM's Mine Defiance Campaign against segregated facilities at the Rustenburg Refinery. Prior to his death he had been charged with using a chair reserved for whites in the refinery's canteen. Njuza was one of the founding members of NUM in the Rustenburg region. His funeral gathered about 10 000 people and was met with repression from the Bophuthatswana police and army. One of NUM's Elijah Barayi Memorial Training Centre's conference rooms was named after him and the union holds a yearly Jeffrey Nzimane Njuza Memorial Lecture. 'Police Beat NUM Members after Funeral of Defiance Victim',

NUM News, December 1989, p. 8. 'NJUZA, Nzimene Jeffrey', *Truth Commission Special Reports*, accessed 28 June 2017, http://sabctrc.saha.org.za/victims/njuza_nzimene_jeffrey.htm.

9   NUM, Secretariat Report, PWV Regional Conference, 2005, pp. 6, 9.

10 NUM, Secretariat Report, PWV Regional Conference, 2011, p. 81.

11 NUM, Secretariat Report, Carletonville Regional Conference, 2005, p. 7.

12 NUM, Secretariat Report, PWV Regional Conference, 2005, p. 7.

13 NUM, Secretariat Report, Carletonville Regional Conference, 2005, p. 6.

14 NUM, Regional Committee Report, Carletonville region, 28 September 2011, pp. 58–64.

15 NUM, Annual Report, 5th National Congress, 1987, pp. 41–51.

16 NUM, Biennial Report, 6th National Congress, 1989, pp. 56–57.

17 South Africa, which had been the top world producer of gold for most of the twentieth century, yielded its rank to China in 2007 and is now fifth behind China, Australia, the USA and Russia. From nearly 400 tonnes of gold produced in 2002, it fell to about 200 tonnes in 2011. In the meantime the total workforce in gold decreased from 199 000 in 2002 to 146 000 in 2011, including contractors. Chamber of Mines, *Mining Facts & Figures*, 2012, accessed 14 August 2017, http://www.chamberofmines.org.za/industry-news/publications/facts-and-figures/send/17-facts-and-figures/143-facts-and-figures-2012.

18 Theto Mahlakoana, 'NUM Report Details Its Many Failures', *Business Day*, 8 June 2017.

19 NUM, Secretariat Report, 9th National Congress, 1997, p. 44.

20 NUM, Secretariat Report, 11th National Congress, 2003, pp. 1, 33–34.

21 This NUM region was created after the merger of the union's Wits and Westonaria regions in the early 1990s.

22 Capps, 'Victim of Its Own Success?'.

23 Mbuyiseli Hibana, secretary, NUM Carletonville region, interview, Carletonville, 2 December 2011.

24 NUM, Draft Report, Rustenburg Regional Conference, 2008, p. 6.

25 Archie Palane, head of corporate affairs and transformation, Samancor, interview, Johannesburg, 21 May 2012.

26 Gwede Mantashe, '"A Good Union": The National Union of Mineworkers', *South African Labour Bulletin* 30 (2006), p. 37.

27 Sapa, 'Union Bosses in Court for Fraud', *News24* archives, 15 March 2007, accessed 28 June 2017, http://www.news24.com/SouthAfrica/News/Union-bosses-in-court-for-fraud-20070314. The three former leaders were eventually acquitted: Sapa, 'Former NUM Members to Take Union to Court', *Times Live*, 25 January 2010, accessed 15 December 2013, http://www.timeslive.co.za/business/article276600.ece/Former-NUM-members-to-take-union-to-court?commentsPage=true.

28 NUM, Secretariat Report, 12th National Congress, 2006, p. 8.

29 NUM, Secretariat Report, Rustenburg Regional Conference, 2011, p. 8.

30 A 'mining house coordinator' is an elected union official at a given mining company who is in charge of coordinating NUM's activities in that particular company, as well as of organising meetings and supporting the relationship between the union and management.

31 Reuters, 'Amplats Likely to Sell or Shut Union Mine', *Mail & Guardian*, 14 January 2013, accessed 28 June 2017, http://mg.co.za/article/2013-01-14-amplats-to-lose-union-mine. After 2012 Anglo Platinum announced massive retrenchments as well as its intention to sell its loss-making operations.

32 The role of national leaders present at regional conferences is pivotally about making sure that 'institutional rites' are respected. Rites are here meant to legitimise processes that are in part arbitrary and in part planned, as shown by Pierre Bourdieu, 'Les Rites Comme Actes d'Institution', *Actes de la Recherche en Sciences Sociales* 43 (1982).

33 Richard Mahoha, chairperson, NUM Rustenburg region, interview, Rustenburg, 28 November 2011.

34 NUM, '30 years of unbroken revolutionary trade unionism struggle', Secretariat Report, 14th National Congress, 2012, p. 78.

35 Informal conversation, NUM PWV Regional Conference, 2011.

36 NUM, Secretariat Report, 12th National Congress, 2006, p. 7.

37 In 2009, the income derived from membership fees was R187 million, 80% of which came from mining. Union expenditures broke down as follows: accommodation and seminars (14%); affiliation fees (7%); computer expenses (1%); consultant fees (3%); legal fees (12%); motor vehicle expenses (18%); printing (2%); rental-offices (6%); rent, office, equipment (3%); repairs and maintenance (1%); salaries, wages and contributions (24%); telephone, fax and cellular costs (2%); training and development (1%); travelling (5%). NUM, 'A revolutionary union for a conscious membership', Secretariat Report, Central Committee, Johannesburg, 2010, p. 54.

38 At Lonmin, for instance, NUM and management had apparently not entered into such an agreement. One shaft steward I met there complained about this because, he argued, non-members also benefited from NUM work. Moreover, he told me, his branch – Karee, which was losing members after the 2011 wildcat strike – would have benefited from an agency fee that would have encouraged mineworkers to rejoin NUM.

39 Sonia Bendix, *Industrial Relations in South Africa*, 4th edition (Cape Town: Juta, 2001), p. 265.

40 See, in particular, chapter 3: 'The Labor Union and Economic Freedom'. Mancur Olson, *The Logic of Collective Action: Public Goods and the Theory of Groups* (Cambridge, MA: Harvard University Press, 2002).

41 NUM, National Executive Committee Meeting, 'Organising', 7 September 1991, p. 57.

42 NUM, National Executive Committee Meeting, 23–24 March 1994, pp. 1–4.

43 The 1992/1993 gold agreement signed by NUM and the Chamber of Mines states: 'Agency Shop to be further discussed. Anglo has agreed to begin discussions with NUM to deal with "free riders" – the non-members of NUM who still get the benefits that are negotiated by NUM. An arrangement similar to an Agency Shop has been implemented at Harmony Gold Mine – all non-NUM member are contributing 1% of wages to a "Collective Bargaining Fund". Half of this money will go direct to NUM to meet bargaining expenses in connection with Harmony.' At the time, only 42% of gold mineworkers were NUM members. NUM Collective Bargaining Department, Summary for Report Backs. The 1992/3 wage agreements between NUM and Chamber of Mines Gold Mines, 1992, p. 2.

44 Douglas Gininda, secretary, NUM Randfontein branch, interview, Randfontein, 30 June 2010.

45 NUM, Draft Report, Rustenburg Regional Conference, 18–19 October 2008, p. 21.

46 NUM, Secretariat Report, Central Committee, 2008, p. 17.

47 NUM, Secretariat Report, Central Committee, 2011, p. 19.

48 David Macatha, NUM treasurer general, speech given at NUM 14th National Congress, 24 May 2012.

CHAPTER 6

1   Hannah Arendt, *Between Past and Future: Six Exercises in Political Thought* (New York: Penguin Books, 2006), see chapter 3.
2   Richard Sennett, *Authority* (New York: W.W. Norton, 1993), p. 4.
3   E.P. Thompson studied food riots in eighteenth-century England and showed that they were triggered not only and objectively speaking by 'soaring prices, by malpractices among dealers, or by hunger'. He argued instead that there was at the time 'a pattern of social protest which derives from a consensus as to the moral economy of the commonwealth in times of dearth'. In other words, 'these grievances operated within popular consensus as to what were legitimate and what were illegitimate practices. This in its turn was grounded upon a consistent traditional view of social norms and obligations, of the proper economic functions of several parties within the community, which, taken together, can be said to constitute the moral economy of the poor'. Edward Palmer Thompson, *Customs in Common* (London: Penguin Books, 1993), pp. 188, 246.
4   When declared illegitimate, leaders can be rightfully deposed or even killed. These options are helpful in understanding some responses to failed leadership in a context such as that of the mines. The principle of legitimacy attached to power has been used to allow disobedience, resistance and the resort to violence in diverse historical, political and geographic contexts. North of Africa, contemporary forms of political Islam such as that preached by influential Egyptian Muslim Brother Sayyid Qutb considered violence a legitimate response to illegitimate rulers.
5   Arendt, *Between Past and Future*, 93.
6   Jared Sacks, 'Marikana Prequel: NUM and the Murders That Started It All', *Daily Maverick*, 12 October 2012, accessed 29 June 2017, http://www.dailymaverick.co.za/opinionista/2012-10-12-marikana-prequel-num-and-the-murders-that-started-it-all#.UymQPl6nf-k.
7   Alexander et al., *Marikana*.
8   The NUM leadership qualities I list hereafter are based on recurring organisational trends and conceptions I observed and are neither exclusive of one another nor equally shared by all. They can nevertheless be conceived as core leadership qualities that are well shared union-wide and complementary insofar as my interviewees' regular mention of them, in one order or another, and because they generally fit what is taught to aspiring leaders in the organisation. This said, every leader also has his or her own leadership 'style', as they say in NUM.
9   Bhongo Mvimvi, full-time shaft steward, Cooke 3, NUM Randfontein Branch, interview, Cooke 3 mining hostels, 1 July 2010.
10   Goodwell Tshitshiba, secretary, Mponeng Branch, interview, 22 November 2011.
11   NUM branch office bearer at Lonmin, interview, 26 October 2011.
12   Sennett, *Authority*, p. 18.
13   Archie Palane, head of corporate affairs and transformation, Samancor, interview, Johannesburg, 21 May 2012.
14   'Baleni on Lonmin Killings and Violence', video posted on NUM's official website via YouTube, 20 August 2012, accessed 4 October 2014, http://www.youtube.com/watch?v=1eLzskhdYwY.
15   Course pack distributed to participants in NUM leadership development course convened by the NUM education and training unit, EBMTC, Johannesburg, 10–14 October 2011, pp. 14–15.

16   See the website of Bob and Sally Garratt's company, Garratt Learning Services, which has been active in South Africa, for more details. Accessed 18 August 2017, http://garrattlearningservices.com/About.htm.

17   Frans Baleni, 'Social Governance Critical in Organisation Building', *South African Labour Bulletin* 28 (2004), p. 12.

18   Elijah Chiwota, 'Struggle Not Over Yet: An Interview with Nehawu's Suraya Jawoodeen', *South African Labour Bulletin* 35 (2011), pp. 12–13.

19   John P. Kotter, 'What Leaders Really Do', *Harvard Business Review*, 'Best of HBR', December 2001.

20   See, for instance, James Jaspers, *The Art of Moral Protest: Culture, Biography, and Creativity in Social Movements* (Chicago: University of Chicago Press, 1999).

21   NUM, 'Intermediate Steward Manual', NUM Education and Training Department, Johannesburg, 2006, pp. 7, 3.

22   NUM, 'Participants Manual', stewards' induction training course, 2005, pp. 106–109.

23   Jaco Joubert, human resources manager for North Shafts, Impala Platinum mine, interview, 8 June 2015.

24   Douglas Gininda, secretary, NUM Randfontein branch, interview, Randfontein, 30 June 2010.

25   Goodwell Tshitshiba, secretary, NUM Mponeng branch, interview, Mponeng Gold mine, 22 November 2011.

26   Mez Ramatena, treasurer, NUM Impala Services branch, interview, Impala Platinum mine, 20 October 2011.

27   In some cases, however, such pay increases can be awarded to more branch leaders, as was the case at Lonmin where the worst 2012 strike took place. There, the top five members of each NUM branch committee were appointed on a full-time basis at the same rate of pay they had enjoyed immediately prior to their election, although Annexure D of the recognition agreement entered into between the union and the company prescribed the payment of a monthly allowance to full-time branch office bearers 'to make up the difference between the full-time shop steward's current total guaranteed pay and R14 000 per month'. 'Recognition Agreement between Lonmin Platinum … and National Union of Mineworkers', signed at Marikana, 25 July 2011, pp. 19–20, 39.

28   Greg Marinovich, 'Conflict of Interest, Inc: Mining Unions' Leaders Were Representing Their Members While in Corporations' Pay', *Daily Maverick*, 24 April 2013, accessed 29 June 2017, http://www.dailymaverick.co.za/article/2013-04-24-conflict-of-interest-inc-mining-unions-leaders-were-representing-their-members-while-in-corporations-pay/#.U0QZasdU_-k. NUM subsequently responded to Greg Marinovich's article in NUM, 'NUM's Response to *Maverick*', press release, 25 April 2013. It is worth recalling here that NUM negotiates its leaders' wages on an individual basis with employers for national office bearers and a few regional office bearers only (usually regional chairpersons and secretaries). NUM officials argue that the fact that union representatives remain employees of their companies – that is, technically workers and not permanent union employees – is part of worker control.

29   NUM, Secretariat Report, 11th National Congress, 2003, p. 9.

30   NUM shaft stewards committee member, Lonmin Karee branch, interview, Marikana, 16 May 2012.

31   In his foreword to the 2006 edition of the NUM Intermediate Steward Manual, Frans Baleni wrote the following, which reveals a lot about the national leaders' actual expec-

tations and how they are comforted by or even informed by SWOP reports: 'It has to be brought to your attention that the NUM membership profile is changing, and therefore, we are expected to adapt and respond to the repositioned members' needs. It is common cause that we now recruit and organise members in the white colour category. These members are skilled and professionals, they expect to get quality service of a particular nature.' Note the interesting lapsus linguae 'white colour' instead of 'white collar'. NUM, 'Intermediate Steward Manual', p. iii.

32   The concept is understood here within the Bourdieusian analytical framework, as a set of dispositions to act. Pierre Bourdieu, *Le Sens Pratique* (Paris: Minuit, 1980).

33   Pierre Bourdieu, *La Distinction: Critique Sociale du Jugement* (Paris: Minuit, 1979), p. 1.

34   It is not random that Amcu's leader Joseph Mathunjwa, going back to his membership during wage negotiations at the end of the 2014 landmark platinum strike, was reported as having said to thousands of mineworkers: 'The world called you uneducated … But you taught the entire world a lesson.' Kwanele Sosibo, 'Mathunjwa Pats Self on Back after Amcu Strike Ends', *Mail & Guardian*, 23 June 2014, accessed 28 June 2017, http://mg.co.za/article/2014-06-23-mathunjwa-pats-self-on-back-after-amcu-strike-ends.

35   Bourdieu, *La Distinction*, pp. 5–6.

36   Before delegates gathered at the 2011 Rustenburg regional conference, he made at least three references to the words of the English poet. He first stated: 'Kings are born kings, some have weaknesses.' Later on he quoted words from *Julius Caesar*: 'Cowards die many times before their deaths.' Finally he made a more awkward reference to *Twelfth Night*: 'The best for my foes, the worst for my friends.'

37   For a recent South African discussion of Bourdieusian theory see Karl von Holdt and Michael Burawoy, *Conversations with Bourdieu: The Johannesburg Moment* (Johannesburg: Wits University Press, 2012).

38   Manin, *Principes*, p. 125.

39   Manin, *Principes*, p. 169.

40   This was well observed by Michels, who wrote: 'With the appearance of professional leadership, there ensues a great accentuation of the cultural differences between the leaders and the led. Long experience has shown that among the factors which secure the dominion of minorities over majorities – money and its equivalents (economic superiority), tradition and hereditary transmission (historical superiority) – the first place must be given to the formal instruction of the leaders (so-called intellectual superiority).' Michels, *Political Parties*, p. 107.

41   Buhlungu, *Paradox of Victory*.

42   NUM, Secretariat Report, Central Committee, 2011, p. 8.

43   Buhlungu, *Paradox of Victory*, pp. 117–118.

44   Frans Baleni, NUM general secretary, interview, NUM head office, Johannesburg, 12 July 2010.

45   NUM legal officer, interview, NUM head office, Johannesburg, 14 June 2010.

46   Mthembeni Gula, secretary of the health and safety sub-committee, NUM Impala South branch, interview, 20 October 2011.

47   Meshack Moeng, deputy secretary, NUM Impala South branch, interview, 20 October 2011.

48   Branch office bearer, NUM Murray & Robert's Kroondal-Marikana branch, interview, 30 November 2011.

49   Claude Grignon and Jean-Claude Passeron, *Le Savant et Le Populaire: Misérabilisme et Populisme en Sociologie et en Literature* (Paris: Seuil, 1989).

50   Allen, *History of Black Mineworkers*, pp. 92–93.
51   One merely has to consult union documents produced in the regions and even more at branch level to see that the English literacy skills of NUM leaders are often not this good.
52   Interestingly, in French one often talks about the 'électeur stratège' – literally, the strategist elector – in reference to Anthony Downs' rational theory of electoral choice. Anthony Downs, *Une Théorie Economique de la Démocratie* (Bruxelles: Université de Bruxelles, 2013). Also see the original version of the book: Anthony Downs, *An Economic Theory of Democracy* (New York: Harper and Brothers, 1957).
53   Jerry Ndamase, secretary, NUM Karee branch, interview, Karee Hostels, Lonmin-Marikana, 17 May 2012.
54   Lonmin, Information Sheet, September 2012.
55   Natasha Marrian and Allan Seccombe, 'Amcu Wants "Majority Status" at Lonmin', *Business Day Live*, 6 March 2013, accessed 29 June 2017, http://www.bdlive.co.za/national/labour/2013/03/06/amcu-wants-majority-status-at-lonmin.
56   These three interviews were conducted with Lonmin members, 16 May 2012.
57   Mponeng member, interview, 18 May 2012.
58   Dhiraj Nite and Paul Stewart (eds), *Mining Faces: An Oral History of Work on Gold and Coal Mines in South Africa, 1951–2011* (Johannesburg: Fanele, Jacana, 2012), pp. 3–4.
59   Nite and Stewart, *Mining Faces*, p. 254.
60   Amcu shaft steward, interview, Impala Platinum mine, 8 June 2015.

CHAPTER 7

1   Moodie, 'Leadership', pp. 66–68.
2   Eddie Majadibodu, head of NUM production pillar, interview, NUM head office, 10 June 2010.
3   Frans Baleni, NUM general secretary, interview, Johannesburg, 12 July 2010.
4   NUM Youth Forum Seminar, EBMTC, 14 October 2011, observation notes.
5   Steve Biko, *I Write What I Like: Selected Writings* (Chicago: University of Chicago Press, 2002).
6   Ronel Swart, 'Towards a Prospectus for Freirean Pedagogies in South African Environmental Education Classrooms: Theoretical Observations and Curricular Reflections' (MEd thesis, University of Pretoria, 2009), pp. 14–16.
7   Rehana Muhammad, 'The People's Education Movement in South Africa – A Historical Perspective' (MEd thesis, Rand Afrikaans University, 1996). See also Fhulu Nekhwevha, 'The Influence of Paulo Freire's "Pedagogy of Knowing" on the South African Education Struggle in the 1970s and 1980s', in *History of Education*, ed. Kallaway, pp. 134–144.
8   Menzi Melrose Mthwecu, 'The Role of Trade Unions in Adult Basic Education and Training: A Case Study of the National Union of Mineworkers in South Africa' (EdD thesis, University of Massachusetts – Amherst, 1996), pp. 36–41.
9   See the Paulo Freire Project website: http://cae.ukzn.ac.za/PauloFreireProject.aspx, accessed 30 June 2017.
10   NUM, National Executive Committee Meeting, 8–9 December 1990, pp. 15, 20.
11   NUM, Secretariat Report, 11th National Congress, 2003, pp. 53–57.
12   The NUM education and culture department was incepted in 1984 and its five principal objectives, which I have summarised in points (i) and (ii), are well expressed in NUM, Biennial Report, 6th National Congress, 1989, pp. 29–30. The programme of work of

the department was coordinated by Kgalema Motlanthe from the NUM head office, and it shows that beyond training courses for shaft stewards, mass education was largely limited to 'cultural activities' aimed at preserving 'the rich cultural traditions of our members'.

13 Michels, *Political Parties*, p. 70.

14 NUM, National Executive Committee Meeting, 27 November 1993, pp. 55–57.

15 Abet is a basic education and training framework for adults in South Africa, comprising language literacy and numeracy modules on a four-level continuum. The negotiation, planning and implementation of Abet programmes in the mines was studied in depth by the late Menzi Mthwecu; see his 'Role of Trade Unions'.

16 Mthwecu, 'Role of Trade Unions', p. 78. See pp. 78–82, as well as pp. 90ff. for a chronological summary of how Abet spread through Cosatu and NUM structures.

17 Mthwecu, 'Role of Trade Unions', p. 1.

18 Mthwecu, 'Role of Trade Unions', p. 2. Note that this figure can be contested. For instance, in a NUM report quoting from the 1996 Population Census, the literacy level in the mining sector is estimated to be 68.5%: NUM, Education Secretariat Report, National Policy Conference, 6–8 February 2003, p. 25. This figure is consistent with the 68% level of 'functional literacy' estimate for the overall population of South Africa at the time, as well as in 2001. See John Aitchison and Anne Harley, 'South African Illiteracy Statistics and the Case of the Magically Growing Number of Literacy and ABET Learners', *Journal of Education* 39 (2006), p. 91. For further information on Abet and the notion of illiteracy in South Africa, see Parliamentary Monitoring Group, 'What is ABET', 2002, accessed 30 June 30 2016, http://www.pmg.org.za/docs/2002/appendices/020917abet.htm.

19 Mthwecu, 'Role of Trade Unions', p. 57.

20 Mthwecu, 'Role of Trade Unions', pp. 2–3.

21 Mthwecu, 'Role of Trade Unions', p. 77.

22 NUM, Secretariat Report, Special Congress, Johannesburg, 2004, p. 4.

23 NUM, Secretariat Report, Kimberley Regional Conference, 2008, p. 23.

24 Bezuidenhout et al., *Meeting Expectations*, pp. 99–100.

25 As dictated by the Skills Development Act No. 97 of 1998, the South African government created the Mining Qualification Authority (MQA) to drive skills development in the mining sector.

26 Department of Mineral Resources, *Broad-Based Socio-economic Empowerment Charter for the South African Mining Industry* (Pretoria: Department of Mineral Resources, Republic of South Africa, 2002).

27 Department of Mineral Resources, *Mining Charter Impact Assessment Report* (Pretoria: Department of Mineral Resources, Republic of South Africa, 2009), p. 5.

28 Speech by Susan Shabangu at the launch of the Mining Charter Review and Scoreboard, Pretoria, 13 September 2010.

29 Ngoako Matsha, 'Mineworker Graduates with an MBA', *NUM News*, August 2012, p. 3.

30 These two quotes (the first from 'female alumni winner, Nancy Makatseng') are from a JB Marks Alumni Award promotional clip downloaded at http://www.mic.co.za/, 23 April 2014.

31 Buhlungu, *Paradox of Victory*, pp. 109–111.

32 JB Marks Education Trust Fund, home page: http://www.jbmarksedutrust.co.za/index.php, accessed 18 April 2014.

33   The Amwu was formed in 1941/42 with a view to organising African mineworkers. It was involved in and eventually destroyed by the 1946 black mineworkers' strike. NUM often pictures itself as the heir of this early organisation even though, as Allen notes, 'when Ramaphosa and a small group of supporters met at the end of August 1982 to establish a trade union and give it a name, none had been aware that the AMWU had ever existed'. Allen, *History of Black Mineworkers*, p. xxv. On NUM-claimed affiliation with Amwu, see NUM, '1946, Five Brave Days', *NUM Information Series* (Johannesburg: Research, Information and Publication Department of NUM, no date, probably 1986). On the 1946 strike and the part the Amwu played in it, see T. Dunbar Moodie, 'The Moral Economy of the Black Miners' Strike of 1946', *Journal of Southern African Studies* 13 (1986).

34   JB Marks Education Trust Fund official web site: http://www.jbmarksedutrust.co.za/index.php, accessed 18 April 2014. The fund is administered by a board of trustees which includes several NUM officials and staff members. The board was chaired by Frans Baleni at the time.

35   Nite and Stewart, *Mining Faces*.

36   After he had been retrenched in 1997, Mathebula, a father of nine, ended up living in a township and he explained that 'I have tried to do things to earn a living until now. I don't have any skill and at school I only learned a little as I dropped out in standard five (the final year of primary schooling)'. His interview in Nite and Stewart's book ends with the same complaint about his retrenchment package. See Nite and Stewart, *Mining Faces*, pp. 193–194, 204.

37   Since 1997, 'the fund has enabled 750 bursars to graduate with mainstream tertiary qualifications (including 15 medical doctors) and disbursed R96m to more than 2,500 beneficiaries, with 600 students in progress'. Mineworkers Investment Trust, official website, accessed 18 April 2014, http://www.mit.org.za/index.php/2013–12–06–11–08–35/jb-marks.

38   NUM, Secretariat Report, Kimberley Regional Conference, 2008, p. 24.

39   NUM, Secretariat Report, Kimberley Regional Conference, 2008, pp. 26–27.

40   Mineworkers Investment Trust, Annual Report, February 2012, p. 10.

41   NUM, Secretariat Report, Rustenburg Regional Conference, 2011, p. 55.

42   NUM, Secretariat Report, 11th National Congress, 2003, p. 26.

43   Mineworkers Investment Trust, Annual Report, February 2012, pp. 11, 17.

44   Joseph Morallana, regional coordinator, NUM PWV region, interview, Johannesburg, 29 June 2010.

45   The EBMTC is not the only vehicle of trade union education in South Africa. The Ditsela Workers' Education Institute, a joint project launched by Cosatu, Fedusa (the Federation of Unions of South Africa) and Nactu (the National Council of Trade Unions) in 1996, is another such institution.

46   EBMTC, official website, accessed 19 April 2014, http://Ebmtc.co.za/?page_id=106.

47   Mineworkers Investment Trust, official website, accessed 19 April 2014, http://www.mit.org.za/index.php/beneficiaries/Ebmtc.

48   'The Training Centres are able to self-generate income averaging R9 million per year … In 2009 EBMTC was rated to be a tourism venue by the South African Tourism Grading Council and is now offering accommodation to tourists at both facilities'. EBMTC, accessed 21 April 2014, http://www.mit.org.za/index.php/beneficiaries/Ebmtc.

49   Mineworkers Investment Trust, Annual Report, 2012, p. 21.

50   In 2009, 'a total of 34 courses were offered … with nearly 1000 students in attendance from NUM regions in the country and also from outside of South Africa; Botswana,

DRC [Democratic Republic of Congo], Ghana, Mozambique, Nigeria, Swaziland and Zimbabwe. Around 40% of learners are female with on-going efforts to encourage a higher attendance. The majority of attendees are still from the mining sector but there has been a steady improvement in members from construction and the energy fields.' EBMTC, accessed 21 April 2014, http://www.mit.org.za/index.php/beneficiaries/ Ebmtc.

51 Mercy Sekano, executive director of the EBMTC, interview, Johannesburg, 3 October 2011.
52 NUM, NUM Education Strategic Plan 2005–2010, no publication date but probably 2005, pp. 3–5, 9–11.
53 NUM, NUM Education Strategic Plan 2005–2010, p. 6.
54 MQA, official website, accessed 21 April 2014, http://www.mqa.org.za/content. asp?subID=1.
55 Mercy Sekano, executive director of the EBMTC, interview, Johannesburg, 3 October 2011.
56 On the official website of the Department of Higher Education and Training, FET Colleges (public and private), are described as follows: 'Further Education and Training courses are vocational or occupational by nature meaning that the student receives education and training with a view towards a specific range of jobs or employment possibilities. Under certain conditions, some students may qualify for admission to a University of Technology to continue their studies at a higher level in the same field of study as they were studying at the FET College.' FET Colleges South Africa, official website, accessed 19 April 2014, http://www.fetcolleges.co.za/.

CHAPTER 8

1 NUM, Secretariat Report, Central Committee, 25–27 April 2002, Bloemfontein, p. 12.
2 NUM shaft stewards committee member, Lonmin Karee branch, interview, Marikana, 16 May 2012.
3 'RDP houses', which are sometimes also referred to as 'matchboxes', are housing units the South African government built in large numbers under the aegis of the Reconstruction and Development Programme (1994). They were designed to solve the housing crisis by giving proper shelter to residents living in the townships erected in suburban areas under apartheid, as well as in rural settlements. Between 1994 and 2000, the ANC-led government built more than one million such houses to accommodate five million people out of an estimated 12.5 million people without proper housing. Tom Lodge, *Politics in South Africa: From Mandela to Mbeki* (Cape Town: David Philip, 2002), p. 57.
4 These words are those of a local NUM leader who asked to remain anonymous. The interview was conducted in 2012.
5 Cosatu, 'Gulf between Rich and Poor Widening', press release, 6 December 2010.
6 Mpho Raborife, 'Amplats's Griffith Apologises for Fair Pay Comments', *Mail & Guardian*, 17 May 2014, accessed 6 July 2017, http://mg.co.za/article/2014–05–17-amplatss-griffiths-apologises-for-fair-pay-comments.
7 Angelique Serrao and Lebogang Seale, 'Amcu Leader's Life of Luxury', *The Star*, 19 May 2014, accessed 6 July 2017, http://www.iol.co.za/news/politics/amcu-leader-s-life-of-luxury-1.1690081.
8 'I Did Not Steal from Anyone – Joseph Mathunjwa', *City Press*, 19 May 2014, accessed 6 July 2017, http://www.citypress.co.za/news/steal-anyone-joseph-mathunjwa/, or http://

www.news24.com/Archives/City-Press/I-did-not-steal-from-anyone-Joseph-Mathun-jwa-20150429.

9   See Fiona Forde's biography of Malema, *An Inconvenient Youth: Julius Malema and the 'New' ANC* (Johannesburg: Picador Africa, 2011). The foreword to the book, by Achille Mbembe, offers an interesting reading of the character whom he describes as an embod-iment of 'lumpen radicalism'.

10 Sapa, 'Malema: EFF is SA's Future Ruling Party', *Mail & Guardian*, 17 May 2014, accessed 6 July 2017, http://mg.co.za/article/2014-05-17-malema-eff-is-sas-future-ruling-party.

11 Richard Banégas and Jean-Pierre Warnier, 'Nouvelles Figures et du Pou-voir', *Politique Africaine* 82 (2001).

12 Judith Hayem, ' "When You're Successful, You Must Give Back to the Community!" Suc-cessful, Rich and Poor: Three Key Notions for the Understanding of a Generation', paper presented at the 4th European Conference on African Studies, Uppsala, 17 June 2011.

13 In the same way as Weber considered the ideal of the capitalist entrepreneur, that of the bureaucrat, or that of the charismatic leader. Max Weber, *From Max Weber: Essays in Sociology*, translated and edited by H.H. Gerth and C. Wright Mills (New York: Oxford University Press, 1946), p. 59. Weber's analyses in terms of 'ideal', which he most com-monly applied to collectives (for instance, bureaucracies and religions), does not in any way constitute a normative attempt to conceptualise society; rather it features as a meth-odological tool, a fictional construction designed to reach a more accurate and refined understanding of it. His goal through what merely consists of an intellectual simplifi-cation was thus to accentuate distinctive features to give sociological consistency to the often vague categories used by historians or social scientists.

14 Lipset et al., *Union Democracy*, pp. 219–222.

15 Renée Grawitsky, independent journalist and researcher, interview, Johannesburg, 15 May 2012. When I met her, Grawitsky was working on an official biography of Motlatsi.

16 Moodie, 'Who was Lira Setona?', p. 61.

17 Moodie, 'Outraged Feelings', pp. 68–70.

18 'The pastoral leader does not nominate. Instead, he gathers his followers together, guides and leads them. This is the power that seeks to do good, beneficent power, directing the conduct of its followers, and bringing them together as individuals in a mutual rela-tionship of responsibility. For the pastoral leader, wielding power is a duty, pursued with zeal, devotion and endless application, offering care to others but denying it to oneself. Leadership is defined not as an honour but rather as a burden and effort. The leader puts himself out for, acts, works and watches over all his followers – and each of them as well. He acts not like a judge but a healer. Followers are expected to work on their own behaviour, to obey, but willingly so, because the aim is their own salvation. In a word, redemption.' Moodie, 'Leadership', pp. 66–68.

19 Buhlungu, *Paradox of Victory*, pp. 122–123, 125, 127, 137. For a summary of his typol-ogy, see the table entitled 'Categories of full-time officials in post-1973 unions', p. 126.

20 Buhlungu, *Paradox of Victory*, p. 129.

21 Course pack distributed to participants in the NUM Leadership Development course convened by the NUM education and training unit, Elijah Barayi Memorial Training Centre, Johannesburg, 10–14 October 2011, 'Activity 9: Leadership Styles', unpaginated.

22 By 'ethos' I mean here that Ecliff Tantsi's personal inclination is not towards militancy. He presents himself as a strategist, a negotiator and a professional, which he is indeed.

23 Luc Boltanski, *Les Cadres: La Formation d'un Groupe Social* (Paris: Minuit, 1982). The English translation of the book – Luc Boltanski, *The Making of a Class: Cadres in French*

Society (New York: Cambridge University Press, 1987) – retained the French 'cadre' that matches several English terms (the words 'manager', 'professional', 'administrator' and 'executive' are all close but non-synonymous). Interestingly, while Boltanski considers 'cadres' as a 'social group', the English translation chose the much more connoted notion of 'class', which Boltanski does not, however, avoid, discussing the definitions of the 'middle' and the 'working' 'classes' at length.

24 Boltanski, *Les Cadres*, pp. 476, 477–482.
25 It would have been useful here to dig deeper into the interactions between NUM leaders and mining managers, to show how their respective subjectivities and ethos intertwine in their regular interactions. My observations of wage negotiations and interviews with mine managers shed some light on this process, which I cannot detail here. For more insights on this, see Botiveau, 'Negotiating Union', Part 3.
26 Andre Janse van Vuuren, 'Where Does Baleni's Loyalty Lie?', *City Press*, 10 February 2013, accessed 6 July 2017, http://www.citypress.co.za/business/where-does-balenis-loyalty-lie/. See NUM's right of reply: Lesiba Seshoka, 'NUM Still a Worthy Labour Union', *City Press*, 17 February 2013, accessed 6 July 2017, http://www.citypress.co.za/business/num-still-a-worthy-labour-union/.
27 Frans Baleni, NUM general secretary, interview, Johannesburg, 12 July 2010.
28 Baleni, 'Social Governance', p. 12.
29 Between 2003 and 2006 Baleni also held the position of nonexecutive director and chair of the tender committee at Eskom, South Africa's electricity parastatal.
30 Matserane wa Mapena, 'Trade Union Education in the Real World Educating Poem', in NUM, Education & Training 2010, booklet.
31 In my interviews with him, as well as when I observed his performance as a union chief negotiator, Tantsi showed regular concern about members' evaluation of his moves. His 'leadership style', as I elaborate in what follows, shows that he is careful not to lose touch with the grassroots, where, he knows, his representative power originates. On the notion of 'accountability', see Adam Przeworski, Susan C. Stokes and Bernard Manin (eds), *Democracy, Accountability, and Representation* (Cambridge: Cambridge University Press, 1999).
32 Zwelitsha Ecliff Tantsi, NUM national education secretary, interview, NUM head office, 17 June 2010.
33 Zwelitsha Ecliff Tantsi, NUM national education secretary, interview, NUM head office, 12 September 2011.
34 Ecliff Tantsi told me he was interviewed on several occasions by 'a woman from Leaders' Quest', which describes itself as 'a social enterprise committed to improving the quality and impact of leaders around the world … Our growing global community connects more than 6,000 leaders. We work with people to integrate social purpose with company performance. We mentor high-calibre leaders, from CEOs to grassroots organisers, and we empower some of the poorest in society to drive positive change.' Accessed 27 May 2014, http://www.leadersquest.org/who-we-are/.
35 At the end of 2012, NUM represented most Northam employees and was the only union to have sufficient representation to bargain with the company since Uasa, Solidarity and Amcu did not have enough members there (the recognition threshold being 33.3%). Northam Platinum Limited, Annual Integrated Report, 2013, p. 63.
36 This idea should nonetheless be tempered since NUM allegedly lowered its demands in the course of the strike and asked that '50% of these demands must be met in the current

financial year and the other 50% in the next'. NUM, 'Northam Platinum on the Brink of Collapse as Workers Strike through Christmas', press release, 13 December 2013.

37 Carol Paton, 'Lesson to be Learnt from Northam Strike Debacle', *Business Day*, 28 January 2014, accessed 16 February 2014, http://www.bdlive.co.za/national/labour/2014/01/28/lesson-to-be-learnt-from-northam-strike-debacle. After the strike settlement, NUM issued a triumphant press release: NUM, 'Northam Platinum Strike Ends in Triumph for NUM Members', press release, 17 January 2014.

38 'NUM: Even Animals Are Treated Better than Us', *Mail & Guardian*, video footage, 26 November 2013, accessed 30 August 2017, http://mg.co.za/multimedia/2013-11-26-num-even-animals-are-treated-better-than-us.

39 See the Myburgh Commission report on the July and August 1996 violence, which left 42 workers dead at Gold Fields and Northam mines: 'Report of the Commission of Enquiry into the Recent Violence and Occurrences at the East Driefontein, Leudoorn and Northam Mines, 5 October 1996'.

40 Paul Dunne, CEO of Northam Platinum, interview, Johannesburg, 18 June 2015.

41 Zwelitsha Ecliff Tantsi, NUM national education secretary, interview, 17 June 2015.

42 Alistair Anderson, 'Month-Long Strike Ends at Samancor Chrome', *Business Day*, 28 March 2012, accessed 7 July 2017, http://www.bdlive.co.za/articles/2012/03/27/month-long-strike-ends-at-samancor-chrome. NUM, 'Samancor's Four Week Long Strike Ends', press release, 27 March 2012.

43 One mining company official I met in 2011 confessed that although employers would, of course, prefer not to have strikes, a two- or three-day industrial action was fine and considered to be the right length of time, from an employer's point of view. The same official added that the internal politics of trade unions sometimes meant that they had to wage strikes to show their muscle – in 2011, for instance, Baleni's strike was also an answer to a recent and successful Numsa strike led by Irvin Jim, one of Baleni's rivals in Cosatu.

44 See Margaret Mead's classic study, *Culture and Commitment: A Study of The Generation Gap* (London: Bodley Head, 1970).

45 Clive Glaser, *The ANC Youth League* (Johannesburg: Jacana, 2012); Raphaël Botiveau, 'The ANC Youth League or the Invention of a South African Youth Political Organisation', IFAS Working Papers 10, French Institute of South Africa, Johannesburg, 2007.

46 On the question of youth in several African contexts, see Filip De Boeck and Alcinda Honwana (eds), *Makers and Breakers: Children and Youth in Postcolonial Africa* (Trenton NJ: Africa World Press, 2005), including the editors' introduction and Jean and John Comaroff's 'Reflections on Youth'.

47 Pierre Bourdieu, *Questions de Sociologie* (Paris: Minuit, 1984), p. 144.

48 Jean and John Comaroff, 'Réflexions sur la Jeunesse, du Passé à la Postcolonie', *Politique Africaine* 80 (2000).

49 NUM, '30 years of unbroken revolutionary trade unionism struggle', Secretariat Report, 14th National Congress, 2012, p. 34.

50 Note that in ANC-aligned organisations, a member is generally statutorily conceived as 'young' up until the age of 35.

51 Collin Mohala, regional coordinator, NUM Carletonville region, interview, NUM Carletonville regional office, 21 June 2010. I could not verify this information in union documents, but a 2004 amendment of the NUM constitution added: 'Only workers who have been members in good standing for an unbroken period of five years or who have been stewards before are eligible to stand for a position of a branch office bearer.' This clearly prevents incoming union members from directly accessing power positions

within the union. NUM, Constitutional Amendments, Special Congress 2004, p. 12. The above-mentioned time limitation seems to have subsequently been brought down to three years, as stipulated in the NUM constitution amended in 2009.

52 Richard Mahoha, chairperson, NUM Rustenburg region, interview, 28 November 2011.

53 NUM branch office bearer at Lonmin, interview, 26 October 2011.

54 Sibusiso Mhlala, chairperson, NUM Murray & Roberts Kroondal-Marikana branch, interview, 30 November 2011.

55 He was none other than Sithethi Mxhasi, a veteran NUM organiser from the 1980s (see Part I).

56 Branch office bearer, NUM Murray & Robert's Kroondal-Marikana branch, interview, 30 November 2011.

57 Koos Nkotsi, chairperson, NUM Impala Services branch, interview, Johannesburg, 11 October 2011.

58 I use his example for it is probably the most emblematic one of this leadership type. During my fieldwork I met several other senior NUM leaders whose leadership style would also be consistent with this ideal. They included, for instance, Thamsanqa Joko, chairperson of the NUM PWV region, and Mbuyiseli Hibana, secretary of NUM Carletonville region.

59 In 2007, Senzeni Zokwana was elected unopposed to the presidency of the 20-million-worker-strong International Federation of Chemical, Energy, Mine and General Workers' Unions (Icem). The Icem merged with the IndustriALL Global Union in 2012, which now represents 50 million workers in 140 countries.

60 On the question of 'masculinities' in mining, see chapters 1 and 4 in Moodie and Ndatshe, *Going for Gold*. One of the 'transformation'-related issues most consistently promoted by NUM leaders has been the right for women to work in mining – a males-only environment. See Asanda P. Benya, 'Women in Mining: A Challenge to Occupational Culture in Mines' (MA thesis, University of the Witwatersrand, 2009).

61 *Report of the Commission of Inquiry into Safety and Health in the Mining Industry Vol. 1*, 1995, electronic copy by David W. Stanton, October 2003, pp. 11–14, accessed 31 August 2017, http://www.cwbpi.com/AIDS/reports/LeonCommissionV1.pdf.

62 'Tenderpreneur' is a South African neologism that refers here to the way Julius Malema and others became multimillionaires through accumulating tenders awarded by local, provincial and national government.

63 Raphaël Botiveau, 'Inheritance and Invention: The Case of the African National Congress Youth League after Apartheid', paper presented at the One Hundred Years of the ANC: Debating Liberation Histories and Democracy Today Conference, Johannesburg, 23 September 2011, accessed 31 August 2017, http://www.sahistory.org.za/sites/default/files/RBotiveau_Paper_100%20Years%20of%20the%20ANC_22-9-2011.pdf).

64 Writing about the relationship between the 1950s ANC Youth League and its mother body, the ANC, Edward Feit explained that 'the political clash of generations is seldom clear-cut. In this case, a majority of the youth and the aged allied against an aging leadership and a minority of the young.' Edward Feit, 'Generational Conflict and African Nationalism in South Africa: The African National Congress, 1949–1959', *The International Journal of African Historical Studies* 5 (1972), p. 183.

65 One NUM employee I met at head office, who had been following the genesis of the Youth Forum, confirmed that it had emerged as some NUM youth wanted a dedicated structure to address specific issues but that it was then taken over by the old guard in a move to control and intimidate the youth. A couple of weeks before the Youth Forum seminar took place in Johannesburg on 14–15 October 2011, I had met one of

the participants. A convinced communist who showed obvious support for the 'legit-imist elders' on various occasions when I met him, apart from at the seminar, he told me that senior leadership had entrusted him with the mission to explore the possibility of launching a youth organ. Peterson Siyaya, informal conversation, NUM Rustenburg regional conference, Bela Bela, 29 September 2011.

66   A NUM employee in charge of the membership desk presented PowerPoint slides on the composition of the union's membership to delegates during the Youth Forum seminar in October 2011. It showed that more than 100 000 NUM members were young work-ers. In his report to the 2012 national conference, Frans Baleni estimated that about 54 % of NUM members were aged between 19 and 41. NUM, '30 years of unbroken rev-olutionary trade unionism struggle', Secretariat Report to the 14th National Congress, 2012, p. 34.

67   'The Hour of Youth Strikes at NUM', draft programme of action distributed at the NUM Youth Forum seminar, Johannesburg, 14–15 October 2011.

68   NUM, 'NUM Launches Its Youth Forum', press release, 8 May 2013.

CHAPTER 9

1   This, however, did not prevent Ramaphosa, in the context of the struggle against apart-heid (during which the ANC and the SACP were banned) and during the cold war, from preaching in favour of the class struggle and claiming to represent the working class. NUM's early bias towards communism was also linked to its connection with its Brit-ish homonym, whose secretary general, Arthur Scargill, belonged to the Communisty Party. Note that at the time, many if not most top anti-apartheid leaders, both inside and outside South Africa, belonged to the SACP.

2   This dimension is linked to a clear goal of the SACP, which states that 'the impera-tive of communists [is] not to isolate themselves as a narrow clique, but to be active within "every revolutionary movement"'. SACP, Political Report to the 13th Congress of the South African Communist Party, 11–15 July 2012, p. 7. The strategy includes the deployment of communist cadres to key positions in the trade union movement, the ANC and the State.

3   For a summary of the position of the SACP within the Tripartite Alliance over the past twenty years, see Botiveau, 'Longevity of the Tripartite Alliance'.

4   Goodwell Tshitshiba, secretary, NUM Mponeng branch, interview, 22 November 2011.

5   Sithethi Mxhasi, regional coordinator, NUM Rustenburg region, interview, 25 October 2011.

6   NUM branch office bearer at Lonmin, interview, 26 October 2011.

7   Meshack Moeng, deputy secretary, NUM Impala South branch, interview, 20 October 2011.

8   When I first met him in 2005, Buti Manamela, national secretary of the YCL, in fact told me that 'part of our role as the YCL is to demystify political involvement' and attract the youth. This, however, does not prevent the youth organisation, which was relaunched in 2003 (the original organisation had been banned in 1950), from displaying Stalinist ten-dencies and the YCL was allegedly 'purged' after Manamela's re-election for a third term had been contested on the basis of fraud allegations. Manacled Mataboge, 'Purge of League's Lumpen', *Mail & Guardian*, 4 March 2010, accessed 7 July 2017, http://mg.co.za/article/2011-03-04-purge-of-leagues-lumpen.

9   Over the past decade the SACP has nevertheless dramatically increased its membership, which, at the time of writing, was in the region of 150 000 card holders. Carol Paton, 'The Meteoric Rise and the Compromises of the SACP', *Business Day Live,* 16 April 2013, accessed 7 July 2017, http://www.bdlive.co.za/opinion/2013/04/16/the-meteoric-rise-and-the-compromises-of-the-sacp. On the ANC, note that most members are not active members but just cardholders and that membership figures tend to increase in the period that precedes the Party's five-yearly national conferences.

10   Bhongo Mvimvi, full-time shaft steward, Cooke 3, NUM Randfontein branch, interview, 1 July 2010.

11   Tumi Mokgatle, full-time shaft steward, smelter section, NUM Impala Minpro branch, interview, Impala Platinum mine, 19 October 2011.

12   Buhlungu, *Paradox of Victory*, p. 127.

13   Mantashe, 'A Good Union'.

14   NUM, Secretariat Report, 12th National Congress, 2006, p. 3.

15   Gwede Mantashe, 'When the Rain Comes, It Falls for Everybody', *South African Labour Bulletin* 20 (1996), p. 27.

16   NUM, 13th National Congress Resolutions, as discussed and adopted by the National Congress, 28–30 May 2009, Gallagher Estate Convention Centre, p. 39.

17   Mercy Sekano, executive director of the EBMCT, interview, Yeoville, 3 October 2011.

18   Frans Baleni, NUM general secretary, interview, NUM head office, Johannesburg, 12 July 2010.

19   Antonio Gramsci, *Guerre de Mouvement et Guerre de Position*, ed. Razmig Keucheyan (Paris: La Fabrique, 2011), pp. 147, 157–158.

20   The two exchanged their respective views in a series of four articles and responses: Sakhela Buhlungu, 'Rebels without a Cause of Their Own? The Contradictory Location of White Officials in Black Unions in South Africa, 1973–94', *Current Sociology* 54 (2006); Johann Maree, 'Rebels with Causes: White Officials in Black Trade Unions in South Africa, 1973–94: A Response to Sakhela Buhlungu', *Current Sociology* 54 (2006). Sakhela Buhlungu, 'Whose Cause and Whose History? A Response to Maree', *Current Sociology* 54 (2006); Johann Maree, 'Similarities and Differences between Rebels with and without a Cause', *Current Sociology* 54 (2006).

21   Jabu Gwala and Mike Murphy, 'The Role of "Intellectuals" in Trade Unions: A Discussion', *South African Labour Bulletin* 18 (1994), p. 51.

22   Madoda Sambatha, NUM head of the parliamentary pillar, interview, Cape Town, 3 August 2010.

23   Mmanaledi Mataboge, 'Supra Mahumapelo Elected as North West ANC Leader', *Mail & Guardian*, 13 February 2011, accessed 4 September 2017, http://mg.co.za/article/2011–02-13-supra-mahumapelo-elected-as-north-west-anc-leader.

24   NUM, Regional Secretariat Report, Carletonville Regional Conference, 2005, p. 38.

25   This is probably in part explained by the history of the SACP, which lived in exile and operated underground for forty years and did not have open access to the working class, hence preventing the latter from receiving communist ideas and identifying as a class.

26   See, for instance, Charles van Onselen, 'Worker Consciousness in Black Miners: Southern Rhodesia, 1900–1920', *Journal of African History* 14 (1973).

27   It is worth recalling here that while in Marx's view the class struggle as the engine of history preceded the Party, in Lenin's analysis of the Russian situation characterised by the absence of a proletariat, it is the Party that implicitly became the engine of history as producer of class and of the class struggle.

28 NUM, Secretariat Report to the Rustenburg Regional Conference, 2011, p. 89.

29 Douglas Gininda, secretary NUM Randfontein branch, interview, 30 June 2010.

30 NUM, Rustenburg Region Secretariat Report, Rustenburg Regional Conference, 2006, p. 6.

31 NUM, Participants Manual Political School 2009, presented by Khaya Blaai, 14–18 September 2009. The following list of 'acknowledgements' appears on page 2: 'Cosatu, SACP, ANC, Karl Marx, Govan Mbeki, Patrick Bond, Michael Leibowitz, Joe Slovo, Ben Fine and Alfredo Saad-Fildo's *African Communist*, Vladimir Lenin's *State and the Revolution*, Jack Rasmus, Anwar Shikh's *An Introduction to the History of Crisis Theories*, Kwame Nkrumah, Frederick Engels.'

32 NUM, SACP, NUM/SACP Joint Political Education Programme 2012: Reading Material, produced and consolidated by Madoda Sambatha (NUM) and Malesela Maleka (SACP), through internet research.

33 'We can admit that the fundamental distinctions be, in the moral order, the good and the evil; the beautiful and ugly in the aesthetic order; in economics, the useful and harmful or, for instance, the profitable and non-profitable. The question that then arises is to know if such a simple criterion exists for politics … The specific distinction of politics, to which political acts and motives can be reduced, is the discrimination of the friend and the enemy. It provides an identification principle with the value of criterion and not an exhaustive or comprehensive definition.' Carl Schmitt, *La Notion de Politique, Suivi de Théorie du Partisan* (Paris: Flammarion, 1992), pp. 63–64.

34 'Baleni on Lonmin Killings and Violence', video statement shot and edited by Livhuwani Mammmburu, posted on YouTube 20 August 2012, accessed 5 September 2017, http://www.youtube.com/watch?v=1eLzskhdYwY&feature=player_embedded.

35 'Frans Baleni – General Secretary, South African National Union of Mineworkers', interviewed in *Hardtalk*, BBC World Service, 26 November 2012. Accessed 14 September 2017, http://www.bbc.co.uk/programmes/p010pd5l.

36 Rapule Tabane, 'Amcu a Group of Vigilantes and Liars, Say Alliance Bosses', *Mail & Guardian*, 17 May 2013, accessed 7 July 2017, http://mg.co.za/article/2013–05–17–00–amcus-no-union-its-just-vigilantes-and-liars-say-alliance-bosses.

37 Sapa, 'NUM to Eradicate the Enemy Within: Baleni', *The Sowetan*, 27 May 2013, accessed 7 July 2017, http://www.sowetanlive.co.za/news/2013/05/27/num-to-eradicate-the-enemy-within-baleni.

38 NUM, 'Ill-informed Mathunjwa Must Stop Lying about Our President', press release, 19 May 2014.

39 See James Guillaume's foreword to Carlo Cafiero, *Abrégé du 'Capital' de Karl Marx* (Marseille: Le Chien rouge, 2008).

40 'I state: 1° that there shall be no solid revolutionary movement without a stable *organisation of leaders* to ensure the continuity of work; 2° that the larger the mass spontaneously drawn into the struggle, forming the base of the movement and participating to it, the more pressing the *need* to have such an organisation …; 3° that such an organisation must be mostly composed of men whose profession is the revolutionary activity.' This quote is from Lenin's *What is to be Done?* (1902), in Cohen, *Siècle des Chefs*, p. 31. Interestingly, Cohen almost identifies leadership and communism: 'to be a Bolshevik', he writes, 'it is to be a leader'; pp. 419–424.

41 Cohen, *Siècle des Chefs*, p. 447.

42 Frans Baleni, NUM general secretary, interview, NUM head office, Johannesburg, 12 July 2010. Note the reference to the SWOP surveys, which in Baleni's mind are a model of consultation.

43 Frans Baleni, NUM general secretary, interview, NUM head office, Johannesburg, 12 July 2010.

44 NUM, Secretariat Report, Rustenburg Regional Conference, 2006, no page number, p. 10 from first page.

45 NUM, Draft Report for the Rustenburg Regional Conference, 2008, pp. 23–24.

46 Baleni, 'Social Governance', pp. 12–13.

47 Organising: 'Activity Report for the period 06–29 October 1993', in NUM, National Executive Committee Meeting, 27 November 1993, pp. 71–72.

48 NUM, Secretariat Report, 11th National Congress, 2003, pp. 15–16.

49 NUM, Secretariat Report, 11th National Congress, 2003, p. 1.

50 NUM, Secretariat Report, 11th National Congress, 2003, pp. 5–6.

51 NUM, Secretariat Report, Special Congress, 2004, p. 7.

52 During the Rustenburg 2011 regional conference, a pro-Mantashe leader like Madoda Sambatha did not hesitate, for instance, to criticise delegates because, instead of pushing the motion of deceased Rustenburg chairperson Lazarus Ditshwene's deputy, Eliott Moloi, they decided to nominate other leaders for the position left vacant.

53 NUM, 'Resolutions adopted at the 9th National Congress, 1997', 10th National Congress, 2000, p. 18.

54 Mandy Rossouw, 'Newsmaker: Mantashe – Baas van die Plaas', City Press, 23 December 2012, accessed 7 July 2017, http://www.citypress.co.za/news/newsmaker-mantashe-baas-van-die-plaas/.

55 Allen, History of Black Mineworkers, pp. 434, 547–550.

56 'NUMSA Wants More Workers in ANC Leadership', Sapa, 22 July 2010.

57 Gwala and Murphy, 'Role of "Intellectuals" in Trade Unions', p. 53.

58 Jan de Lange, 'The Rise and Rise of Amcu', Miningmx, 2 August 2012, accessed 7 July 2017, http://www.miningmx.com/special_reports/mining-yearbook/mining-yearbook-2012/A-season-of-discontent.htm.

59 Alexander Beresford, 'Comrades "Back on Track"? The Durability of the Tripartite Alliance in South Africa', African Affairs 108 (2009), p. 399.

60 These included the dismantling of NUM substructures dedicated to education and health and safety at national and regional levels to avoid weakening the decision-making centres. Instead, Mantashe proposed to have one or two additional office bearers in charge of education and health and safety elected to the union's main national and regional structures. Another important item on the constitutional reform agenda involved abolishing the branch annual general meeting, which posed problems insofar as it duplicated another local decision-making body, the branch conference, and caused misunderstandings and troubles in NUM branches (where the annual meeting was often done away with in practice; see chapter 4). NUM, Secretariat Report, Special Congress, 2004, pp. 4–6.

61 NUM, Constitutional Amendments, Special Congress, 2004, pp. 12, 14, 22.

62 Gwede Mantashe, 'NUM Matures to Adulthood', interview with South African Labour Bulletin 28 (2004), p. 43.

63 Mantashe, 'NUM Matures to Adulthood'.

64 Matuma Letsoalo, 'NUM Digs in for Battle', Mail & Guardian, 19 May 2006.

65 Eddie Majadibodu, head of NUM production pillar, interview, NUM head office, 10 June 2010.

66 Letsoalo, 'NUM Digs in for Battle'. In a 2008 article, Buhlungu and Bezuidenhout wrote: 'The year before this fracas became public, we conducted research commissioned by NUM on the quality of their services to members … We were struck by the extent to which some branches and regions were openly divided. While more complex in reality, these divisions were sometimes expressed as cleavages between ethnic groups, more specifically speakers of Xhosa and Sotho. Added to this mix were issues of citizenship, since many Sotho speakers in the mining industry are migrant workers from South Africa's neighboring State Lesotho. At one branch in the Free State region, members told us that they feared for their lives, since some mineworkers were carrying guns. At this specific branch, the elections for local leadership were about to happen, and two factions competed for dominance. Indeed, the branch constitution was under dispute, since some members wanted a certain level of literacy and numeracy to be a precondition for eligibility. This was also seen as being directed at specific opponents. It seems as though "succession battles" take place not only at the level of national politics, or even in the national structures of unions, but also among the building blocks of union structures: their branches.' Buhlungu and Bezuidenhout, 'Union Solidarity', p. 264.

67 'Police Intervene in NUM Office Protest', *Mail & Guardian*, 4 June 2006, accessed 7 July 2017, http://mg.co.za/print/2006-06-04-police-intervene-in-num-office-protest.

68 Archie Palane, former NUM deputy general secretary, interview, Johannesburg, 21 May 2012.

CHAPTER 10

1 Frans Baleni, NUM general secretary, interview, NUM head office, Johannesburg, 12 July 2010.

2 'Opening Address at the National Congress of NUM by NUM President Senzeni Zokwana', 14th National Congress, 2012, p. 4.

3 Abraham Seaketso, Amcu mining house coordinator, Impala Platinum, interview, 8 June 2015.

4 NUM, '30 years of unbroken revolutionary trade unionism struggle', Secretariat Report, 14th National Congress, 2012, p. 79.

BIBLIOGRAPHY

Adler, Glenn and Eddie Webster, eds. *Trade Unions and Democratization in South Africa, 1985–1997*. Johannesburg: Wits University Press, 2000.

Adler, Glenn and Eddie Webster. 'Challenging Transition Theory: The Labor Movement, Radical Reform, and Transition to Democracy in South Africa'. *Politics & Society* 23 (1995): 75–106.

Aitchison, John and Anne Harley. 'South African Illiteracy Statistics and the Case of the Magically Growing Number of Literacy and ABET Learners'. *Journal of Education* 39 (2006): 89–112.

Alexander, Peter, Lekgowa, Thapelo, Mmope, Botsang, Sinwell, Luke and Bongani Xezwi. *Marikana: A View from the Mountain and a Case to Answer*. Johannesburg: Jacana, 2012.

Allen, Victor Leonard. *The History of Black Mineworkers in South Africa, Vol. 3: Organise or die, 1982–1994*. Keighley: The Moor Press, 2003.

Arendt, Hannah. *Between Past and Future: Six Exercises in Political Thought*. New York: Penguin Books, 2006.

Baleni, Frans. 'Social Governance Critical in Organisation Building'. *South African Labour Bulletin* 28 (2004): 12–13.

Baleni, Frans. 'Strategic Unionism in the New South Africa'. *South African Labour Bulletin* 20 (1996): 79–81.

Banégas, Richard and Jean-Pierre Warnier, 'Nouvelles Figures de la Réussite et du Pouvoir'. *Politique Africaine* 82 (2001): 5–23.

Bannon, John K. *Who the Hell Wants to be in Platinum? An Illustrated History of Impala Platinum Holdings Limited*. Johannesburg: Impala Platinum, 2012.

Barchiesi, Franco. *I Sindicati Indipendenti Sudafricani: Bibliografia*. Bologna: Centro Amilcar Cabral, Bologha: II Nove, 1994.

Barchiesi, Franco. 'Orientamenti Metodologici e Bibliografici per lo Studio del Sindacalismo Indipendente Sudafricano'. *Africa* 48 (1993): 70–91.

Bendix, Sonia. *Industrial Relations in South Africa*. Cape Town: Juta, 2001.

Benya, Asanda P. 'Women in Mining: A Challenge to Occupational Culture in Mines'. MA thesis, University of the Witwatersrand, 2009.

Beresford, Alexander. 'Comrades "Back on Track"? The Durability of the Tripartite Alliance in South Africa'. *African Affairs* 108 (2009): 391–412.

Bezuidenhout, Andries. 'New Patterns of Exclusion in the South African Mining Industry'. In *Racial Redress and Citizenship in South Africa*, edited by Kristina Bentley and Adam Habib, 179–208. Pretoria: HSRC Press, 2008.

Bezuidenhout, Andries, Bischoff, Christine and Themba Masondo. *Meeting Expectations? A Research Report on the State of Servicing in the National Union of Mineworkers*. Johannesburg: SWOP Institute, 2010.

Bezuidenhout, Andries and Sakhela Buhlungu. 'From Compounded to Fragmented Labour: Mineworkers and the Demise of Compounds in South Africa'. *Antipode* 43 (2010): 237–263.

Bezuidenhout, Andries and Sakhela Buhlungu. 'Old Victories, New Struggles: The State of the National Union of Mineworkers'. In *State of the Nation: South Africa 2007*, edited by Sakhela Buhlungu, John Daniel, Jessica Lutchman and Roger Southall, 245–265. Cape Town: HSRC Press, 2007.

Bezuidenhout, Andries, Buhlungu, Sakhela, Hlela, Hlengiwe, Modisha, Geoffrey and Dinga Sikwebu. *Research Report on NUM Servicing*. Johannesburg: SWOP Institute, 2005.

Bezuidenhout, Andries, Kenny, B., Masha, G., and H. Tshikalange. *Servicing the NUM: A Report of Surveys Conducted with NUM Branches in the PWV, Highveld and Rustenburg Regions*. Johannesburg: SWOP Institute, 1998.

Biko, Steve. *I Write What I Like: Selected Writings*. Chicago: University of Chicago Press, 2002.

Boltanski, Luc. *Les Cadres: La Formation d'un Groupe Social*. Paris: Minuit, 1982.

Botiveau, Raphaël. 'La Langue de Ceux d'en Dessous: Les Bases Morales des Mobilisations de Mineurs dans la Platinum Belt Sud-Africaine'. In *Quand l'Industrie Proteste: Fondements Moraux des (In)Soumissions Ouvrières*, edited by Amin Allal, Myriam Catusse and Montserrat Emperador Badimon. Rennes: PUR, forthcoming.

Botiveau, Raphaël. 'Negotiating Union: South Africa's National Union of Mineworkers and the End of the Post-apartheid Consensus'. PhD thesis, Université Paris 1 Panthéon-Sorbonne, La Sapienza Università di Roma, 2014.

Botiveau, Raphaël. 'Longevity of the Tripartite Alliance: The Post-Mangaung Sequence'. *Review of African Political Economy* 40 (2013): 620–627.

Botiveau, Raphaël. 'The ANC Youth League or the Invention of a South African Youth Political Organisation'. IFAS Working Papers 10. Johannesburg: IFAS, 2007.

Bourdieu, Pierre. *Questions de Sociologie*. Paris: Minuit, 1984.

Bourdieu, Pierre. 'Les Rites Comme Actes d'Institution'. *Actes de la Recherche en Sciences Sociales* 43 (1982): 58–63.

Bourdieu, Pierre. *Le Sens Pratique*. Paris: Minuit, 1980.

Bourdieu, Pierre. *La Distinction: Critique Sociale du Jugement*. Paris: Minuit, 1979.

Bourdieu, Pierre. 'Sur le Pouvoir Symbolique'. *Annales* 32 (1977): 405–411.

Bourdieu, Pierre, and Jean-Claude Passeron. *La Reproduction: Eléments pour une Théorie du Système d'Enseignement*. Paris: Minuit, 1970.

Buhlungu, Sakhela. *A Paradox of Victory: Cosatu and the Democratic Transformation in South Africa*. Pietermaritzburg: University of KwaZulu-Natal Press, 2010.

Buhlungu, Sakhela. 'The Decline of Labor Studies and the Democratic Transition'. *Work and Occupations* 36 (2009): 145–161.

Buhlungu, Sakhela. 'The Rise and Decline of the Democratic Organizational Culture in the South African Labor Movement, 1973 to 2000'. *Labor Studies Journal* 34 (2009): 91–111.

Buhlungu, Sakhela. 'Gaining Influence but Losing Power? Cosatu Members and the Democratic Transformation of South Africa'. *Social Movement Studies* 7 (2008): 31–42.

Buhlungu, Sakhela. 'Rebels without a Cause of Their Own? The Contradictory Location of White Officials in Black Unions in South Africa, 1973–94'. *Current Sociology* 54 (2006): 427–451.

Buhlungu, Sakhela, ed. *Trade Unions and Democracy: Cosatu Workers' Political Attitudes in South Africa*. Cape Town: HSRC Press, 2006.

Buhlungu, Sakhela. 'Whose Cause and Whose History? A Response to Maree'. *Current Sociology* 54 (2006): 469–471.

Buhlungu, Sakhela. 'The Building of the Democratic Tradition in South Africa's Trade Unions after 1973'. *Democratization* 11 (2004): 133–158.

Buhlungu, Sakhela. 'The Big Brain Drain: Union Officials in the 1990s'. *South African Labour Bulletin* 18 (1994): 25–32.

Buhlungu, Sakhela and Andries Bezuidenhout. 'Union Solidarity under Stress: The Case of the National Union of Mineworkers in South Africa'. *Labor Studies Journal* 33 (2008): 262–287.

Buhlungu, Sakhela, Brookes, Mick and Geoffrey Wood. 'Trade Unions and Democracy in South Africa: Union Organizational Challenges and Solidarities in a Time of Transformation'. *British Journal of Industrial Relations* 46 (2008): 439–468.

Buhlungu, Sakhela and Malehoko Tshoaedi, eds. *Cosatu's Contested Legacy*. Cape Town: HSRC Press, 2012.

Butler, Anthony. *Cyril Ramaphosa*. Johannesburg, Oxford: Jacana, James Currey, 2007.

Capps, Gavin. 'Victim of Its Own Success? The Platinum Mining Industry and the Apartheid Mineral Property System in South Africa's Political Transition'. *Review of African Political Economy* 39 (2012): 63–84.

Chinguno, Crispen. 'Marikana and the Postapartheid Workplace Order'. Working Paper 1. Johannesburg: SWOP Institute, 2013.

Chinguno, Crispen. 'Continuities and Discontinuities in Repertoires of Strike Violence in Post-apartheid South Africa: Cases from Rustenburg Platinum Mines'. Paper presented at the International Mining History Congress, Johannesburg: 19 April 2012.

Chiwota, Elijah. 'Struggle Not Over Yet: An Interview with Nehawu's Suraya Jawoodeen'. *South African Labour Bulletin* 35 (2011): 12–13.

Cohen, Yves. *Le Siècle des Chefs: Une Histoire Transnationale du Commandement et de l'Autorité (1890–1940)*. Paris: Éditions Amsterdam, 2013.

Collins, Deanne. 'An Open Letter to Johnny Copelyn and Marcel Golding'. *South African Labour Bulletin* 21 (1997): 79–80.

Comaroff, Jean and John Comaroff. 'Réflexions sur la Jeunesse, du Passé à la Postcolonie'. *Politique Africaine* 80 (2000): 90–110.

Cooper, Linda. 'The Trade Union as a "Learning Organisation"? A Case Study of Informal Learning in a Collective, Social-Action Organisational Context'. *Journal of Education* 39 (2006): 27–46.

Cooper, Linda, Andrew, Sally, Grossman, Jonathan and Salim Vally. ' "Schools of Labour" and "Labour's Schools": Worker Education under Apartheid'. In *The History of Education under Apartheid, 1948–1994: The Doors of Learning and Culture Shall Be Opened*, edited by Peter Kallaway, 111–133. Cape Town: Pearson Education South Africa, 2002.

Copelyn, John. 'Seizing the Moment: Union Investment Companies'. *South African Labour Bulletin* 21 (1997): 74–78.

Cosatu. *The Report of the September Commission on the Future of the Unions to the Congress of South African Trade Unions*. Johannesburg: Cosatu, 1997.

Crozier, Michel. *Le Phénomène Bureaucratique: Essai sur les Tendances Bureaucratiques des Systèmes d'Organisation Modernes et sur leurs Relations en France avec le Système Social et Culturel*. Paris: Seuil, 1971.

Crozier, Michel and Erhard Friedberg. *L'Acteur et le Système: Les Contraintes de l'Action Collective*. Paris: Seuil, 1977.

Crush, Jonathan. 'Migrancy and Militance: The Case of the National Union of Mineworkers of South Africa'. *African Affairs* 88 (1989): 5–23.

Crush, Jonathan, Ulicki, Theresa, Tseane, Teke and Elizabeth Jansen van Veuren. 'Undermining Labour: The Rise of Sub-contracting in South African Gold Mines'. *Journal of Southern African Studies* 27 (2001) : 5–31.

De Boeck, Filip and Alcinda Honwana, eds. *Makers and Breakers: Children and Youth in Postcolonial Africa*. Trenton, NJ: Africa World Press, 2005.

Dexter, Philip. 'Union Investment towards a Political Strategy'. *South African Labour Bulletin* 21 (1997): 71–73.

Donham, Donald L. *Violence in a Time of Liberation: Murder and Ethnicity at a South African Gold Mine, 1994*. Durham, NC: Duke University Press, 2011.

Downs, Anthony. *An Economic Theory of Democracy*. New York: Harper and Brothers, 1957.

Edelstein, J. David and Malcolm Warner. 'Research Areas in National Union Democracy'. *Industrial Relations* 16 (1977): 186–198.

Feit, Edward. *Workers without Weapons: The South African Congress of Trade Unions and the Organization of the African Workers*. Hamden: Archon Books, 1975.

Feit, Edward. 'Generational Conflict and African Nationalism in South Africa: The African National Congress, 1949–1959'. *The International Journal of African Historical Studies* 5 (1972): 181–202.

Fiorito, Jack. 'Union Renewal and the Organizing Model in the United Kingdom'. *Labor Studies Journal* 29 (2004): 21–53.

Fletcher, Bill and Richard W. Hurd. 'Beyond the Organizing Model: The Transformation Process in Local Unions'. In *Organizing to Win: New Research on Union Strategies*, edited by Kate Bronfenbrenner, Sheldon Friedman, Richard W. Hurd, Rudolf A. Oswald and Ronald L. Seeber, 37–53. Ithaca NY: ILR Press, 1998.

Forde, Fiona. *An Inconvenient Youth: Julius Malema and the 'New' ANC*. Johannesburg: Picador Africa, 2011.

Forrest, Kally. *Metal That Will Not Bend: National Union of Metalworkers of South Africa 1980–1995*. Johannesburg: Wits University Press, 2011.

Friedberg, Erhard. 'La Dynamique de l'Action Organisée'. In *Les Organisations: État des Savoirs*, edited by Philippe Cabin, 51–56. Auxerre: Sciences Humaines Éditions, 1999.

Friedman, Michelle. *'The Future is in the Hands of the Workers': A History of Fosatu*. Johannesburg: University of the Witwatersrand Historical Papers Labour Archive Project, 2011.

Frommer, Franck. *How PowerPoint Makes You Stupid: The Faulty Causality, Sloppy Logic, Decontextualized Data, and Seductive Showmanship that Have Taken Over Our Thinking*. New York: New Press, 2012.

Gaxie, Daniel. 'Rétributions du Militantisme et Paradoxes de l'Action Collective'. *Swiss Political Science Review* 11 (2005) : 157–188.

Gaxie, Daniel. 'Économie des Partis et Rétributions du Militantisme'. *Revue Française de Science Politique* 27 (1977) : 123–154.

Giraud, Baptiste. ' "Le Syndicalisme Saisi par le Management": Les Conditions de Production d'une Expertise Managériale de l'Action Syndicale au Prisme de Ses Investissements Diversifiés'. *Politix* 79 (2007): 125–147.

Glaser, Clive. *The ANC Youth League*. Johannesburg: Jacana, 2012.

Golding, Marcel. 'Pioneers or Sellouts? Exploring New Lands'. *South African Labour Bulletin* 21 (1997): 85–90.

Gramsci, Antonio. *Guerre de Mouvement et Guerre de Position*. Edited by Razmig Keucheyan. Paris: La Fabrique, 2011.

Gramsci, Antonio. *Scritti sul Sindacato*. Milano - Roma: Sapere Edizioni, 1975.

Grignon Claude and Jean-Claude Passeron. *Le Savant et le Populaire: Misérabilisme et Populisme en Sociologie et en Littérature*. Paris: Seuil, 1989.

Guillaume, Cécile and Sophie Pochic. 'La Professionnalisation de l'Activité Syndicale: Talon d'Achille de la Politique de Syndicalisation à la CFDT?'. *Politix* 85 (2009) : 31–56.

Gumede, William Mervin. *Thabo Mbeki and the Battle for the Soul of the ANC*. Cape Town: Zebra Press, 2005.

Gwala, Jabu and Mike Murphy. 'The Role of "Intellectuals" in Trade Unions': A Discussion. *South African Labour Bulletin* 18 (1994): 50–54.

Hacking, Ian. 'Making Up People'. *London Review of Books* 28 (2006): 23–26.

Hacking, Ian. *The Social Construction of What?* Cambridge, MA: Harvard University Press, 1999.

Hayem, Judith, ' "When You're Successful, You Must Give Back to the Community!" Successful, Rich and Poor: Three Key Notions for the Understanding of a Generation'. Paper presented at the 4th European Conference on African Studies, Uppsala, 17 June 2011.

Hayem, Judith. *La Figure Ouvrière en Afrique du Sud*. Johannesburg, Paris: IFAS, Karthala, 2008.

Heller, Frank, Pusić, Eugen, Strauss, George and Bernhard Wilpert. *Organizational Participation: Myth and Reality*. Oxford: Oxford University Press, 1998.

Hirschsohn, Philip. 'From Grassroots Democracy to National Mobilization: Cosatu as a Model of Social Movement Unionism'. *Economic and Industrial Democracy* 19 (1998): 633–666.

Hood, Christopher. 'A Public Management for All Seasons?'. *Public Administration* 69 (1991): 3–19.

Hughes, Everett Cherrington. *Men and Their Work*. London: The Free Press of Glencoe, Collier-Macmillan Limited, 1964.

Hyman, Richard. *Marxism and the Sociology of Trade Unionism*. London: Pluto Press, 1971.

Iheduru, Okechukwu C. 'Organised Labour Globalisation and Economic Reform: Union Investment Companies in South Africa'. *Transformation* 46 (2001): 1–31.

Jaspers, James. *The Art of Moral Protest: Culture, Biography, and Creativity in Social Movements*. Chicago: University of Chicago Press, 1999.

Kallaway, Peter, ed. *The History of Education under Apartheid, 1948–1994: The Doors of Learning and Culture Shall Be Opened*. Cape Town: Pearson Education South Africa, 2002.

Lambert, Robert and Edward Webster. 'The Re-emergence of Political Unionism in Contemporary South Africa'. In *Popular Struggles in South Africa*, edited by William Cobbett and Robin Cohen, 20–41. London: James Currey, 1988.

Leger, Jean and Phillip van Niekerk. 'Organisation on the Mines: The NUM Phenomenon'. In *South African Review III*, edited and compiled by South African Research Service, 68–78. Johannesburg: *Ravan Press*, 1986.

Lipset, Seymour Martin, Trow, Martin A. and James S. Coleman. *Union Democracy: The Internal Politics of the International Typographical Union*. New York, London: The Free Press, Collier-Macmillan Limited, 1968.

Lodge, Tom. *Politics in South Africa: From Mandela to Mbeki*. Cape Town: David Philip, 2002.

Lodge, Tom. *Black Politics in South Africa since 1945*. Johannesburg: Ravan Press, 1990.

Majadibodu, Eddie. 'Progressive and Dynamic: NUM Always Improving Service to Members'. *South African Labour Bulletin* 36 (2012): 19–21.

Mamdani, Mahmood. *Citizen and Subject: Contemporary Africa and the Legacy of Late Colonialism*. Princeton, NJ: Princeton University Press, 1996.

Manin, Bernard. *Principes du Gouvernement Représentatif*. Paris: *Flammarion*, 2012.

Mantashe, Gwede. 'The Decline of the Mining Industry and the Response of the Mining Unions'. MA thesis, University of the Witwatersrand, 2008.

Mantashe, Gwede. '"A Good Union": The National Union of Mineworkers'. *South African Labour Bulletin* 30 (2006): 36–39.

Mantashe, Gwede. 'NUM Matures to Adulthood'. *South African Labour Bulletin* 28 (2004): 43.

Mantashe, Gwede. 'When the Rain Comes, It Falls for Everybody'. *South African Labour Bulletin* 20 (1996): 24–31.

Maree, Johann. 'Rebels with Causes: White Officials in Black Trade Unions in South Africa, 1973–94: A Response to Sakhela Buhlungu'. *Current Sociology* 54 (2006): 453–467.

Maree, Johann. 'Similarities and Differences between Rebels with and without a Cause'. *Current Sociology* 54 (2006): 473–475.

Maree, Johann. 'The Cosatu Participatory Democratic Tradition and South Africa's New Parliament: Are They Reconcilable?'. *African Affairs* 97 (1998): 29–51.

Markham, Coletane and Monyaola Mothibeli. 'The 1987 Mineworkers Strike'. *South African Labour Bulletin* 13 (1987): 58–75.

Mead, Margaret. *Culture and Commitment: A Study of the Generation Gap*. London: Bodley Head, 1970.

Michels, Robert. *Sociologie du Parti dans la Démocratie Moderne: Enquête sur les Tendances Oligarchiques de la Vie des Groupes*, translated by Jean-Christophe Angaut. Paris: Gallimard, 2015.

Michels, Robert. *Political Parties: A Sociological Study of the Oligarchical Tendencies of Modern Democracy*. New Brunswick, NJ, London: Transaction Publishers, 1999.

Misra, Neeta. 'Strategic Unionism: The Political Role of the Congress of South African Trade Unions (Cosatu) in South Africa and What It Means for Black Workers'. PhD thesis, Massachusetts Institute of Technology, 2008.

Mitchell, Timothy. 'The Work of Economics: How a Discipline Makes its World'. *European Journal of Sociology* 46 (2005): 297–320.

Mitchell, Timothy. *Rule of Experts: Egypt, Techno-Politics, Modernity*. Berkeley: University of California Press, 2002.

Moodie, T. Dunbar. 'Social Movement Unionism: From Enthusiasm to Delivery – A Response to Gay Seidman'. *South African Review of Sociology* 43 (2012): 81–86.

Moodie, T. Dunbar. 'Becoming a Social Movement Union: Cyril Ramaphosa and the National Union of Mineworkers'. *Transformation* 72/73 (2010): 152–180.

Moodie, T. Dunbar. 'Comprehending Class Compromise in the History of Class Struggle on the South African Gold Mines: Variations and Vicissitudes of Class Power'. *South African Review of Sociology* 41 (2010): 99–116.

Moodie, T. Dunbar. 'Leadership of a Special Type: NUM at Vaal Reefs'. *South African Labour Bulletin* 34 (2010): 66–68.

Moodie, T. Dunbar. 'Outraged Feelings Burst Forth: Mineworkers at Vaal Reefs'. *South African Labour Bulletin* 33 (2009/2010): 68–70.

Moodie, T. Dunbar. 'Managing the 1987 Mine Workers' Strike'. *Journal of Southern African Studies* 35 (2009): 45–64.

Moodie, T. Dunbar. 'Who was Lira Setona? Why Should We Care?'. *South African Labour Bulletin* 33 (2009): 60–62.

Moodie, T. Dunbar. 'The Moral Economy of the Black Miners' Strike of 1946'. *Journal of Southern African Studies* 13 (1986): 1–35.

Moodie, T. Dunbar with Vivienne Ndatshe. *Going for Gold: Men, Mines and Migration.* Berkeley: University of California Press, 1994.

Mthwecu, Menzi Melrose. 'The Role of Trade Unions in Adult Basic Education and Training: A Case Study of the National Union of Mineworkers in South Africa'. EdD thesis, University of Massachusetts – Amherst, 1996.

Muhammad, Rehana. 'The People's Education Movement in South Africa – A Historical Perspective'. MEd thesis, Rand Afrikaans University, 1996.

Muiiler-Jentsch, Walther. 'Trade Unions as Intermediary Organizations'. *Economic and Industrial Democracy* 6 (1985): 3–33.

Nekhwevha, Fhulu. 'The Influence of Paulo Freire's "Pedagogy of Knowing" on the South African Education Struggle in the 1970s and 1980s'. In *The History of Education under Apartheid, 1948–1994: The Doors of Learning and Culture Shall Be Opened*, edited by Peter Kallaway, 134–144. Cape Town: Pearson Education South Africa, 2002.

Nite, Dhiraj and Paul Stewart, eds. *Mining Faces: An Oral History of Work on Gold and Coal Mines in South Africa, 1951–2011.* Johannesburg: Fanele, Jacana, 2012.

Oberry, Ingrid. 'NUM Tests Legal Strategies'. *Work in Progress* 33 (1984): 17–20.

Olson, Mancur. *The Logic of Collective Action: Public Goods and the Theory of Groups.* Cambridge, MA: Harvard University Press, 2002.

Panitch, Leo. *Social Democracy and Industrial Militancy.* Cambridge: Cambridge University Press, 1976.

Phakathi, Sizwe Timothy. 'Membership–Leadership Conflict within a Trade Union on a South African Gold Mine: A Worker Perspective and Reflection on Marikana'. *Global Labour Column* 140 (2013): unpaginated.

Philip, Teresa Kate. 'Enterprise Development on the Margins: Making Markets Work for the Poor?'. PhD thesis, University of the Witwatersrand, 2006.

Piketty, Thomas. *Capital in the Twenty-first Century.* Cambridge, MA: The Belknap Press of Harvard University Press, 2014.

Pretorius, Paul, Molahlehi, Edwin and Clive Thompson, 'Report of the Commission of Enquiry into Events at the Bafokeng North Mine during March 1992'. Document in author's possession.

Przeworski, Adam, Stokes, Susan C. and Bernard Manin, eds. *Democracy, Accountability, and Representation.* Cambridge: Cambridge University Press, 1999.

Pudal, Bernard. *Prendre Parti: Pour une Sociologie Historique du PCF.* Paris: Presses de la FNSP, 1989.

Reddy, Micah. 'Tswana Mineworkers, Industrial Unrest and "Worker Consciousness" on the Platinum Mines of Bophuthatswana in the Early 1990s'. Paper presented at the International Mining History Congress, Johannesburg, 19 April 2012.

Rocker, Rudolf. *Anarcho-Syndicalism.* Edinburgh, Oakland, LA: AK Press, 2004.

SALB correspondent. 'Union Investment, New Opportunities, New Threats'. *South African Labour Bulletin* 20 (1996): 33–39.

SALB correspondent. 'Impala: Gencor Strikes Again'. *South African Labour Bulletin* 11 (1986): 15–16.

SALB correspondent. 'UCAR Minerals in Bophuthatswana'. *South African Labour Bulletin* 9 (1984): 99–103.

Schiavone, Michael. 'Social Movement Unions and Political Parties (in South Africa and the Philippines): A Win-Win Situation?'. *African and Asian Studies* 6 (2007): 373–393.

Schmitt, Carl. *La Notion de Politique, Suivi de Théorie du Partisan*. Paris: Flammarion, 1992.

Sefalafala, Thabang. 'Union Splits on the Mines: A Case Study of Legal Voice at Driefontein East Gold Mine, Carletonville, Gauteng (2010)'. Honours thesis, University of the Witwatersrand, 2010.

Seidman, Gay. 'Social Movement Unionism: From Description to Exhortation'. *South African Review of Sociology* 42 (2011): 94–102.

Sennett, Richard. *Authority*. New York: W.W. Norton, 1993.

Séverin, Marianne and Pierre Aycard. 'Who Is Governing the "New" South Africa? Elites, Networks and Governing Styles (1985–2003)'. In *Ten Years of Democratic South Africa Transition Accomplished?*, edited by Philippe Guillaume, Nicolas Péjout and Aurélia Wa Kabwe-Segatti, 14–37. Johannesburg: IFAS, 2006.

Sikwebu, Dinga. 'NUM Aims to Remain "Champ Of Champs"'. *South African Labour Bulletin* 29 (2005/2006): 26–27.

Sitas, Ari. 'African Worker Responses on the East Rand to Changes in the Metal Industry, 1960–1980'. PhD thesis, University of the Witwatersrand, 1983.

Smith, Janet and Tromp Beauregard. *Hani: A Life Too Short*. Johannesburg and Cape Town: Jonathan Ball Publishers, 2009.

Stewart, Paul. 'The 2012 Strike Wave, Marikana and the History of Rock Drillers in South African Mines'. *Global Labour Column* 121 (2013): unpaginated.

Stewart, Paul. 'Labour Time, Worker's Control and Exploitation: A Moment in the Practical Production Politics of a Group of Rock Drill Operators on a South African Platinum Mine'. Paper presented at the 7th Global Labour University Conference, University of the Witwatersrand, Johannesburg, 28–30 September 2011.

Streek, Barry. 'Organizing the Struggle: Cyril Ramaphosa, General Secretary, National Union of Mineworkers'. *Africa Report* 31 (1986): 10–14.

Swart, Ronel. 'Towards a Prospectus for Freirean Pedagogies in South African Environmental Education Classrooms: Theoretical Observations and Curricular Reflections'. MEd thesis, University of Pretoria, 2009.

Thompson, Edward Palmer. *Customs in Common*. London: Penguin Books, 1993.

Turner, Rick. *The Eye of the Needle: Towards Participatory Democracy in South Africa*. Johannesburg: Ravan Press, 1978.

Vally, Salim, wa Bofelo, Mphutlane and John Treat. 'Worker Education in South Africa: Lessons and Contradictions'. *McGill Journal of Education* 48 (2013): 469–490.

Van Niekerk, Phillip. 'NUM First Legal Mine Strike'. *South African Labour Bulletin* 10 (1984): 11–20.

Van Onselen, Charles. 'Worker Consciousness in Black Miners: Southern Rhodesia, 1900–1920'. *Journal of African History* 14 (1973): 237–255.

Von Holdt, Karl. 'Social Movement Unionism: The Case of South Africa'. *Work, Employment & Society* 16 (2002): 283–304.

Von Holdt, Karl. 'Strategic Unionism: The Debate'. *Southern Africa Report* 8 (1993): 36.

Von Holdt, Karl and Michael Burawoy. *Conversations with Bourdieu: The Johannesburg Moment*. Johannesburg: Wits University Press, 2012.

Von Lieres, Bettina. 'The 1987 NUM Strike'. BA thesis, University of the Witwatersrand, 1988.

Voss, Kim and Rachel Sherman. 'Breaking the Iron Law of Oligarchy: Union Revitalization in the American Labor Movement'. *American Journal of Sociology* 106 (2000): 303–349.

Walton, Richard E. and Robert B. McKersie. *A Behavioural Theory of Labor Negotiations: An Analysis of a Social Interaction System.* New York: McGraw-Hill, 1965.

Weber, Max. *Économie et Société, Tome 1: Les catégories de la sociologie.* Paris: Pocket, 1995.

Weber, Max. *From Max Weber: Essays in Sociology,* translated and edited by Hans H. Gerth and C. Wright Mills. New York: Oxford University Press, 1946.

Webster, Edward. 'South African Labour Studies in a Global Perspective, 1973–2006'. *Labour, Capital and Society* 37 (2004): 258–282.

Webster, Edward. 'The Rise of Social-Movement Unionism: The Two Faces of the Black Trade Union Movement in South Africa'. In *State, Resistance and Change in South Africa,* edited by Philip Frankel, Noam Pines and Mark Swilling, 174–196. London: Croom Helm, 1988.

Webster, Edward. *Cast in a Racial Mould: Labour Process and Trade Unionism in the Foundries.* Johannesburg: Ravan Press, 1985.

Webster, Eddie and Glenn Adler. 'Towards a Class Compromise in South Africa's "Double Transition": Bargained Liberalization and the Consolidation of Democracy'. *Politics & Society* 27 (1999): 347–385.

Webster, Edward and Sakhela Buhlungu. 'Between Marginalisation and Revitalisation? The State of Trade Unionism in South Africa'. *Review of African Political Economy* 100 (2004): 39–56.

Webster, Edward, Buhlungu, Sakhela and Andries Bezuidenhout. *Work and Organizations.* Oxford: Oxford University Press, 2003.

Webster, Edward and Karl von Holdt, eds. *Beyond the Apartheid Workplace: Studies in Transition.* Pietermaritzburg: University of KwaZulu-Natal Press, 2005.

Wood, Geoffrey. 'Organizing Unionism and the Possibilities for Perpetuating a Social Movement Role: Representivity, Politics, and the Congress of South African Trade Unions'. *Labor Studies Journal* 26 (2002): 29–49.

Zikalala, Snuki. 'Impala Platinum: No Easy Road to Collective Bargaining'. *South African Labour Bulletin* 16 (1992): 26–39.

INDEX

Page numbers in *italics* indicate figures and tables.

Printed and bound by CPI Group (UK) Ltd, Croydon, CR0 4YY

16/04/2025

14658440-0005